FOUR CENTURIES OF QUILTS

FOUR CENTURIES OF QUILTS

The Colonial Williamsburg Collection

LINDA BAUMGARTEN

KIMBERLY SMITH IVEY

THE COLONIAL WILLIAMSBURG FOUNDATION
WILLIAMSBURG, VIRGINIA

in association with

YALE UNIVERSITY PRESS, NEW HAVEN AND LONDON

25 24 23 22 21 20 19 18 17 16   2 3 4 5

Library of Congress Cataloging-in-Publication Data

Colonial Williamsburg Foundation.

 Four centuries of quilts : the Colonial Williamsburg collection / Linda Baumgarten, Kimberly Smith Ivey.

   pages cm

 Includes bibliographical references and index.

 ISBN 978-0-87935-264-6 (hardcover : alk. paper) (CWF) — ISBN 978-0-300-20736-1 (Yale) 1. Quilts—Catalogs. 2. Quilts—Virginia—Williamsburg—Catalogs. 3. Colonial Williamsburg Foundation—Catalogs. I. Baumgarten, Linda, author. II. Ivey, Kimberly Smith, author. III. Title.

 NK9102.W55C653 2014
 746.46074'7554252—dc23

                                                                        2013049064

Colonial Williamsburg is a registered trade name of The Colonial Williamsburg Foundation, a not-for-profit educational institution.

The Colonial Williamsburg Foundation
PO Box 1776
Williamsburg, VA 23187-1776
colonialwilliamsburg.org

Published in association with
Yale University Press
302 Temple Street
PO Box 209040
New Haven, CT 06520-9040
yalebooks.com/art

Printed in Malaysia

Designed by Shanin Glenn

Jacket front: Detail of Honeysuckle Quilt, figure 106

Jacket back: Detail of Silk Corded Quilt, figure 14; detail of Williamsburg Appliquéd, Pieced, and Embroidered Quilt, figure 69; detail of Quaker Friendship Album Quilt, figure 120; detail of Housetop Quilt, figure 146

Frontispiece: Detail of Star of Bethlehem Quilt, figure 91

Dedication page: Detail of Botanical Album Quilt, figure 122

Contents page: Detail of Pieced and Stuffed-Work Irish Chain Quilt, figure 79

In Memory of Our Parents

GILBERT AND IRENE BAUMGARTEN

JAMES AND OCIE JOSEPHINE SMITH

Remember me.

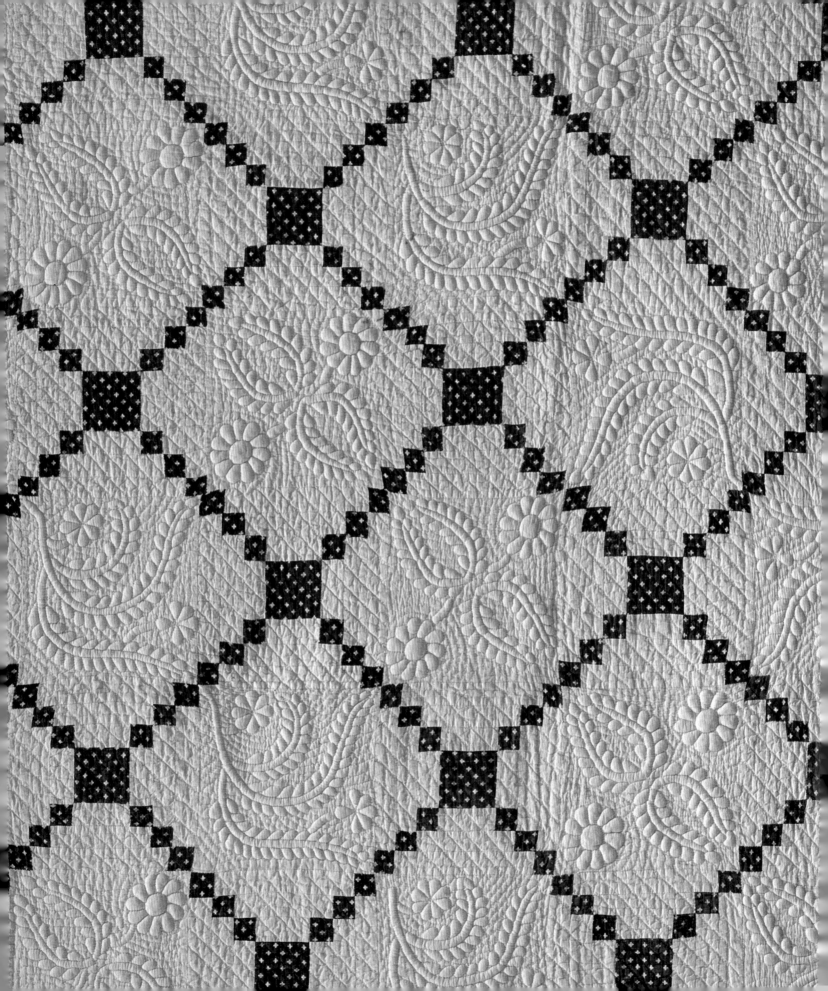

TABLE of CONTENTS

FOREWORD

FOREWORD

In the winter of 1857, three dozen members of the Leigh Street Baptist Church in Richmond, Virginia, collaborated on the production of a colorful album quilt. Nearly nine feet square, the stylish bedcovering was made for presentation to the Reverend Edward Jefferson Willis. The quilters' motivation remains unclear. Their work may have been in celebration of Willis's appointment as pastor, or it may have commemorated completion of the congregation's imposing church. That the quilt was a gift of the wider congregation is suggested by the disparate ages and socioeconomic situations of the needlewomen. Their number included widow Ann Burke, in her sixties and living with her banker son-in-law; the spinster McCoull sisters (Ann, Mary, and Julia), middle-aged and sharing a small house in the city's First Ward; and twelve-year-old Emma Woodfin, residing with her parents.[1]

All thirty-six squares of the Willis quilt bear inscriptions. Most were written in ink, but one was executed in cross-stitch and two were custom printed. Each of the quilters added her name to the block she made, and several dated their work or noted its production in Richmond. Most incorporated relevant Bible verses. Young Emma Woodfin's block was inscribed in part "Suffer little Children to come unto me." Several dedicatory notes were included as well. Sarah Starke's square was simply addressed "To Her Pastor" while Sylvia Libby's was offered "As a token of respect." Clearly produced in a spirit of generosity and affection, the quilt must have been prized by the Willis

family since it exhibits little evidence of wear. Still brilliant today, the textile was carefully preserved and handed down through the family for a century and a half until it entered the Colonial Williamsburg collection in 2013.

Like many eighteenth-, nineteenth-, and twentieth-century quilts, this one is both a work of art and a historic document. Exhibiting stuffed work, embroidery, chintz appliqués, piecing, and a number of other techniques, the quilt nicely illustrates the aesthetic choices and needlework skills of Richmond women and girls on the eve of the Civil War. At the same time, its inscriptions provide keys to information about the community of faith that engendered its fabrication and the social and economic standings of the congregants. That a few squares were machine quilted even reveals something about the swift acceptance of that new technology in antebellum Richmond.

Despite its remarkable attributes, the Willis quilt is not unusual in holding such illuminating clues to our past. Most of the more than 150 quilts examined in *Four Centuries of Quilts: The Colonial Williamsburg Collection* offer similar glimpses of early American and British social, artistic, and craft traditions. One need only know how to interpret the evidence. Authors Linda Baumgarten and Kimberly Smith Ivey are ideally suited for that role. They share a passion for historic textiles, and each has many years of research and scholarship to her credit. Their vision and intellectual curiosity are at the core of this volume. Yet the work could not have been undertaken without the generosity

Richmond Appliquéd Friendship Album Quilt, female members of the Leigh Street Baptist Church, Richmond, Virginia, 1857, cottons with ink and cotton embroidery threads, 105 x 105 in. (267 x 267 cm), Museum Purchase, 2013.609.8. Signature album quilts made up of individually signed blocks became especially popular after 1845. Also known as friendship quilts, these album quilts were often created as gifts. This large appliquéd friendship quilt was made by female members of the Leigh Street Baptist Church in Richmond, Virginia, for their pastor, the Reverend Edward Jefferson Willis (1820–1891).[2] Assembled in a block-by-block construction, sometimes referred to as "quilt-as-you-go" or "potholder," the quilt consists of blocks that were individually pieced and/or appliquéd, layered, quilted, and edge finished prior to being assembled as one entire quilt. Some blocks were also embellished with stuffed areas and/or embroidery stitches. Each block is finished in a one-half-inch folded strip of green cotton. The blocks are quilted in a variety of floral patterns. Some are machine quilted, perhaps indicating how technologically up-to-date the maker was.

of Mary and Clinton Gilliland and the Turner-Gilliland Family Fund of the Silicon Valley Community Foundation. We gratefully acknowledge their magnanimous decision to fund the research, design, and production of this book. We also acknowledge with thanks the DeWitt Wallace Fund for Colonial Williamsburg, which supports the curating, conservation, and exhibition of the Foundation's notable collections.

Ronald L. Hurst
The Carlisle H. Humelsine Chief Curator
The Colonial Williamsburg Foundation

notes for FOREWORD

1 James L. Apperson household, 1850 U. S. census, Preston, Henrico, VA, page 452B, National Archives and Records Administration (NARA) microfilm M432, roll 951, digital image as found on Ancestry.com (2009); "Virginia, Select Marriages, 1785–1940," s.v., "Mary Ann Burke," online database, Ancestry.com (2014); Ann Mccaull household, 1860 U. S. census, Richmond Ward 1, Henrico, VA, page 104, NARA microfilm M653, roll 1352, digital image as found on Ancestry.com (2009); Mary Fulcher household, 1860 U. S. census, Upper Revenue District, Hanover, VA, page 514, NARA microfilm M653, roll 1350, digital image as found on Ancestry.com (2009).

2 Rev. Edward J. Willis marker, digital image as found on findagrave.com, Find a Grave memorial #6020065, record added December 9, 2001.

INTRODUCTION

INTRODUCTION

Colonial Williamsburg's superb collection of bed quilts numbers about 250 examples and spans almost four hundred years, from 1600 to the late twentieth century. Quilts are an important part of the textile collection, which also includes woven and nonquilted bedcovers and hangings, household linens, schoolgirl samplers and other needlework, printed and woven study fragments, and clothing. Collected from around the world, the quilts originated in India, continental Europe, the United Kingdom, colonial America, and, later, the United States. Some were made in the homes by women (and the occasional man) for their families while others came from workshops where skilled male and female quilters executed the ideas of professional designers to create quilts for sale.

The American-made quilts in the collection are especially noteworthy. They date from the eighteenth to the twentieth century and display a variety of techniques, colors, and materials, including boldly patterned worsted wholecloth examples, brilliantly pieced and appliquéd works of art, and pristine white bedcovers. The diverse quilts made by Anglo-American, Amish, Mennonite, Pennsylvania German, African American, and Hawaiian quilt makers reveal the multicultural nature of American society.[1]

Colonial Williamsburg first began collecting quilts in 1930 when textiles were needed to furnish the restored and reconstructed houses that were part of Virginia's colonial capital. Eighteenth-century quilts and accurate reproductions graced tall-post beds in the Governor's Palace (fig. 1),

the George Wythe House, the Peyton Randolph House, and other sites where the history of Williamsburg was

Figure 1 Reproduction Worsted Wholecloth Quilt covering tall-post bedstead in the Governor's Palace, Williamsburg, Virginia. Adapted from an antique in the Colonial Williamsburg collection (see fig. 32), the reproduction bedcovering was designed by Beth Gerhold and handmade by volunteers Charleen Perry, Bobbi Finley, Jane Bergstralh, Mary Lou Rowe, Martha Bjick, Nan Losee, and participants in a quilting workshop held by Colonial Williamsburg in 2009. Jim Mullins enlarged the digital pattern taken from the antique to quilt size in preparation for transferring the pattern to the cloth. The wool batting came from Colonial Williamsburg's rare breed sheep.

Figure 2 Pieced Bedcover, Jewett Washington Curtis (1847–1927), Mill Plain, Washington, ca. 1895, wools, 64½ x 51 in. (164 x 130 cm), Museum Purchase, 1993.609.2. Although piecing and quilting are often considered women's work, men also produced outstanding examples of intricate needlework. Jewett Washington Curtis was a musician in the Civil War. Prior to marrying and settling on a farm in rural Washington State, he had been a career soldier stationed for a time in Alaska. Curtis may have seen other pieced examples made by soldiers using wool uniform scraps, a tradition that originated in Great Britain. Curtis assembled almost eleven thousand small pieces of heavy woolens and hand pieced them using backstitches with narrow seam allowances about one-sixteenth inch in width. Once believed to be a table covering, this pieced top may have been the childhood bedcover of the maker's son Clark Edward Curtis, according to the recollections of a descendant. The bedcover does not have batting or backing.[2]

interpreted. Quilts were used as important interior furnishings and continue to be displayed in several furnished buildings.

With the building of the Abby Aldrich Rockefeller Folk Art Center in 1957 and the DeWitt Wallace Decorative Arts Museum in 1985, now consolidated into the Museums of Colonial Williamsburg, the quilts could be exhibited in modern galleries as artistically significant artifacts, as well as household furnishings. The Abby Aldrich Rockefeller Folk Art Museum houses most of the American-made examples from the nineteenth and twentieth centuries. Earlier quilts made in America, England, Europe, and India are exhibited at the DeWitt Wallace Decorative Arts Museum. In addition to viewing physical exhibitions in the Museums of Colonial Williamsburg, scholars and enthusiasts can study the quilt collection online.[3]

Colonial Williamsburg's quilt holdings are enhanced through the generous gifts of collectors, such as Mrs. Jason (Peggy) Westerfield and Foster and Muriel McCarl, and other individuals who choose to share their family treasures with the world through their generous donations to the museum and whose names are listed with the quilt entries. Ironically, although Abby Aldrich Rockefeller collected a number of folk art paintings, sculptures, and schoolgirl silk-embroidered pictures that she eventually donated to Colonial Williamsburg, she did not collect significant quantities of quilts, and the museum has no quilts or coverlets from Mrs. Rockefeller.[4] The first full-size quilt acquired by the Abby Aldrich Rockefeller Folk Art Museum came in 1972 (see fig. 84), fifteen years after the museum opened, but the collection of American-made quilts has grown steadily ever since.

WHAT IS A QUILT?

Quilts vary considerably in materials, techniques, and designs over the almost four hundred years represented in the Colonial Williamsburg collections. Most quilts are made as a sandwich of two textiles with a filling called the *batting*, or *wadding*, to add warmth. Today many quilters use synthetic battings, but historically quilts were usually filled with the unspun fibers of wool or cotton. The three layers

of a quilt are typically fastened together by stitching that creates checks, parallel lines, contours around the pattern on the quilt top, or more decorative designs. Most hand quilting is done with running stitches moving up and down through all three layers to connect them. A few historical quilts were made with backstitches that could be touching to give a continuous solid line or spaced to resemble a dashed line, the latter known as *half backstitches* (fig. 3).

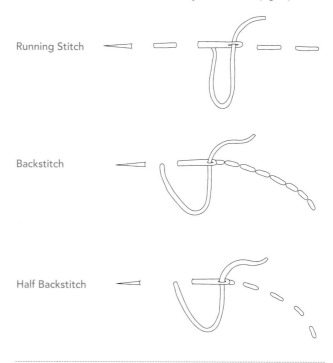

Figure 3 Stitches used in quilting: running stitch, backstitch, and half backstitch. To determine the number of stitches per inch for quilts published in this book, the authors counted the stitches visible on the top of the quilt within a one-inch length.

Sometimes, quilts were simply tied with threads knotted at regular intervals to hold the layers together (see figs. 193, 194, 203). Although tied bedcovers are usually called *comforters*, or *comforts*, not *quilts*, there is historical precedent for considering tying as part of the quilting repertoire. In the eighteenth century, tied upholstery tufting was often referred to as *quilting*. In addition, early mattresses were sometimes called *quilts*, probably because they were layered with stuffing and tufted, much like quilted upholstery.[5] This early use of terms suggests caution when interpreting early eighteenth-century inventories since a reference to a "quilt" might actually mean a mattress.

Quilts can be categorized by their tops, which are usually more decorative than their backings. The top may be lengths of uncut fabric, usually called *wholecloth;* embroidered; pieced; appliquéd; or a combination of several techniques. The filling also affects the finished appearance of the quilt. Battings are usually evenly applied fibers. Sometimes extra fibers are inserted to raise specific areas above the surface, with or without an allover batting. Fillings can also be separate spun cords drawn between stitched channels. After quilting, the raw edges of the bedcover have to be finished. Most finishing involves one of three techniques: applying a separate binding or woven tape, turning the edges in toward each other and stitching, or extending one side (usually the backing) around to the other side to form an edge finish.

Some makers signed and/or dated their quilts or individual blocks. They used a number of techniques, including "writing" with the quilting stitches themselves, signing in ink, stamping with a precut ink stamp, stenciling, and marking with embroidery, the last usually cross-stitched.

Although they occasionally looked alike and shared certain design features, handmade quilts and woven coverlets were very different in their construction. Coverlets were woven on looms, usually by male professionals, using a number of different weave structures, including overshot, double weave, and figured and fancy weaves such as Beiderwand and tied Beiderwand (see fig. 4). Except for hemming the raw edges, joining the woven pieces at a center seam, or attaching separate fringe, coverlets had no hand stitching as part of their construction.

Quilt Names

Quilt makers and scholars today often identify pieced and appliquéd patterns by name, but the practice of naming quilt patterns apparently is of relatively recent origin. Judging from surviving sources, it appears that pattern naming first began in the eighteenth century. A 1798 letter from a New England schoolgirl mentioned quilt pieces in the "Mariner's Compass" pattern, in addition to a "Geometrical piece."[6]

Figure 4 Detail of Coverlet, Samuel Hippert (active 1833–1841), Elizabethtown, Pennsylvania, 1836, wool and cotton, 89 x 79 in. (226 x 201 cm), gift of Col. and Mrs. James W. Roy, 1974.609.4. Weaver Samuel Hippert combined a pattern of lilies and compass stars in the main field of his tied Beiderwand coverlet with paired birds, trees, and stars in the border. The paired goldfinches, or thistle finches, often referred to by their German name of *distelfinks,* are separated by flowering trees, or homs. Similar motifs were sometimes borrowed for bed quilts, such as that made by Sara Keplar (fig. 5).

Sometimes the pattern name was a reference to what the design resembled, such as the rows of triangles that call to mind Flying Geese or the nine small pieces of Nine Patch. Quilt names document familiarity with biblical stories and characters, such as Star of Bethlehem, Joseph's Coat, and Job's Tears. Women referenced their personal beliefs and political persuasions by naming patterns Whig Rose and Slave Chain. In the late nineteenth and early twentieth centuries, printed patterns in ladies' magazines often included names selected by the authors.

Today's scholars and quilters have identified thousands of pattern names to aid in categorizing and studying quilts. Whatever the source, quilt names changed with the time and place, and the same pattern often went by several different names, depending on the makers. For example, the pattern known as Trip Around the World in the wider community became known as Sunshine and Shadow in the insular Amish community (see fig. 139). For this

Figure 5 ABC Quilt, Sara Keplar, probably eastern Pennsylvania, 1851, cottons with cotton embroidery threads, 8 running stitches per inch, 84 x 70 in. (213 x 178 cm), Museum Purchase, partially funded by the Quilt Conservancy, 2007.609.2. The quilt maker naively interpreted motifs favored by Pennsylvania coverlet weavers. The outer border consists of birds and flowering tree motifs that are reminiscent of the finches and flowering trees seen on many figured and fancy woven coverlets. The center field of forty-eight eight-pointed stars is surrounded by an inner border of mirrored alphabets and the signature line "SARA • KEPLAR • 1851." Although a number of Sara(h) Keplars can be identified in Pennsylvania, this quilt maker's exact identity is not known.

publication, the authors have chosen commonly used pattern names to aid in the identification of the quilts. In most cases, however, it is not known whether the quilt makers used pattern names.

QUILTING AND SOCIETY

The activity of quilting often invited social interaction as people joined together around a large frame to fasten the layers of a quilt together with intricate hand stitches (fig. 6). Communal quilt gatherings, later called *quilting bees*, were known in the eighteenth century as *quiltings*.

Figure 6 *The Quilting Party*, artist unknown, United States, 1854–1875, 19¼ x 26 in. (49 x 66 cm), oil, pencil, paper, and plywood, from the collection of Abby Aldrich Rockefeller, gift of David Rockefeller, 1937.101.1. Quilting parties allowed extra hands to assist in the stitching process. It was not unusual for men and children to participate in quilting parties, especially after the quilt was finished. Gossip, music, dancing, and eating all speeded the stitching and made the event a festive one. The unidentified folk artist of this painting copied an illustration in the October 21, 1854, issue of *Gleason's Pictorial Drawing-Room Companion*. The original print was titled *A Quilting Party in Western Virginia*.

Written records illuminate the role of quilting as an important part of social interaction. According to her diary, Elizabeth Porter Phelps of Hadley, Massachusetts, often quilted with friends and relatives. In 1788, when she was rushing to finish a quilt for her sixteen-year-old son, Porter, to take to Harvard College, the middle-aged housewife enlisted the help of a relative and a neighbor. On October 26, she wrote, "Thursday sister Warner and Mrs. Shipman here to help me Quilt a Bed quilt for Porter. Fryday here again."

The communal work around the quilting frame proceeded quickly, and by Saturday Elizabeth took the quilt off the frame. Elizabeth had relied on her network of female friends and relatives to speed the quilting.[7]

Elizabeth Phelps's diary also reveals that quilting activity ebbed and flowed, depending on her personal responsibilities and life stage. When she was a young unmarried woman, Elizabeth quilted an average of six times a year just prior to her marriage, and usually with friends. Elizabeth or a friend often stayed overnight at the other's house to quilt over a period of several days. After she married and began rearing her young family, the busy housewife was able to quilt less than once a year. Even so, in May 1778 she got out to the Ebenezer Marshes', where "many people [were] there a Quilting." As her children grew older and more self-sufficient, Elizabeth quilted about twice a year on average. This is the period when she made son Porter a quilt to take to Harvard. The cycle repeated itself as Elizabeth's girls grew up and began to go out quilting frequently as part of *their* social lives as unmarried young ladies. On July 21, 1793, "the girls [went] quilting at Mr. Eleazar Porters and many others."[8]

The daughters of Martha Ballard, a midwife from Maine, also attended social quiltings. On November 10, 1790, "my Girls had Some Neighbours to help ym quilt a Bed quilt. 15tn Ladies, they began to quillt at 3 h pm, finisht & took it out at y Evn. there were 12 Gentlemen took Tea. they Danced a little while after Supper."[9]

Frances Baylor Hill, a young unmarried gentry woman living at Hillsborough plantation in King and Queen County, Virginia, recorded in her diary on July 24, 1797, that Aunt Temple was "very busy fiscing [fixing] her bedquilt in the fram[e]." (Notice here the use of the term *bedquilt* to specify a quilted covering for the bed. The term *quilt* in the period could also refer to a quilted petticoat.) On July 26, Frances wrote, "Aunt Temple and my-self went to work on the quilt by times, we had Cousin P Gwathmey[,] Camm Garlick, Nancy & Becky Aylett, Mrs & Miss Polly Turner, Miss Caty Pollard & Mrs Simons to help us, we quilt'd a great deal and was very merry." The next day Frances recorded that she and Aunt Temple did not accomplish as much, probably because they had "a number of fine water mellons & Peach's a plenty of Biscuit & Cake fine eating and merry quilting." On Friday they "spent the day agreable eating drinking and quilting" with visits from a number of male cousins. On Saturday they "got the quilt out early in the day and then the girls all went to making edging."[10] Clearly, quilt gatherings were a way to combine fun with useful activity. They were particularly important to help unmarried girls socialize and to meet eligible young men.

In the nineteenth century, quilting as a social activity continued among people of all social stations, from those in the slave quarters to wealthy householders. In fact, quilts based on individual squares rather than overall designs became very popular for communal work. Each person could make a block or more to be incorporated into the larger design. In the 1840s and 1850s, signature and album quilts became especially popular. Made by a group of people, album quilts had blocks or pieces that were usually signed and dated. The quilt was then assembled and quilted and finally presented to an honoree such as a bride, a minister, or an individual leaving the community (see figs. 118–120).

The tradition of quilting get-togethers continued into the twentieth and twenty-first centuries. Young Mary Kouba attended a quilting bee at her grandmother's house in rural Vernon County, Wisconsin, around 1943, almost two centuries after Elizabeth Porter Phelps had attended her quilting parties in Massachusetts. As an adult, Mary Kouba Baumgarten recalled the event: "My grandmother was having an old-fashioned quilting bee. The quilt was stretched on a quilt frame and was a bed-size quilt. The ladies that were gathered included my great-aunts and my grandmother's neighbors. All in all, about six ladies. I was playing on the floor under the quilt and bumped or touched someone. My mother chased me out."[11] Mary's great-grandparents were Czech-Americans who settled in Wisconsin. Mary continued to quilt most of her life.

Louisiana P. Bendolph, a descendant of slaves, also played under the quilting frame while her mother and other relatives quilted in their Alabama home in the 1960s (see p. 239). Louisiana later became a quilter herself.[12] Even today, quilt makers and quilt students reenact a long tradition when they gather in clubs, guilds, and church halls to make quilts for a fund-raising raffle or to give away to the needy half a world away.

Something about quilts still speaks to people today, whether it is the creation of beauty from small pieces, giving of oneself through a special gift, connecting with a past ancestor through a surviving quilt or textiles, or recording history by making something useful from the fragments of outdated but fondly remembered fabrics (see fig. 183). Quilts often mark important life events: the arrival of a new baby, a wedding, a child leaving home for school or military service, or the influx of a deceased parent's old clothing and furnishings—all can inspire quilters to commemorate the event (fig. 7). One of this book's authors collected her son's T-shirts to make a quilt to send along with him to college. The other author has collected a stash of neckties, scraps, and other fabrics, some saved from the clothing of her deceased parents, intending to make a memory quilt.

To some, quilts are striking objects to be hung on the wall like modern art, capable of uplifting and inspiring through their extraordinary artistic achievement. To others, quilts speak of family, friends, memory, and tradition. Historic quilts record in a tangible way the artistic achievements of those who have lived before. Museums preserve and display quilts in part to help illuminate the stories and lives of people who often go unrecorded—housewives and anonymous professional quilters. Their stories and achievements put our own stories into historical perspective and become part of our own history.

CONVENTIONS Dimensions are listed with the height or length first, followed by width. Metric dimensions are rounded off to the nearest centimeter. Stitches are counted as the number of stitches visible on the top surface within a one-inch length.[13] Where birth and death dates of quilters are known, they are given; the absence of dates means they are not yet determined. Most of the drawings of quilting patterns omit the background quilted lines for clarity.

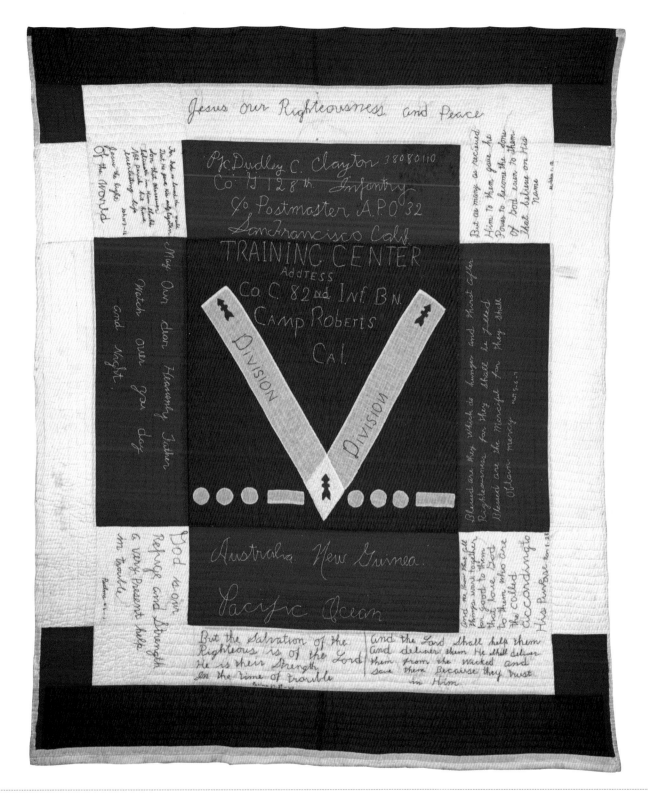

Figure 7 World War II Quilt, friend or relative of Dudley Clayton (1919–1953), Texas, ca. 1945, cottons with cotton embroidery threads, 3 running stitches per inch, 80¾ x 67 in. (205 x 170 cm), Museum Purchase, 1994.609.1. Although she did not sign her work, the quilt maker may have been Kate Dunlap Clayton (Mrs. Hence Clayton), the mother of Dudley Clayton, whose name and military address are written prominently in outline stitches on the face of the quilt, along with Bible verses, prayers for his safety during World War II, and a large V for victory. Clayton served as a rifleman and earned two bronze stars for the Papua New Guinea campaigns; he was discharged in March 1945 and worked as an auto glass installer in Amarillo, Texas. He remained unmarried and died at age thirty-four from accidental asphyxiation.[14]

1   The Colonial Williamsburg quilt collection is divided into two related groupings. The grouping of pre-1830 quilts consists mostly of American examples and imported British quilts that influenced what early Americans made. The pre-1830 grouping also includes continental European and Indian examples that had considerable influence on Anglo-American fashions of the day. The second grouping consists of American quilts, most of them postdating 1830. These are part of the Abby Aldrich Rockefeller Folk Art Museum (AARFAM) collection, designated by 609 as part of the accession number. The AARFAM collection represents American untrained or amateur "folk" artists. Colonial Williamsburg does not collect studio art quilts or those by modern trained fiber artists.

2   This quilt was first published in the Lang 2012 American Quilt Calendar (2011), produced by the Lang Company, Waukesha, WI, with captions written by Linda Baumgarten and Kimberly Ivey. The quilt was exhibited at the Shelburne Museum in 2012 and published in Jean M. Burks and Joe Cunningham, *Man-Made Quilts: Civil War to the Present* (Shelburne, VT: Shelburne Museum, 2012), 35. The biographical information for Jewett Curtis comes from the following sources: Jewett Curtis household, 1900 U. S. census, Preston, Clark County, WA, enumeration district 27, page 3A, National Archives and Records Administration microfilm, T623, roll 1742, digital image as found on Ancestry.com (2004); and U. S. National Cemetery Interment Control Forms, 1938–1962, AI 2110-B, Records of the Office of the Quartermaster General, 1774–1985, record group 92, National Archives at College Park, MD, online database, digital image as found on Ancestry.com (2012). In the census, Jewett is listed as a fifty-seven-year-old head of household who was born in 1848 in Vermont. In 1900 he was living with Mary, twenty-three; Clark E., five; and James C., two months.

3   Accessible on eMuseum at emuseum.history.org.

4   The Museum of Fine Arts, Houston, TX, owns the only quilt known to have been in Abby Aldrich Rockefeller's collection: a Baltimore album quilt, ca. 1840s (45.4).

5   John Locke used the term *quilts* as the equivalent to *mattresses:* "Let his [a child's] *Bed* be *hard,* and rather Quilts than Feathers." *Some Thoughts Concerning Education,* 5th ed. (London, 1705), 32 (section 22).

6   Eliza Southgate to Robert Southgate, January 9, 1798, in *A Girl's Life Eighty Years Ago: Selections from the Letters of Eliza Southgate Bowne,* ed. Clarence Cook (New York: Charles Scribner's Sons, 1887), 15.

7   "The Diary of Elizabeth (Porter) Phelps," ed. Thomas Eliot Andrews, *New England Historical and Genealogical Register* 119 (October 1965): 300. Porter left for college on November 5.

8   "The Diary of Elizabeth (Porter) Phelps," ed. Thomas Eliot Andrews, *New England Historical and Genealogical Register* 118 (October 1964): 304; and "The Diary of Elizabeth (Porter) Phelps," ed. Thomas Eliot Andrews, *New England Historical and Genealogical Register* 120 (July 1966): 206. For a lengthy analysis of Elizabeth Porter Phelps's diary, see Marla R. Miller, "'And others of our own people': Needlework and Women of the Rural Gentry," in *What's New England about New England Quilts?* ed. Lynne Z. Bassett (Sturbridge, MA: Old Sturbridge Village, 1999), 19–33.

9   *The Diary of Martha Ballard, 1785–1812,* ed. Robert R. McCausland and Cynthia MacAlman McCausland (Camden, ME: Picton Press, 1992), 176.

10 "The Diary of Frances Baylor Hill of 'Hillsborough,' King and Queen County, Virginia (1797)," ed. William K. Bottorff and Roy C. Flannagan, *Early American Literature Newsletter* 2, no. 3 (Winter 1967): 38.

11 Mary Kouba Baumgarten, conversation with author (Baumgarten), December 6, 2004. The quilting bee she described occurred in Chicken Valley where Mary's grandmother Albena G. Levy lived. Albena's daughter Marie Levy Kouba Verbsky was Mary's mother. The women at the bee also included Mary's great-aunt Helen Housner.

12 See Louisiana P. Bendolph, "A New Generation of 'Housetops,'" in *Gee's Bend: The Architecture of the Quilt,* ed. Paul Arnett, Joanne Cubbs, and Eugene W. Metcalf Jr. (Atlanta, GA: Tinwood Books, 2006), 189.

13 Some quilt makers count running stitches on the top and multiply by two to arrive at the number of stitches on both top and bottom of the quilt. The authors did not use this method.

14 This quilt was published in Sue Reich, *World War II Quilts* (Atglen, PA: Schiffer, 2010), 163. The biographical information on Dudley Clayton is from the following sources: John C. Kuehl, Veterans Services officer, Department of Veterans Affairs, to Barbara Luck, March 14, 1997, Object file 1994.609.1, Department of Collections, Colonial Williamsburg Foundation (hereafter "CWF object file"); Texas Department of Health, death certificate no. 602, Dudley C. Clayton (1953), Bureau of Vital Statistics, Amarillo; Dudley C. Clayton, Enlisted Record and Report of Separation, March 26, 1945, Houston, TX (copy received from Department of Veterans Affairs, March 1997); and Amarillo, Texas, City Directory, 1928, "Hence Clayton," U. S. City Directories, 1821–1989, online database, digital image as found on Ancestry.com (2011).

CHAPTER 1

INDIAN

Chapter 1

INDIAN

For centuries India was famous for the production of fine cotton textiles, silk embroidery, and quilts. Long before Europeans began trading directly with the country, India had a thriving textile trade throughout Southeast Asia and as far away as Greece, Rome, and Egypt. A fragment of mordant-dyed cotton found in the Indus Valley has been dated by radiocarbon analysis to before 1700 BC, and by the fifth century BC, Greek authors were writing about the trade in Indian cottons.[1]

Portuguese adventurers opened trade with India by the early 1500s and developed a flourishing traffic in goods that included luxury quilts, such as those from Bengal (see fig. 11). Although the Portuguese preceded them in the direct Indian trade by almost a hundred years, the Dutch, British, and French eventually entered the market. Chartered in 1600, the British East India Company imported Indian textiles and quilts into England and ultimately into the American colonies. The Dutch and English gained ascendency after the Portuguese were expelled from India following a 1632 battle with the Mughals.

Some of the trade textiles were inexpensive goods consisting of plain, striped, and block-printed cottons known by names such as calicoes, seersuckers, ginghams, patches, muslins, and baftas. The most desired, however, were brilliantly colored and patterned cottons that had been mordant painted and dyed, and thus were colorfast. These usually were called *chintz*, a word that originally meant speckled or spotted. In 1755, Samuel Johnson's *Dictionary*

of the English Language defined "chints" as "cloath of cotton made in India, and printed with colours." As Europeans ultimately developed their own printed textile industries, the category of chintz included cottons printed in Europe as well as in India. The Portuguese word for spotted or speckled gave rise to the term *pintado* to refer to painted Indian cottons. Sometimes panels designed as bed hangings or counterpanes were called *palampores*, a word derived from the Portuguese *palang posh*, meaning bedcover (see fig. 12).

The finest Indian chintzes were colored and patterned through painstakingly slow methods. Different colors required different processes. To achieve reds, pinks, lavenders, and black, dyers hand painted the design with mordants, or color fixatives, and then dyed the textile with chay, a root that yields a dye capable of producing red and a number of other colors; the final color depended on the chemical composition of the mordant. For blue, workers used wax to resist the dye in all the areas except those to be blue and dyed the textile in an indigo solution. To add yellow, workers usually painted the patterned textile with yellow dye in areas intended to be yellow, and for green, they painted yellow over previously dyed blue. The final step was glazing the textile with rice paste and polishing the surface. Between every step of the production, the textile had to be cleared, or cleaned, of dye or wax residue.[2] The resulting textiles were famous for their beauty and the fastness of their colors. Edward Terry, a visitor to India around 1615, published his observations on the textile manufactures and trade of India and described the cottons stained with flowers and figures, "which are so fixed in the cloth, that no water can wash them out."[3]

In addition to producing textiles for clothing and home furnishings, Indians made a variety of quilts, some of which are known only through documentary records. "The natives there," wrote Edward Terry, "show very much ingenuity in their curious manufactures." Among their products were quilts of three different varieties: "quilts of their stained cloth, or of fresh coloured taffata lined with their pintadoes, or of their sattin lined with taffata, betwixt which they put cotton wool, and work them together with silk. Those taffata or sattin quilts are excellently stitched by them, being done as evenly, and in as good order, as if they had been drawn out for them for their direction, the better to work them."[4]

What did these early quilts look like? "Quilts of their stained cloth" referred to wholecloth quilts made with cotton on both sides, at least one side being patterned cotton, that is, chintz. Quilts made of "fresh coloured taffata lined with their pintadoes" would have had silk on one side and printed or mordant-painted cotton on the other (see fig. 8).[5] Terry's quilts made of "sattin lined with taffata, betwixt which they put cotton wool, and work them together with silk" would have combined silk on both front and back with cotton fiber batting between the two silk layers, all stitched with silk quilting threads.[6] ("Cotton wool" was period terminology for fibers from the cotton plant, which resembled sheep's wool.) Other travelers mentioned all-white quilts made in India, in addition to the colored and printed examples described by Terry. In 1609, an English merchant in the East Indies trade wrote back to England that "quilts ready made both of white calicoes and of all sorts of painted stuffs are to be had in abundance, and very reasonable."[7]

Indian workers also produced exceptional silk embroidery, some of it incorporated into quilts. Embroiderers in the Bengal region produced early pictorial quilts using naturally yellow tussah silk as the embroidery thread (see fig. 11). In 1618, the minutes of the British East India Company described a "Bengalla" quilt "embroidered all over with pictures of men and crafts in yellow silk."[8] Very

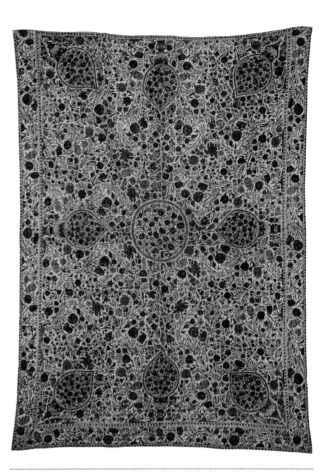

Figure 8 Quilt, maker unknown, Coromandel Coast, India, 1700–1725, cotton and silk, 122 x 93 in. (311 x 236 cm), Victoria and Albert Museum, London, IS.12-1976. Quilts such as this eighteenth-century example are similar in materials to those described by Edward Terry the century before. This example has chintz on one side quilted to red silk on the opposite side.

different embroidered quilts, from the south-central Deccan area, incorporated silk floss and metallic thread embroidery on cotton grounds quilted with silk (see fig. 10). Workers in the area around Gujarat produced yet another variety of embroidery, rendered with chain stitches made using a fine hook; surviving examples, however, are typically not quilted (see fig. 9).

As Indian textiles gained popularity in Britain, weavers began to fear for their livelihoods and petitioned for protection. The government responded with a 1700 law banning the importation of most chintz cottons. Excepted from the ban were plain white cottons and printed textiles for reexport. The law was widely ignored, and subsequent legislation enacted in 1720 prohibited wearing and using chintzes in the home in England.

Wealthy American colonists in the seventeenth century shared British citizens' desires for fashionable Indian goods. As early as 1655, Virginian Peter Walker owned an "East Indyan Quilte." Ironically, colonial Americans were apparently unaffected by the British chintz prohibitions. Because chintzes brought into Britain could be legally reexported, colonial settlers enjoyed access to textiles that were banned for use back in Britain. In Yorktown, Virginia, a tavern keeper had "1 India Calaco quilt" on his bed at the time his inventory was taken in 1716. The bed, with its chintz quilt, mattress, bolster, and other textiles, was valued at six pounds sterling. In Boston in 1720, Judge Samuel Sewall ordered "a good fine large Chintz Quilt well made" for his daughter who was recently married. And in 1729, Governor William Burnett of Massachusetts owned an "India silk quilt." At twenty-five pounds sterling, Burnett's bed and its "chints" hangings were more than twice as valuable as any of his other beds. Americans' appetite for Indian textiles continued throughout the century. In the 1770s, American merchants openly advertised in the *Virginia Gazette* newspaper that they had fine imported Indian chintz for sale. In London during the same time, however, Mrs.

David Garrick was fighting to get her Indian chintz panels released from customs officials who had confiscated the goods as illegal.[9]

Figure 9 Detail of Bed Counterpane, maker unknown, Gujarat region, 1725–1740, cotton with silk embroidery threads, 120 x 123 in. (305 x 312 cm), Museum Purchase, 1963-134. Indian embroiderers used hooks to work extremely fine chain stitches. The design for the vase of flowers was probably drawn in Europe and sent to India to be copied.

BED QUILT ADAPTED FROM A FLOOR SPREAD

FIGURE 10

This large bed quilt, probably adapted from a floor spread designed for use in India, combines rosettes and palmettes inspired in part by Persian textiles. The hybrid nature of the textile is indicative of the lively transmission of textiles and design sources in the region. Indians made textiles not only in their own traditions but also in designs to appeal to specific export markets, a concept that sounds modern but actually has its origins many hundreds of years ago.

The embroidery combines floss silk and metallic threads with backstitch quilting in geometric designs filling the cotton ground, all worked through thin cotton batting and coarse cotton backing. The corners were cut out to accommodate the posts of a tall-post bed. Strips of the removed narrow floral borders were reapplied to edge the cutouts, and the quilt was cut down across the top.

A related example is in the Victoria and Albert Museum, London, and yet another quilt with a similar center motif was once in the collection of Nostell Priory, Yorkshire, England.[10]

Figure 10a Detail.

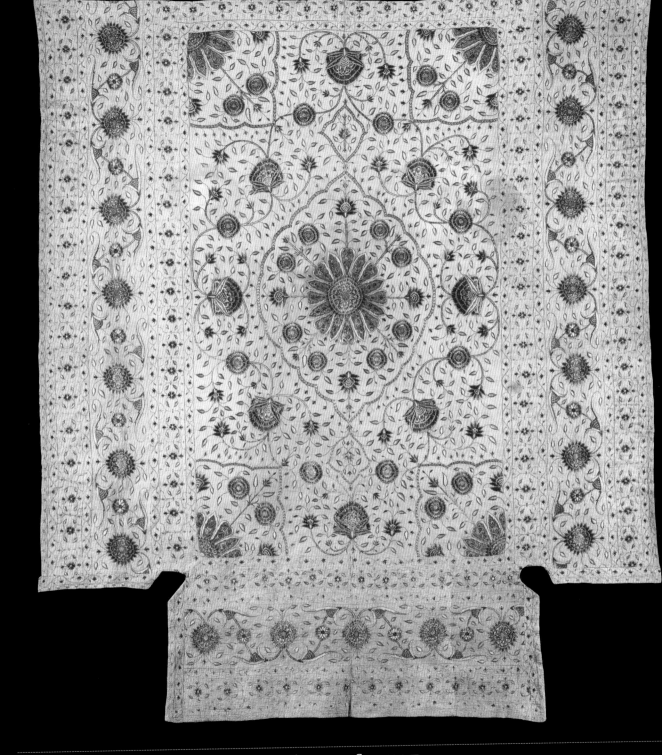

Bed Quilt adapted from a Floor Spread FIGURE 10

Maker unknown

Deccan region, India, 1730–1750

Cottons; silk and metallic embroidery threads

11–12 backstitches per inch

114 x 96 in. (290 x 244 cm)

Museum Purchase, 1959-250

FIGURE 11

Although the pale-yellow silk embroidery of this example is much worn, the design nevertheless reveals exotic creatures and a hunting scene in which men riding elephants spear their prey. Within a central roundel, the suggestion of a diamond is formed by the repetition of a winged figure that Westerners might view as a kind of mermaid but in India would be recognized as Matsya, one of the incarnations of the Hindu god Vishnu. A rectangular inner border features a quarter round inside each corner, and several outer borders teem with energetic scenes of hunters and animals.

The embroidery and quilting were done with tussah silk, which is naturally yellow in color, not dyed. The design was first worked with silk chain stitches through the white cotton top only. Then the decorated top was layered with extremely thin cotton batting and coarser cotton interlining and quilted in small scrolls and tight leafy vines that appear to pucker the ground slightly. The quilt has a loose linen backing fastened only at the outer edges. The backing must have been applied in England at a relatively early date since Indians did not typically use linen. Yellow-and-white Indian quilts such as this influenced English needlework styles, and early in the eighteenth century, it became fashionable to embroider with yellow silk (see figs. 24, 26).

A cloth label sewn to the linen backing reads, "This Quilt belonged to / Catherine Colepepper afterwards / Lady Fairfax / & matches with the Cushions" (fig. 11a). Catherine Colepepper, or Culpeper, who married Thomas Fairfax, fifth Lord Fairfax, inherited Leeds Castle in Kent, England, as well as the proprietorship of a vast tract of land in Virginia. Given the early date of the embroidered bedcover, Lady Fairfax could have inherited it from her ancestors. Her 1719 estate inventory includes several quilts, but none described in enough detail to determine whether this was one of them.[11] Another possibility is that the quilt came with the castle. An earlier resident of Leeds Castle, Sir Richard Smythe, had a brother, Sir Thomas Smythe, who was a founder of the East India Company and governor of the company from 1606 to 1621.[12] Perhaps the quilt came to Leeds Castle by virtue of Sir Thomas Smythe's trading activities and remained there when the castle came into the possession of the Culpeper family.

Colonial Williamsburg donor Cora Ginsburg purchased the quilt from an English dealer in the twentieth century. Although Lord Fairfax did travel to Virginia, as he administered his wife's Northern Neck lands, there is no evidence that the quilt was ever in Virginia. Nevertheless, Lord Fairfax would have been familiar with this or similar quilts. Indeed, written sources show that other colonial American families owned Indian quilts, possibly of this type. The embroidered cushions referred to in the label do not survive but were probably similar to the pillows that coordinate with two English silk-embroidered quilts in the Colonial Williamsburg collection (see figs. 25a, 27).

Related examples are in the collections of several museums, including the Victoria and Albert Museum, London; the Museu Nacional de Arte Antiga, Lisbon, Portugal; and the Tokugawa Art Museum, Nagoya, Japan.[13]

Figure 11a Detail of the quilt with corner turned up, revealing the handwritten label on the back of the quilt. Notice the fine yellow silk chain stitching with textural needlework in the background.

Embroidered Quilt FIGURE 11

Maker unknown

Bengal, India, 1600–1625

Cottons, Linen; silk embroidery threads

12–16 backstitches per inch

106 x 88 in. (269 x 224 cm)

Gift of Cora Ginsburg, 1987-551

QUILT MADE FROM A CHINTZ PALAMPORE

A central tree bearing a variety of flowers rises from a rocky mound and is surrounded on three sides by a border of additional flowers and C-scroll stems flowing from cornucopias. Although often considered typically Indian, the flowering tree motif derived from a hybrid of influences, including Chinese, Persian, and European, as well as Indian. As early as 1643, British East India Company directors sent instructions to India regarding the best colors to sell in England, and by 1662, the directors were sending out British patterns to be copied in India. Scholars have noted the close relationship between the exotic trees on English crewel embroidery and the flowering branches on chintzes, concluding that an already-established taste in needlework motifs may have influenced the Indian products, rather than the reverse (see fig. 12a).[14]

The Indian-made mordant-painted and resist-dyed panel, probably originally sized and designed to be a bed curtain, was cut down at the top and extended in width to make a bed quilt by the addition of greenish-yellow silk borders. The whole was quilted in a diamond pattern with guilloche borders through cotton batting and coarse cotton backing. The quilting stitches are gold-colored silk thread in the borders and natural linen thread in the chintz areas. The quilting was probably done in Europe, possibly France. The Cooper-Hewitt National Design Museum in New York also has a quilt with a chintz center and extensions of silk.[15]

Acquired in 1930, the bedcover was one of the first quilts purchased by Colonial Williamsburg. Vendor Elinor Merrell of New York specialized in what her letterhead referred to as "Old Chintzes," many of which she purchased in Europe, especially in France.

Figure 12a Curtain panel, "MM," England, 1701, linen-cotton mixture with wool embroidery threads, 96 x 54 in. (244 x 137 cm), Museum Purchase, 1958-631. Designs and influences flowed back and forth between England and India. Crewel wool embroidery in the flowering tree pattern was fashionable in England and may have influenced the designs on some India chintz palampores. This panel was inscribed at the top edge "BEGAN NOV 3 1701 MM." The needleworker's identity is not known.

Quilt made from a Chintz Palampore FIGURE 12

Maker unknown

Center panel India, quilted in Europe, 1770–1790

Cottons, silks, linen

5–6 running stitches per inch

119 x 112½ in. (302 x 286 cm)

Museum purchase, 1930-690

1   Ruth Barnes, Steven Cohen, and Rosemary Crill, *Trade, Temple and Court: Indian Textiles from the Tapi Collection* (Mumbai: India Book House, 2002), 12. For more about Indian quilts, especially those exported to the Netherlands, see An Moonen, *A History of Dutch Quilts* (Utrecht, NETH: Van Gruting, 2010).

2   For detailed descriptions of the mordant-painting and dyeing process, see John Irwin and Katharine B. Brett, *Origins of Chintz* (London: Her Majesty's Stationery Office, 1970) and Rosemary Crill, *Chintz: Indian Textiles for the West* (London: V & A Publishing, 2008).

3   Edward Terry, *A Voyage to East-India; Wherein Some Things Are Taken Notice of, in Our Passage Thither, but Many More in Our Abode There, within That Rich and Most Spacious Empire of the Great Mogul: Mixt with Some Parallel Observations and Inferences upon the Story, to Profit as well as Delight the Reader* (1655; repr., London, 1777), 108–109.

4   Ibid., 127.

5   In addition to the quilt shown in fig. 8, the Victoria and Albert Museum has a chintz quilt with plain cotton lining, dated ca. 1720–1750 (Circ.465-1912).

6   A small silk quilt attributed to the vicinity of Goa is in the Los Angeles County Museum of Art collection; although not made of taffeta reversing to satin, this silk quilt may be related to the type described in Terry's account. It is unlikely that the quilt was made in the port city of Goa but may have been sold or exported from there. The quilt was a gift of Cora Ginsburg, published in Sandi Fox, *Wrapped in Glory: Figurative Quilts and Bedcovers, 1700–1900* (London: Thames and Hudson; Los Angeles, CA: Los Angeles County Museum of Art, 1990), 14–17.

7   *Letters Received by the East India Company from Its Servants in the East,* ed. Frederick Charles Danvers, vol. 1, *1602–1613* (London: Sampson Low, Marston, 1896), 29.

8   India Office Archives, Court Book IV, p. 135, as quoted in John Irwin and Margaret Hall, *Indian Embroideries,* vol. 2 of *Historic Textiles of India at the Calico Museum* (Ahmedabad, IND: S. R. Bastikar on behalf of Calico Museum of Textiles, 1973), 35.

9   Inventory of Peter Walker, Northampton County, VA, Deeds, Wills, and Inventories, no. 5 (1654–1655), Virginia State Library, Richmond; "Inventory of Estate of Richard Grimes, December 5, 1716," York County, VA, probate records, as transcribed in

Colonial Williamsburg's digital library, accessed March 9, 2012, http://research.history.org/DigitalLibrary.cfm; *The Diary of Samuel Sewall,* ed. M. Halsey Thomas, vol. 2, *1709–1729* (New York: Farrar, Straus and Giroux, 1973), 954n37; "An Inventory of the Personall Estate of His Excelencey William Burnett Esqr, Deceased Late Governour of the Province of the Masachusetts Bay," October 13, 1729, Suffolk County, Massachusetts, Probate Court; Purdie and Dixon's *Virginia Gazette* (Williamsburg), January 30, 1772; Rind's *Virginia Gazette* (Williamsburg), May 12, 1774; Dixon and Hunter's *Virginia Gazette* (Williamsburg), May 8, 1778; and Christopher Gilbert, *The Life and Work of Thomas Chippendale* (London: Studio Vista, 1978), 1:240, 2:29.

10 Victoria and Albert Museum (IM.2-1912). The Nostell Priory quilt was sold in 1991. The sale catalog suggested it was English and dated 1700 to 1730, although it appears Indian from the photograph. Sotheby's, *Fine Dolls, Teddy Bears, Automata, Mechanical Musical Instruments, Tinplate and Diecast Toys, Robots, Games, European Costume and Textiles,* September 17–18, 1991 (London: Sotheby's, 1991), lot 440.

11 David A. H. Cleggett, *History of Leeds Castle and Its Families* (1990; Maidstone, Kent, UK: Leeds Castle Foundation, 1992), 119–123.

12 Ibid., 79.

13 See Satarupa Dutta Majumder, "Satgaon Quilts: A Study," in *Textiles from India: The Global Trade,* ed. Rosemary Crill (Calcutta, IND: Seagull Books, 2006), 316–328; and John Irwin, "Indo-Portuguese Embroideries of Bengal," *Art and Letters: The Journal of the Royal India, Pakistan and Ceylon Society,* n.s., 26, no. 2 (1952): 65–73. The authors thank Sandi Fox for lending copies of these articles from her research archives. See also John Guy, *Woven Cargoes: Indian Textiles in the East* (London: Thames and Hudson, 1998), fig. 218.

14 Crill, *Chintz,* 14–15.

15 In addition to the quilt with silk borders (1968-79-1), the collection at Cooper-Hewitt has a chintz quilt with extensions of French floral-patterned, block-printed cotton (1969-128-1). See Alice Baldwin Beer, *Trade Goods: A Study of Indian Chintz in the Collection of the Cooper-Hewitt Museum of Decorative Arts and Design, Smithsonian Institution* (Washington, DC: Smithsonian Institution Press, 1970), 79, 97.

CHAPTER 2

SILK CORDED

CHAPTER 2

SILK CORDED

A group of distinctive and colorful silk quilts has long puzzled scholars. The quilts are made of silk on both front and back in a bold cord-quilting technique. The cord fillings are soft, loosely spun cotton rolls measuring between one-quarter and three-eighths inch in diameter, or about seven to ten millimeters. Unlike these silk examples, most English and continental European corded quilts are made of white linen or cotton in dense yet delicate designs, and the manner of construction is apparent. After stitching channels through two layers of fabric, quilters inserted thin, tightly spun cords through holes opened in the coarser backing fabric, leaving clear evidence of the technique in the form of holes and projecting cords (see fig. 27). In contrast, the quilts from the silk corded group are much bolder in scale and are completely reversible. The delicate silks show no evidence that cords were inserted through the backs after stitching the channels; the stuffing cords must have been laid in during the quilting process.

The Colonial Williamsburg Foundation collection includes two examples of the genre, one complete quilt and one fragment, and similar quilts exist in numerous other collections in the United States and around the world.[1] In addition to sharing the same technique and materials, many of the surviving quilts feature similar motifs: a ship or ships in full sail; roundels enclosing profile faces, some wearing turbans; fighting soldiers in armor; human figures hunting animals such as boars; eight-petal flowers; and

guilloche, or figure-eight, bands that delineate borders. Some of the quilts include double-headed eagles; interlacing tracery or arabesques; arcaded architectural elements; and scenes or characters from mythology, such as Neptune, Triton, and Orpheus charming the animals.

The silk corded quilts are generally assigned dates from the late 1500s to around 1610, based on the style of clothing worn by the human figures and the designs of the ships.[2] The iconography and stylistic elements can be compared with other decorative arts about the same time, such as early woodcut maps and map cartouches, which illustrate similar land and sea creatures and wavy lines to suggest water in the seas (see fig. 13).

The question of where the quilts were made remains a bigger mystery. In past years, museums and collections have cataloged them as being from Germany, Italy, Sicily, Marseilles, Portugal, India, and Indo-Portugal, the last including objects made in India under the patronage and influence of the Portuguese, who dominated Indian trade through Goa until the mid-seventeenth century. The quilts were apparently widely disseminated by sea. Examples have been found from Cornwall in England to the French coast and Italy.

The travel account of Edward Terry, who visited India in 1615, confirms that silk quilts with cotton fillings were made in that country for export (see chap. 1), and by the second half of the seventeenth century, orders went out from England to India for silk quilts by the hundreds.[3]

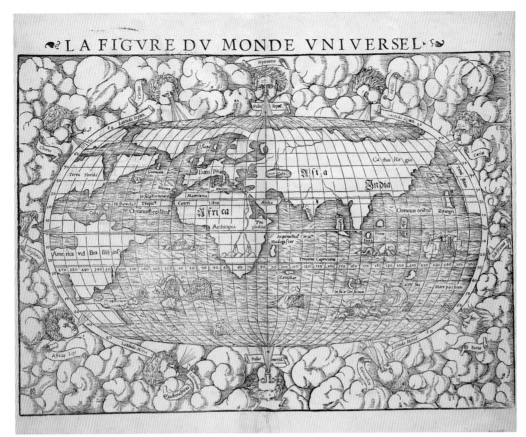

LA FIGVRE DV MONDE VNIVERSEL

Judging from these references, quilts made in the same materials as the silk corded group were being made in India: silk fronts and backs stitched with silk and with cotton filling. The surviving quilts in the silk corded group do appear to show Indian influence in their designs, especially compared with seventeenth-century embroideries from Bengal (see fig. 11). Many of the Bengal embroidered quilts feature center circular medallions, human and animal figures, hunting scenes with men spearing animals, and sea creatures.

There are problems with an Indian attribution, however. Assuming that Edward Terry knew the correct identity of satin and taffeta, his seventeenth-century description matches the quilts in the silk corded group with respect to fiber (silk with cotton filling) but not to weave structure. Most of the quilts in the silk corded group are made with thin plain-woven silk, not the shiny float-weave satin or ribbed-weave taffeta indicated by Terry.[4]

There may be another problem with an Indian attribution. Quilts from Winterthur Museum and from Colonial Williamsburg have undergone dye testing that identifies the yellow as weld, a dye believed to be unknown in early Indian textiles.[5] The dye evidence is not conclusive, however, because records show that European textiles were imported into Goa during Portuguese domination. Further, English traders sent dyers and weavers to Goa later in the seventeenth century.[6]

If an India origin is in question, what other locations are possible? Scholar Margaret Renner Lidz has made a compelling case for the quilts' origin on the island of Chios, one of the Greek Islands that was controlled by Genoese merchants until 1566 and then was taken over by the Ottoman Turks. The attribution is based on early period references to quilt making on the island as well as to iconographical relationships among art, architecture, and quilt designs. Lidz also pointed to the important Battle of Lepanto, fought in 1571 between the Ottoman Turks and the Christian alliance called the Holy League. This battle had great symbolic importance in the West because it disproved the previous belief that the Ottomans were invincible. Some of the ships on the quilts, especially those apparently shooting cannons, may refer to that battle.[7]

The group of silk corded quilts raises a number of questions. If the quilts are not Indian, based on the dye evidence and weave structure, where *are* the Indian silk quilts that were described as being made in great numbers in the seventeenth century? Did Indians make quilts using imported silks or dyestuffs, such as weld, thus explaining the non-Indian dyestuff?

Another question begging for an answer is whether the silk corded quilts were made at one location or in several different areas. The standardized materials and designs in many of the quilts suggest that those examples, at least, must have been made in close-knit workshops. Not all the

surviving examples, however, are drawn or quilted with the same level of detail or skill. It is possible that some quilts were made by professionals working in different workshops or even different countries, one copying or influencing the other.[8]

Given the wide geographical area where the quilts have been found and their designs, they were intended for export to an international audience familiar with Greco-Roman legends and iconography and possibly made somewhere in the Mediterranean or Aegean Sea area. Chios remains a strong possibility, although still conjecture until a firmly documented example is found. The Indo-Portuguese trading area of Goa cannot be ruled out as a possible origin, at least for some of the quilts.

SILK CORDED QUILT

FIGURE 14

This impressive quilt is filled with human and animal images. A large central roundel features a sailing ship that is surrounded by fish and two men perched on cloud-like islands. Four circles within the inner border each enclose a profile head, the designs possibly taken from coins or medals. The narrow borders feature classical guilloche bands, similar to cables or figure eights also seen in a number of later quilts. The quadrants and wider borders are filled with hunting scenes almost lost in the foliage (fig. 14a). In each quadrant, a knight on horseback waves a sword and carries a shield while his companion hound runs down a deer. In the outer borders, men on foot attack wild boars, and in the corners, double-headed eagles fill the spaces.

The quilt is reversible, made of thin yellow weld-dyed silk on one side and correspondingly thin blue silk on the other. As with the other silk corded quilts, loosely spun rolls of cotton are stitched into channels with no additional batting. The silk textiles making up the quilt are woven in plain weave and measure about thirty-two inches wide between the selvages.

Colonial Williamsburg purchased the quilt from the New York–based company of Cora Ginsburg LLC. The company acquired it at auction in London, where it had been consigned by a French owner.

Figure 14a Detail of quilting pattern. The foliage imagery and background wavy lines have been omitted for clarity.

Silk Corded Quilt   Figure 14

Maker unknown

Possibly Mediterranean or Aegean Sea area,
ca. 1600

Silks, cotton

7–10 running stitches per inch

107½ x 96½ in. (273 x 245 cm)

Museum Purchase, 2005-94

FIGURE 15

Made from thin silks of solid red and solid yellow with cotton cording between, this textile is a fragment of a much larger quilt. Many of the motifs were taken from classical stories and iconography, including the god Triton, who is shown blowing his horn, and the sea god Neptune, or Poseidon, who stands on a swimming dolphin (fig. 15a). The swimming man can be related to a number of other decorative arts and suggests Leander swimming across the Hellespont to his lover Hero. A similar motif is depicted in a second-century mosaic found at the Baths of Neptune in Ostia, not far from Rome, which shows a naked swimming man surrounded by dolphins. That is not to suggest that the quilt maker necessarily copied mosaics, however, because the motif of a swimmer was also used in northern European map iconography.

Although the fragmentary guilloche border matches that in figure 14, the design is otherwise quite different. Instead of having its design organized around a center roundel or horizontal band, this fragment is a mélange of seemingly scattered figures. Like several other quilts in the silk corded group, this fragment features ships sailing on water depicted as wavy quilting lines. The pennants with crescent motifs indicate that the ships are Turkish since the single crescent was part of various Ottoman pennants and flags from 1453 into the nineteenth century. It is tempting to suggest that the ships represent the 1571 Battle of Lepanto between Turks and Christians. Did the missing half of the quilt show more of the battle? By the late 1500s, the Ottoman Empire had extended to include the eastern Mediterranean, north to present-day Hungary and southwest to Iran and Egypt. The areas of the eastern Mediterranean—indeed, the entire Mediterranean—would have shared a long-standing Greco-Roman cultural influence, also seen in this fragment, yet they would have been keenly aware of the Turkish, given the nearness and influence of that major power. Perhaps this quilt fragment supports an eastern Mediterranean origin for at least some of the group.

Figure 15a The quilted motifs. The background wavy lines have been omitted for clarity.

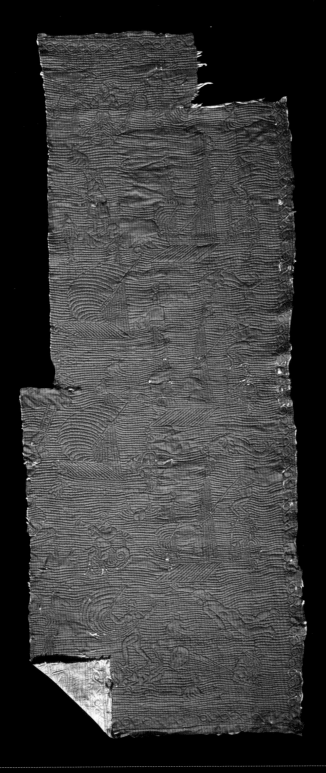

Silk Corded Quilt Fragment Figure 15

Maker unknown

Possibly Mediterranean or Aegean Sea area, ca. 1600

Silks, cotton

11–14 running stitches per inch

90 x 37 in. (229 x 94 cm)

Bequest of Grace Hartshorn Westerfield, 1974-650

Material from this chapter from Linda Baumgarten, "The Mystery of Silk Cord Quilts," paper presented at a meeting of the American Quilt Study Group, International Quilt Study Center & Museum, Lincoln, Nebraska, April 2009.

1   Silk corded quilts are found in museum and private collections worldwide, including Winterthur Museum, Garden & Library, DE (1954.49); the Royal Ontario Museum, Toronto (971.143 and 971.349); the Victoria and Albert Museum, London (T62-1937, CIRC 94-1937, T207-1953, 349-1886, and T296-1967); the Art Institute of Chicago (1960.889); the International Quilt Study Center & Museum, Lincoln, NE (2009.014.0003 and 2009.012.0004); the Wadsworth Atheneum Museum of Art, Hartford, CT (W.A. 1977.71); the Musée des Arts Décoratifs de l'Océan Indien, Saint-Louis, Réunion (inv. 996-1022); the Los Angeles County Museum of Art (M.87.229); private collection, discovered at Truro, ENG, by the British Quilters' Guild (see Pauline Adams and Bridget Long, "Traditions of Quilting," in Janet Rae et al., *Quilt Treasures of Great Britain: The Heritage Search of the Quilters' Guild* [Nashville, TN: Rutledge Hill Press, 1995], 64–135, esp. figs. 56–57); and a quilt once in the collection of Cora Ginsburg and sold at Sotheby's in 2005, present whereabouts unknown. The authors thank Titi Halle and Leigh Wishner for sending a photograph of this example and for information about similar quilts. See also Kathryn Berenson, *Marseille: The Cradle of White Corded Quilting* (Lincoln, NE: International Quilt Study Center & Museum, 2010), 44–47.

2   Two silk corded quilts from the collections of the Royal Ontario Museum (ROM), Toronto, were examined by ROM specialist curators and the author (Baumgarten) on October 2, 2006. Deepali Dewan saw Persian-Islamic design influences. She pointed out that the women flanking a musician look Indian with their triangular skirts. The piece was probably not Indian, however, although Portugal was a possibility. Peter Kaellgren suggested that Goa be considered as the origin. This city was a center for Western style and culture. Corey Keeble identified the ships as stylized three-masted square riggers, a European type of ship, with crow's nests at the tops. After first considering whether the ships might be 1650–1750, he said they rather date closer to ca. 1600. The costumes are soldiers' clothing and armor, with the helmets of the burgonet and comb morion types. The date of the soldiers' clothing appears to be 1590–1610. Keeble identified the round shields as types associated with Iberian Peninsula soldiers and suggested that the profile heads in medallions probably came from medals. Many of the motifs in the ROM quilts are also seen in the two Colonial Williamsburg examples.

3   Edward Terry, *A Voyage to East-India; Wherein Some Things Are Taken Notice of, in Our Passage Thither, but Many More in Our Abode There, within That Rich and Most Spacious Empire of the Great Mogul: Mixt with Some Parallel Observations and Inferences upon the Story, to Profit as well as Delight the Reader* (1655; repr., London, 1777), 127; and Vilhelm Slomann, *Bizarre Designs in Silks: Trade and Traditions* (Copenhagen, DEN: Ejnar Munksgaard, 1953), 148–149.

4   Quilts in the Chicago Art Institute and Los Angeles County Museum of Art, however, are made of silk satin.

5   Penelope Walton Rogers, York, ENG, analyzed the dyes in Colonial Williamsburg's yellow quilt 2005-94 in 2000 and 2003, before the quilt was acquired by CWF. Rogers found that the blue is indigotin, which can be derived from woad or indigo; the yellow consists of luteolin and apigenin, characteristic of weld. Rogers and colleagues have found weld in European, Persian, and Egyptian textiles but not in textiles known to be of Indian origin. According to Linda Eaton, curator at Winterthur Museum, Garden & Library, the silks in the Winterthur quilt measure about twenty-nine inches wide, and the dyes are weld reversing to redwood, the latter probably brazilwood.

6   Slomann, *Bizarre Designs in Silks*, 90, 110–111. Although Peter Kaellgren, the Royal Ontario Museum's specialist in Indian art, suggested Goa as a possible source, Rosemary Crill, curator of Indian artifacts at the Victoria and Albert Museum, London, suggested that the quilts in the group are *not* Indian. In fact, Crill had never seen an all-silk quilt she felt confident was Indian, despite the early references to them. Conversation with author (Baumgarten), July 5, 2005.

7   Margaret Renner Lidz, "The Mystery of Seventeenth-Century Quilts," *Antiques* 154, no. 6 (December 1998): 834–843. In this article, Lidz was among the first to publish a thorough analysis of the quilts and their origins.

8   Several examples that the author (Baumgarten) has not examined in person appear to have more detail in the figures, more sensitive designing, and larger areas of stuffing. These include the quilt at the Musée des Arts Décoratifs and Sotheby's 2005 quilt (see note 1).

Chapter 3

European Calico

EUROPEAN CALICO

The history of British and continental European printed cottons reflects in large part the influence of imported Indian cottons (see figs. 16, 17 and see chap. 1). Patterned Indian cottons were bright, colorful, exotic, comfortable to wear, washable, and colorfast. They became so popular that British and Continental textile printers quickly tried to copy them, although it took a number of years for Europeans to match the competition and to perfect their own printing technologies.

Printed cotton quilts and counterpanes were practical and fashionable. To help determine how common cotton quilts were before 1800 and what they looked like, scholars turn to household estate inventories. Although relatively few quilts were described with any detail in American inventories of the seventeenth and eighteenth centuries, those quilts that were described reveal what was considered fashionable, valuable, and worthy of special note. Of those quilts that were described by material, many were made of the cotton material known as calico.

What was calico? During the seventeenth century and

Figures 16 and 17 Details of two floral printed textiles, (left) probably France, ca. 1785, linen-cotton mixture, 81 x 40 in. (206 x 102 cm), Museum Purchase, 1955-427; (right) India, 1710–1720, cotton, 13¾ x 21¾ in. (35 x 55 cm), gift of F. Schumacher and Company, 1978-194. English and other European printers copied the colors and designs of imported Indian cottons but used block printing and penciling instead of the more labor-intensive techniques used in India. The French textile (left) was block printed with madder colors, after which pencil blue and yellow were added to create green; the Indian textile (right) was mordant painted and resist dyed.

the first half of the eighteenth century, *calico* usually meant cotton cloth imported from India. By the second half of the eighteenth century, the term included European cottons as well. Nevertheless, as late as 1755, Samuel Johnson's *Dictionary of the English Language* defined *calico* as "an Indian stuff made of cotton; sometimes stained with gay and beautiful colours." The distinction between *calico* and *chintz* is often confusing because their definitions and word usage changed over time (see chap. 1). Calico could be white, dyed, or printed. Although the term *chintz* was usually reserved for the finest Indian mordant-painted cotton textiles, *calico* and *chintz* were sometimes used interchangeably, especially by the late eighteenth century. Throughout the period under discussion, then, the word *calico* came to refer to many different kinds of cotton, whether Indian or English, whether white, dyed, or multicolored; they could be patterned by a number of different techniques from India as well as Europe. In this chapter, the focus is on quilts made of European eighteenth-century printed cotton calicoes.

One variety of calico, called *patch* or *patches,* may cause confusion for quilt scholars. In Virginia in 1789, Thomas Nelson of Yorktown, Virginia, had "4 patch callico quilts" worth eight British pounds in his estate inventory.[1] The word *patch* here does not necessarily refer to patch*work,* or piecing, but almost certainly to the textile. Patches arrived in America through the export trade and were widely advertised in eighteenth-century newspapers: "India Patches," "chinces, callicoes, [and] *India* patches," "callicoes & chints, english, & india patches."[2] The contexts suggest that patches were cotton yard goods that were typically printed.

Trade records and inventories attest that American colonists, although separated from commercial centers by an ocean, were able to acquire textiles from Europe and as far away as India beginning in the early years of settlement. These imports included cotton yard goods as well as finished quilts. Seventeenth-century Boston appears to be typical of other urban areas in its use of cotton wholecloth quilts at an early date. First, it should be noted that bed rugs woven or embroidered with heavy wool outnumber quilts by almost twelve to one in early Boston-area inventories. Nevertheless, six of the thirteen quilts listed in the

surveyed inventories were made of calico, and one was further described as "painted," almost certainly a reference to Indian mordant-painted and dyed cotton; one quilt was described as "East India," a term that could indicate Indian cotton calico or one of the embroidered quilts made in India at the time (see figs. 10, 11); five of the quilts were silk; and one quilt was described simply by the color white. No quilts in the inventory survey were identified as wool.[3]

In Woodbury, Connecticut, between 1727 and 1800, 440 quilts out of 545 were unidentified as to their color or material. Of those quilts for which a material was given, however, 51 were calico, the most commonly mentioned textile in this group of inventories. One of the calico quilts was described as "pice'd [pieced]," and another was blue and white. Blue was an especially popular color for quilts in Woodbury. Forty-nine quilts were described simply as blue, but no additional identification was given, so neither the fiber nor the pattern (or lack of it) can be determined. Five quilts were made of worsted wool materials, possibly similar to the quilts illustrated in chapter 5.[4]

In York County, Virginia, between 1700 and 1765, only about one in five inventories surveyed included bed quilts of any type, and, like inventories in other regions, most did not specify what the quilts looked like. Out of 174 quilts, 160 were not identified as to color or material. Once again, however, calico appears to have been called out for special notice. Eight quilts were described as "callico" or "calico" (one described as "India" calico); four were silk (one of the four was silk patchwork); one quilt was made of Holland, a linen textile; and one was described as yellow. No wool or worsted quilts were listed.[5]

Although they give valuable information, inventories tell only part of the story. Some people whose inventories did not list quilts may actually have owned them, subsumed under the general phrase "bed and furniture" or "bed and bedding." The inventories also prompt questions about why the percentage of wool quilts appears to be so low, despite their physical survival in relatively high numbers (see chap. 5). In all likelihood, many of the quilts not otherwise described were made of wool worked in simple florals, grids, or zigzag lines—functional but unremarkable bedcovers probably not considered worthy of special note. But why

PLATE XII.　　　　　　　Engraved for the SUPPLEMENT.　　　　　Facing Calico printing

Figure 18 Facing "Calico-printing," from John Barrow, *A Supplement to the New and Universal Dictionary of Arts and Sciences* (London, 1754), plate 12, © The British Library Board. At the center and right, English workmen use blocks to print mordants for madder dye onto the textile. At the left, women paint, or "pencil," blue and yellow to create blue, yellow, and/or green (the last achieved by combining blue with yellow).

were calico quilts specifically listed more often than any other textile for more than one hundred years? The answer lies in the fact that calico quilts were both fashionable and increasingly available.

Although the earliest calico quilts were probably made of Indian cotton, British and Continental printers quickly sought to imitate the popular Indian printed cottons using their own linens or imported white Indian cottons for the ground fabrics and madder dye instead of Indian chay (fig. 18). Printing in Britain was initially stimulated by prohibitions on Indian imported cottons enacted in 1700. Due to the combined effects of imported cottons and British imitations of Indian goods, however, other textile industries were adversely affected, and they petitioned for relief. The relatively young printing business in Britain was dealt a blow by a 1721 law that sought to protect other textiles by prohibiting all-cotton printed textiles, whether domestically produced or Indian imports, except for blue cottons and printed cottons made specifically for export.[6] From that time until the passage of new legislation in 1774, British printers could legally sell to local customers prints only on textiles with linen warps and cotton wefts.

The challenge for printers came not in simply applying color or ink but in printing in such a way that the colors were fast, not subject to fading or running. An English engraver named William Sherwin is credited with patenting

a method for colorfast printing in 1676, effectively starting the important British textile printing industry. Printers in France and Holland were developing similar technology at about the same time.[7] Unlocking and perfecting the complex secrets of colorfast printing relied on knowledge of dye chemistry. The dyestuff madder, for example, which produced colors ranging from black and brown to more lively shades of reds, pinks, and purples, required mordants, chemical color fixatives, to remain fast to light and washing. The finest Indian cottons had been patterned by the labor-intensive process of hand painting the mordants, but Europeans turned to the quicker methods of block printing and, later, copperplate and roller printing. To successfully print, however, the mordants had to be thickened for adhesion during printing. Once European printers had developed methods to properly thicken the mordants, they were able to apply a different mordant for each color in the desired pattern on the textile. Before dyeing in madder, the mordant-printed textile was aged in a warm, humid atmosphere and subjected to baths of cow dung and water to remove the excess mordants and thickener. Finally the textile was dyed in madder, which produced a number of colors, depending on the strength and composition of the mordants used. The colors remained fast where the mordant had penetrated the cloth but could be cleared, or washed out, from those areas not printed with mordant.

In contrast to dyeing or printing with madder, coloring textiles with indigo blue required entirely different techniques. A vat dye, indigo needed to be in solution (often involving stale urine) to chemically reduce the dyestuff and allow it to penetrate the textile in the vat. When the textile was removed and exposed to the oxygen in air, the blue color oxidized on the textile and became colorfast. Repeated dipping created darker blue shades. In order to achieve a pattern with indigo, the dyestuff had to be prevented from penetrating where the textile was to remain white with either wax (the method used in India) or another resist paste, such as clay. Europeans also experimented with chemical methods to resist the indigo. Because of the expense of labor in England and on the Continent, indigo-resist printers developed block printing, rather than hand painting, to apply a resist paste. The use of resist paste led to the term *paste work* for these textiles.

Indigo-resist cottons were considered part of the calico family of textiles during the eighteenth century. An indigo-resist textile in the Albany Institute of History and Art in New York is stamped with a British excise stamp and the word "callicoe" (1948.31). Colonial Williamsburg has two textiles from the same yardage (fig. 19).

The special chemistry of indigo made it difficult to combine blue with other colors, which would have been ruined in an indigo vat. The Indian technique of applying wax to all areas intended to remain white or another color was deemed impractical in Britain, and by the 1730s printers developed pencil blue, a method of painting or brushing small details of indigo directly onto the textile. To prevent the indigo from oxidizing immediately on the brush, chemicals were required to retard oxidation long enough for the (mostly female) workforce of pencillers to apply the indigo to the textile with quick brush strokes (fig. 18). The rapid brushing process is still visible in many penciled textiles, which often have drips of blue and irregular streaks in blue areas.

China blue was another chemically sophisticated technique for printing patterns with indigo. China blue printers mixed ground indigo with thickeners and copperas, a chemical retardant. The mixture was printed on the textile, which was then dipped into alternating chemical vats to reduce

Figure 19 Detail of indigo-resist textile, Indian cotton, probably printed in England, ca. 1766, cotton, 39½ x 114 in. (100 x 290 cm), pattern repeat 46½ in. (118 cm), Museum Purchase, 1955-257, 2. Printed in two shades of indigo blue, this textile shows a printer's error in placing the blocks used to create the resist pattern. This textile was once part of the yardage now in the Albany Institute of History and Art that has a 1766 British excise stamp and the word "callicoe" on the bolt end (1948.31). The textile has a history of use in Albany, New York, in the eighteenth century.

the indigo with lime and then to reoxidize it with ferrous sulphate. This dipping process rendered the blues colorfast where the ground indigo had been applied.

Printers also advanced methods for applying color to textiles through the use of engraved copper plates, which had been used to print ink on paper for years. For textiles, however, the issues of washability and colorfastness had to be solved. An Irish printer named Francis Nixon is credited with developing the first commercially successful method for thickening mordants to the right consistency for printing from engraved copper plates. By printing with mordants for madder colors or China blue for indigo, the colors were fast to washing and light. Developed about 1752, the copperplate printing technique quickly spread to England by 1756 and to France not long after. Copperplate printing resulted in fine-line designs similar in appearance to engravings on paper. The textiles were not only colorfast, but they also captured considerable pictorial detail within long repeats (see fig. 20).[8] Copperplate prints were usually a single color—red, purple, sepia, black, or blue on white—

due to the difficulty of accurately registering the fine lines over each other for printing additional colors.

At the end of the eighteenth century, roller printing advanced the speed with which cotton textiles could be patterned. In Britain, William Bell patented a roller-printing machine in 1783 with improvements in technology over previous machines. Although Bell's machine eventually made cylinder printing commercially successful, it did not entirely eliminate other printing methods. Printers continued to use blocks and copperplates well into the nineteenth century, despite the increasing use of rollers for printing. Often, block printing was used in conjunction with early roller prints to give added pattern or color.

Figure 20 Copperplate-Printed Wholecloth Quilt, textile printed by Talwin & Foster, quilt maker unknown, Bromley Hall, Middlesex, England, probably quilted in America, 1765–1775, linen-cotton mixture, linens, and wool with silk embroidery threads, 6 running stitches per inch, 94 x 94 in. (239 x 239 cm), Museum Purchase, 1973-3. The bold pattern of cockatoos perched on meandering branches was printed on fabric with linen warp and cotton weft, in accordance with British law before 1774. The maker used linen running stitches to quilt the bedcover in a pattern of zigzag lines. The batting is a thin layer of wool, and the backing an old reused linen sheet that still bears the brown silk cross-stitched initials of the original owner.

FIGURE 21

The cotton top of this wholecloth quilt is printed with two shades of indigo and quilted to a homespun woolen backing through woolen batting with linen thread in a zigzag pattern. The pieced-up top suggests that older fabric may have been reused to make the quilt. Although similar white-ground indigo resists are more often found in New York, this quilt has a documentable history in Connecticut.

About the QUILT MAKER AND HER FAMILY

The quilt descended in the family of Julia Evelina Smith, later Mrs. Amos Parker, of Glastonbury, Connecticut, who willed it to her friend Mrs. James Noble, from whom it descended to the latter's granddaughter, Mrs. Theodore Loomis Noble Harding. According to Mrs. Harding, her grandmother and Julia Smith (later Parker)[9] had formed a deep friendship through their mutual interest in women's suffrage. Julia Smith Parker's 1883 will described the bed quilt as being 120 years old and made by her grandmother before her marriage. Assuming Julia was correct about the age of the bequeathed quilt, it was made in or before 1766. Most likely, then, the quilt maker was Julia's maternal grandmother, Abigail Johnson, who married,

first, David Hickok in 1766. (She later married Eleazer Mitchell in 1786 after her first husband's death.) Not only do the dates of the first marriage fit Julia's recollections, but also this grandmother lived long enough to have personally related the quilt's history to her granddaughter. In fact, Grandmother Abigail lived with the Smith family as an elderly widow.[10]

The quilt would have been used by Julia Smith and her sister Abby, who shared their family home, Kimberly Mansion, in Glastonbury, Connecticut, prior to Julia's marriage. The quilt maker's two granddaughters were fascinating characters in their own right. Julia was a classical scholar who translated the Bible from the original languages. Julia and Abby were antislavery activists, but their fame came when they protested high taxes on their property, especially in light of the fact that, as women, they did not have the right to vote. They argued that this was "taxation without representation." The city impounded the sisters' cows in 1874 to cover unpaid taxes, although they were able to buy back the cows and eventually won the battle against the local tax assessors.[11] They never enjoyed the right to vote, however, because women's suffrage did not come about until 1920.

INDIGO-RESIST WHOLECLOTH CHILD'S QUILT

FIGURE 22

One side of this quilt has a bold floral design in two shades of indigo blue on white. Similar white-ground indigo resists have often been attributed to New York printers, as numerous examples have been found there. Indeed, this quilt descended in the Van Rensselaer family from Albany, New York. The existence of indigo-resist yardage carrying a British excise stamp from 1766 appeared to suggest that at least some of the indigo-resist textiles were British made (see fig. 19). Further research suggested that the stamp referred to foreign, not English, calicoes and that the indigo-resist textiles were the

products of India.[12] Most likely the stamp indicates cottons woven in India and exported as white yardage to be printed in England or elsewhere.

The reverse of the quilt has a China blue block-printed design of rococo ornaments enclosing castles and flowers on a background of scalloped dots that suggest quilting. Despite the stitchlike quality of the design, the quilter did not "follow the dots" on the backing. Instead, he or she stitched a central roundel, quarter rounds in the interior corners, and fans, ignoring the textile patterns entirely. The textiles and batting are cotton, quilted with linen thread.[13]

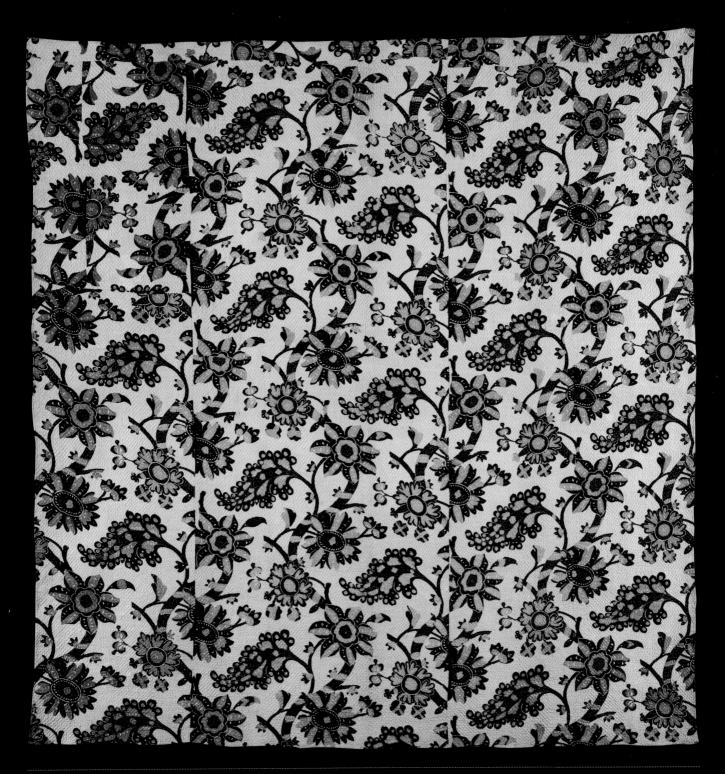

Indigo-Resist Wholecloth Quilt FIGURE 21

Indigo-Resist Wholecloth Child's Quilt   Figure 22

Maker unknown

Textiles probably England, quilted
in England or New York, 1750–1770

Cottons, linen

6–7 running stitches per inch

46½ x 36½ in. (118 x 93 cm)

Museum Purchase, 1955-175

Although printed textiles usually adorned the faces of quilts, some bedcovers were made with calico for the backing. The use of a printed textile on the back of a silk-faced quilt appears to have originated in India, and the fashion continued in the Philadelphia community of Quaker quilters in the second and third quarters of the eighteenth century.[14] The cotton backing of this quilt was block printed with two madder colors of black and red with the addition of pencil blue in a design of lacy oval frames, each enclosing a vignette with a well, reclining deer, and crane. Flowers fill in the remaining spaces. Although the origin of this printed textile is not known, it must have been imported.

The stitched design (fig. 23a) in this superbly preserved quilt is typical of those in other quilts and quilted petticoats made by Philadelphia Quakers.[15] The quilt features a center roundel, gadrooned vases with thin double handles, pomegranates and tulips at the ends of long stems, and inward-curving C-scroll leafy vines terminating in single flower heads. The ribbed silk face is quilted to the cotton backing through a batting of woolen fibers using silk running stitches. It is possible that the quilt design was drawn by a Philadelphia schoolteacher or professional designer (see also fig. 153).[16]

About the QUILT MAKER According to the family in which the quilt descended, Ann Jones made this quilt within the year she married Enoch Flower at Philadelphia Monthly Meeting on December 24, 1736.[17] It is not known whether she made the quilt in anticipation of her marriage or after.

Figure 23a Quilting pattern.

WHOLECLOTH QUILT BACKED WITH PRINTED COTTON FIGURE 23

ANN JONES FLOWER (MRS. ENOCH FLOWER) (CA. 1711–1775)

PHILADELPHIA, PENNSYLVANIA, CA. 1736

SILKS, COTTON, WOOL

10–12 RUNNING STITCHES PER INCH

103½ X 95 IN. (263 X 241 CM)

MUSEUM PURCHASE, 1976-59

1   "Inventory of Estate of General Thomas Nelson, June 2, 1789," York County, VA, probate records, as transcribed in Colonial Williamsburg's digital library, accessed March 13, 2012, http://research.history.org /DigitalLibrary.cfm.

2   *Boston Weekly News-Letter,* April 15, 1736; *Boston Gazette, or Country Journal,* May 26, 1755; and *Boston-Gazette, and Country Journal,* September 1, 1760. Florence Montgomery suggested that *patch* may have come from "panches, an Indian printed cloth." *Textiles in America, 1650–1870: A Dictionary Based on Original Documents, Prints and Paintings, Commercial Records, American Merchants' Papers, Shopkeepers' Advertisements, and Pattern Books with Original Swatches of Cloth* (1984; New York: W. W. Norton, 2007), 318.

3   Linda R. Baumgarten, "The Textile Trade in Boston, 1650–1700," in *Arts of the Anglo-American Community in the Seventeenth Century,* Winterthur Conference Report 1974, ed. Ian M. G. Quimby (Charlottesville: University Press of Virginia for the Henry Francis du Pont Winterthur Museum, 1975), 262. Inventories were surveyed in three periods of five years each: 1650–1655, 1670–1675, and 1690–1695.

4   Robert G. Stone, ed. *Connecticut Quilts: Bed Quilt Entries Listed in Woodbury Connecticut Probate Inventories, 1720–1819* (Lee's Summit, MO: Fat Little Pudding Boys Press, 1998), 11–19. The worsted quilts were identified as follows: one each of shalloon, calamanco, and tammy and two of "woosted."

5   The statistics come from 415 estate inventories from York County, VA, between 1700 and 1765, which have been digitized and made available online at Colonial Williamsburg's Digital History site: http://research.history.org/DigitalLibrary.cfm. This online database does not include all York County inventories but is a representative selection. Gloria Seaman Allen surveyed York County, VA, inventories from 1780 to 1840 and found that the percentage of quilt owners hovered around 12–17% of decedents between 1780 and 1820 but then increased dramatically to 39% in the 1820s and 44% in the 1830s. Calico remained popular, according to Allen, only being eclipsed by Marseilles quilts by the 1790s. *First Flowerings: Early Virginia Quilts* (Washington, DC: DAR Museum, 1987), tables B-1 and C-1.

6   For more detail on printing history and techniques, see Florence M. Montgomery, *Printed Textiles: English and American Cottons and Linens, 1700–1850* (New York: Viking, 1970); also Deryn O'Connor and Hero Granger-Taylor, *Colour and the Calico Printer: An Exhibition of Printed and Dyed Textiles, 1750–1850* (Surrey, ENG: West Surrey College of Art and Design, 1982). For new research on indigo resist, see Mary E. Gale and Margaret T. Ordoñez, "Indigo-Resist Prints from Eighteenth-Century America: Technology and Technique," *Clothing and Textiles Research Journal* 22, nos. 1/2 (2004): 4–14, 45.

7   Victoria and Albert Museum, *English Printed Textiles, 1720–1836* (London: Her Majesty's Stationery Office, 1960), 1.

8   Although some have credited French printers with developing copperplate printing (so-called *toiles de Jouy*), research indicates that Francis Nixon of the Drumcondra printworks outside Dublin first developed the technique in 1752. Victoria and Albert Museum, *English Printed Textiles,* 2–3; and Montgomery, *Printed Textiles,* 28–29.

9   Julia Smith married Amos A. Parker in 1879 at the age of 87, well after her activist career and her sister's death.

10 The grandmother on Julia's father's side was Ruth Hollister, who married Isaac Smith in Glastonbury in 1758. Biographical information for Julia Smith Parker and her family comes from Mrs. Theodore Loomis Noble Harding and the following sources: Julia E. S. Parker, will, dated March 26, 1883, codicil dated March 4, 1884, proved 1886, Hartford District Estate files 1881–1915, LDS#1831750, Connecticut State Library, Hartford; Emily Sampson, *With Her Own Eyes: The Story of Julia Smith, Her Life, and Her Bible* (Knoxville: University of Tennessee Press, 2006), 1–12; *Dictionary of American Biography,* s.v. "Smith, Abby Hadassah"; Charles Nelson Hickok, comp., *The Hickok Genealogy: Descendants of William Hickocks of Farmington, Connecticut* (Rutland, VT: Tuttle Publishing Company, 1938), 36–38, 72–73, 120; "Deaths" (for Abigail Mitchell), *Connecticut Courant* (Hartford), February 22, 1831; Lafayette Wallace Case, comp., *The Hollister Family of America; Lieut. John Hollister of Wethersfield, Conn., and His Descendants* (Chicago: Fergus Printing Company, 1886), 730–734. The authors thank Jerry Seagrave in History and Genealogy, Connecticut State Library, for assistance.

11 National Register of Historic Places Inventory–Nomination Form, Kimberly Mansion, Glastonbury, Hartford County, CT, U. S. Department of the Interior, National Park Service, digital image as found on nps.gov/nr, accessed July 10, 2013.

12 Amelia Peck, ed., *Interwoven Globe: The Worldwide Textile Trade, 1500–1800* (New York: Metropolitan Museum of Art, 2013), 295.

13 The quilt was once in the collections of the Albany Institute of History and Art. Sections of the border were quilted with cotton thread, possibly indicating later repairs. A reversible copperplate-printed quilt in the Metropolitan Museum of Art, New York, (45.145) is quilted in a similar pattern with fan shapes and a center panel; the quilt is said to be English based on that quilt pattern. See Amelia Peck, *American Quilts and Coverlets in the Metropolitan Museum of Art,* new ed. (New York: Metropolitan Museum of Art and MQ Publications USA, 2007), 126–127.

14 For a discussion of Indian silk quilts with printed cotton backings, see p. 13. The Mifflin family quilt at Winterthur Museum (1960.0787) has a silk front backed with red and black block-printed cotton.

15 Four related quilts have been identified thus far: bed quilt, owned by Elizabeth Coates Paschall, Philadelphia Museum of Art (PMA) (1932-45-124); quilted petticoat, worn by a member of the Roberts family, PMA (1900-49); bed quilt, said to be a ca. 1746 wedding gift to Sarah Mifflin Jones, PMA (1952-75-1); and a bed quilt, owned by Sarah Logan, Stenton, James Logan's historic house in Philadelphia (1975.3.8).

16 Based on their positions as teachers in the Philadelphia Quaker community, the particular students they taught, the motifs on their needlework, and a petticoat made by Ann, Elizabeth Marsh or her daughter, Ann, may have designed this quilt as well as others of the same style from the same community. See Linda Baumgarten, "Vase-Pattern Wholecloth Quilts in the Eighteenth-Century Quaker Community," in *Uncoverings 2015,* ed. Lynne Zacek Bassett (Lincoln, NE: American Quilt Study Group, 2015), 7–34.

17 William Wade Hinshaw and Thomas Worth Marshall, *Encyclopedia of American Quaker Genealogy* (Ann Arbor, MI: Edwards Brothers, 1938), 2:362, 567. The quilt descended in the female line to Ann Wheeler from her mother, Ann Jones Flower, and then to E. F. Paul, Mary P. Lownes, Sallie W. Morris, Mary Paul Morris, and lastly Patricia Paul Brown Mills.

EARLY EMBROIDERED

CHAPTER 4

EARLY EMBROIDERED

S ome of the most beautiful quilts in the Colonial Williamsburg collection were stitched in England in the late seventeenth century through the first half of the eighteenth century, a time when tall-post beds were often lavishly furnished with yards of expensive textiles, including bedcoverings that matched or echoed the designs of the curtains and valances. The workmanship was exquisite, and the materials included rich silk embroidery and quilting on fine, closely woven linens and cottons. Quilts such as these were sometimes given as wedding gifts among the gentry and were probably saved and cherished as much for sentimental reasons as for their beauty.[1]

These quilts and counterpanes were usually the products of anonymous professionals who embroidered for a living. Although their handwork is highly valued today, the work of embroiderers was neither glamorous nor remunerative in the eighteenth century. Robert Campbell's 1747 *London Tradesman* described the environment in which women and some men engaged in professional embroidery and quilting, working long days for low wages in the workshops of "lace-men," who hired many of the embroiderers. The shop owners oversaw the work and provided the expensive materials. According to Campbell, embroiderers needed special skills because embroidery "is an ingenious Art, requires a nice Taste in Drawing, a bold Fancy to invent new Patterns, and a clean Hand to save their Work from tarnishing." Furthermore, "an Embroiderer ought to have a Taste for Designing, and a just Notion of the Principles of Light and Shade, to know how to range their

Colours in a natural Order, make them reflect upon one another, and the whole to represent the Figure in its proper Shade."[2]

Campbell pointed out that, despite such high ideals for the trade, few workers had the skill of drawing, and for that reason, both embroiderers and quilters relied on professional designers called "Pattern-Drawers" to create the outlines for their work.[3] In the case of embroiderers, "they have their Patterns from the Pattern-Drawer, who must likewise draw the Work itself, which they only fill up, with Gold and Silver, Silks or Worsteds, according to its Use and Nature." Campbell explained that pattern drawers worked for a variety of trades, perhaps explaining the consistency of designs from one medium to the other: pattern drawers were "employed in drawing Patterns for the Callico-Printers, for Embroiderers, Lace-workers, Quilters, and several little Branches belonging to Women's Apparel. They draw Patterns upon Paper, which they sell to Workmen that want them."[4]

The designs and colors of early eighteenth-century embroidery frequently betray influence from Indian imports. Pale-yellow silk stitches on white cotton grounds echo Bengal embroidered quilts, except that Indians used naturally yellow tussah silk, not dyed silk. Designs with a central lobed medallion and a quarter round in each corner similarly show the influence of India (see figs. 10, 11).

A number of techniques can be seen in English professionally embroidered quilts of the late seventeenth and early eighteenth centuries. Some bedcovers were heavily embellished with silk embroidery stitches, with the spaces between motifs worked in backstitched repeat patterns through the top textile and a coarser interlining fabric, a style probably inspired by Indian imports. This technique is sometimes referred to as flat, pseudo, or false quilting because the English quilts lack any fiber batting. The coarse interlining might be considered the equivalent to batting, however, since the bedcovers were eventually backed to hide the reverse of the embroidery stitches, resulting in a three-layered end product. Some embroidered quilts combined silk embroidery with cord quilting, such as the elaborate quilt with two matching pillow covers in figures 26 and 27.

EMBROIDERED COUNTERPANE OR QUILT

FIGURE 24

This subtle but stunning bedcover was embroidered with gold-colored silks that create a shimmering effect reminiscent of metallic gold strapwork and repoussé raised ornamentation. A professional embroiderer used satin, padded satin, stem, running, straight, and split stitches, along with clusters of French knots, to create the primary design with a lobed center medallion and quarter rounds in the corners. The intervening spaces were filled with stylized flowers, leaves, and scrollwork, and the ground quilted with backstitches in a pattern of interlocked circles. The stitching was worked through two layers, the fine linen top and coarser linen interlining, without any batting. In the border extensions, the floral pattern was drawn on the top fabric in black ink while the backstitched quilting design was drawn with light red ink. Both are still visible in areas where the embroidery has worn away. The use of red ink would have enhanced the golden yellow color and avoided the darkening effect that sometimes occurs when light colors are embroidered over black ink outlines.[5] The quilt has been altered over time by the addition of border extensions to the sides, top, and bottom. These were probably the original bed valances, stitched to the quilt to enlarge it years after the set of bed hangings was first made, possibly after the rest of the set had worn out. The backing and satin binding are modern replacements.

The bedcover has a history of ownership until 1957 by Mrs. Berkeley Levett of Sidmouth, England, whose late husband had been an equerry, or a gentleman usher, to Edward VII.[6] Given its early date, the quilt would have been owned by an eighteenth-century ancestor of one of the Levetts.

Figure 24a Detail of the yellow silk embroidery and background quilting stitches.

Embroidered Counterpane or Quilt FIGURE 24

MAKERS UNKNOWN

ENGLAND, 1690–1720

LINENS; SILK EMBROIDERY THREADS

26 BACKSTITCHES PER INCH

83 X 78 IN. (211 X 198 CM)

MUSEUM PURCHASE, 1957-158

EMBROIDERED QUILT

FIGURE 25

The gold, brown, and black silks of this small bedcover give an effect of energetic movement as the leaves and stems curl and twist against the backstitched ground. A professional embroiderer used satin and split stitches, couching, French knots, and a variety of decorative fillings. The background was quilted with gold-colored silk backstitches in half-inch diamonds. The black inked outlines of the design, drawn directly on the plain-woven cotton ground, are still visible under the embroidery and quilting. All of the embroidery was worked through the top and two different interlining materials: one section of the quilt was interlined with coarse linen, and another section, as well as the pillows, with cotton.

Three graduated embroidered pillows survive with the quilt (fig. 25a). The pillows have plain linen backs and cotton-stuffed inserts that are old but probably not original. Two of the pillows were tagged with old paper labels reading "Pillowcover belonging to old Embroidered Quilt / Date 1700 / Miss Dilkes." The identity of Miss Dilkes has not been determined.

The survival of matching cushions is not unique. A quilt in the collections of Winterthur Museum has matching pillows, and another embroidered quilt with a matched set of three pillows survives in the collections of Longleat House, Wiltshire, England. Like the Colonial Williamsburg examples, the Longleat pillows are graduated in size and were apparently intended to be piled in a pyramid at the foot of the bed. The Longleat set was made in 1733 for the wedding of Lady Louisa Carteret, who married the second Viscount Weymouth.[7]

Close examination shows subtle but clear differences among the embroidered pillows in the Colonial Williamsburg set, indicating that they were made in a professional studio with more than one hand at work. The largest pillow was quilted with twenty-three to twenty-four backstitches per inch; the middle pillow with twenty-six stitches per inch; and the smallest pillow, intended to be stacked on top of the pyramid and therefore most visible, with thirty to thirty-two stitches per inch. The bedcover itself averages about twenty-five stitches per inch. Differences can be observed in some of the embroidery details as well. Flowers that were outlined with a series of French knots on two of the pillows were worked with bullion knots on the smallest pillow.

According to Cora Ginsburg, who sold them to Colonial Williamsburg, the quilt and pillows originally came from Stoke Edith, a village in Herefordshire, England. The set had been in the collection of the Honorable Mrs. Nellie Ionides, a twentieth-century collector and connoisseur who lived in Sussex, England.[8]

Figure 25a Embroidered Pillows, makers unknown, England, 1700–1725, cottons and linens with silk embroidery threads, 23–32 backstitches per inch, 16¼ x 21 in. (41 x 43 cm), 13¾ x 18½ in. (35 x 47 cm), and 11 x 15 in. (28 x 38 cm), Museum Purchase, 1964-454, 2–4. Judging from perceptible differences in technique and stitches per inch, the set was probably embroidered in a large workshop with a number of hands at work.

Embroidered Quilt   Figure 25

Maker(s) unknown

England, 1700–1725

Cottons, linens; silk embroidery threads

25 backstitches per inch

74 x 58 in. (188 x 147 cm)

Museum Purchase, 1964-454, 1

EMBROIDERED AND CORDED QUILT AND TWO PILLOW COVERS

FIGURE 26   FIGURE 27

Luxurious yellow silk embroidery and dense cord quilting give this quilt the elegance appropriate to a fine English state bed, which would have been hung with full-length curtains of coordinating embroidery or woven silk. The quilt's design centers on a diamond-shaped medallion with four pendants, with related quarter medallions and pendants in the four corners and a nine-inch-wide border, all embellished with freely embroidered flowers in split and stem stitches with French knot accents. The design shows influence from imported Indian counterpanes in the use of pointed medallions and yellow color (see chap. 1). The ground of the quilt is a lavish pattern of raised cord quilting in coiling stems, leaves, and abstracted flowers, all achieved by parallel rows of backstitches through which cotton cords were drawn from the back.

Freely embroidered areas of the quilt were interlined with loosely woven wool for padding and stability; the wool was not used behind the cord-quilted areas, only behind the center medallion, quarter medallions, and borders. In the spaces between the embroidered motifs in the noncorded areas, parallel rows of yellow silk running stitches were worked through the top linen and the woolen interlining and pulled tight to gather up the ground fabric slightly (fig. 26a). This use of gathering stitches served two purposes. From a functional standpoint, the running stitches controlled potential puffs and puckers created by the adjacent cord quilting, the denseness of which tends to draw in the fabric where it is worked. The running stitches and wool padding also evened out the thickness of the quilt. From a stylistic point of view, the yellow stitches echoed the yellow silk allover quilting found in many fashionable Indian quilts (see fig. 11).

The pillow covers were not made with wool interlining or gathered quilting, probably because their smaller size resulted in less puckering around the cord quilting. The pillows were likely embroidered by a different individual in the workshop.

Figure 26a The detail shows cord quilting and areas of embroidery that are surrounded by running stitches to gather up the ground between flowers.

Embroidered and Corded Quilt and Two Pillow Covers   Figures 26 and 2

Makers unknown

England, 1700–1725

Linen, cotton, wool; silk embroidery threads

22–28 backstitches per inch

Quilt 93½ x 88½ in. (237 x 225 cm)

Pillow Covers each 15 x 26½ in. (38 x 67 cm)

Gift of Mrs. J. S. Frelinghuysen, 1941-260 and 1941-261, 1–2

The bottom pillow cover is shown inside out to reveal the back of the cord quilting and needlework.

1 Naomi Tarrant suggested that embroidered bedcovers like the example in the collections of National Museums Scotland were sometimes given as wedding gifts. She referred to similar examples in the Victoria and Albert Museum, London, and Longleat House, Wiltshire, ENG, with such histories. *Textile Treasures: An Introduction to European Decorative Textiles for Home and Church in the National Museums of Scotland* (Edinburgh: National Museums of Scotland Publishing, 2001), 95.

2 R[obert] Campbell, *The London Tradesman* (London, 1747; repr., New York: Augustus M. Kelley, 1969), 153–154, 213.

3 Most pattern drawers are anonymous. The name of one pattern drawer, John Stilwell, is known from his signature on a woman's embroidered waistcoat in the Fashion Museum, Bath, ENG (4750/2). The garment is embellished with exotic birds and flowers; the background is quilted in a backstitched grid pattern, typical of the quilting found on several English bedcovers in the Colonial Williamsburg collection. Stilwell signed his work on the lining of the garment, "John Stilwell Drawear att ye Flaming Soord in Russell Street Cov. [Covent Garden]." See John L. Nevinson, "John Nelham,

Embroiderer," *Bulletin of the Needle and Bobbin Club* 65, nos. 1/2 (1982): 15, 17–19, esp. 18 and fig. 8.

4 Campbell, *London Tradesman*, 115, 153, 213.

5 A closely related quilt in the collections of Winterthur Museum also has the primary design drawn in black and the quilting lines drawn in red. The quilt has a matching pillow cover. See Linda Eaton, *Quilts in a Material World: Selections from the Winterthur Collection* (New York: Abrams in association with the Henry Francis duPont Winterthur Museum, 2007), 120–121.

6 Charles Angell to John M. Graham, August 9, 1957, CWF object file 1957-158. Angell misspelled the name as "Levell" but identified Berkeley as an "Equerry to the late King Edward VII." Berkeley Levett held the position of gentleman usher in the 1920s and early 1930s. Mrs. Berkeley Levett was Sibell Lucia Bass. *Who Was Who, 1941–1950*, s.v. "Levett, Maj. Berkeley John Talbot."

7 For the Longleat set, see Thomasina Beck, *The Embroiderer's Flowers* (Devon, ENG: David & Charles, 1992), 46. For the Winterthur cushions, see Eaton, *Quilts in a Material World*, 121.

8 *Antiques* 83, no. 3 (March 1963): 298–299.

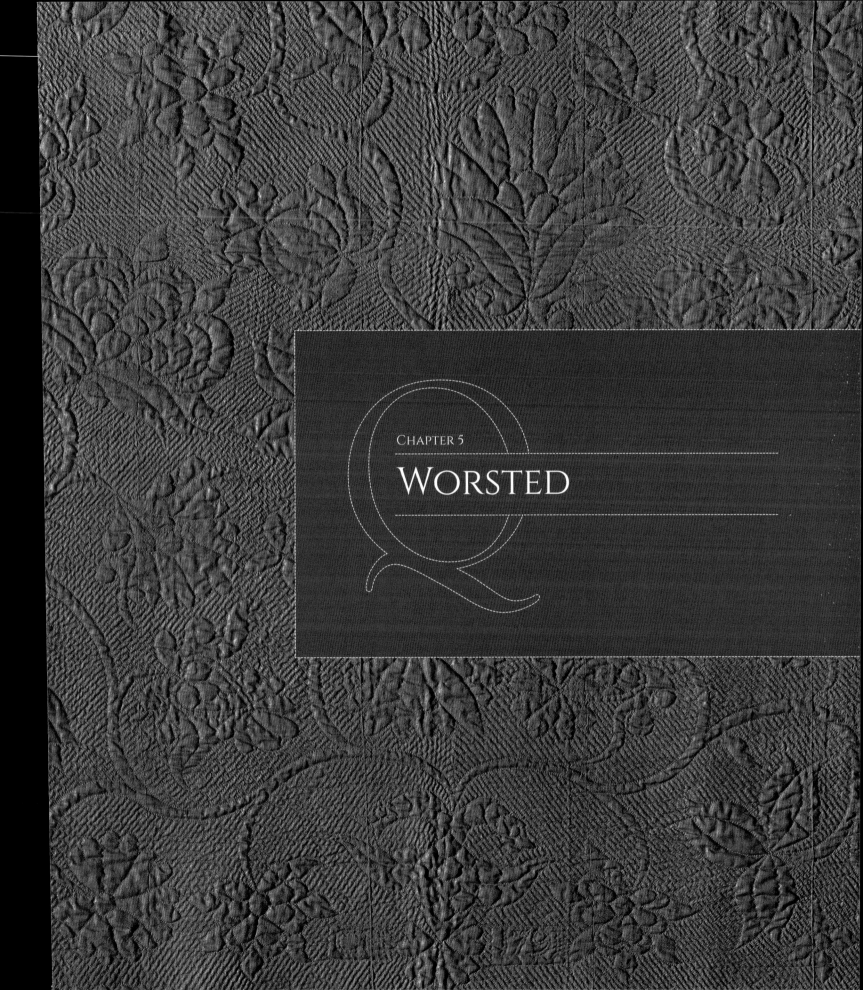

WORSTED

CHAPTER 5

WORSTED

Many women quilted wholecloth bedcovers using wool textiles for the tops, stitching lengths of woven fabric together to make a single piece large enough for the entire top. With wholecloth quilts, especially those using solid-colored materials, the decoration came entirely from the stitches that held the layers together. Some women drew their own designs while others relied on local artists or copied imported English quilts.

A relatively large number of wool wholecloth quilts survives. Often, the quilt tops were made from glazed worsteds, called *tammy, calamanco,* and *shalloon*.[1] These textiles were woven from fine, long wool fibers known as worsteds and pressed after weaving to give a glaze that rivaled silk in sheen. This treatment made the textiles permanently shiny and crisp and enhanced the visibility of the quilting. Because the glazing process required heavy machinery, it was done by the textile manufacturer, not by the quilter. Glazed worsteds often retain permanent creases in the fabric from being folded in the press and subjected to great pressure; these creases are still visible in some quilts (see fig. 29). Worsted wool treated in this way was made in England and shipped around the world, although a few American weavers produced glazed worsted textiles locally.

Merchants throughout the colonies not only sold the yard goods for women to construct their own bedcovers, but they also sold imported quilts—most likely wool wholecloth examples made in workshops around London—in a variety of standardized widths.[2] In 1760, for example, a Boston merchant advertised "6-4, 8-4, 9-4 and 10-4 bed quilts." The following year the same merchant described his merchandise as "6 7 8 9 & 10 qr. Bed Quilts."[3] (The use of quarters was a standard measuring system in the eighteenth century. A quarter was one-quarter of a yard, or nine inches; therefore, a "10-4," or "10 qr.," quilt was ninety inches wide.) Imported quilts likely influenced the designs of quilts made in the home.

Some American women continued to make and use wool quilts throughout the nineteenth century, but new textile innovations gradually made wool quilts less desirable. Developments in factory spinning and textile printing technologies caused patterned cottons to become more popular than wool for quilts. The cotton products not only were colorful, but they also were washable. Although chintzes and printed calicoes had always been fashionable for luxury quilts, nineteenth-century factory-made cottons became increasingly available to the average household and less costly than cottons had been prior to mechanization. Jacquard-woven coverlets also offered a relatively inexpensive alternative to handmade quilts. Coverlets made from wool and cotton by professional weavers were as colorful and warm as quilts and required less handwork on the part of the customer (see fig. 4). Finally, white cotton coverlets, counterpanes, and quilts surged in fashion by the end of the eighteenth century; they suited the new lighter aesthetics of the emerging neoclassical style while also being washable (see chap. 6).

INDIGO QUILT BACKED WITH OVERSHOT COVERLET

FIGURE 28

Because textiles were expensive, many eighteenth-century Americans altered, recycled, and reused their old clothing and textiles when they went out of fashion or became somewhat worn. This twill-woven glazed worsted quilt retains a beautiful quilted pattern despite being worn and fragile (fig. 28a). However, this quilt is even more important for its reused backing, an old coverlet made of yellow wool and natural linen in a diamond-pattern overshot weave (fig. 28b). Although many overshot coverlets woven with factory-spun cotton warps survive from the nineteenth century, only a handful of early linen-and-wool examples can be dated before 1800. The coverlet was too small to line the entire quilt, so the quilt maker pieced out the back of the quilt with fragments of a recycled mustard-color woolen blanket, one piece marked in blue silk with the original owner's initials, PI.

The quilt was purchased from a Richmond-based dealer who acquired many artifacts in the south.

Figure 28a Quilting pattern.

Figure 28b Detail of the linen-and-wool homespun coverlet reused as the backing of the indigo wool quilt.

Indigo Quilt backed with Overshot Coverlet   Figure 28

Maker unknown

America, 1780–1800, backing 1750–1780

Wools, linen-wool mixture; silk embroidery threads

6 running stitches per inch

99 x 85 in. (251 x 216 cm)

Museum Purchase, 1986-140

ROSE WHOLECLOTH QUILT

The maker of this bedcover, known only by the initials CH quilted into the center bottom, created an undulating asymmetrical pattern of large-scale flowers and leaves that brings to mind designs of the early to middle eighteenth century. However, the 1791 date stitched next to the initials reveals that some quilters retained conservative designs even after neoclassical design had influenced decorative arts. The quilt helps scholars assign dates to related quilts with similar characteristics.

The face of the quilt is made of plain-woven glazed worsted that retains the creases from the glazing process. The plain-woven brown backing is a combination of linen warp and wool weft, sometimes called *linsey-woolsey,* and the filling is wool fibers. All of the layers are stitched with wool running stitches.

The quilt came from Connecticut-based dealers.

Figure 29a Quilting pattern.

PINK WHOLECLOTH QUILT

The brilliant pink worsted is further enhanced by oversize quilted leaves and flowers. Although the design areas appear to be stuffed with extra filling, no additional batting was added beyond a layer of wool fiber spread evenly throughout the quilt. The stuffed appearance occurs because the background diagonally quilted lines, not shown in the drawing, pull the textile in, causing the nonquilted areas to puff up. The use of glazed worsted in the plain-woven top enhances the effect because the crisp glazed texture holds its shape without flattening. The quilt's backing is light-orange plain-woven wool that has been heavily napped to give it a fuzzy surface, and the quilting threads are wool. The cutout corners accommodated the posts of a tall bedstead.

The quilt came from the 1966 estate sale of collector Mrs. Austin P. Palmer of New Hampshire.[4]

Figure 30a Quilting pattern.

Rose Wholecloth Quilt Figure 29

"CH"

America, probably New England, 1791

Wools, linen-wool mixture

9–12 running stitches per inch

93 x 87½ in. (236 x 222 cm)

Museum Purchase, 1959-129

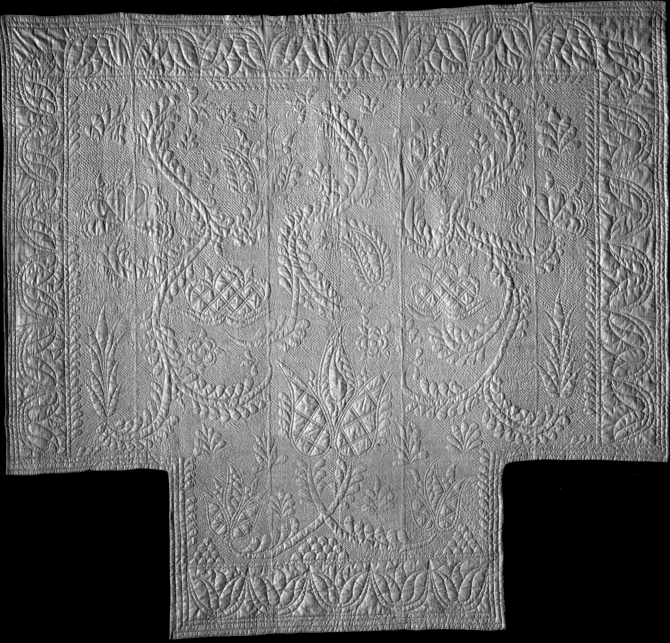

Figure 31

Green Wool Quilt

America or England, 1740–1790

100 x 87 in. (254 x 221 cm)

Museum Purchase, 1954-715

Figure 32

Blue Wool Quilt

New England, 1740–1775

94 x 95 in. (239 x 241 cm)

Museum Purchase, 1954-757

Figure 33

Dark-Indigo Wool Quilt

America, possibly New England, 1750–1790

94 x 88½ in. (239 x 225 cm)

Museum Purchase, 1962-190

Figure 34

Pink Wool Quilt

America, 1750–1800

94 x 87 in. (239 x 221 cm)

Museum Purchase, 1952-204, 1

Patterns from Wool Wholecloth Quilts

Figure 35

Bright-Pink Wool Quilt with Silk Stitching

America, probably New York, 1740–1790

103 x 98 in. (262 x 249 cm)

Museum Purchase, 1959-11

Figure 36

Yellow Wool Quilt

America, 1750–1820

102 x 96 in. (259 x 244 cm)

Museum Purchase, 1953-951

Figure 37

Green-and-Blue Reversible Wool Quilt

Probably America, 1760–1790

105¾ x 95½ in. (269 x 243 cm)

Museum Purchase, 1951-224

Figure 38

Aqua Wool Quilt

America, possibly New England, 1770–1790

100 x 97 in. (254 x 246 cm)

Anonymous gift, 1971-1369

Figure 39

Blue Wool Quilt

America, possibly New England, 1780–1830

101¾ x 90½ in. (258 x 230 cm)

Museum Purchase, 1957-121

Figure 40

Green Wool "LG" Quilt

America, 1790–1830

98 x 96 in. (249 x 244 cm)

Museum Purchase, 1952-86

Figure 41

Light Blue-Green Wool Quilt

America, 1820–1840

91½ x 83½ in. (232 x 212 cm)

Museum Purchase, 1960-903

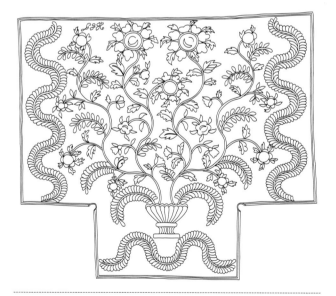

Figure 42

Blue Wool-and-Cotton Quilt

America, 1790–1830

94½ x 110½ in. (240 x 281 cm)

Museum Purchase, 1952-116

Patterns from Wool Wholecloth Quilts

Figure 43

Brownish-Yellow Wool Quilt Fragment

America, 1800–1830

82 x 68 in. (208 x 173 cm)

Bequest of Grace Hartshorn Westerfield, 1974-340

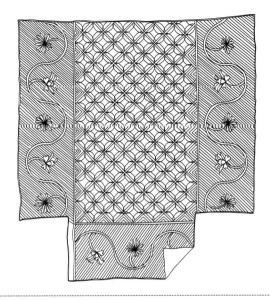

Figure 44

Rust-Brown Wool-and-Cotton Quilt

America, probably New England, 1800–1830

105 x 95 in. (267 x 241 cm)

Gift of Mr. and Mrs. John Batdorf, 1985-26

Figure 45

Rust-Red Wool-and-Cotton Quilt

America, possibly Pennsylvania, 1800–1840

102 x 89½ in. (259 x 227 cm)

Museum Purchase, 1952-336

Figure 46

Rust-Red Wool Quilt

America or Wales, UK, 1800–1830

91 x 77 in. (231 x 196 cm)

Museum Purchase, 1953-396

1   Linda Eaton, curator of textiles at Winterthur Museum, has examined documented pieces of glazed worsted textiles in dated swatch books and has discovered that those identified as calamanco were a 4:1 broken twill, similar in appearance to satin; shalloon was twill-woven thin glazed wool; and tammy was plain-woven glazed wool. Linda Eaton to author (Baumgarten), e-mail message, July 26, 2011.

2   Robert Campbell's 1747 *London Tradesman* describes professional stitching in London, one of the source locations for the ready-made quilts shipped to the American colonies. According to Campbell,

"They [quilted petticoats] are made mostly by Women, and some Men, who are employed by the Shops and earn but little. They quilt likewise Quilts for Beds." *The London Tradesman* (London, 1747; repr., New York: Augustus M. Kelley, 1969), 213.

3   *Boston-Gazette, and Country Journal*, June 30, 1760; and Supplement to the *Boston-Gazette, and Country Journal*, January 12, 1761.

4   Mrs. Palmer was formerly married to DeWitt C. Howe.

5   For photographs and more information about the quilts, go to Colonial Williamsburg's website emuseum.history.org.

CHAPTER 6

WHITE

Chapter 6

White

In an era without automatic washing machines, electric irons, or permanent-press fabrics, owning pristine white textiles was a sign of gentility and high status. The royal governor of Virginia Lord Botetourt had white quilts on two of his most expensive chintz-curtained beds in 1770.[1] The governor was following fashionable British practice, for the well-known cabinetmaker and upholsterer Thomas Chippendale supplied white calico quilts for many of his wealthiest English clients to use on their best bedsteads. The quilt Chippendale provided for the damask-curtained, domed state bed at Harewood House in 1773 was especially fine: "An exceeding large Superfine white Callico Quilt extra work."[2] Snowy white quilts remained in fashionable use for centuries.

White quilts were produced in diverse styles. Because the tops were not pieced or appliquéd, solid-white quilts can be considered wholecloth, but they are usually distinguished by how their battings are applied. Like the more colorful worsted wholecloths shown in chapter 5, some white cotton and linen quilts had battings applied in an even thickness between the top and bottom layers. Quilting stitches worked through even-thickness battings, however, did not show up as well on soft cottons and linens as they did on stiff worsteds, which tended to puff up around the stitching. For that reason, quilters working with cottons and linens often employed corded or stuffed-work quilting methods. Cords or additional batting inserted from the back made the designs stand out in higher relief.[3]

Although white quilts were made in many locations around the world, by amateurs and professionals alike, the port city of Marseilles in southern France became famous for a style of white raised-work quilts made of delicate cord quilting using fine white cottons or linens, sometimes further embellished with knot stitches (now called *French knots*) to give additional texture (see fig. 47).[4] The name *Marseilles* was originally given to products made in the city in this style although, eventually, the name became associated with a variety of white quilted products made in France and elsewhere, whether by hand or on a loom.

Charles Germain de Saint-Aubin, designer to French King Louis XV, described the work of eighteenth-century professional Marseilles stitchers in his book, *L'Art du Brodeur.* Working with a frame to hold the pieces taut, Marseilles quilters stitched motifs through two layers of textiles. On the top was a fine white textile that Saint-Aubin described as either "batiste" or "mousseline." At that time, batiste was made of fine linen, and mousseline, or muslin, was cotton. The top textile was backed with stronger, coarser material. After stitching the outlines, workers turned the layered textile over and pushed cotton fibers or cords between the two textiles from the back to make the motifs stand out in relief. Finally, they embroidered knots ("nœuds de fil") on the front of the quilted piece, creating a textural effect. Judging from surviving examples, quilting of this type was especially well suited for smaller clothing items that required washing, such as men's waistcoats,

Figure 47 Marseilles Cord-Quilted Cover, maker unknown, France, probably Marseilles, 1720–1740, linens and cottons with linen embroidery threads, 26–32 backstitches per inch, 33 x 30 in. (84 x 76 cm), anonymous gift, 1971-1340. Almost hidden in the twining foliage of this very small quilted piece are double-headed eagles, a running deer, exotic birds, unicorns, and a turkey worked with white backstitches and French knots. The piece is made of fine white linen and coarser linen on the back, stitched through both layers with linen threads, and stuffed from the back with cotton cords. The linen lace edging and cotton dimity extension appear to be later additions. The twentieth-century collector Mrs. DeWitt Clinton Cohen purchased the textile in Austria.

children's layettes, caps, women's stomachers (triangular gown fronts), comfortable waistcoats and bedgowns worn by women during the lying-in period following childbirth, and, to use Saint-Aubin's term, "meubles de bains," or furnishings for the bath. According to Saint-Aubin, Marseilles quilters also made wholecloth quilts and quilted clothing with allover battings of carded cotton, some stitched with "soie" (silk) and some with "fil" (linen thread) in shell, square, and mosaic patterns.[5] Although the cord-quilting techniques used by Marseilles workers had existed much earlier, French workers brought the work to technical perfection and helped popularize it.

Quilters throughout continental Europe, Great Britain, and the American colonies imitated French styles, often referring to the imitations by the term *Marseilles* or one of its variant spellings, such as Marsailles, Mersails, Marcels, Marsyle, or Marcella. As scholar Clare Rose stated, "'Marseilles' referred to the style of the work, not its place of origin." The term was not used consistently, but in general it referred to white cotton and white linen products with raised areas. London haberdashers retailed patterns and thread for working "French Quilting" in England.[6] American women also had access to designs and materials for making items in the fashionable quilting style. As early as 1712, George Brownwell or his wife taught "French Quilting" in Boston, Massachusetts.[7] In Charleston, South Carolina, in 1749, a merchant imported the materials for making Marseilles quilted waistcoats, complete with the pattern already drawn: "*Just imported,* in Capt. *Ball* and Capt. *White,* from *London* . . . mens chints waistcoats drawn for *marseilles quilting,* with cotton for the same."[8] The following year, teacher-proprietors of a French school advertised their services to their Charleston clientele, stating that "they draw for *Marseilles* quilting and all kinds of embroidery, at a reasonable rate."[9]

Around the middle of the eighteenth century, English manufacturers began to experiment with weaving bedcovers and yardage using soft, loosely spun cotton as the filling in a three-layer textile, thus bypassing hand stitching altogether. This technique of quilting in the loom became

known as "Marseilles quilting," probably to capitalize on the popularity of the fashionable handmade products. The development of woven quilting was supported by prizes from the Society for the Encouragement of Arts, Manufactures, and Commerce. The first winner was Robert Elsden, who invented the technique for making clothing items and counterpanes "Work'd in a Loom" in 1745, and in 1760, another weaver submitted his specimen of "English wove Quilting in Imitation of the French" to the society.[10] By the mid-1760s, the work was well enough established to receive notice in an American newspaper. The June 6, 1765, *Georgia Gazette* of Savannah carried a notice that "the business of quilting bed-carpets [bedcovers] and petticoats, which formerly the females engrossed, is now totally going into a different channel, the weavers in Spittalfields [east end of London] having struck upon a method of quilting in their looms, which is much cheaper and neater than any person with a needle can do." Despite the claims in the advertisement, woven quilts did not replace hand quilting, but the new products nevertheless became popular as yardage, petticoats, and finished full-size bedcovers (see fig. 48). By 1766, merchants in Williamsburg, Virginia, offered for sale "Marseilles quilting" that probably referred to yard goods since the context includes many other textiles by the yard.[11] Although the early developments in quilted weaving had occurred near London, the English cotton industry eventually settled in Lancashire in northern England. Marseilles woven yardage and one-piece white cotton bedcovers, produced in England as well as America, continued in widespread use throughout the nineteenth century (see fig. 54). The woven bedcovers, variously called *counterpanes* or *quilts,* retained the descriptive name of *Marseilles* after the hand-stitched French products.

Ironically, although woven quilting had been developed to imitate handwork, some women later copied the designs on the fashionable woven products when they stitched their own white quilts at home, bringing the process full circle (see fig. 53). Mrs. D. Baker of New Bedford, Massachusetts, won a prize for her meticulously hand-stitched white quilt in 1841, made "in imitation of Marseilles."[12]

Figure 48 Doll Wearing Underwear, maker unknown, England, ca. 1770, wood, hair, gesso, paint, glass, linen, cotton, baleen, and silk, 22 in. tall (56 cm), Museum Purchase, 1966-169, 1966-170. This carved and painted wooden doll came with a complete set of underwear beneath her silk gown: a linen shift, cotton-and-baleen stays, two petticoats, and a pocket. One of the petticoats and the pocket were made of white cotton Marseilles quilting, woven in a tiny diamond pattern, typical of the quiltings produced by the yard in the region around Manchester, Lancashire, England.

FIGURE 49

This white cotton quilt is a marriage of quilts from two different centuries.[13] The center portion has a cotton face, backing, and batting and is quilted in a grid with a guilloche border using linen thread. The wide attached borders were made from different white cotton with a design consisting of a series of arches enclosing unicorns, cavorting animals, oversize birds in trees, and flowering bushes. Unlike the central portion with its overall batting, the borders were decorated in the cord-quilting technique, with no batting between the raised cotton-corded channels. The borders are quilted with linen thread in running stitches.

Salvaged from an earlier quilt, the borders were added to a white calico quilt that almost certainly dates to the eighteenth century. The splicing probably occurred in the nineteenth century. Although compromised as a museum piece, the bedcover preserves two fragments that might otherwise have been lost. Rarely do relatively plain early calico quilts, such as this center, survive. The borders, equally important, are probably rare seventeenth-century remnants of a Portuguese quilt.[14] Given the presence of linen stitching threads, the quilting was done in Europe, rather than India, where silk or cotton would have been used.

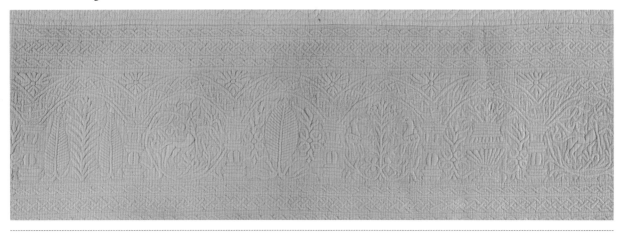

Figure 49a Detail.

Figure 49b A partial drawing shows the intricate foliage and animals that were part of the earlier quilt.

Wholecloth and Corded Quilt Figure 49

Makers unknown

Europe, eighteenth century, borders possibly Portugal,
seventeenth century, spliced together later

Cottons, linens

6–7 running stitches per inch in center, 8–9 running
stitches per inch in borders

86 x 84 in. (218 x 213 cm)

Museum Purchase, 1936-57

CORDED QUILT

FIGURE 50

The center of this white corded quilt features a large vase of flowers standing on a mound and enclosed in an octagonal frame. The design echoes the widespread fashion for floral still-life paintings and prints from the late seventeenth century into the first half of the eighteenth century. Similar motifs appear in many decorative arts, including textiles embroidered in India (see fig. 9).

The quilt was constructed in England or Ireland using a cord-quilting technique. Two layers of white textiles, a fine cotton face and coarser linen backing, were quilted in channels with linen running stitches and then given dimension by drawing cotton cords through the channels from the back. The vase of flowers in the center medallion is fully corded though the remainder of the quilt is more sparsely corded in design areas only.

The quilt descended from the 2nd Earl of Kingston, Robert King (1754–1799), and his wife, Caroline Fitz-Gerald King (1754–1823). Based on its apparent date, the quilt must have been handed down from an earlier member of the FitzGerald or King family. It eventually descended to Mr. and Mrs. William King, who sold it to Colonial Williamsburg through the auspices of Doris Langley Moore in 1952. Colonial Williamsburg also purchased other textiles once used by the countess, including linen sheets and napkins bearing her cross-stitched mark CK under a coronet (fig. 50b).[15]

Figure 50a (left) Backlighted view.

Figure 50b Detail of mark on Bed Sheet, Ireland or England, ca. 1770, linen with silk embroidery threads, 104 x 142½ in. (264 x 362 cm), Museum Purchase, 1952-665, 1. Typical of bed sheets in the eighteenth century, this one is constructed with quarter-inch hems and is not decorated, except for the owner's initials intended for laundry inventory purposes.

Corded Quilt   <small>Figure 50</small>

Maker unknown

England or Ireland, 1730–1750

Cottons, linens

18–20 running stitches per inch

101 x 94 in. (257 x 239 cm)

Museum Purchase, 1952-668

Maternity Ensemble made from Quilt

FIGURE 51

This rare ensemble consists of a jacket, petticoat, and vest designed for maternity wear. The sleeveless vest, which was made with adjustable lacings at the center back, was worn under the jacket and served to fill in the expanded front during pregnancy. The petticoat was cut slightly longer in front than in back to accommodate the projection of the belly, and the waistband, fitted with adjustable tape ties above deep slits on either side, allowed the wearer to expand or overlap the waist size as needed. Given the expense of clothing in the eighteenth century, it is not surprising that the ensemble was made to function equally well for a woman after delivery. The new mother could set aside the vest and lace the jacket closed, creating a fashionable daytime suit (fig. 51a).

The ensemble itself was cleverly designed for functionality, and its construction from an old bed quilt was equally innovative. In cutting apart the quilt to make the garment pieces, the dressmaker positioned the quilt's borders at the petticoat's hem and brought the side borders around to the front, where they were butted together to form a

visual panel down the center (figs. 51b, 51c). The original quilt was made of fine white cotton quilted through a thin, even layer of cotton batting and coarser cotton backing using linen quilting threads. Consisting of a simple grid with narrow floral and scroll borders, the quilt's design and construction suggest that it was made in the home, not by a professional quilter. Given its unremarkable design and plain white color, the calico quilt might have been lost to history had it not been remade into a garment late in the eighteenth century.

Figure 51a Ensemble shown without vest. After the baby was born, the wearer could set aside the vest and wear the jacket and petticoat as a two-piece ensemble.

Figures 51b and 51c To construct the petticoat, the seamstress joined the borders of the quilt at the center front to create a decorative panel.

MATERNITY ENSEMBLE MADE FROM QUILT   FIGURE 51

MAKER UNKNOWN

ENGLAND, 1780–1795, USING AN EARLIER QUILT

COTTONS, LINENS

11 RUNNING STITCHES PER INCH

PETTICOAT CIRCUMFERENCE 100 IN. (254 CM)

MUSEUM PURCHASE, 1936-666, 1–3

SMALL CORDED QUILT

FIGURE 52

This lovely quilt is worked in cord quilting delineated in white linen thread with closely spaced backstitches. Soft cotton cords drawn between the cotton front and back layers raise the floral pattern in slight relief, although the quilter did not add the knot stitches that often characterize Marseilles quilted objects. Worked into the center is the date 1788 and the letter B (or LB), but their significance is unknown. If the piece was made by an anonymous quilter in a professional workshop, the initial(s) may be that of the client rather than the maker. The quilt is bound with narrow linen tape.

Small quilts were not necessarily used by children. In France, a quilt such as this served either as a *vanne,* placed on top of a larger bedcover for decoration, or a *couvre-pieds,* a foot cover for lounging.[16]

Colonial Williamsburg purchased the quilt from a New York dealer.

Figure 52a Backlighted view.

CORDED AND STUFFED-WORK QUILT

FIGURE 53

Lucy Daniel must have been familiar with woven Marseilles bedcovers considering the similarity of her layout with that of English-made examples. In her handmade cotton quilt, Lucy used closely spaced cord quilting to fill the ground spaces between the scattering of flowers and undulating borders that were raised from the surface in the stuffed-work technique, achieved by the addition of cotton batting inserted from the back side after stitching the channels and outlines with cotton quilting threads. Such techniques were taught in fashionable girls' schools and by private needlework instructors. The quilt is bound with narrow white linen edging.

About the QUILT MAKER Using needle skills she may have learned as a child working a sampler, Lucy Daniel signed and dated her quilt on the upper border of the back side using tiny brown silk cross-stitches that read "Lucy Daniel May I 1801." Historical records support the family tradition that the quilt was made for Lucy's wedding, for just twenty days after dating her quilt, she married Mathew Kemp. Lucy was the daughter of Beverley and Milly Tarpley Daniel of Middlesex County, Virginia.[17]

Figure 53a Detail of back showing Lucy Daniel's name and date.

Small Corded Quilt Figure 52

Maker unknown

France, possibly Marseilles, 1788

Cottons, linens

21–24 backstitches per inch

58 x 48 in. (147 x 122 cm)

Museum Purchase, 1953-317

CORDED AND STUFFED-WORK QUILT FIGURE 53

LUCY DANIEL (B. 1778)

MIDDLESEX COUNTY, VIRGINIA, 1801

COTTONS, LINEN; SILK EMBROIDERY THREADS

9–11 RUNNING STITCHES PER INCH

88½ X 89¾ IN. (225 X 228 CM)

MUSEUM PURCHASE, THE FRIENDS OF COLONIAL WILLIAMSBURG
COLLECTIONS FUND, 2001-765

MARSEILLES WOVEN BED QUILT OR COUNTERPANE

Woven in one piece on a wide loom, this bed counterpane is an excellent example of nineteenth-century bedcovers made in the loom-woven technique and usually called Marseilles, after the city where white hand quilting was famous. The central rosette and medallion are set within a large square, with stags, hounds, and birds in the quarters. The single border at the top and bottom and the double borders at the sides feature repeated anthemia, fashionable neoclassical motifs typical of the 1820s. The quilt came with a fragment of block-printed cotton in a bold and colorful pillar print, which came from the hangings on the same bed (fig. 54a).

According to family history, this was the bridal quilt of Emily Hannah Badger (1806–1882) when she married Levi Bull Smith (1806–1876) in 1827. Born in Maine, Emily Badger had gone as a teenager to live with her aunt in Reading, Pennsylvania. There she met and eventually married Levi Smith, a Princeton graduate and lawyer, who later went into the iron business. The couple settled near Reading and became the parents of ten children.[18]

Figure 54a Fragment of the block-printed cotton that was used for bed curtains on Emily and Levi Smith's marriage bed, maker unknown, England, ca. 1827, 20¾ x 11¾ in. (53 x 30 cm), gift of Beatrix T. Rumford, 1999-220.

EAGLE STUFFED-WORK QUILT

The patriotic spread eagle at the center of this quilt holds in its beak a banner that reads "E PLURIBUS UNUM," translated as "from the many, one," the motto selected in 1776 to appear on the Great Seal of the United States. Two overflowing cornucopias below the eagle associate America's bounty and prosperity with political unity. The stylized flag has thirteen rosette flowers, probably a reference to the thirteen original colonies. (The number of stars, or flowers in this case, depicted on a quilt or coverlet is not an accurate indicator of the date of a piece.) The folded triangles around the edges suggest the trimmings on fashionable clothing of the 1820s and 1830s and may indicate the date of this quilt, although eagle-design quilts continued to be popular later in the nineteenth century. Decorative tassels around all four sides are stitched in the hollows between the triangles and at their tips.

The quilt was purchased from a Michigan farm estate sale.

Marseilles Woven Bed Quilt or Counterpane Figure 54

Weaver unknown

England, probably 1827

Cottons

117 x 109½ in. (297 x 278 cm)

Gift of Beatrix T. Rumford, 1999-219

Eagle Stuffed-Work Quilt Figure 55

Maker unknown

United States, 1820–1855

Cottons

10–12 running stitches per inch

94 x 94 in. (239 x 239 cm)

Museum Purchase, 1981.609.2

1 "An Inventory of the Personal Estate of His Excellency Lord Botetourt Began to be Taken the 24th of October 1770," as transcribed in Graham Hood, *The Governor's Palace in Williamsburg: A Cultural Study* (Williamsburg, VA: Colonial Williamsburg Foundation, 1991), 289. The original document can be found at the Library of Virginia, Richmond, in the O. A. Hawkins Collection of Virginiana, 1770–1877, acc. no. 14038, personal papers collection.

2 Christopher Gilbert, *The Life and Work of Thomas Chippendale* (London: Studio Vista, 1978), 207; see also pp. 183, 188, 191, and 231. The Harewood quilt cost £8 15s.

3 Some people refer to corded and stuffed-work quilting by the Italian word *trapunto,* meaning to embroider. The term does not show up in early British or American documents, however, and was apparently not used in English-speaking areas to refer to quilted textiles until the twentieth century.

4 Marseilles had been a thriving center of hand quilting and needlework using imported cotton textiles well before the seventeenth century. The city enjoyed special privileges that encouraged the textile industry to flourish. It was allowed to continue importing cottons from India while the rest of France was subject to import-export legislation intended to protect local industries from foreign competition. In 1669, the French king declared Marseilles a free port, which allowed shipping without entry and exit fees. Even during times of prohibition, evidence suggests that merchants smuggled Marseilles quilting into Britain and the American colonies. For more information, see Kathryn Berenson, *Marseille: The Cradle of White Corded Quilting* (Lincoln, NE: International Quilt Study Center & Museum, 2010), 50, 89; Kathryn Berenson, *Quilts of Provence: The Art and Craft of French Quiltmaking,* 2nd ed. (Washington, DC: Archetype Press, 2003); Clare Rose, "The Manufacture and Sale of 'Marseilles' Quilting in Eighteenth Century London," *Bulletin du CIETA (Centre International d'Étude des Textiles Anciens)* 76 (1999): 104–113; Clare Rose, "Quilting in Eighteenth-Century London: The Objects, the Evidence," *Quilt Studies* (2000): 11–30; Jacqueline M. Atkins, "From Lap to Loom: The Transition of Marseilles White Work from Hand to Machine," *Chronicle of the Early American Industries Association, Inc.* 54, no. 1 (March 2001): 9–19; and Lynne Z. Bassett and Jack Larkin, *Northern Comfort: New England's Early Quilts, 1780–1850* (Nashville, TN: Rutledge Hill Press, 1998), 79–86.

5 Charles Germain de Saint-Aubin, *L'Art du Brodeur* (Paris, 1770) translated by Nikki Scheuer as *Art of the Embroiderer* (Los Angeles and Boston: Los Angeles County Museum of Art and David R. Godine, Publisher, 1983), 29. Saint-Aubin used the term *brodeur,* or *embroiderer* in English, to describe the workers and the work, which involved some embroidery techniques.

6 Rose, "Quilting in Eighteenth-Century London," 25.

7 *Boston News-Letter,* March 2, 1712. Lynne Zacek Bassett suggested that Mrs. Brownwell served as the instructor for classes held in her husband's house. See *Massachusetts Quilts: Our Common Wealth* (Hanover and London: University Press of New England, 2009), 25.

8 *South-Carolina Gazette* (Charleston), April 7, 1749.

9 Abraham Varnod and Mary Irwin advertising in the *South-Carolina Gazette* (Charleston), January 15, 1750. The authors thank Kathy Staples for bringing this reference to their attention.

10 Rose, "Manufacture and Sale of 'Marseilles' Quilting," 109.

11 Merchants Balfour & Barraud advertising in Purdie and Dixon's *Virginia Gazette* (Williamsburg), July 25, 1766.

12 Bassett and Larkin, *Northern Comfort,* 84–86.

13 This quilt was the design source for the popular modern matelassé bedspreads sold by Colonial Williamsburg under the name William and Mary.

14 The Victoria and Albert Museum, London, has a related quilt identified as being Portuguese, 1600s (T.121-1916).

15 *The Complete Peerage, or A History of the House of Lords and All Its Members from the Earliest Times,* s.v. "Kingston: Robert (King), Earl of Kingston."

16 Kathryn Berenson to author (Baumgarten), e-mail message, March 2, 2012.

17 John Otto Yurechko, *Christ Church Parish Register, Middlesex County, Virginia, 1553–1812* (Westminster, MD: Family Line Publications, 1996), 218, 236.

18 Emily Ellsworth Clymer, "Meet Your Ancestors," unpublished family history compiled in 1976, CWF object folder 1999-219; Morton L. Montgomery, *History of Berks County in Pennsylvania* (Philadelphia: Jas. B. Rodgers Printing Company, 1886), 1155–1157; "U. S., Sons of the American Revolution Membership Applications, 1889–1970," s.v. Samuel Smith Hill Jr., online database, digital image as found on Ancestry.com (2011); and Levi B. Smith household, 1870 U. S. census, population schedule, Reading, Ward 7, Berks, PA, page 101A, National Archives and Records Administration microfilm M593, roll 1307, digital image as found on Ancestry.com (2009).

Paper Template

PAPER TEMPLATE

Although most surviving pre-1800 quilts are wholecloth or embroidered examples (see chaps. 1–6), some quilters also made use of the technique of piecing, or patchwork. It is tempting to assume that pieced quilts were born out of necessity and made of fabric scraps cobbled together haphazardly for warmth. On the contrary, inventory and object research shows that for functional warmth most British and colonial householders used wool blankets or pile-woven bed "rugs," not quilts. The earliest pieced quilts were actually decorative and expensive, carefully planned, and made more for show than function (see fig. 56).

Patchwork can also be documented in early written sources and literature. Scholars have found reference to patchwork as early as the seventeenth century, and a 1703 play described a foppish man who helped ladies with their patchwork.[1] By 1726, in Jonathan Swift's "Voyage to Lilliput" from *Gulliver's Travels*, the main character's clothing was pieced together from the narrow strips woven on the Lilliputians' tiny looms. Gulliver described his pieced-up clothing as looking like the "Patch-Work made by the Ladies in *England*, only that mine were all of a Colour."[2] This portrayal suggests not only that patchwork was very familiar to the author and his readers by 1726 but also that patchwork could be defined as consisting of multicolored pieces.

Americans followed British precedent and did patchwork at an early date. An eighteenth-century pieced silk hand-screen in the Danvers Historical Society, Massachusetts, has an American history.[3] Probate inventories confirm that early Americans also owned patchwork quilts, probably made by the ladies of the family. In Virginia in 1731, James McKindo had "a patch work Quilt" on one of his curtained beds.[4] In 1747, Colonel Henry Lee's three patchwork quilts were described as "callico," a type of fine cotton (see chaps. 2 and 3). He also owned four "very old"

Figure 56 Pieced Bedcover, "IN," England, 1726, silks and papers, McCord Museum, Montreal, Canada, gift of Mrs. Albert Ayer M972.3.1. The quilt was probably brought to Canada from England at an early date.

quilts and one "old" quilt.[5] In 1757, Sarah Green owned "I Silk Patch Work Quilt" valued the same as a round table in the hall. Green's inventory also listed silk chair bottoms, suggesting that she had access to fine materials with which to make a pieced quilt.[6] By the last quarter of the eighteenth century, many more references to patchwork quilts can be found in American estate inventories.[7] Written sources must be read with caution, however. General Thomas Nelson's "4 patch callico quilts" may refer to an Indian or European printed cotton textile called *patch,* or *patches,* rather than to a piecing technique.[8]

The patchwork quilts documented by the early American inventories probably resembled surviving British examples of the same date (see fig. 56).[9] The British examples were worked in elaborately pieced patterns using fine textiles folded over paper templates. In paper-template piecing, the various textiles making up a quilt top were folded over precut paper shapes. The edges of the textiles were basted to hold them in place to the papers, and then the units were stitched together at the very edges using an overcast technique (fig. 57). This process was in contrast to piecing in which right sides were placed together and the pieces stitched from the back, leaving a narrow seam allowance. Sometimes the paper templates were left in place, but often the basting stitches were pulled out and the papers removed prior to quilting. The technique is often referred to as *mosaic patchwork* or *honeycomb,* the latter referring to the popular hexagonal shapes (fig. 58).[10]

The survival of several rare dated quilts proves that women in England were piecing over paper templates at least by the early eighteenth century. A silk patchwork quilt at the McCord Museum of Montreal is dated 1726 in the piecing and has paper templates (fig. 56). A silk quilt top or coverlet in the collection of the British Quilters' Guild is even earlier, made with the date 1718 pieced into it, along with geometric shapes, hearts, and human figures, all folded over paper templates prior to stitching together edge to edge.[11]

Although piecing by stitching right sides together eventually became the norm, some quilters continued to use the paper-template technique well into the nineteenth century. By the twentieth century, some quilters were using papers inside quilts for another purpose. The widespread availability of inexpensive newspapers and magazines meant that paper could be used as a cheap substitute for things like insulation in crudely constructed cabins or even as a substitute for quilt batting rather than as a method for achieving elegant accuracy with expensive textiles (see fig. 157).[12]

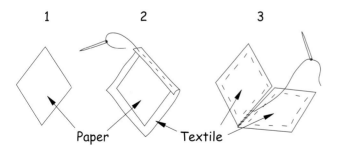

Figure 57 Drawing of paper-template piecing technique. The textile is cut to shape slightly larger than the paper template, folded over the template, and basted in position. Then the prepared shapes are stitched together at the edges. The basting stitches and paper can be removed prior to quilting.

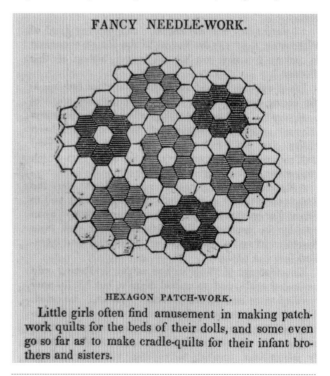

Figure 58 Hexagon patchwork illustration from "Fancy Needle-Work," *Godey's Lady's Book,* vol. 10, January 1835, 41. An article in a popular ladies' magazine suggested that the hexagonal pattern, which often went by the name "honey-comb patch-work," was one of the prettiest forms of patchwork. Old books or letters were suggested for the paper templates.

One-inch hexagons form the main part of this cotton quilt top, which is bordered by triangles and dagger shapes. All of the pieces were stitched with linen thread and backed by plain white paper templates, without any printing or writing apparent. The border is especially well designed in its use of carefully cut striped textiles positioned to give the suggestion of a fringed border all around. At the center, bird and flower appliqués were stitched down over their cut edges using wool embroidery threads; the raw edges were not folded under.

The use of hexagons in pieced quilts occurred relatively early in America. In Frederick County, Virginia, in 1808, two quilts sold as part of personal property were described as "two quilts Made with patchwork one a Sexagon (or so denominated) the other of Squares of Callico and Muslin."[13] The person describing the quilt apparently did not know that the proper term for a six-sided figure is *hexagon*, not "sexagon."

Noted illustrator Tasha Tudor (fig. 59a) recounted that one of her grandmothers made this quilt top and that as a child Tasha admired the pretty textiles in it. The dates of the textiles suggest, however, that the quilt top must have been made by an earlier ancestor and handed down in the family. Although unfinished, with papers in place and basting stitches still visible on the top, the bedcover once had a relatively modern backing machine stitched around the edges. This modern backing undoubtedly protected the fragile paper templates over the years.

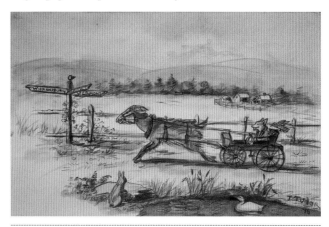

Figure 59a *Caleb Corgi Going to Williamsburg*, Tasha Tudor, Williamsburg, Virginia, 1996, charcoal on paper, 9¼ x 14 in. (23 x 36 cm), anonymous gift, 1997.201.2. In 1996, Tasha Tudor visited Williamsburg, where she did this charcoal drawing. She later donated to the Colonial Williamsburg Foundation the pieced bedcover and a number of costumes from her superb collection.

HEXAGON-PIECED QUILT

This scintillating quilt is constructed from thousands of precisely cut and stitched cotton hexagons, each measuring about 1⅜ inches across. The edges of the hexagons were butted and stitched, a technique consistent with paper-template piecing, although no papers appear to have survived. By carefully selecting dark and light printed cottons and alternating them with white, the quilt maker created hexagonal abstract "flowers" that appear to radiate from the center against a white ground. The pieced top is quilted to thin cotton batting and white cotton backing with linen running stitches.

Family tradition attributes the quilt to Hester Ann Tilman Johnson (1867–1951), wife of Reuben Johnson of Fluvanna County, Virginia.[14] Given the apparent date of the quilt, however, it must have been made by an earlier ancestor. The family traces their Virginia roots back to the seventeenth century.

Hexagon-Pieced Cotton Quilt Top   Figure 59

Ancestor of Tasha Tudor (born Starling Burgess)

New England, 1800–1840

Cottons, papers, linen; wool embroidery threads

83 x 72 in. (211 x 183 cm)

Gift of Tasha Tudor, 2000-131

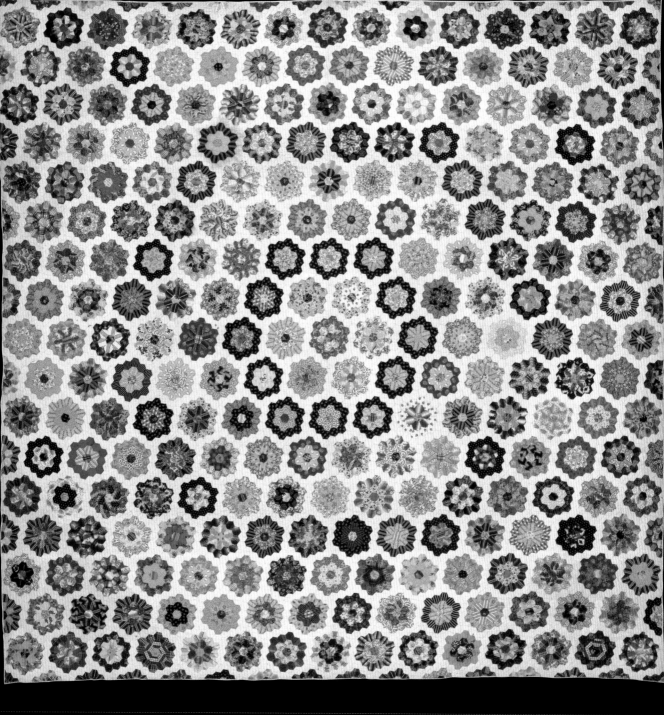

Hexagon-Pieced Quilt FIGURE 60

Member of the McCrary, Tilman, or Johnson family

Fluvanna County, Virginia, 1835–1850

Cottons, linens

8–10 running stitches per inch

112 x 110½ in. (284 x 281 cm)

Museum Purchase, 1999.609.1

FIGURE 61

The brilliantly colored hexagonal motifs of this unfinished silk quilt top stand out in jewel-like fashion against the black background, which is also formed by hexagons. Originally pieced around paper templates, the quilt top retains only a few papers still attached to the silks. The piecing was done with silk threads.

About the QUILT MAKERS A typewritten tag stitched to the edge records the family tradition that a teenage boy and his sisters worked together to piece this quilt top. Apparently, the tedious task did not suit the young man, for the tag reads, "Silk Quilt top cut and pieced by Louis Phillippi /and four sisters in Philadelphia in 1863. / This was the cause of his running away from home and / joining the Union army at the age of 14" (fig. 61a). Inked onto the center pink hexagon is the family name of "Phillippi," corroborating the family of origin (fig. 61b). Louis Phillippi (b. ca. 1849) was the only boy among the children of Henry Phillippi (sometimes spelled Phillipie) and Elizabeth Clampitt Phillippi of Philadelphia. Louis survived the Civil War and moved to Missouri, where he became a bookkeeper (fig. 61c).[15]

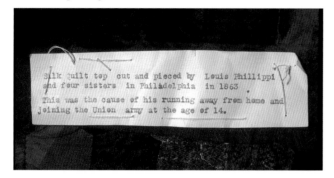

Figure 61a Detail. The typewritten family history asserts that the Phillippi siblings worked together to do the piecing. Louis allegedly ran away to fight in the Civil War to avoid having to work on the quilt.

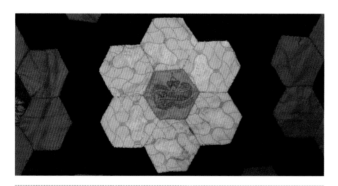

Figure 61b Detail showing the name "Phillippi."

Figure 61c Louis Phillippi as an adult, ca. 1880, courtesy Olivene Hargrave.

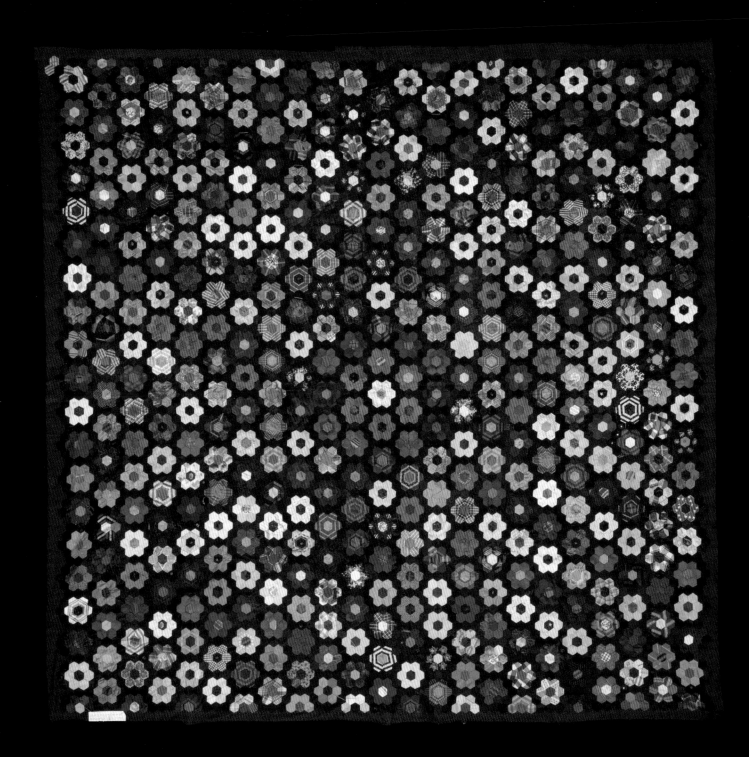

Hexagon-Pieced Silk Quilt Top FIGURE 61

Members of the Phillippi Family

Philadelphia, Pennsylvania, ca. 1863

Silks, papers; ink inscription

92 x 87 in. (234 x 221 cm)

Museum Purchase, 2004.609.2

FIGURE 62   FIGURE 63

These rare documents offer extremely important evidence of early piecing and appliqué, techniques that became much more common one hundred years later. Originally the bedcover must have had black borders on at least three sides, possibly all four. Now, only one black border remains in place, and a small fragment of removed border survives. Although the silk pieces are too small to date with precision, they appear to originate between 1690 and 1730. Along with the variety of patterned and plain silk pieces, the quilt is embroidered and appliquéd with silk and metallic threads.

Figure 62a Detail. Back view of paper templates inside the quilt top.

The piecing silks were folded and basted over carefully cut recycled geometric paper templates, which allowed the maker to achieve great precision (fig. 62a). Still remaining in place inside the quilt top, the papers include accounts; newspapers or pages from books, one referring to a date of 1652 in the text; and handwritten letters from as early as 1672. The fact that all the papers are written in English corroborates the English origin of the quilt. The dates on the papers are not indicative of the date of the piecing,

however, as the papers probably originated many years before they were cut up for the purpose. On the reverse, various linen and silk-wool mixed fabrics form individual linings behind each large square, suggesting that the pieced units were worked independently, backed separately, and joined last. The basting and piecing were done with both linen and silk threads. Because this bedcover does not have any batting and is not quilted, it might be argued that it is not a true quilt but rather a counterpane or coverlet. There are, however, three layers: pieced top, papers, and backings.

The outer border, inner bands, and some of the blocks feature appliquéd and embroidered animals, flowers, and people in clothing styles of the late seventeenth and early eighteenth century, probably drawn from published sources. The rider on horseback, for example, may have been inspired by an illustration published in England in the seventeenth century by John Nieuhoff, former ambassador of the Dutch East India Company to China (fig. 62b).

Figure 62b *The Young Viceroy of Canton Beginning a March against Rebels in Qvangsi, a Province of China,* from the portfolio *Collections of Costumes of Various Nations,* probably London, ca. 1600, hand-colored drawing, © British Library Board. This figure of a man on horseback may have been used as a model for the block in the top center of the quilt. The image would have been familiar to well-read quilt makers because it was used as an illustration in John Nieuhoff's book *An Embassy from the East-India Company of the United Provinces, to the Grand Tartar Cham, Emperor of China,* translated into English and first published in London in 1669.

PIECED QUILT AND BORDER FRAGMENT FIGURES 62 AND 63

MAKER(S) UNKNOWN

ENGLAND, 1700–1730

SILKS, PAPERS, SILK-WOOL MIXTURES, LINENS;
SILK AND METALLIC EMBROIDERY THREADS

QUILT 71½ X 63 IN. (180 X 160 CM)

BORDER FRAGMENT 9¾ X 29 IN. (25 X 74 CM)

MUSEUM PURCHASE, 2005-1, A–B

1   Clare Browne located a 1695 London household inventory that included "1 patchwork Counterpain & 2 stooles of ye same." See "Making and Using Quilts in Eighteenth-Century Britain," in *Quilts 1700–2010: Hidden Histories, Untold Stories*, ed. Sue Prichard (London: V & A Publishing, 2010), 41. Browne points out that the use of the term *patchwork* in relation to stool coverings is ambiguous and may refer to appliqué. Although the early use of the term *patchwork* may have included appliqué in some instances, in this chapter the term will be used to refer to pieced designs. The 1703 play is *Tunbridge-Walks* by Thomas Baker, cited by John Styles, "Patchwork on the Page," in Prichard, *Quilts 1700–2010*, 49.

2   Jonathan Swift, *Gulliver's Travels: A Facsimile Reproduction of a Large-Paper Copy of the First Edition (1726) Containing the Author's Annotations and with an Introduction by Colin McKelvie, M.A.* (Delmar, NY: Scholars' Facsimiles and Reprints, 1976), 109.

3   See Lynne Zacek Bassett, ed., *Massachusetts Quilts: Our Common Wealth* (Lebanon, NH: University Press of New England, 2009), 7.

4   "Inventory of Estate of James McKindo 1731 July 19," York County, VA, probate records, as transcribed in Colonial Williamsburg's digital library, accessed February 2, 2012, http://research.history.org/DigitalLibrary.cfm.

5   "Inventory of the Estate of Colo Henry Lee," September 1, 1747, Westmoreland County, VA, Records and Inventories, Settlements of Estates, No. 2, 1746–1752, Library of Virginia, Richmond, microfilm reel 30.

6   "Inventory of the Estate of Sarah Green 1759 May 21," York County, VA, probate records, as transcribed in Colonial Williamsburg's digital library, accessed February 2, 2012, http://research.history.org/DigitalLibrary.cfm. Sarah's quilt was valued at 21s. 6d.; "3 Silk Chair bottoms" in the hall were valued at 2s. 6d.

7   For more information on American eighteenth- and early nineteenth-century silk pieced quilts, see Deborah E. Kraak, "Early American Silk Patchwork Quilts," in *Textiles in Early New England: Design, Production, and Consumption*, ed. Peter Benes (Boston: Boston University, 1999), 7–28.

8   "Inventory of Estate of General Thomas Nelson, June 2, 1789," York County, VA, probate records, as transcribed in Colonial Williamsburg's digital library, accessed March 14, 2012, http://research.history.org/DigitalLibrary.cfm. Nelson's quilts were valued at eight pounds sterling. For a definition of the textile called *patch*, see Florence M. Montgomery, *Textiles in America, 1650–1870: A Dictionary Based on Original Documents, Prints and Paintings, Commercial Records, American Merchants' Papers, Shopkeepers' Advertisements, and Pattern Books with Original Swatches of Cloth* (1984; New York: W. W. Norton, 2007), 318.

9   For examples of British eighteenth-century pieced quilts, see Browne, "Making and Using Quilts," 28, 29, 31, 40, 41, 42.

10 Virginia Gunn, "Victorian Silk Template Patchwork in American Periodicals, 1850–1875," in *Uncoverings 1983*, ed. Sally Garoutte (Lincoln, NE: American Quilt Study Group, 1984), 9–23; and International Quilt Study Center & Museum, *Elegant Geometry: American and British Mosaic Patchwork* (Lincoln, NE: International Quilt Study Center & Museum, 2011).

11 The entire 2003 issue, no. 5, of *Quilt Studies* was devoted to the 1718 silk patchwork coverlet.

12 John Beardsley described the cabins of African Americans in Gee's Bend, AL: "Inside, walls are plastered with newsprint to keep out winter drafts." John Beardsley, William Arnett, Paul Arnett, and Jane Livingston, *The Quilts of Gee's Bend* (Atlanta, GA: Tinwood Books in association with the Museum of Fine Arts, Houston, 2002), 26.

13 Frederick County, VA, Deed Book 31, 1808–1809, September 29, 1808, pp. 232–233, Library of Virginia, Richmond, microfilm reel 17.

14 Reuben E. Johnson household, 1920 U. S. census, Cunningham, Fluvanna, VA, enumeration district 92, page 8A, National Archives and Records Administration (NARA) microfilm T625, roll 1889, digital image as found on Ancestry.com (2010); and West Virginia Deaths Index, 1853–1973, s.v. "Hester Tillman Johnson," online database, Ancestry.com (2011).

15 Henry Phillippi household, 1850 U. S. census, Southwark Ward 4, Philadelphia, PA, page 313A, NARA microfilm M432, roll 822, digital image as found on Ancestry.com (2009); Louis Phillippi, 1890 U. S. census, veterans schedule, Festus and Joachim, Jefferson, MO, enumeration district 324, page 3, NARA microfilm M123, roll 27, digital image as found on Ancestry.com (2005); and Louis Phillippi household, 1880 U. S. census, Joachim, Jefferson, MO, enumeration district 192, page 79D, NARA microfilm T9, roll 695, digital image as found on Ancestry.com (2010). Family descendant Olivene Hargrave identifies the four sisters as Katheran, Anna, Florence, and Henretta.

Early Appliquéd

EARLY APPLIQUÉD

Appliquéd quilts are created by cutting out shaped pieces of fabric and stitching them onto a ground textile. Frequently, the raw edges of the cut pieces are folded under and sewn with blind, or hidden, stitches. Sometimes the edges are fastened with more decorative stitches, such as buttonhole or blanket stitches. Appliquéd motifs can be layered and gathered to create dimension and texture.

Three subgroups of appliquéd quilts exist. Some appliquéd quilts are created from fabric cut to shape using paper or tin patterns; in some instances the appliqué is created in much the same way as a child cuts out a paper snowflake from a folded piece of paper (see chap. 12). In reverse, or underlaid, appliqué, the design is created by fabric laid behind cutout areas of the ground textile or appliquéd shapes. This technique is found in the elaborate mid-nineteenth-century album quilts produced in the Baltimore region (see chap. 14). A third technique of cutting out design elements, such as flowers, trees, and birds, from printed cotton, or chintz, and using them for appliqué is often known today as *chintz appliqué* and *chintzwork*. *Broderie perse*, French for "Persian embroidery," is another term associated with this technique, although it usually suggests the use of more decorative stitches in the application of the printed textiles. The quilts discussed in this chapter were created with chintz appliqué. In many examples the appliquéd

Figures 64, 65, and 66 Appliquéd Quilt Squares, makers unknown, details of figure 74. These three quilt squares illustrate how quilt makers could individualize their work by mixing and matching printed designs and carefully placing design elements. Each of these squares begins with the same vase of flowers, but the results differ depending on the addition of birds, butterfly, and floral elements.

designs were attached with decorative buttonhole or blanket stitches. The ground fabrics are mostly plain cottons. However, two examples in the Colonial Williamsburg collection have pattern-woven cotton grounds (see figs. 70, 127).

It took time, patience, and skill to create a successfully designed and executed chintzwork quilt. By cutting apart fabric design elements and rearranging them into new appliquéd designs on a larger plain ground fabric, the quilt maker made a small amount of fabric go a long way (figs. 64–66). Some early chintzwork quilts, like Mary Galt's (fig. 69), contain expensive Indian mordant-painted and dyed cottons. Most chintzwork quilts were created from fashionable home-furnishing printed cottons, which were also used for bed and window hangings and covers for

seating furniture. By the second decade of the nineteenth century, printed cotton panels were created specifically for making quilts (see fig. 72a).[1]

Many early nineteenth-century chintzwork quilts were worked in a framed center-medallion format—a style associated with English and Welsh quilt-making traditions. The design was based on a dominant central element in a small field framed by multiple borders (see fig. 67). Often the design was arranged within a framework of concentric squares and diamonds, and sometimes the center frame was on point (see fig. 68).[2] Center-frame quilts produced after about 1830 usually have larger fields and narrower borders than earlier ones (see figs. 71, 72).

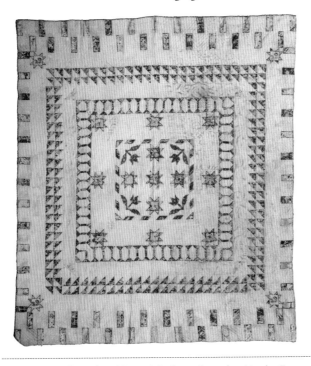

Figure 67 Appliquéd and Pieced Quilt, attributed to Martha Frances Dabney Collier (Mrs. Thomas Collier), Virginia, ca. 1795, cottons with linen embroidery threads, 9 running stitches per inch, 82 x 75 in. (208 x 190 cm), gift of Jan Bennett-Collier, 2006-158. The maker of this framed center-medallion quilt illustrated her sense of humor and ingenuity by using printed tulip-patterned brown cotton in the appliquéd tulip motifs in the corners of the central square. The quilt is backed in plain cotton and bound in a narrow printed cotton strip. The outer border is quilted in chevron patterns in cotton threads. Other quilting patterns include double diagonal parallel lines, undulating vine and flowers, alternating concentric swags, and outline of appliqué. The quilt descended in the Collier family of Virginia. Family tradition states that the quilt "took a premium in the Fair at Waco Texas in the year 1874 as the oldest quilt in the states and for the many designs in which it is quilted."[3]

Figure 68 Appliquéd, Pieced, Stuffed, and Corded Quilt, possibly a member of the Philhower family, possibly Norfolk, Virginia, ca. 1800, cottons and linen with wool and silk embroidery threads, 9 running stitches per inch, 80 x 76 in. (203 x 193 cm), gift of Mr. and Mrs. Lewis S. Philhower, 1963-71. Typical of early appliquéd quilts made in the Chesapeake region of Virginia, this one was worked in a format of concentric squares with the center frame set on point. In addition to pieced, appliquéd, stuffed, and corded techniques, the quilt was embellished with buttonhole and other embroidery stitches. The quilt maker created a sculptured effect of highlights and shadows with areas of stuffed and corded vines, flowers, and leaves. The bedcover is further quilted in patterns of outline and vertical and diagonal parallel lines. It is backed in plain cotton and bound in a one-half-inch folded strip of white cotton.

WILLIAMSBURG APPLIQUÉD, PIECED, AND EMBROIDERED QUILT

FIGURE 69

Mary Galt's framed center-medallion quilt consists of expensive pieced and appliquéd Indian mordant-painted and dyed cottons and multicolor English block-printed linen-cotton mixtures. That Mary made the most of her valuable textiles is evident in how she skillfully pieced and placed patches of printed cloth. For example, the wide floral border surrounding the concentric center squares is made up of small diamonds and triangles of alternating plain and printed fabrics. Some of the small diamonds with printed designs are carefully pieced. The result is the illusion that one whole piece of costly printed cloth was used in the creation of the large border.

In the center of the quilt is a silk-embroidered cornucopia worked in herringbone and outline stitches and flowers appliquéd with buttonhole stitches. A symbol of prosperity and wealth, the cornucopia motif appears on another early appliquéd Virginia quilt in the Colonial Williamsburg collection (see fig. 68). The quilt is backed with a linen-cotton mixture and bound in a one-half-inch folded strip of linen, which also has been pieced in numerous places. The outer border and areas of printed fabric are quilted in a diamond pattern with linen thread in about ten running stitches per inch. Plain areas are finely quilted with linen thread in various floral sprig motifs in fourteen to twenty running stitches per inch (figs. 69a, 69b).

About the QUILT MAKER The quilt is the earliest Virginia-made quilt in the Colonial Williamsburg collection. It descended in the notable Galt family of Williamsburg and was probably made by Mary W. Taylor Galt, second wife of James Galt (1748–1800), a silversmith, keeper of the public jail, and supervisor of the Public Hospital, an institution for persons with mental illness.[4]

It is remarkable that Mary found the time and energy to stitch such an intricate and lovely quilt. In addition to James's four children from his first marriage, Mary and James had eleven of their own, two of whom were twins. The couple's eleventh child was born two months after James's death in 1800. Mary's quilt must have provided a much-needed outlet from the monotony of housework and child rearing. Her death date of November 28, 1813, is recorded in a family Bible along with these words of praise: "She was a fond Mother and a good Wife."[5]

It's likely that Mary Galt received help with the quilting from her older daughters and/or servants. However, not all quilters were so fortunate. In an 1822 letter, Lucy Ambler of Fauquier County, Virginia, protested that she had little help in finishing her mother-in-law's quilt:

> I have put a bed quilt in frame and you know that must be a tedious job. The quilt was commenced by Mr. Amblers mother and I think I am bound to finish it. Catherine and Elizabeth Ambler are staying with me and they occasionally assist me though not much.[6]

Figures **69a** and **69b** Drawings of floral sprig motifs quilted on the squares of plain cotton.

Figure **69c** James Galt House, Williamsburg, Virginia. This charming one-story cottage with dormers was the home of James and Mary Galt. It originally stood on the grounds of the Public Hospital and was the only eighteenth-century building to escape destruction in the disastrous fire of 1885. It was eventually moved to its present location on Tyler Street.

Williamsburg Appliquéd, Pieced, and Embroidered Quilt Figure 69

Probably Mary W. Taylor Galt (Mrs. James Galt) (ca. 1761–1813)

Williamsburg, Virginia, ca. 1790

Cottons, linens, linen-cotton mixtures; silk and linen embroidery threads

10–20 running stitches per inch

87 x 87 in. (221 x 221 cm)

Museum Purchase, 1978-23

FIGURE 70

This framed center-medallion quilt consists of an eight-pointed chintzwork star set within two closely spaced concentric diamonds and surrounded by seven concentric square borders. The center medallion set on point is a characteristic seen in other Virginia and North Carolina quilts. By the 1840s, pieced eight-pointed stars were a popular motif on Shenandoah Valley quilts.[7]

The quilt is made of multicolor block- and roller-printed cottons on an unusual ground consisting of two different pattern-woven white cotton fabrics and a plain cotton fabric. The chintz patches are appliquéd in cotton and linen buttonhole stitches, and the bedcover is quilted in cotton running stitches in clamshell and grid patterns (fig. 70a). The cotton fringe is woven and knotted. Note that Polly did not waste her work by putting the fringe where it would not be seen; the top of the quilt would have been hidden by a bolster and pillows. The cotton backing was brought to the front to form a narrow edge finish where there is no fringe.

About the QUILT MAKER The quilt descended in the Abney family of the Shenandoah Valley of Virginia in a home called Solitude in the Staunton area of Augusta County. A family treasure, it was lovingly referred to as "The Quilt" and thought to have been created by Polly Abney Kinney. It is possible that Polly or another family member also stitched a silk embroidered picture of Palemon and Lavinia in the Colonial Williamsburg collection.[8] The needlework is signed "Mary Abney" and attributed to Rockbridge, a neighboring county. "Polly" was a nickname for "Mary."

Figure 70a Detail. The quilt maker used buttonholes stitches in linen and cotton to attach the cutout printed cottons.

Shenandoah Valley Appliquéd and Pieced Quilt Figure 70

Attributed to Polly Abney Kinney

Probably Augusta County, Virginia, ca. 1825

Cottons; cotton fringe; linen and cotton
embroidery threads

9 running stitches per inch

107½ x 96 in. (273 x 244 cm)

Museum Purchase, 1987-763

PETERSBURG APPLIQUÉD QUILTS

FIGURE 71　　FIGURE 72

The products of professional quilters, these two framed center-medallion quilts share some of the same printed textiles. The unusual width and format of the smaller quilt may indicate that it served as a covering for a table rather than a bedstead. The appliquéd motifs, which were finely worked in buttonhole stitches, were set within frameworks of lattice-patterned sashing (fig. 71a). The quilt is backed in plain white cotton and bound back to front with three-fourths-inch multicolor printed tape. The cover retains some of the original pencil lines for the quilting pattern, which consists of chevron, or zigzag, patterns in the sashing and border and outline patterns around the appliqués.

The larger quilt was symmetrically designed and also appliquéd with finely worked buttonhole stitches. The framed center medallion is not made up of individually appliquéd patches cut from larger pieces, as in earlier appliquéd quilts. Rather, the center medallion was created from an entire square of printed cotton produced just for the construction of a bedcover (figs. 72a, 72b). A popular design, similar printed squares are found on appliquéd bedcovers made in Baltimore and on at least two quilts from North Carolina.[9] The bedcover was meticulously quilted in chevron, or zigzag, patterns in the outer border and small diamonds, diagonal lines, and outline quilting patterns elsewhere. It was backed in plain white cotton and finished in such a way as to create a narrow stiff binding. A strip of cotton was folded under on the front edge and turned to the back side and attached. A second line of stitching along the edge of the quilt created a finished binding resembling piping. This unusual method of finishing a quilt is similar to hemming and finishing techniques associated with dressmaking and may reflect the training of the Boyle sisters as professional dressmakers.

Figure 71a Detail of appliqué.

The quilts were owned by D'Arcy Paul (1793–1874) and Elizabeth Scrosby Cooke Paul (1794–1865) of Petersburg, Virginia.[10] A merchant, D'Arcy was a leading citizen of the town, serving as president of the board of directors for the Petersburg Female College.[11] Family tradition states that D'Arcy commissioned the quilts from two unmarried sisters named Boyle who made their living stitching and selling quilts. Written in ink on the quilt backing is the inscription "B. Roper / from her grandmother / E. S. Paul." Both quilts were given by Elizabeth to Elizabeth ("Bettie") Paul Roper (1846–1912), her granddaughter.[12] They descended through the family until they became partial gifts to Colonial Williamsburg.

About the QUILT MAKERS The Boyles were actually five spinster sisters—Hannah (ca. 1808–1877), Emily J. (ca. 1810–1879), Melvina A. (ca. 1814–1885), Rosina (ca. 1818–1883), and Jane (1823–1903)—who resided with their brother, Joseph John Boyle (ca. 1815–1889), a carpenter, on Pine Street in Petersburg. They were the children of James Boyle and Jane Harding Boyle. James operated a soap and candle manufactory in the town. Emily, Melvina, Rosina, and Jane were, at least at one point, mantua-makers, or dressmakers. Their oldest sister, Hannah, kept house.[13] No other quilts have been identified as the work of the sisters, but the skill in the design and execution of these quilts strongly suggests that there must be more.

Figures 72a and 72b Printed Textile Panel (left), Great Britain, ca. 1820, cotton, 25½ in x 25 in. (65 x 64 cm), bequest of Grace Hartshorn Westerfield, 1974-550; detail of Petersburg Appliquéd Quilt, 1991-645 (right). Printed cotton panels were exported as yardage from British printers. A panel could be used uncut as the center medallion of a quilt, or the motifs could be cut out and arranged in various designs as a quilt center. This unused panel (left) is the same design that appears in the center of the larger Boyle quilt (right). Achsah Wilkins selected a similar panel as the center of her Baltimore bedcover (fig. 127), only she did not use the pineapple corners, perhaps saving them for another quilt.

PETERSBURG APPLIQUÉD QUILT FIGURE 72

THE BOYLE SISTERS

PETERSBURG, VIRGINIA, CA. 1840

COTTONS

10–12 RUNNING STITCHES PER INCH

116½ X 115 IN. (296 X 292 CM)

PARTIAL GIFT OF MR. AND MRS. PHILIP ROPER JR., 1991-645

FIGURE 73

This large center-medallion appliquéd and pieced quilt consists of seventy-three blocks of alternating pieced Le Moyne stars and chintzwork appliqués of flowers, baskets, birds, and cupids. The edges of the appliqués were turned under and slip-stitched in place with great skill in following the outline of the printed elements. The blocks are defined by a two-and-a-half-inch sashing of blue printed cotton. The cutout corners of the quilt accommodated the posts of a tall-post bedstead. The quilt is bound in two pattern-woven cotton tapes—a green-and-white check and a green-and-white stripe. The bedcover is backed in plain cotton and quilted in patterns of diagonal lines in the sashing and stars, floral motifs in plain areas, and outline of the appliqué.

Figure 73a Before conservation and the after results can be seen in this detail of a quilt square. The entire quilt could not be wet-cleaned because of its original glaze, fugitive dyes, and fragile fabrics dyed with iron mordants. The off-white ground fabric was cleaned by hand with deionized water on cotton swabs—a very slow and tedious process.

The quilt represents the stylistic transition in quilt making from chintzwork appliquéd quilts in a framed center-medallion format to a compartmentalized, or album quilt, format that was popular with many quilt makers by the mid-1840s. Yet, the skill in the piecing and quilting of the bedcover suggests that it was the work of one maker, and not several, as was the case with many album quilts at this time. The centers of the star blocks where eight diamond points join together were precisely sewn. In order to create star blocks that lie flat like these, the diagonal of the corner square must equal the outer measurement of the background triangle. No points of the stars were cut off to fit within a block, and the star blocks vary by only one-eighth of an inch.

The quilt descended in the Fitzgerald, Maury, and Bruce families of Virginia and was once owned by Sophie Clapham Bruce Maury (1864–1946), who was born at Berry Hill, located near South Boston in Halifax County, Virginia.[14] Built in the 1840s for James Coles Bruce, one of Virginia's most affluent planters, Berry Hill was, and still is today, a premier monument of the American Greek Revival (fig. 73b). This splendid quilt of pieced stars and finely appliquéd flowers, birds, and baskets would have been an appropriate cover to grace a bedstead of such a fine example of architecture.

Figure 73b Berry Hill Plantation, Halifax County, Virginia, courtesy Library of Congress. The stately Parthenon-like dwelling of Berry Hill in Virginia's Southside was originally the home of the wealthy businessman James Coles Bruce. The mansion, which contained twin stairways in the entrance hall and a pair of drawing rooms, was filled with fine furnishings such as silver finger bowls and gilt wallpaper.

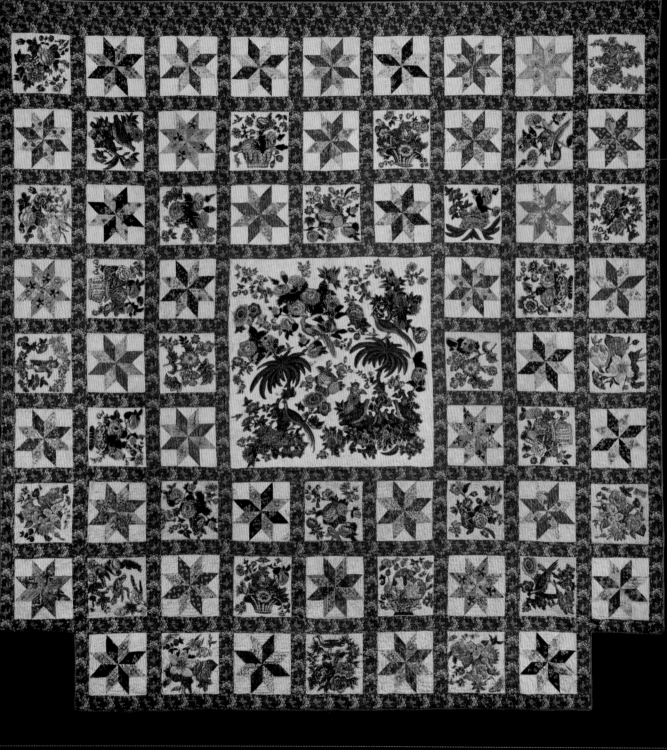

Virginia Appliquéd and Pieced Quilt Figure 73

Probably a member of the Bruce or Maury family

Probably Halifax County or Richmond, Virginia, ca. 1845

Cottons

9–10 running stitches per inch

115 x 111 in. (292 x 282 cm)

Gift of Dabney Herndon Harfst Narvaez in memory
of Alice Fitzgerald Harfst Straughn, 2011.609.1

Appliquéd Quilt Squares

FIGURE 74

Never completed as a quilt, these twenty-five quilt blocks were cut out and appliquéd from floral and bird printed cottons. The edges of the appliquéd motifs were turned to the reverse and slip-stitched in place. Probably made by a group of friends and/or relatives, the squares carry inked dates of 1848, 1849, and 1850 and signatures with the names of men and women from families that were concentrated primarily in Aiken County, South Carolina, and Richmond County, Georgia, located adjacent to each other on the state border.[15] Place names include "B.

Island" (probably Beech Island, South Carolina), "Augusta, Ga.," "Milledgeville, Georgia," and "Charleston, South Car."

One block contains this penned inscription (fig. 74a):

"Beware what earth calls happiness; beware
All joys, but joys that never can expire;
Who builds on less than an immortal base,
Fond as he seems, condemns his joy to death."

The exact relationships among all the signers of the quilt squares are unknown, though some are siblings. The squares descended in the Clarke family.[16]

Figure 74a Detail. This verse is from a long poem written by the English poet Edward Young titled *The Complaint; or, Night Thoughts, on Life, Death, and Immortality*. It was originally published in nine parts between 1742 and 1745 and is best known for the line "Procrastination is the thief of time."

Appliquéd Quilt Squares Figure 74

Family and friends of Mary B. Clarke
(later Mrs. David H. Porter) (b. ca. 1835)

South Carolina and Georgia, 1848–1850

Cottons; ink inscriptions

Approx. 15 x 15 in. (38 x 38 cm) each

Gift of Jane Miller Wright, 2002-73, 1–25

1   For a full discussion of printed panels, see Merikay Waldvogel, "Printed Panels for Chintz Quilts: Their Origin and Use," in *Uncoverings 2013*, ed. Lynne Zacek Bassett (Lincoln, NE: American Quilt Study Group, 2013), 101–131.

2   Research by Gloria Seaman Allen revealed that the diamond within a square format was popular with quilt makers in the Chesapeake region of Virginia and in the Carolinas. She also stated that buttonhole stitches and the addition of decorative embroidery stitches were more often found on quilts from the Virginia Chesapeake than other regions of Virginia. *First Flowerings: Early Virginia Quilts* (Washington, DC: DAR Museum, 1987), 8.

3   Loula Jackson Sleet, great-great-granddaughter of the quilt maker and former owner of the quilt, note to file, n.d., CWF object file 2006-158.

4   The hospital was the first building in North America devoted solely to the treatment of individuals with mental illness. As supervisor, Galt was responsible for the material welfare of the patients.

5   Biographical information for the Galt family is found in entries in the Galt family Bible, John D. Rockefeller, Jr. Library, Colonial Williamsburg Foundation.

6   Lucy Ambler to Sarah T. Massie, August 3, 1822, in "Letters and Other Papers, 1735–1829," *Virginia Magazine of History and Biography* 23, no. 2 (April 1915): 188.

7   Allen, *First Flowerings*, 8.

8   See Kimberly Smith Ivey, *In the Neatest Manner: The Making of the Virginia Sampler Tradition* (Austin, TX, and Williamsburg, VA: Curious Works Press and Colonial Williamsburg Foundation, 1997), 76–80.

9   See Ellen Fickling Eanes, "Chintz Appliqué Quilts," in *North Carolina Quilts*, ed. Ruth Haislip Roberson (Chapel Hill: University of North Carolina Press, 1988), 43, 52. Achsah Goodwin Wilkins used this printed panel on her appliquéd bedcovers produced in Baltimore (see fig. 127).

10 "D'Arcy Paul" on findagrave.com, Find a Grave memorial #28451621, record added July 22, 2008.

11 *Petersburg (VA) Index*, March 7, 1868.

12 "Elizabeth A. Paul Roper" on findagrave.com, Find a Grave memorial #69753334, record added May 13, 2011.

13 John J. Boyle household, 1850 U. S. census, Petersburg, VA, page 342A, National Archives and Records Administration (NARA) microfilm M432, roll 941, digital image as found on Ancestry.com (2009); Hannah Royle household, 1860 U. S. census, South Ward, Petersburg, VA, page 326, NARA microfilm M653, roll 1342, digital image as found on Ancestry.com (2009); Joseph Boyle household, 1870 U. S. census, Ward 3, Petersburg, VA, page 261B, NARA microfilm M593, roll 1643, digital image as found on Ancestry.com (2009); Joseph Boyle household, 1880 U. S. census, Petersburg, Dinwiddie, VA, enumeration district 93, page 357B, NARA microfilm T9, roll 1363, digital image as found on Ancestry.com (2010); and City of Petersburg, VA, Blandford Cemetery Records, entries for James Boyle, Hannah Boyle, Emily J. Boyle, Joseph John Boyle, Melvina A. Boyle, Rosina Boyle, and Jane Boyle, online database, accessed July 24, 2012, http://www.petersburg-va.org/blandford. The ages of the sisters are not consistent in the census records, which suggests that the siblings lied about their ages to the census takers. All five sisters are buried at Blandfield Cemetery in Petersburg, VA. The authors thank Nan Losee for her assistance with the genealogical research.

14 Sophie Clapham Bruce Maury marker, digital image as found on USGenWeb Archives, Tombstone Project, last updated July 21, 2008, http://www.usgwarchives.org/. Sophie Clapham Bruce Maury is buried with her husband, Matthew Fontaine Maury, at Hollywood Cemetery in Richmond, VA.

15 The names and place names are Samuel Clarke, B[eech?] Island; Sarah Ann Clarke; Samuel J. M. Clarke, Ann Helen Clarke, B[eech?] Island; Caroline C. W. Clarke; Ann Helen Hall, Augusta, GA; Ada B. Hall, Augusta, GA; Susan Mira[or Misa] Hall, Augusta, GA; Eliza Catherine Johnson, Charleston, SC; Jane Haywood Johnson, Charleston, SC; Elizabeth Williams; Margaret Miller; Mary H. Shi[rholder?], Milledgeville, GA; M. A. Mills; and H. H. M. Cook.

16 The quilt squares were probably made for Mary B. Clarke before her marriage to David H. Porter in 1855. "South Carolina Marriages, 1641–1965," s.v. "David H. Porter," online database, Ancestry.com (2005). According to her great-granddaughter, Mary was the daughter of Samuel Clarke and the sister of Caroline and Sarah Clarke, whose names appear on the quilt squares. The quilt squares along with a casket engraved "Daisy" descended through the family line of Mary's daughter Jane (b. ca. 1861). Daisy (b. ca. 1866) was one of Jane's younger sisters. Mary Clarke's birth date comes from the 1870 U. S. census, David H. Porter household, Savannah Division 21, Chatham, GA, page 166A, NARA microfilm M593, roll 141, digital image as found on Ancestry.com (2009).

CHAPTER 9

PIECED 1840–1910

PIECED 1840-1910

Quilt making thrived between 1840 and 1910 due in part to the Industrial Revolution's enormous impact on the textile industry. By the 1840s, commercially produced fabrics were available and affordable for many households. Thanks to new manufacturing processes and synthetic dyes, a huge selection of printed cottons became available to quilt makers. A special dye process that resulted in bright-red colorfast fabrics gave quilters a more stable vibrant red, called Turkey red, that would not bleed or fade. More expensive than the red fabrics produced by synthetic dyes that faded, it was a favorite of quilt makers and purchased whenever they could afford it. The popularity of the color duo of red and green between 1840 and 1870 was probably influenced by the availability of Turkey-red fabrics.

The invention of the sewing machine and its availability in the 1840s meant women could spend less time on sewing clothing and everyday household textiles, leaving them more time to spend on quilt making. An 1860 edition of *Godey's Lady's Book and Magazine* applauded the sewing machine as "the queen of inventions" and extolled its benefits, stating, "By this invention the needlewoman is enabled to perform her labors in comfort."[1] Because sewing machines were expensive and highly desirable, women occasionally showed off their new possessions and their skill in using them by machine stitching visible areas on their quilts (see p. xi).

Figure 75 Pieced Pillow Cover, maker unknown, possibly Pennsylvania, probably 1840–1850, cottons and silk, 17¼ x 22¾ in. (44 x 58 cm), bequest of Grace Hartshorn Westerfield, 1974.609.32. This pillow cover illustrates repeating geometric patterns and the ready mixing of differently sized, colored, and scaled prints that characterize much mid-nineteenth-century pieced work. Rectangles, squares, and triangles of different printed cottons were stitched together with three-sixteenth-inch seams. Typical of patchwork pillow covers, only the visible surface of this example was pieced; the back was made from a single piece of printed cotton. Silk ties on the inside of the case held the pillow in place. Like most pillow covers of this date, it is not quilted. Patchwork, or pieced, pillow covers were popular with Pennsylvania Germans.

Quilt makers of this period employed an assortment of construction, embellishment, and finishing techniques in the creation of their quilts. Patchwork, or pieced, quilts were created by stitching together small shapes of fabric to make one larger design. The piecing was often based on repeating patterns, especially geometric ones such as circles, squares, diamonds, triangles, and rectangles (see fig. 75).

Several methods of piecing were used, including the template method discussed in chapter 7 and the foundation method of piecing, which became popular in the last quarter of the nineteenth century. In the foundation method, the quilter begins with a piece of fabric, usually of cotton or linen in the shape of a block, and stitches decorative fabric pieces to the ground fabric eventually covering it up.

This type of piecing is most often found in crazy quilts (see chap. 20) and Log Cabin quilts (see figs. 136, 143). The patchwork quilts illustrated in this chapter used a third piecing technique in which right sides of the fabric were pieced together, leaving a narrow seam allowance. The joined pieces were then pressed open.[2]

PIECED SCRIPTURE QUILT

FIGURE 76

Assembled in a block-by-block construction, sometimes referred to as "quilt-as-you-go," this quilt consists of blocks that were individually pieced, layered, quilted, and edge finished prior to being joined. *The Ladies' Guide to Needle Work, Embroidery, etc.* commented on this quilt-making technique in 1877: "It is a great improvement upon the huge and unwieldy quilting-frames of the days of our grandmothers, to make the patchwork for a quilt in bound squares."[3] The term *potholder* was coined for quilts of this type because each block standing alone as a finished unit resembles a pot holder.[4] This quilt is composed of twenty-eight separate blocks in seven different pieced patterns. Each block is bordered by the same red-and-white printed cotton. The blocks are backed in several varieties of plain unbleached cotton. Typical of block-by-block quilts, the batting is thin, and the quilting pattern is a simple outline pattern.

The quilt is a concrete reminder of religion's importance in nineteenth-century life. The pious unknown quilt maker incorporated twenty-three Bible inscriptions, handwritten in ink on white cotton and centered within symmetrically ordered geometric blocks. The center block with a heart motif bears verses from Jeremiah: "The heart is deceitful above / all things, and desperately wicked: / who can know it? I the Lord search / the heart. __ And I will give them a / heart to know me, that I am the / Lord; and they shall be my peo / ple, and I will be their God / for they shall return unto / me with their whole / heart" (17:9–10 and 24:7). Other verses are from Psalms, Isaiah, Ecclesiastes, Proverbs, and Daniel.[5]

The majority of identified block-by-block quilts originated in New England, especially Maine. Like this one, many contain blocks of more than one pattern and include inscriptions.[6] Unfortunately, although all the inscriptions appear to be in the same hand, this quilt is unsigned, and nothing is known of its provenance.

CRIB SAMPLER QUILT

FIGURE 77

With blocks measuring less than five inches square, this diminutive quilt was intended for an infant's crib or perhaps a large doll bed. The quilt is a true sampler of different piecing techniques, using tiny scraps to create a variety of patterns. Only two of its twenty blocks are exactly alike, and none of them are signed. The diverse blocks give the quilt a visual sophistication that belies its small size. It is backed in a single piece of printed cotton and bound in a floral-printed cotton strip. The quilting was done in elliptical shapes in the borders and sashing and crossed lines in the interior blocks and bars.

The quilt was found on Block Island, Rhode Island, and may have been made there.

Pieced Scripture Quilt Figure 76

Maker unknown

Probably New England, possibly Maine, 1860–1880

Cottons; ink inscriptions

8–9 running stitches per inch

97 x 87 in. (246 x 221 cm)

Gift of George Schoellkopf, 1990.609.2

CRIB SAMPLER QUILT FIGURE 77

MAKER UNKNOWN

PROBABLY RHODE ISLAND, 1880–1910

COTTONS

8 RUNNING STITCHES PER INCH

37¼ X 31¼ IN. (95 X 79 CM)

GIFT OF JOANNE M. AND EMMETT
W. ELDRED, 1984.609.5

FIGURE 78

Featured in the center of this rare example of an early patchwork quilt is a copperplate-printed handkerchief eulogizing George Washington.[7] The unknown maker of the cover used an impressive variety of printed and glazed cottons in the geometric patchwork borders, which frame the handkerchief as a center medallion. Interestingly, Martha Washington favored this design. Two of her surviving quilts in the collection of the Mount Vernon Ladies' Association were pieced with a center medallion framed with patchwork borders. One of her quilts features a brown copperplate-printed historical scene of Penn's Treaty as the center medallion.[8] The outer edge of Colonial Williamsburg's quilt was finished by folding the top and back inwards and stitching them together. It is backed in plain white cotton and quilted in an orange peel, or melon seeds, pattern.

Although nothing is known of the maker, much is known of the quilt's subject. Titled *The Death of General Washington*, the handkerchief in the center of the quilt depicts the nation's first president on his deathbed, attended by his doctors (fig. 78a). A bereaved Martha is seated at the foot of the bed. Surrounding the scene are exalted eulogies praising America's hero. The handkerchief was copied from the print *G. Washington in His Last Illness Attended by Docrs. Craik and Brown* by an unknown artist, which was published in Philadelphia by Pember and Luzarder in 1800.[9] The handkerchief, however, was probably printed in Glasgow, Scotland, later that year. In July 1800, the *New-York Gazette* reported, "In the stores of some of our dry good merchants, we observe a neat tribute to the memory of the illustrious WASHINGTON—It is a pocket handkerchief, lately imported from Glasgow, in Scotland, on which is wrought a scene

representing the Death of the General, attended by his two physicians, Mrs. Washington, and one of his domestics. On each side of the plate are appropriate inscriptions."[10]

The quilt survives in remarkable condition considering the many fragile brown printed textiles used in its construction. The bedcover was clearly cherished as a reminder of the nation's beloved first president and probably used for only special occasions.

Figure 78a Detail. The sudden death of General Washington on December 14, 1799, plunged America into a period of mourning. Honored and revered in life, George Washington became a legend in death. A flood of portraits, poetry, music, art, and textiles dedicated to his memory encouraged the new fashion for mourning in the young republic. The copperplate-printed handkerchief in the center of this quilt is one of the earliest and rarest images of Washington's final hours. It vividly captures the scene at Mount Vernon with realistic details of the bed textiles, fringed dressing table cover, and clothing accessories such as the miniature portrait hanging around Martha's neck.

Pieced Framed Center-Medallion Quilt Figure 78

Maker unknown

Probably mid-Atlantic states, ca. 1810

Cottons

7 running stitches per inch

97 x 98½ in. (246 x 250 cm)

Museum Purchase from the estate of Foster and Muriel McCarl, 2012-172

PIECED AND STUFFED-WORK IRISH CHAIN QUILT

FIGURE 79

Quilts pieced in variations of the Irish Chain pattern abound, but this example's elaborate quilting and stuffed-work designs make it exceptional. Two sizes of small blue-and-white printed blocks have been pieced with larger white rectangles and squares forming a version of the Irish Chain pattern. The large number of missing blue-and-white printed blocks in the top corners suggests that the quilt maker simply ran out of fabric before completing her work. It is likely that these areas were barely visible at the top of the bed over or under the pillows. The smaller, printed blocks are quilted in simple diagonal lines whereas the all-white blocks are stuffed and quilted in two different complex flower and feather, or plume, designs. Similarly elaborate stuffed and quilted designs fill the outermost border, except for clamshell quilting in the two upper corners (fig. 79a). The quilt is backed in plain-woven white cotton and bound in a white cotton tape.

About the QUILT MAKER The bedcover is attributed to Sarah Ann Fulkerson Ewing of Lee County, Virginia, on the basis of family history, which also states that the quilt won first prize at a fair. Sally, as she was called, was the second of ten children born to John and Jeancy Hughes Fulkerson. On August 9, 1826, Sally married William Smith Ewing (1802–1839) of the same county. The Fulkerson and Ewing families had settled early in the rugged, isolated land of Virginia's southwesternmost county. In 1850 the widowed Sally and her two children were living with her mother. Sometime after that Sally and her children moved to Missouri to join other Fulkerson and Ewing family members. Her route was probably through the Cumberland Gap, the key passageway west for pioneers in the lower central Appalachian Mountains. She died in St. Joseph, Missouri, in 1892.[11] The quilt must have made each move with Sally for it descended through the family of Sally's son, Joshua Porter Ewing, to her great-granddaughter, who donated the quilt to the museum. Considering its history, the almost all-white pieced and stuffed-worked quilt survives in beautiful condition.

Figure 79a Detail of quilt and quilting pattern.

Pieced and Stuffed-Work Irish Chain Quilt Figure 79

Sarah Ann Fulkerson Ewing (1805–1892)

Lee County, Virginia, ca. 1840

Cottons

9–10 running stitches per inch

89 x 75 in. (226 x 190 cm)

Gift of Mrs. Milton J. Franklin, 1972.609.2

FLYING GEESE QUILT

FIGURE 80

Flying Geese was a popular pattern with quilters in the early nineteenth century possibly because the abstract triangular shapes of the "geese" appealed to the quilters' sense of fancy. The rows of perfectly aligned triangles recall the annual migrations of geese while the triangular shapes echo the formation in which the birds fly. This example consists of 1,319 pieces of cotton in various printed patterns including checked and striped shirting material. It is backed in cotton printed in a tiny leaf pattern and bound with a folded one-inch-wide striped, twill-woven tape. It is quilted in figure eights and parallel lines.

About the QUILT MAKER According to family history, the quilt was made by Deborah Middleton, later Parry. Written on a slip of paper originally pinned to the quilt is the inscription "This large quilt made / by Gt. Aunt Deborah Parry / (1830–1904) when she / was a girl. / Probably completed about 1842."[12] In 1842, however, Deborah Bunting Middleton would only have been twelve years old when she finished the quilt. In addition, some of the quilt's textiles, such as the paisley border pattern, suggest that the quilt was more likely completed at a later date. If Deborah created her quilt for her wedding trousseau, she waited many years to actually use it. At thirty years old Deborah was living with her parents, Joel and Amy Middleton, in Burlington County, New Jersey. Not until 1875, at the age of forty-five, did she marry Wilson Parry, a sixty-year-old Quaker retail merchant also in Burlington County.[13] In 1880 Deborah and Wilson were living in Chester, New Jersey, with one servant and no children. The quilt descended through Deborah's brother's family.[14]

Figure 80a Detail.

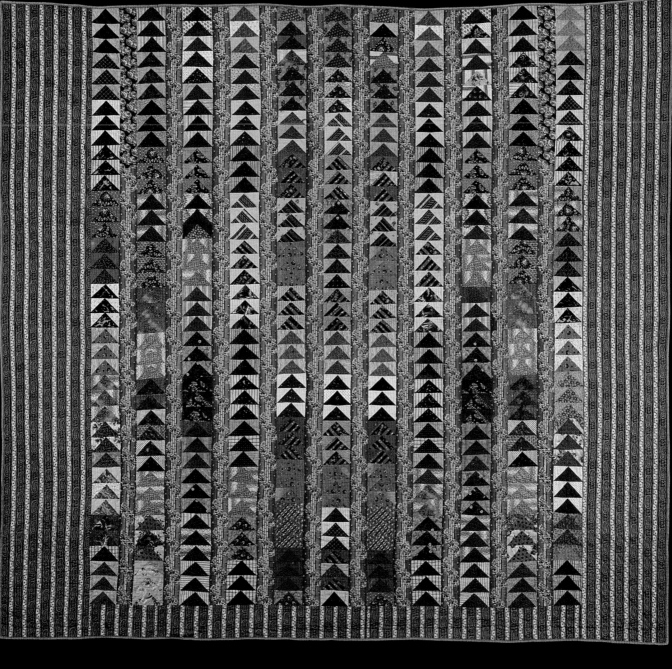

Flying Geese Quilt   Figure 80

Deborah Bunting Middleton (later Mrs. Wilson Parry)
(1830–1904)

New Jersey, 1842–1850

Cottons

7 running stitches per inch

92¾ x 99½ in. (236 x 253 cm)

Gift of Dr. and Mrs. Paul Middleton, 1986.609.22

CHIMNEY SWEEP QUILT

Kate Tupper's quilt consists of twenty-five full blocks, twelve half blocks, and four quarter blocks set on point with floral-printed sashing. It is backed in plain cotton and bound with a one-half-inch beige twill tape. The bedcover is quilted in straight lines that form concentric rectangles, squares, triangles, and diamonds with figure eights in the sashing. Some of the white centers of the blocks are quilted with four-petaled flowers.

One of the most popular patterns for friendship and autograph quilts was the Chimney Sweep, also known as the Friendship Chain. Most quilts constructed in this design feature a signature of a friend or relative in the white fabric forming the center of each block. In this quilt, all but one of the center crosses are blank, leaving the modern viewer to question why.

About the QUILT MAKER In the top center half cross, the quilt is marked in ink "Kate H. Tupper / 1850" (fig. 81a), and the center block is quilted with the date and initials, "18 / K H T / 50." Catherine (Kate) H. Tupper made the quilt when she was sixteen years old. In 1850 Kate was living with her parents, Tristram and Eliza Tupper, and her three younger siblings in Charleston, South Carolina. Her father, who was born in Maine, was a merchant.[15] Kate married Samuel Lord, a prominent Charleston attorney, and is buried with him at Magnolia Cemetery in Charleston, South Carolina.[16]

Figure 81a Detail. Although the Chimney Sweep pattern was a popular design for signature quilts, the only autograph on this quilt is that of the maker, Kate H. Tupper.

Chimney Sweep Quilt FIGURE 81

Kate H. Tupper (1833–1900)

Charleston, South Carolina, 1850

Cottons; ink inscription

6–8 running stitches per inch

99 x 98 in. (251 x 249 cm)

Bequest of Grace Hartshorn Westerfield, 1974.609.26

1   *Godey's Lady's Book and Magazine* 61 (July 1860): 77.

2   Barbara Brackman referred to this type of piecing as the "running stitch method." She said it is sometimes called the American method because it is the most common piecing technique used in the United States. *Clues in the Calico: A Guide to Identifying and Dating Antique Quilts* (McClean, VA: EPM Publications, 1989), 97.

3   The author continued, "Each one is lined, first with wadding, then with calico quilted neatly, and bound with strips of calico. These squares being then sewed together, the quilt is complete." S. Annie Frost, *The Ladies Guide to Needle Work, Embroidery, etc., Being a Complete Guide to All Kinds of Ladies' Fancy Work . . .* (New York: Henry T. Williams, 1877), 128.

4   In her article "One Foot Square, Quilted and Bound: A Study of Potholder Quilts," Pamela Weeks stated, "I needed some way to reference the technique, and the term 'potholder' quilt readily emerged as a recognizable and useful descriptor." In *Uncoverings 2010*, ed. Laurel Horton (Lincoln, NE: American Quilt Study Group, 2010), 133.

5   In Carleton L. Safford and Robert Bishop's description of this quilt, they stated that quilts bearing biblical inscriptions are often known as "Scripture" quilts. *America's Quilts and Coverlets* (New York: Weathervane Books, 1974), 119.

6   Pamela Weeks stated that 78% of the quilts in her research set that have known geographic provenance are attributed to New England, with 33% attributed to Maine. See "One Foot Square, Quilted and Bound," 137.

7   The quilt was published in Safford and Bishop, *America's Quilts and Coverlets*, 120–121.

8   Barbara Tricarico, ed., *Quilts of Virginia, 1607–1899: The Birth of America through the Eye of a Needle* (Atglen, PA: Schiffer, 2006), 44–45.

9   Davida Tenenbaum Deutsch, "Washington Memorial Prints," *Antiques* 100, no. 2 (February 1977): 329.

10 *New-York Gazette* (New York City), July 25, 1800.

11 "U. S. City Directories, 1821–1989," s.v. "Sallie A. Ewing," online database, digital image as found on Ancestry.com (2011); Margaret Ewing Fife, *Ewing in Early America* (Bountiful, UT: Family History Publishers, 2003), 207; Elbert William R. Ewing, *Clan Ewing of Scotland: Early History and Contribution to America: Sketches of Some Family Pioneers and Their Times* (Ballston, VA: Cobden Publishing, 1922), 190; Hattie Byrd Muncy Bales, comp., *Early Settlers of Lee County, Virginia, and Adjacent Counties* (Greensboro, NC: Media, Inc., Printers and Publishers, 1977), 2:743–744; Fancy (Jeancy) Fulkerson household, 1850 U. S. census, District 31, Lee, VA, page 371A, National Archives and Records Administration (NARA) microfilm M432, roll 955, digital image as found on Ancestry.com (2009); and J. P. Ewing household, 1870 U. S. census, Washington, Buchanan, MO, page 693B, NARA microfilm M593, roll 762, digital image as found on Ancestry (2009).

12 CWF object file 1986.609.22.

13 See *Friends' Review* 28, no. 51 (August 7, 1875): 808.

14 Joel H. Middleton household, 1860 U. S. census, Chesterfield, Burlington, NJ, page 837, NARA microfilm M653, roll 685, digital image as found on Ancestry.com (2004); Wilson Parry household, 1870 U. S. census, Chesterfield, Burlington, NJ, page 259, NARA microfilm M593, roll 854, digital images as found on Ancestry.com (2003); and Wilson Parry household, 1880 U. S. census, Chester, Burlington, NJ, enumeration district 19, page 220.4000, NARA microfilm T9, roll 772, digital image as found on Ancestry.com (2005).

15 Tres Tupper household, 1850 U. S. census, St. Michael and St. Phillip Parishes, Charleston, SC, page 99, NARA microfilm M432, roll 850, digital images as found on Ancestry.com (2005). Also, Tristram Tupper household, 1860 U. S. census, Ward 1, Charleston, SC, page 190, NARA microfilm M653, roll 1216, digital images as found on Ancestry.com (2009).

16 Samuel Lord household, 1860 U. S. census, Ward 3, Charleston, SC, page 264, NARA microfilm M653, roll 1216, digital images as found on Ancestry.com (2004); and Samuel Lord and Kate Tupper Lord marker, digital image as found on findagrave.com, Find a Grave memorial #45809056, record added December 26, 2009.

Mariner's Compass

MARINER'S COMPASS

A circle with radiating points has long been a common design in many cultures and decorative arts (see fig. 82). In quilts, the motif was particularly popular from 1825 to 1875. The pattern has been known by a number of names including Sunburst, Rising Sun, and Mariner's Compass, the last coming into general use by the twentieth century.[1] An English quilt dated 1726 is the earliest dated example of this pattern. The earliest American dated Mariner's Compass quilt is 1834.[2] It is not known what the original makers of these quilts called their patterns. However, one Massachusetts schoolgirl used the term in 1798 when she described her lost quilt as a "Mariner's Compass."[3]

The name was probably derived from the decorative images of compass roses and wind roses, both similar in configuration, found on maps, sea charts, and magnetic compasses. The design element of thirty-two points reflects the design and number of points on a compass or wind rose. The points originally, on the wind rose, indicated the directions of the winds. The magnetic compass came into use in the late thirteenth century and retained the same design. As sailors came to trust the magnetic compass, the wind rose gradually evolved into a decorative element on maps and charts filling in vacant spaces in the ocean areas (see fig. 83). Evoking the romance of the sea, the Mariner's Compass pattern may have had special meaning to quilt makers living on the eastern seaboard (see fig. 86).[4]

Figure 82 Pieced Pillow Cover, maker unknown, possibly Pennsylvania, probably 1840–1850, cottons, 17½ x 31½ in. (44 x 80 cm), anonymous gift, 1979.610.4. This variation of the Mariner's Compass pattern required sewing several curved seams, a challenge for any seamstress. Not as well-known today as contemporaneous pieced quilts and rarely quilted themselves, pieced pillow covers were sometimes made to match or coordinate with a particular bedcover. They were especially popular in Pennsylvania.[5] The companion pillow cover presumably made to match this one is now missing, as is any quilt originally associated with them. Although the cover is marked "M C" in red cross-stitches on its reverse, no history of ownership is known.

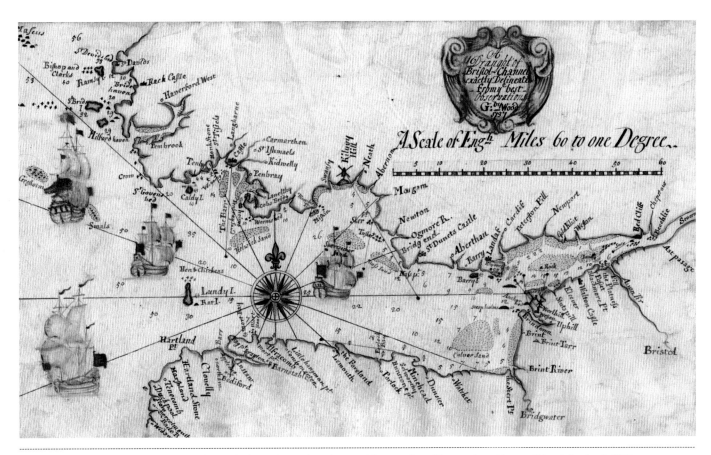

Figure 83 Detail from map *A Draught of Bristol-Channel Exactly Delineated from y.e Best Observations*, George Wood, England, 1737, 8¹⁄₁₆ x 12⁵⁄₁₆ in. (20 x 31 cm), Museum Purchase, 1958-412. The points on the decorative compass rose on this map indicate directions.

BROOKLYN MARINER'S COMPASS QUILT

FIGURE 84

Few examples surpass this Mariner's Compass quilt in the compatibility of the colors and prints represented among its numerous swatches. The quilt consists of sixteen blocks, each containing a thirty-two-point compass within a quilted circle. The bedcover is quilted in doubled concentric circles around each compass, in diamond shapes in the outer border, in overlapping doubled circles in the sashing, and in doubled outlining within the larger compass points. A pattern-woven tape is stitched over the quilt's outer edges. It is backed in plain cotton.

About the QUILT MAKER Although family history attributes the quilt to Clarissa Mary Dodge Marschalk, it is more likely that the quilt was created by her daughter Margaret Dodge Marschalk Sutton since the dates of the printed cottons suggest that the quilt was made after Clarissa died in 1838.[6] Margaret married George Thomas Sutton (1821–1899), a grocer, in 1848, and they lived in a Brooklyn, New York, neighborhood of market men, merchants, and tradesmen. They had seven children, the youngest being Louise Marschalk Sutton (b. 1871). The quilt descended through Louise to a great-grandson of Margaret's, who donated it to the museum.[7]

Brooklyn Mariner's Compass Quilt Figure 84

Attributed to Margaret Dodge Marschalk Sutton
(1826–1907) and possibly designed by Clarissa Mary Dodge
Marschalk (1803–1838)

Brooklyn, New York, 1845–1855

Cottons

12 running stitches per inch

100¼ x 98¾ in. (255 x 251 cm)

Gift of Robert W. Pitt, 1972.609.1

New York Mariner's Compass Quilt

FIGURE 85

Consisting of sixteen blocks of printed, striped, plaid, and plain cottons, this vibrant pieced quilt is a masterpiece of cutting, piecing, and quilt making. As in the previous quilt, the fabrics are precisely cut—in a technique called "fussy cut" by modern quilters—to center motifs within each shape. The quilting pattern follows the piecing, with modified heart shapes filling the white space around each compass. The quilt is backed in white plain-woven cotton and bound in a white pattern-woven three-eighths-inch tape.

About the QUILT MAKER Family history attributes the quilt to Mary Wright Williams, an Irish immigrant to New York City. Mary Wright and John Williams were married in Cork County, Ireland, in 1809.[8] Though their date of emigration is not known, they appear to have been living among other Irish immigrants in New York City by 1850.[9] Interestingly, nothing about the quilt's pattern, technique, or selection of fabrics suggests its maker's close ties with Ireland. Mary's choice of a popular quilt design may, in fact, imply the maker's adaptation or want-to-be assimilation into popular American culture.

Virginia Mariner's Compass Quilt

FIGURE 86

This Mariner's Compass quilt consists of sixteen blocks, each containing a sixteen-pointed star. The blocks are set within a three-inch plaid sashing with three-inch red printed squares at intersections of the sashing. The edge finish consists of a one-fourth-inch red printed-cotton self-binding trim. It is backed in white plain-woven cotton. The bedcover is quilted in double rows of circles, diagonal parallel lines, and botanical elements in the blocks with diagonal parallel lines in the border and sashing.

About the QUILT MAKER Embroidered in cotton threads in the open circles of one row of the compasses are the date 1848 and three sets of initials, including the quilt maker's and those of her future husband, Emanuel Ben Swanger, a German emigrant merchant, whom Ann married in 1856 (fig. 86a). The third set of initials, "CK / MK," has not been identified. These initials probably represent family members, but they are not those of her parents, Nathaniel, a farmer, and Nancy Kellam of St. George's Parish, Accomack County, Virginia.[10] Ann Rebecca Kellam Swanger probably lived her entire life on Virginia's Eastern Shore.[11] Flanked by the Chesapeake Bay to the west and the Atlantic Ocean to the east, Ann's choice of quilt pattern seems quite appropriate.

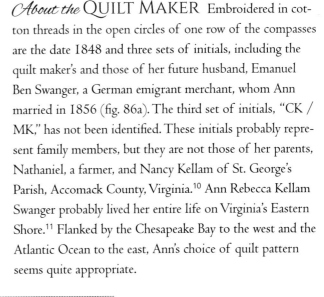

Figure 86a Detail. Ann embroidered the initials of her future husband, Emanuel Ben Swanger, on one of her quilt blocks.

New York Mariner's Compass Quilt Figure 85

MARY WRIGHT WILLIAMS

NEW YORK, NEW YORK, 1845–1855

COTTONS

7–8 RUNNING STITCHES PER INCH

95 X 95 IN. (241 X 241 CM)

MUSEUM PURCHASE, 2008.609.3

Virginia Mariner's Compass Quilt FIGURE 86

Ann Rebecca Kellam (1829–1902)

Accomack County, Virginia, 1848

Cottons; cotton embroidery threads

7–8 running stitches per inch

97½ x 97 in. (248 x 246 cm)

Gift of Dr. and Mrs. John A. Byrd in memory of Grace Floyd Byrd, 2010.609.3

1   Documented by the Kansas Quilt Project is a signed and dated 1878 quilt of this pattern with the name "Virginia Beauty" written on the back. For further discussion of this pattern name, see Barbara Brackman, *Clues in the Calico: A Guide to Identifying and Dating Antique Quilts* (McLean, VA: EPM), 167.

2   Ibid., 170.

3   Eliza Southgate to Robert Southgate, January 9, 1798, in *A Girl's Life Eighty Years Ago: Selections from the Letters of Eliza Southgate Bowne*, ed. Clarence Cook (New York: Charles Scribner's Sons, 1887), 15.

4   For more information on the Mariner's Compass quilt pattern, see Judy Mathieson, "Some Published Sources of Design Inspiration for the Quilt Pattern Mariner's Compass—17th to 20th Century," in *Uncoverings 1981*, ed. Sally Garoutte (San Francisco, CA: American Quilt Study Group, 1982), 11–18.

5   For images of matching pillowcases and quilts with further discussion of pieced and appliquéd pillowcases, see Patricia T. Herr, *Quilting Traditions: Pieces from the Past* (Atglen, PA: Schiffer, 2000), 149–151.

6   A printed calling card for "Mrs." Louise Marschalk Chapman, Margaret's daughter and Clarissa's granddaughter, was pinned to the quilt when the object was acquired; the reverse of the card bears the ink inscription "Designed and made / one hundred years ago by Clarissa Dodge / Marschalk and left / to / Louise Marschalk Chapman."

7   "U.S., Sons of the American Revolution Membership Applications, 1889–1970," s.vv. Margaret Dodge Marschalk, Clarissa Mary Dodge, and George Thomas Sutton, online database, digital image as found on Ancestry.com (2011); Frank F. Chapman household, 1900 U. S. census, Brooklyn Ward 20, Kings, NY, enumeration district 311, page 8B, National Archives and Records Administration (NARA) microfilm T623, roll 1057, digital image as found on Ancestry.com (2004); Theron Royal Woodward, *Dodge Genealogy: Descendants of Tristram Dodge* (Chicago: Lanward Publishing, 1904), 176; George T. Sutton household, 1850 U. S. census, Brooklyn Ward 3, Kings, NY, page 199B, NARA microfilm M432, roll 517, digital image as found on Ancestry.com (2009); George F. Sulton household, 1860 U. S. census, Brooklyn Ward 3 District 1, Kings, NY, page 536, NARA microfilm M653, roll 764, digital image as found on Ancestry.com (2009); George T. Sulton household, 1870 U. S. census, Brooklyn Ward 3, Kings, NY, page 218B, NARA microfilm M593, roll 946, digital image as found on Ancestry.com (2009); and Geo. F. Sutton household, 1880 U. S. census, Brooklyn, Kings, NY, enumeration district 92, page 424D, NARA microfilm T9, roll 846, digital image as found on Ancestry.com (2010).

8   "Irish Records Extraction Database," s.v. "John Williams," online database, Ancestry.com (1999).

9   A John and Mary Williams, presumably this couple, appear in the 1850 federal census in New York City's Fifth Ward. John was a sixty-year-old laborer, and Mary was fifty-six. Their neighbors were born in Ireland or Germany and included tradesmen, laborers, and servants. William Sneider household, 1850 U. S. census, Ward 5, New York, NY, page 261B, NARA microfilm M432, roll 537, digital image as found on Ancestry.com (2009).

10 Barry W. Miles and Moody K. Miles III, *Marriage Records of Accomack County, Virginia, 1854–1895, Recorded in Licenses & Ministers' Returns* (Westminster, MD: Heritage Books, 2006), 53. The 1850 federal census indicates that Nathaniel Kellam was a sixty-two-year-old farmer with real estate valued at two thousand dollars. Listed with him are his wife, Nancy, age sixty-five; Ann R. (the quilt maker), age twenty-one; and Henny R., age six. Nathl Kellam household, 1850 U. S. census, St. George's Parish, Accomack, VA, page 117A, NARA microfilm M432, roll 932, digital image as found on Ancestry.com (2009). The 1870 U. S. census for St. George's Parish in Accomack County lists E. B. Swanger as a merchant and Annie R. as a housekeeper. Five children are listed. E B Swanger household, 1870 U. S. census, St. George's Parish, Accomack, VA, page 232A, NARA microfilm M593, roll 1630, digital image as found on Ancestry.com (2009).

11 Ann Rebecca Kellam Swanger died July 28, 1902, and was interred at Swanger Graves in Locustville in Accomack County, VA. Jean Merritt Mihalyka and Faye Downing Wilson, *Graven Stones of Lower Accomack County Virginia (also Liberty and Parksley Cemeteries)* (Bowie, MD: Heritage Books, 1986), 246.

STAR

The radiating geometric figure known as a star is a centuries-old—even ancient—design motif found in many cultures. Stars often assume symbolic meaning as references to heavenly bodies, religious beliefs, and patriotic themes. In some cultures they represent divine guidance. The imagery for some institutions, such as benevolent societies like the Independent Order of the Odd Fellows and Freemasons, includes specific stars (see fig. 128).[1] The attractive symmetrical shape of the star—whether constructed of five or more points—is especially well suited to the piecing quilt-making process. Ranging from a bold oversize Star of Bethlehem that visually dominates a quilt to a clever star motif created from squares and triangles, a variety of star designs can be constructed using the simple geometric figure as the basis.

Pieced star designs were especially popular in American quilts from about 1840 to 1875. Their popularity may have been due to the influence of the Fancy artistic style, a lively and dynamic period in American art between 1790 and 1840. Fancy was an alternative to the restrained classical style. Characterized by colorful surfaces, exciting patterns, abstracted forms, bright colors, and bold designs, the progressive movement produced many expressive and visually driven household furnishings, including textiles. Designs taken from classical prototypes and nature were replaced with crisp geometric patterns, such as stars. The introduction of the kaleidoscope in 1816 enhanced the decorative vocabulary of Fancy. The influence of the kaleidoscope's wide arrangement of colors and tumbling geometric patterns can be seen on a variety of household furnishings, including woven coverlets and radiating star quilts.[2]

Successful star designs require great skill to cut and piece precisely as well as imagination in manipulating

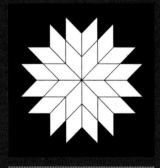

Figure 87 Star design.

Figure 88 Star design.

Figure 89 Star design.

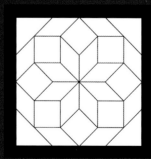

Figure 90 Star design.

colors and printed patterns (see fig. 91). Large and small eight-pointed stars can be created from cut and pieced diamonds (see figs. 87, 94). The impression of movement like that of a pinwheel can be achieved by alternating two dark and light patterned textiles within each star (see figs. 88, 95). Stars cut from the same textile emphasize the outline of the star shape (see fig. 99). An effect of radiation from a center point can be created by repeating the diamonds in bands of color outward (see fig. 94). Orienting striped textiles lengthwise increases the appearance of radiation (see fig. 93).

Some star designs are built on a centered square or a square within a square. The star points are created by triangles. The points are paired instead of radiating equally from a center point (see figs. 89, 96). Other quilts use squares, diamonds, and triangles in combination to form more complex star patterns (see figs. 90, 97).

By the nineteenth century, the meaning of the word *star* had evolved to include someone or something celebrated or distinguished in the arts or a profession. The quilts illustrated here are distinguished examples of their medium—they are stars in their own right.

Figure 91 Star of Bethlehem Quilt, maker unknown, probably Alexandria, Virginia, 1850–1865, cottons, 7 running stitches per inch, 104 x 100 in. (264 x 254 cm), Museum Purchase, 2000.609.1. The unidentified quilt maker responsible for this quilt possessed a good eye for color and mathematical precision. Over 2,192 individual pieces of printed cotton were used to produce the large Star of Bethlehem, also called Lone Star, and the smaller eight-pointed stars and half stars around the sides. Although each diamond used to create the stars is slightly different in shape and size, the meticulous piecing by the maker resulted in a flat, smooth quilt top without puckering—a feat only a very skilled quilter could accomplish. The alternating bands of light and dark diamonds within the stars create a kaleidoscopic effect. The printed floral cotton border is turned to the back and stitched down to create an edge finish. The quilt is backed in roller-printed cotton in a brown floral pattern and quilted in a pattern of parallel lines. A picker purchased the quilt from a family member of the quilt maker, who was from Alexandria, Virginia.[3]

FIGURE 92

Harriet Ann Richards's quilt is notable for its meticulously pieced pattern consisting of seventeen full and six half stars, each radiating from a six-pointed center. Each full star consists of seventy-eight individual diamonds of cotton positioned at sixty degrees to each other. The eye-catching pattern is further enhanced by the brilliant, exceptionally unfaded condition of the printed fabric swatches. The sawtooth inner and outer borders are characteristic of nineteenth-century quilts made in the Shenandoah Valley of Virginia.[4] The deftly executed quilted designs in the border of beautiful floral motifs, turning leaves, and grape clusters are related to at least four other quilts made in Winchester, Virginia, by Amelia Lauck (see figs. 185, 186, 188, 189). The original penciled guidelines for the quilting are still visible, suggesting the quilt was never washed (fig. 92a). The quilt is backed in plain cotton with the backing turned to the front to form a one-fourth-inch binding. It is signed and dated in running stitches: "H A RICHARDS / March 22 / 1840" (fig. 92a).

Store. In 1988 the quilt was unexpectedly discovered in the attic of a Winchester home by a Miller descendant.[5] The quilt probably had never been more than a few miles from its original home until it was donated to Colonial Williamsburg in 1995.

About the QUILT MAKER The daughter of Henry Richards (1779–1853) and Lydia Russell Richards (ca. 1782–1870) of Frederick County, Virginia, Harriet Ann probably created the quilt as part of her wedding trousseau. On September 20, 1842, she became the second wife of Captain George R. Long (ca. 1808–1851). By 1853 the widowed Harriet and her children, Octavia, Catharine, and M. J., were apparently living with her parents.[6] The 1853 will of Harriet's father provided for the "support comfortably at home; my daughter Harriet Long and her children." The will also indicates that the family was well established, owning over seven hundred acres of land and about fifteen slaves. The will lists a "fulling mill tract," "twenty sheep," and a "wool waggon," suggesting that Richards was involved in some type of textile manufacture.[7]

Figure 92a Detail. Harriet Ann Richards signed her quilt in running stitches. The penciled guidelines for the quilting are still visible.

The quilt descended through the family of Harriet's daughter, Mary Jane Long Miller. The Millers had lived in Winchester since before the American Revolution, operating an apothecary shop that later became Miller's Drug

Figure 92b Detail of quilting pattern.

WINCHESTER STARS QUILT FIGURE 92

HARRIET ANN RICHARDS (LATER MRS. GEORGE R. LONG) (1821–1869)

WINCHESTER, VIRGINIA, 1840

COTTONS

9–11 RUNNING STITCHES PER INCH

114 X 103 IN. (290 X 262 CM)

GIFT OF LESLIE CARR MILLER HAAS IN MEMORY
OF HER AUNT MARY LOUISE MILLER BARTON, 1995.609.1

FIGURE 93

The quilt maker's (or makers') skillful use of printed cottons and pattern can be seen in the precise piecing and pleasing color combinations in this example that combines two popular star patterns—Star of Bethlehem and Le Moyne Star. The large and smaller stars in this pieced quilt were constructed of 889 swatches of printed cottons. The bedcover was quilted in dropped diamond and clamshell designs. The front printed-cotton border is turned to the back and stitched in place to form a binding.

Figures 93a and 93b Details. The plain cotton backing is stamped with several inscriptions, which are seen in these details from the reverse. By 1832, the Arkwright Textile Manufactory in Coventry, Rhode Island, included a mill with power looms, a bleachery, and a calico-printing operation.

The quilt is backed in plain cotton fabric that bears stamped inscriptions suggesting the muslin's place of manufacture, processing, and/or wholesale. "Wм. M. COOKE & Co. / ARKWRIGHT / BLEACHERY" and "OCHASSET / MUSLIN" are two of the decipherable stamped inscriptions (figs. 93a, 93b).[8] Although an early cotton mill called the Arkwright Manufacturing Company existed in northern New York, it's more probable that these inscriptions refer to textile production in Rhode Island. During

the 1840s, at least 226 cotton mills existed in Rhode Island, with many located along the Blackstone and Pawtuxet Rivers.[9] The quilt's stamped inscription "ARKWRIGHT BLEACHERY" likely refers to the Rhode Island textile manufacturing of Arkwright in Coventry. Founded in 1809, the mill began operations along the Pawtuxet River in 1810, adding power looms in 1818, a bleachery in 1820, and calico printing in 1832 when William Cooke bought the mill.[10] "OCHASSET" could be a variant spelling for the Pawtuxet River or the Pocasset, a nearby river.

About the QUILT MAKER(S) The quilt is attributed to Sarah and/or Emily Sands, daughters of Joseph Sands, a prosperous merchant who served as treasurer and secretary of Annapolis, Maryland, and Sarah Rawlings Sands. The sisters were certainly adept with their needles. In addition to the quilt, an embroidered white cotton furniture cover and a sampler survive (fig. 93c). The sampler, signed by Sarah Sands and worked about 1816, still hangs on a wall in the Sands family home.[11] Until recently, the pieced quilt and embroidered furniture cover were also in the home, stored with other family textiles and clothing in a chest on the second floor.[12]

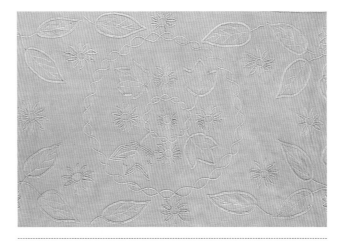

Figure 93c Detail of Embroidered Furniture Cover, Sarah and/or Emily Sands, Annapolis, Maryland, ca. 1830, cottons, 27½ x 42¾ in. (70 x 109 cm), Museum Purchase, 2010.609.2. This embroidered furniture cover, embellished with cotton chain stitches and knitted fringe, may have decorated the top of a chest of drawers or a small table. It was fashionable to have embroidered or quilted tops for a toilet table at which a lady sat to dress in the morning.

Annapolis Star of Bethlehem and Le Moyne Star Quilt · Figure 93

Sarah Sands (ca. 1806–1902) and/or Emily Sands (ca. 1815–1901)

Annapolis, Maryland, ca. 1845

Cottons

8 running stitches per inch

100 x 92½ in. (254 x 235 cm)

Museum Purchase, 2010.609.1

VIRGINIA STAR OF BETHLEHEM AND LE MOYNE STAR QUILT

FIGURE 94

The exact piecing and choice of vibrant fabrics give this quilt its visual appeal. The larger Lone Stars, or Stars of Bethlehem, have carefully cut and pieced diamonds that radiate from the center point in bands of alternating colors. Smaller stars, often called Le Moyne Stars, are simple eight-pointed shapes. All are set within a larger grid of diamonds formed by brilliant blue printed-cotton sashing with yellow printed-cotton pieces at the intersections. The quilt is bound in the same yellow printed cotton, which is also found in some of the quilt patches. It is backed in white plain-woven cotton and quilted in a pattern of parallel lines following the piecing and a single curving leaf, or feather, design in the white areas.

The quilt descended into the Jones and Terry family of Virginia.

PENNSYLVANIA LE MOYNE STAR QUILT

FIGURE 95

By placing colored stars against a white cotton ground, Catharine Knepper Walk created the appearance of stars floating on the surface of this covering, which is quilted in clamshells, diagonal parallel lines, and chevron patterns. The Le Moyne Star pattern was used in the creation of full-size quilts like this one as well as smaller crib quilts for children (see fig. 95a). The quilt is backed and bound in white plain-woven cotton.

About the QUILT MAKER The quilt descended in the donor's family where it had always been attributed to Catharine Knepper Walk, wife of George Walk (1792–1839). They married in 1824. Catharine lived her entire life in Franklin County, Pennsylvania, where her grave is marked by a simple tombstone at the Mount Zion Cemetery in Quincy. In 1850 the forty-five-year-old widowed Catharine was head of a household that included her two sons, John and Samuel. John was a farmer. By 1870 she was living in John's household.[13]

Figure 95a (left) *Baby in Blue Cradle,* artist unidentified, possibly Connecticut, ca. 1840, courtesy National Gallery of Art, 1959.11.3. An eight-pointed star pattern quilt is draped over the foot of the blue cradle in which the baby is sitting.

Figure 95b Detail.

Virginia Star of Bethlehem and Le Moyne Star Quilt Figure 94

Member of the Jones or Terry family

Virginia, 1850–1860

Cottons

6–7 running stitches per inch

104 x 90 in. (264 x 229 cm)

Gift of Thomas R. Terry in honor of Lulie Greenhow Jones Terry, 2002.609.1

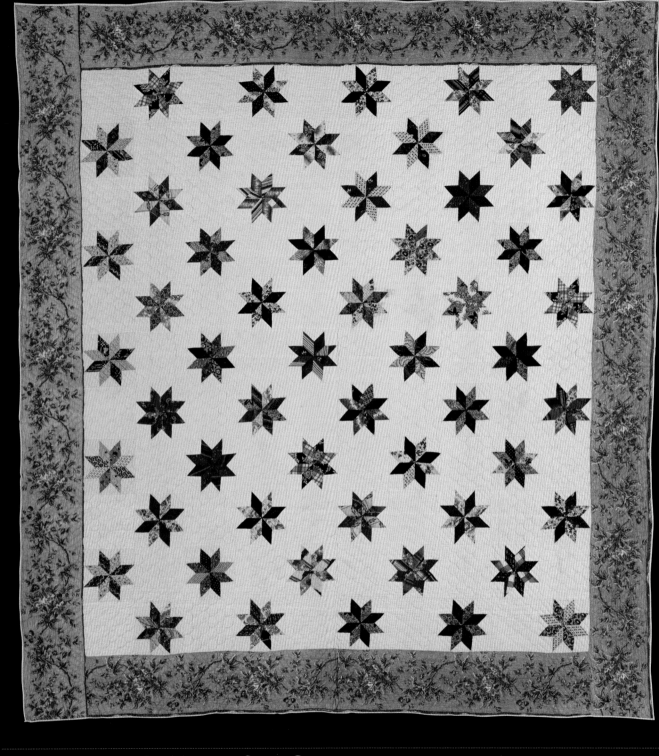

Pennsylvania Le Moyne Star Quilt FIGURE 95

Catharine Knepper Walk (Mrs. George Walk) (1802–1872)

Quincy, Franklin County, Pennsylvania, 1830–1845

Cottons

7–9 running stitches per inch

81½ x 77 in. (207 x 196 cm)

Gift of Grace Bishop, 2005.609.4

STENCILED OHIO STAR QUILT

FIGURE 96

Two techniques were employed in the creation of this bedcovering—piecing and stenciling. Each star was pieced from one square and twelve triangles, giving the effect of a square within a square with four paired points. The pieced-star blocks alternate with white blocks stenciled with stylized flowers and leaves. The quilt is backed in white plain-woven cotton and bound in blue printed cotton. It is quilted in an outline pattern.

Stenciling involves brushing, tamping, or dabbing paint through the openings in a cut stencil onto the ground fabric, which was usually stretched over a padded surface. The colors used for stenciling varied but included ground-up pigments or vegetable dyes thickened with gum arabic and cornstarch. Depending on the dyestuff, the colors might be set using steam. Stencils were made from stiff paper or fabrics treated with substances such as linseed oil, resins, or wax to make them waterproof (fig. 96a). Stencils could also be made from thin wood or tin.

Stenciling was one way to add color and pattern to textiles, as well as furniture, floors, and walls (see fig. 96b). It was fashionable in the early to mid-nineteenth century, especially in New York and New England. Individual stencil patterns could be carefully arranged and positioned to create larger compositions, often using flower, fruit, and bird motifs. In this quilt, the stenciling served as a substitute for more involved and intricate embroidery, appliqué, and piecing.

Figure 96a Stencils, attributed to Stephen D. Shipps, probably Philadelphia, Pennsylvania, ca. 1865, cut paper, 3 x 12½ in. (8 x 32 cm) and 4½ x 12⅞ in. (11 x 32 cm), gift of Mr. and Mrs. George J. Dittmar Jr., 1978.115.2 A–B. Some women designed and created their own stencils. However, professionally cut stencils could be purchased by the mid-1830s. Although many ornamental designs were extremely intricate and required several stencils to complete the motifs, these designs were cut as single stencils to be applied quickly and inexpensively. These examples were originally cut to decorate the backs of chairs.

Figure 96b *Mrs. Jonathan Jaques*, Jacob Maentel (1778–1863), Posey County, Indiana, 1841, watercolor and ink on wove paper, 17¾ x 11⅜ in. (45 x 29 cm), Museum Purchase, 1959.300.7. The lively decoration of this interior suggests the sitter's up-to-date interests. Note the painted blue walls stenciled with medallions and floral sprigs similar to quilt designs, the pair of red curtains, and the woven wall-to-wall carpeting.

STENCILED OHIO STAR QUILT FIGURE 96

MAKER UNKNOWN

POSSIBLY NORTHERN NEW YORK STATE, 1820–1840

COTTONS; PAINT

8 RUNNING STITCHES PER INCH

92 X 81 IN. (234 X 206 CM)

BEQUEST OF GRACE HARTSHORN WESTERFIELD, 1974.609.29

BRUNSWICK STAR QUILT

The basic pieced block of this quilt consists of an eight-pointed star of diamonds surrounded by eight squares, eight diamonds, and four triangles, all creating a larger square on point. The narrow three-fourths-inch binding is from the same textile that forms the alternating blocks in the quilt. The bedcovering is quilted through cotton batting to white cotton backing in patterns of diamonds and parallel lines.

One diamond in the left bottom block is of a patterned fabric that is found nowhere else in the quilt (fig. 97a). It is probable that the quilt maker simply substituted a fabric for one she had run out of or wished to make a quilt block that was totally unique to her. Caution should be used in interpreting this as a "humility block." A humility block is described as one in which a deliberate error was made, such as turning a block sideways or using a different shade or pattern of fabric, as a sign of modesty. They were thought to usually appear in the right bottom quilt corner. This conscious error was supposedly based on the Oriental idea that only the gods or a Supreme Being could create perfection and that it was dangerous and prideful for a human to try. The story is often heard in Oriental rug shops in regard to Persian woven carpets but is considered fictional by most carpet historians and quilt scholars.[14]

The quilt descended through the donor's family of Greene County, Pennsylvania, and Illinois and was believed to have been created by Lucy B. Gregory Moorhead or her mother, Sarah Van Natta Gregory.[15]

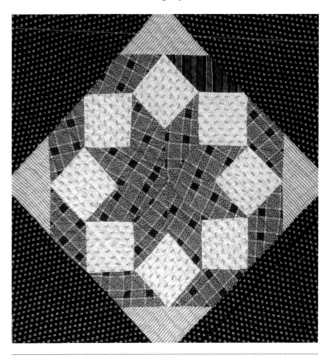

Figure 97a Detail. One diamond in this block is of a patterned cotton found nowhere else in the quilt. The maker may have substituted the textile for one she ran out of.

FEATHERED STAR QUILT

The maker of this vivacious quilt combined red and blue-green printed textiles with solid-white cotton in a pattern of repeated stars in which the points touch those of the adjacent stars by way of pieced diamonds at the tips. Each star is pieced with a square center and eight matching triangles of blue-green, further embellished with smaller red pieced triangles at the edges that give a feathered appearance. In order to make her quilt the correct size, the quilt maker cut up five of the star units and stitched the ten pieces to one side and one end, creating an asymmetrical design. The quilted patterns include feather wreaths, squares, diagonal parallel lines, and diamonds. The quilt is backed in white plain-woven cotton, which has been brought to the front to create a finished edge.

The quilt descended in the donor's family and is thought to have been made by Anna Hopton, who was born in South Carolina and married Thomas Joseph Macon (1839–1917) of Virginia probably around 1870.[16]

Brunswick Star Quilt   Figure 97

Lucy B. Gregory Moorhead (1861–1890) or Sarah Van Natta
Gregory (1840–1869)

Possibly Illinois, 1860–1880

Cottons

6–7 running stitches per inch

76 x 69 in. (193 x 175 cm)

Gift of Mr. and Mrs. Milton Schaible, 1973.609.4

Feathered Star Quilt Figure 98

Possibly Anna Hopton (later Mrs. Thomas Joseph Macon)
(d. 1893)

Southeast United States, possibly Virginia, 1850–1870

Cottons

9–10 running stitches per inch

90 x 76½ in. (229 x 194 cm)

Gift of Mrs. James (Mütter) Hagemann, 1971-3303

Stars and Stripes Pieced Quilt

FIGURE 99

Although the U. S. flag inspired this quilt, its techniques and star shapes differ significantly from the flag itself. Unlike the five-pointed appliquéd stars on most flags, these nontraditional eight-pointed stars, and this quilt in general, are constructed using the piecing technique. Tiny star-patterned and dotted textiles in the blue areas give this boldly graphic design visual appeal. The quilt is backed with white cotton and quilted through thin batting following the geometric shapes of the piecing. Half-inch cotton strips cut on the straight grain are folded over the edges to bind the outer edges of the quilt, leaving a quarter-inch visible on the front.[17]

This quilt was made as a patriotic Union statement during the American Civil War, with the thirty-four stars representing the number of states in the Union by 1861, including those states that had seceded at the beginning of the war. A pattern for a similar "Stars and Stripes Bed-Quilt" was published in the July 1861 issue of *Peterson's Magazine*, a popular periodical for ladies (fig. 99a). The author hoped to inspire readers to document their Union sympathies through their quilting.

The quilt was in the collection of Muriel and Foster McCarl of Beaver Falls, Pennsylvania, but its nineteenth-century history is not known.

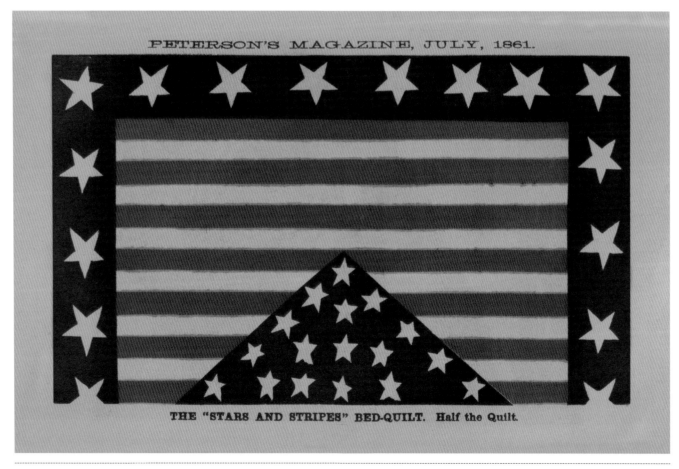

Figure 99a Stars and Stripes Bed-Quilt Pattern, designer unknown, United States, from *Peterson's Magazine*, July 1861. This colorful design from *Peterson's Magazine* gave the reader half of a quilt design intended to be mirrored and enlarged to full bed-quilt size. Like the Colonial Williamsburg quilt, the pattern had thirty-four stars at the center, although *Peterson's* used the standard five-pointed stars.

STARS AND STRIPES PIECED QUILT FIGURE 99

MAKER UNKNOWN

UNITED STATES, PROBABLY 1861–1863

COTTONS

6 RUNNING STITCHES PER INCH

92 X 91¾ IN. (234 X 233 CM)

MUSEUM PURCHASE FROM THE ESTATE OF FOSTER AND MURIEL MCCARL, THE FRIENDS OF COLONIAL WILLIAMSBURG COLLECTIONS FUND, 2012.609.4

1. Five-pointed stars are seen in Odd Fellows imagery, and the Masonic Seal of Solomon is a six-pointed star.

2. For an in-depth discussion of the Fancy artistic style and the influence of the kaleidoscope on the decorative arts, see Sumpter Priddy, *American Fancy: Exuberance in the Arts, 1790–1840* (Milwaukee, WI: Chipstone Foundation, 2004).

3. A similar Star of Bethlehem quilt made by Mary Louisa House Standiford, who lived on King Street in Alexandria, VA, is in the collection of the Virginia Quilt Museum, Harrisonburg. See Joan Knight, *Virginia Quilt Museum* (Charlottesville, VA: Howell Press, 2002), 25. Note, however, that the quilt information is incomplete in the label.

4. Sawtooth borders and zigzag patterns (such as Streak of Lightning and Delectable Mountains) were popular with the quilters of the Shenandoah Valley possibly because they mimic mountain shapes, a familiar sight to quilters living in the valley. The Blue Ridge Mountain range is to the east, the Alleghany to the west, and the Massanutten Mountains divide the valley. Their presence is omnipotent and is felt in almost all aspects of life in the Shenandoah Valley. For other quilts associated with the valley and depicting zigzag patterns, see Knight, *Virginia Quilt Museum*, 6, 11, 12, 17, 66.

5. The donor, Mrs. Louis Haas (née Leslie Carr Miller), found the quilt in the attic of her aunt's house at the time of her aunt's death. Her aunt was Mrs. Lewis Neil Barton (née Mary Louise Miller). Mrs. Haas recorded the line of descent of the quilt as from the maker of the quilt to her daughter, Mrs. Godfrey Lewis Miller (née Mary Jane Long), from Mary Jane Long Miller to George Frederick Miller, her brother-in-law, from George Frederick Miller to Godfrey Otto Miller, his son, from Godfrey Otto Miller to his daughter, Mary Louise Miller, from Mary Louise Miller to her niece Leslie Carr Miller, the donor.

6. Harriett Long, 1870 U. S census, mortality schedule, Winchester, Frederick, VA, line 17, National Archives and Records Administration (NARA) microfilm T1132, roll 10, digital image as found on Ancestry.com (2010); "Virginia, Marriages, 1740–1850," s.v., "Harriet A. Richards," online database, Ancestry.com (1999); "Virginia, Deaths and Burials Index, 1853–1917," s.v. "Henry Richards," online database, Ancestry.com (2011); Lydia Richards, 1870 U. S census, mortality schedule, Winchester, Frederick, VA, line 16, NARA microfilm T1132, roll 10, digital image as found on Ancestry.com (2010); and George R. Long household, 1850 U. S. census, Winchester, Frederick, VA, page 281B, NARA microfilm M432, roll 945, digital image as found on Ancestry.com (2009).

7. Henry Richards, will dated September 30, 1853, Frederick County Will Book 23, p. 508, Winchester-Frederick County Courthouse, Winchester, VA.

8. For a pieced quilt with printed marks on the back that reference the Franklin Mills and Arkwright Bleachers, Rhode Island, see [Bridget Long], *Elegant Geometry: American and British Mosaic Patchwork* (Lincoln, NE: International Quilt Study Center & Museum, 2011), 32.

9. Linda Welters, "Cultural Legacies," in *Down by the Old Mill Stream: Quilts in Rhode Island*, ed. Linda Welters and Margaret T. Ordoñez (Kent, OH: Kent State University Press, 2000), 29.

10. Clare M. Sheridan, librarian, American Textile History Museum, to author (Ivey), e-mail message, April 2, 2010; and Linda Welters and Margaret Ordoñez, "Early Calico Printing in Rhode Island," in *Uncoverings 2001*, ed. Virginia Gunn (Lincoln, NE: American Quilt Study Group, 2001), 74–81.

11. For a full description and image of the sampler, biographical information, an image of the quilt makers, and partial obituaries for Emily and Sarah Sands, see Gloria Seaman Allen, *A Maryland Sampling: Girlhood Embroidery, 1738–1860* (Baltimore, MD: Maryland Historical Society, 2007), 54–56.

12. A ca. 1755 black walnut and yellow pine side chair, once part of a set of at least twelve, also descended in the Sands family and is now in the Colonial Williamsburg collection (2010-26).

13. "Catharine Knepper Walk" on findagrave.com, Find a Grave memorial #71883966, record added June 23, 2011; "George Walk" on findagrave.com, Find a Grave memorial #71883950, record added June 23, 2011; Catharine Walk household, 1850 U. S. census, Quincy, Franklin, PA, page 407A, NARA microfilm M432, roll 782, digital image as found on Ancestry.com (2009); and John Walk household, 1870 U. S. census, Quincy, Franklin, PA, page 528A, NARA microfilm M593, roll 1346, digital image as found on Ancestry.com (2009).

14. Humility blocks have also sometimes been thought to be part of the Amish quilting tradition. However, research by quilt historians has revealed that the intentional creation of humility blocks in old Amish quilts is a myth. In fact, an intentional mistake would be saying just the opposite by showing the arrogance of a quilt maker who has to try to make a mistake in her work that would otherwise be perfect. In her research, Barbara Brackman found no nineteenth-century references to humility blocks; the first she located is in Florence Peto's 1949 book *American Quilts and Coverlets*. "The Deliberate Error: By Design—or Actually by Chance?" *Quilter's Newsletter Magazine* no. 203 (June 1988): 34–35, 62.

15. A written history provided by the quilt's donor states that the quilt was owned by her grandmother Lucy B. Gregory Moorhead, who was born in Greene County, PA, in 1860. After the death of her father in Libby Prison, Lucy and her mother, Sarah Van Natta Gregory, moved to Illinois in 1863 where Lucy married Warren Moorhead in 1881. She died in 1890 leaving one daughter, "Little Mabel," the donor's mother. It is not known if the quilt was made by Lucy or her mother. "Lucy B Gregory Moorhead" on findagrave.com, Find a Grave memorial #33195558, record added January 24, 2009; and "Sarah E VanNatta Gregory" on findagrave.com, Find a Grave memorial #5604663, record added July 11, 2001.

16. "Anna H Macon" on findagrave.com, Find a Grave memorial #93374956, record added July 10, 2012; "Thomas Joseph Macon" on findagrave.com, Find a Grave memorial #83272186, record added January 11, 2012; and T. J. Macon household, 1880 U. S. census, Bermuda, Chesterfield, VA, enumeration district 64, page 24C, NARA microfilm T9, roll 1361, digital image as found on Ancestry.com (2010). Anna Hopton Macon and her husband, Thomas, are buried in Hollywood Cemetery in Richmond, VA.

17. The quilt was published in 1974 with the later date of ca. 1890 and a Hawaiian attribution. See Carleton L. Safford and Robert Bishop, *America's Quilts and Coverlets* (New York: Weathervane Books, 1974), 140.

CHAPTER 12

APPLIQUÉD 1840-1930

APPLIQUÉD 1840-1930

By the early 1840s, the framed center-medallion format of appliquéd quilts changed to compartmentalized designs made of individual appliquéd blocks combined into an overall design. A popular format was the four block, which consisted of four large blocks approximately thirty inches square framed by a border or series of borders (see fig. 100). Fashionable motifs for appliquéd quilts during this time included fruit and flowering trees, grape vines, flowers, swags, baskets, and birds in many shapes and sizes. Some appliqués, such as the legs and eyes of birds, were embellished with cotton and wool threads, as well as inked flourishes (see fig. 101). Stuffing added dimension to some areas of the appliqués (see fig. 109). By the 1870s, synthetic dyes produced a wide variety of colors for the quilter to choose from. Unfortunately, the new dyes were not as reliable as the old vegetable dyes, and many faded to a dull tan when exposed to light or washing (see fig. 112). Some of the appliqués discussed here were created from fabric cut to shape using paper or tin patterns; others were created in much the same way as cutting out a paper snowflake from a folded piece of paper.

Figure 100 Roses and Princess Plumes Four-Block Quilt, maker unknown, United States, 1860–1880, cottons with wool embroidery threads, 7 running stitches per inch, 84 x 82 in. (213 x 208 cm), gift of Miriam R. LeVin, 1974.609.3. The unknown maker of this quilt created a center-medallion bedcover by combining four center blocks of roses and rosebuds with three differently patterned borders of floral, undulating vine of princess plumes, and zigzags. The same vibrant and intricately patterned red paisley print is used for all of the appliquéd swatches, except for the central four roses and the foliage jackets from which the numerous scattered buds emerge. The result is a bedcover with unusual cohesiveness for one with such varied appliqué work. Dark-green embroidered wool threads form the topknots and arrow-like stems of the scattered buds. The quilt is bound in strips of the predominant paisley fabric and backed in two different small-scale printed cottons. It is quilted in an overall design of two-inch diamonds.

Figure 101 Cherry Tree and Birds Quilt, maker unknown, possibly Connecticut, 1920–1930, cottons with cotton and silk embroidery threads, 5–6 running stitches per inch, 80 x 77 in. (203 x 196 cm), gift of Mr. and Mrs. Jason Berger, 1979.609.3. Two favored motifs in nineteenth-century American needlework—birds with fruit trees and meandering grapevines—appear on this appliquéd quilt. Supplementary cotton embroidery threads form the birds' eyes and the twigs in some of their beaks. The muted color scheme, the overall fan quilting pattern, and the single piece of top ground fabric, however, are clues to the quilt's later date.[1] The quilt's white plain-woven cotton backing has been rolled to the front and machine stitched in place to form the binding. According to the donor, the quilt was from the Byron family of Bethel, Connecticut, and was made by one of Mrs. Byron's grandmothers.

VIRGINIA FLORAL WREATH QUILT

FIGURE 102

Floral and vine wreaths were appliquéd motifs on quilts. This quilt consists of sixteen full and four half blocks of green and golden-brown floral wreaths with angular shapes and edges, similar to patterns known as President's Wreath and Martha Washington's Wreath. The blocks are divided by a bold solid-green sashing. A wide printed-cotton border of angular and abstract shapes completes the quilt. The quilt's narrow binding was formed by rolling the plain-woven cotton backing over to the front. Within the appliquéd blocks, the quilting pattern follows the outline of the wreath. The floral border is quilted in groups of parallel diagonal lines that alternate direction.

About the QUILT MAKER Found in Norfolk, Virginia, the quilt is said to have been created by Fanny Butt, a member of the well-known Butt family of that area.[2] The Colonial Williamsburg Foundation also owns an 1811 sampler stitched by Sarah Bruce Butt, possibly the quilt maker's sister (fig. 102a).[3]

Figure 102a Sampler, Sarah Bruce Butt, Norfolk County, Virginia, 1811, silk and linen, 24¼ x 16¾ in. (62 x 43 cm), Museum Purchase, 1989-34. Sarah Bruce Butt was the daughter of Nathaniel and Frances Butt of Norfolk County, Virginia. Sarah may have been the sister of quilt maker Frances (Fanny) Butt.

LYRES AND SWAGS QUILT

FIGURE 103

The maker of this quilt limited herself to repeating the motif of a lyre sixteen times without any separating bands, or sashing. More often the lyre was one of a number of appliquéd motifs used to decorate the individual blocks of an album quilt (see chap. 14).[4] The appliquéd lyres on this quilt are turned toward each other so the quilt can be "read" from either direction when placed on a bed. Swags, tassels, and bows in autumnal colors ornament the outer border. The quilting pattern follows the outline of the appliqué. The quilt is bound in a strip of green cotton and backed in white plain-woven cotton.

The harp-like musical instrument known as a lyre was a popular decorative motif in nineteenth-century furnishings. The graceful motif was revived in the eighteenth and nineteenth centuries with other designs from ancient Greek art, lending notions of classical artistic achievement and democratic ideals. The lyre was also used in Masonic ritual and symbolism.

The quilt is said to have descended in the Moore family, longstanding residents of York County, Virginia, since the eighteenth century. It is one of the few nineteenth-century quilts documented from York County.

VIRGINIA FLORAL WREATH QUILT   FIGURE 102

Lyres and Swags Quilt FIGURE 103

Probably a member of the Moore family

York County, Virginia, 1845–1860

Cottons

8–9 running stitches per inch

92 x 92 in. (234 x 234 cm)

Museum Purchase, 2008.609.7

FIGURE 104   FIGURE 105

Two sisters made these quilts for their nephews.[5] Christiann Rauch alternated sixteen blocks of traditional floral wreaths of red and green with red rosettes, or sunflowers, around the edges with nine white blocks set on point. The border consists of an undulating leafy green vine. Appliquéd in bright red and green, the quilt is signed "CR" and dated "1849" in fine red cross-stitches (fig. 104a). The white blocks between the wreaths are expertly hand quilted with curving leaves, or princess plumes, and floral wreaths, and the border is quilted in pairs of parallel lines. The plain cotton backing fabric is rolled to the front to create a binding.

Ann Margaret Rauch used sixteen blocks of a traditional double-tulip pattern in her exuberant quilt of brilliant pink, yellow, and green. An inner border of triangles in a sawtooth configuration and an outer border of undulating vine of eight-petal yellow rosette flowers add to the quilt's sense of lively movement. As did her sister Christiann, Ann Margaret signed and dated her quilt in red cross-stitches, "M.R." and "18 . 49" (fig. 105a). The bedcover is quilted in squares on point, pairs of diagonal lines, and outline. The face fabric is rolled to the plain cotton backing to create a binding.

About the QUILT MAKERS According to the family history, two spinster sisters, Christiann Rauch and Ann Margaret Rauch, made quilts in 1849 for their nephews, John Emmanuel Hade (1844–1910) and Jacob Henry Hade (b. ca. 1847) (figs. 104/105b, 104/105c). The nephews were the sons of the youngest sister, Sarah (1814–1909), who married Jacob Hade around 1841. By 1849, the widowed Sarah was raising three children under the age of eight, with the youngest, Jacob, born after his father's death in 1846. The two quilts remain together to this day; both gifts from the family. They survive in excellent condition, possibly because they were seldom used. No evidence exists to indicate that John or Jacob married. The quilts descended through the children of their older sister, Anna Elizabeth Hade.[6]

Figure 104/105b John Emmanuel Hade, courtesy Sandra F. and Harry Fisher.

Figure 104/105c Jacob Henry Hade, courtesy Sandra F. and Harry Fisher.

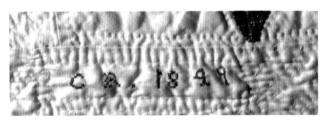

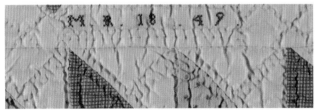

Figures 104a and 105a Details. Both sisters used red cross-stitches to sign and date their quilts.

Wreath and Princess Plumes Quilt Figure 104

Christiann Rauch (ca. 1807–1883)

Franklin County, Pennsylvania, 1849

Cottons; cotton embroidery threads

9–10 running stitches per inch

98 x 98 in. (249 x 249 cm)

Gift of Sandra F. and Harry Fisher, 2008.6091

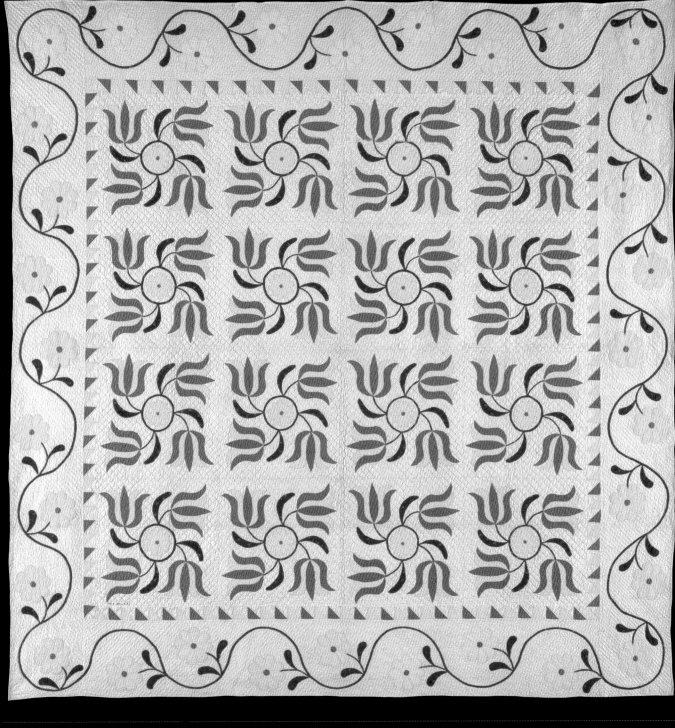

TULIP QUILT FIGURE 105

ANN MARGARET RAUCH (CA. 1811–1882)

FRANKLIN COUNTY, PENNSYLVANIA, 1849

COTTONS; COTTON EMBROIDERY THREADS

9 RUNNING STITCHES PER INCH

85¼ X 85¼ IN. (217 X 217 CM)

GIFT OF SANDRA F. AND HARRY FISHER, 2008.609.2

FIGURE 106

This red-and-green appliquéd and stuffed quilt is composed of twenty blocks in a variation of the Honeysuckle design. The quilt is backed in white plain-woven cotton and bound in a strip of the same. It is quilted in running stitches in patterns including outline, leaves and vine, diamonds, circles, and flowers. Marked in running stitches on the front left center of the quilt is the signature "E A R / May 4th 1857" for Ellen Ann Raywalt, a schoolteacher who created the quilt just four months before her marriage to Albert H. Ansley in Steuben, New York, on October 28, 1857 (fig. 106a).[7] Honeysuckle has been associated with devotion, love's bond, and belonging to one another—appropriate symbols for a quilt Ellen probably created as part of her wedding trousseau.

Figure 106a Ellen Ann Raywalt Ansley, courtesy Ernest Ansley.

About the QUILT MAKER Shortly after their marriage, the young newlyweds moved to northern Virginia where Albert Ansley and his father, William Ansley Jr., owned adjoining farms one mile north of the Fairfax County Courthouse. Letters written by Ellen to her family she left behind in New York provide a colorful glimpse into her life as a newlywed. In January 1858, Ellen cheerfully described to her parents the activities of a young bride as

she "commenced housekeeping in earnest." She wrote to sister Hannah in June of that year grumbling about the Virginia weather as "sunshiny & *hot* sometimes unmercifully so especially when I have much work around the hot stove." She admitted, however, that "it is a heap better than walking a mile or two through the broiling sun to some dingy schoolhouse to care for the score or two of young hopefuls there assembled." In a testament to the constant ritual of keeping house that most Victorian women suffered, Ellen explained to her sister that she had been "engaged in performing the various duties for housekeeping such as ironing mending patching or darning cooking & eating & washing dishes, which together with preparing for company pretty well filled up all my working hours." Ellen also wrote of wanting to get her carpet done that spring for she feared there would be much mopping to do if she did not (see fig. 106b).[8]

By the spring of 1861, Ellen had more to fear than dirty floors! She was a Yankee living in a southern community that witnessed the first southern bloodshed of the American Civil War. Growing tensions between the North and South resulted in open warfare in April 1861, and in late May Virginia ratified secession from the Union. Albert and Ellen Ansley with their two young children fled the troubled Virginia community, eventually making their way back to Yates County, New York, to start a new life.[9] Our quilt maker died of yellow fever in 1865, leaving three children behind to be raised by her husband, who remarried within the year.[10]

Figure 106b Detail. Rag Rug, maker unknown, United States, 1860–1890, cotton, 69 x 43 in. (175 x 109 cm), Museum Purchase, 1996.609.6. In letters written to her sister, Ellen Raywalt Ansley described ripping old pants and cutting rags for making carpets. Her carpets likely looked similar to this one, which is made from old rags stitched together. The rags were used as the weft, or filling, in hand-woven rugs.

HONEYSUCKLE QUILT FIGURE 106

ELLEN ANN RAYWALT (LATER MRS. ALBERT HENRY ANSLEY)
(1833–1865)

STEUBEN COUNTY, NEW YORK, 1857

COTTONS

7–12 RUNNING STITCHES PER INCH

84¾ X 69¾ IN. (215 X 177 CM)

GIFT OF ERNEST ANSLEY, 2000.609.5

WHIG ROSE QUILT

FIGURE 107

Rows of full-blown roses, in shades of pink with large yellow centers, each with eight rosebuds, alternate with rows of eight-pointed stars to create a charming variation of the Whig Rose pattern in this quilt. Unlike in most rose designs, each of these roses has been pieced in eight sections, each section itself pieced three times in shades of pink. The bright-yellow center is appliquéd, as are the stars and the border of serrated swags.[11] The quilt is bound with a plain cotton strip on the bias and backed in plain white cotton. It is intricately quilted in patterns of large squares and medallions of flowers, in addition to outline.

The Whigs, an American political party formed in 1834, is believed to be the source of the name of the appliquéd design. Although by 1856 the party had been succeeded by the Republican Party, the Whig Rose pattern remained popular throughout the second half of the nineteenth century.

About the QUILT MAKERS The donors' history states that this quilt was made by two sisters, Sarah and Harriet Robinson, but research revealed that Harriet was actually the daughter of Thomas and Sarah Robinson, who were born in Maryland and by 1840 were living in Indiana.[12] Thomas and Sarah's son John Larne Robinson was elected to the Thirtieth, Thirty-First, and Thirty-Second Congresses (March 1847–March 1853).[13] Perhaps the political implication of the pattern's name appealed to the mother's and daughter's pride in their family's political involvement. The quilt descended to Harriet's two spinster granddaughters, Blanche Louise Barbour (1882–1971) and Anna Violet Barbour (1884–1968), who were both distinguished citizens in their own right.[14]

VASE AND TULIP APPLIQUÉD FOUR-BLOCK QUILT

FIGURE 108

The unknown quilt maker used two construction techniques—appliqué and stuffed work—and a four-block format to create this bedcover. Four identical large fluted vases of tulips, berries, and birds form the central motifs with tiny vases of flowers, leaves, and berries as borders. The designs were appliquéd in place using blind stitches. Some stems and the bird legs were created with chain and satin stitches. All the berries were stuffed or padded. Quilted in running stitches in triple parallel lines on the diagonal, the quilt is dated 1862 in outline stitches on the reverse. It is bound in the same green cotton that was used in the vases and foliage and backed in plain-woven cotton.

The red-and-green color scheme and the vase and tulip design are characteristic of Pennsylvania quilts and coverlets. Over thirty nineteenth-century quilts in this design and color scheme have been documented—many of them with provenances that associate them with Pennsylvania or Ohio. Although no published quilt patterns are known to exist from this early date, quilt makers did share ideas and hand-drawn patterns, some of which were carried with settlers who migrated west. The vase and tulip design of this quilt has been known by many pattern names over the years, including Pot of Flowers, Tulip Pot, Potted Tulip, Pride of Iowa, and Our Pride.[15]

Whig Rose Quilt   Figure 107

Attributed to Sarah Robinson (1772–1859) and Harriet
Robinson (later Mrs. Samuel Barbour) (1810–1901)

Indiana, 1840–1850

Cottons

9 running stitches per inch

94½ x 93½in. (240 x 237 cm)

Gift of the Misses Louise and Violet Barbour, 1965-224

Vase and Tulip Appliquéd Four-Block Quilt Figure 108

Maker unknown

Possibly Pennsylvania or Ohio, 1862

Cottons; cotton and silk embroidery threads

9 running stitches per inch

81 x 78½ in. (206 x 199 cm)

Gift of Edwin and Barbara Braman, 1997.609.1

BIRDS AND TREES QUILT

FIGURE 109

The quilt maker's careful planning of this quilt is reflected in the consistency of its fabric selections and in its ordered layout: two motifs from the central medallion were picked up and alternately repeated to form an inner border, each motif strategically placed to fill its allotted space. The use of stylized birds with treelike foliage is similar to the distelfink and hom (goldfinch, or thistle finch, and tree of life) motif that was popular on nineteenth-century Pennsylvania figured and fancy woven coverlets (see fig. 4). The Turkey-red-and-green color scheme with accents of chrome orange, or "cheddar," is also associated with quilts made in eastern and central Pennsylvania, as are the four geometric sunbursts.[16]

The openness of the overall design gives this quilt a fresh, light quality that is lost in more complex examples.

The grapes in the outer border, for instance, have been interpreted as sprigs rather than heavy clusters. The designer's clever solution for filling the empty corners of her quilt also deserves mention: only there do the heavy border leaves fall to the outside of the vine, thereby anchoring the design and drawing attention to the bedcover's outermost edges.

Some of the appliquéd motifs, such as the grapes and large berries, are stuffed. Providing additional dimension are the finely embroidered veins in the leaves and details in the birds' tails, feet, eyes, and combs. The bed quilt is backed in plain-woven white cotton with a one-fourth-inch-wide binding of plain-woven white cotton. The quilting pattern consists of a single row of outline stitching around each appliqué, with an overall grid of squares set on the diagonal filling the remainder of the background.

TULIP CROSS CRIB QUILT

FIGURE 110

The floral design of this crib-size quilt is appliquéd in a pattern usually known as Tulip Cross or Cock's Comb. Occasionally full-size quilts were cut down for use on babies', children's, and even dolls' beds, but the top patterns of such adaptations were seldom proportioned to their reduced dimensions. That is not the case in this example where the bold floral spray fills the center while birds effectively lengthen the design to a rectangular format. The eyes of the birds were created by a punched eyelet stitch. The quilt is bound in a red cotton strip and backed with the same plain-woven cotton as is found on the front. It has an overall quilted pattern of one-inch diamonds.

About the QUILT MAKER The use of the flower motif in the shape of a cross with birds is characteristic of Pennsylvania German quilts. This example has a family history in Indiana, but the makers were German so likely shared some of the same design traditions.[17] The quilt was purchased from an Indianapolis dealer who had obtained it at a Richter family sale in Indiana in 1984 where it was attributed to Alma Richter and the date of 1854. Born in 1898, Alma was the daughter of August and Lizzie Richter of Ripley County, Indiana. Living with them in 1900 was Alma's German-born eighty-five-year-old grandmother, Anna Richter, who had immigrated to the United States in 1841. It's probable that Anna or another female family member was the maker of the quilt.[18]

Birds and Trees Quilt Figure 109

Maker unknown

Possibly Lancaster County, Pennsylvania, 1840–1880

Cottons; cotton and silk embroidery threads

9 running stitches per inch

83 x 74 in. (211 x 188 cm)

Museum Purchase, 1979.609.1

TULIP CROSS CRIB QUILT   FIGURE 110

MEMBER OF THE RICHTER FAMILY, POSSIBLY ANNA RICHTER

SUNMAN, RIPLEY COUNTY, INDIANA, 1850–1860

COTTONS; COTTON EMBROIDERY THREADS

8–11 RUNNING STITCHES PER INCH

45⅛ X 35⅛ IN. (115 X 89 CM)

MUSEUM PURCHASE, 1985.609.1

Adam and Eve Quilt

FIGURE 111

The unknown maker of this quilt combined nine large appliquéd rectangles into a charming, unified design of fruit trees, potted flowers, birds, domestic animals, and scenes. Large roses of Sharon flank the center rectangle that contains animals cavorting beneath a fruit tree with potted flowering vines on which twin eagles perch. The most prominent vignette depicts Adam and Eve, wearing calico aprons instead of fig leaves, beneath a tree entwined with the tempting serpent. The appliquéd swatches are secured in two methods: some were turned under and overcast with stitches; in others the raw edges were left exposed and secured with blanket stitches. Embroidered details in the figures and flowers consist of blanket, chain, and knot stitches with couched short lengths of thread. The quilt is bound in a solid-red cotton strip, except at top right where a tan cotton was substituted. It is backed in coarse plain-woven cotton. The cover is quilted in triple diagonal lines throughout the background and in outline stitching within the appliquéd motifs.

Shades of tan are used extensively throughout the quilt and may seem a surprising color choice, particularly for stems and vines. Some late nineteenth-century quilts assumed such coloration through the fading of synthetic green dyes in their swatches. Although the color scheme here appears to be purposeful and evidence of fading is minimal, it is possible that the tans were originally a vibrant green.

Nothing is known of the quilt maker. The donors acquired the quilt in the West Virginia-Pennsylvania-Ohio border area.[19] The existence in a private collection of an almost-identical quilt with a date of 1891 suggests a similar date for this example.[20]

Eagle and Cherries Quilt

FIGURE 112

In this quilt four large spread eagles are arranged symmetrically around a center medallion, creating an impressive abstract quality. Yet the eagles appear to have fanned tails like those of peacocks and rooster combs on their heads. The torsos of their bodies are made up of shields. Probably the gray-white fabric pieces are faded from their originally much brighter green or blue, creating a final impression of delightful whimsy. The bedcover is backed in alternating strips of yellow-and-red calico and blue-and-white calico. The quilting pattern consists of squares on point in the field and outer border, overlapping circles in the inner border of red, outline in the sawtooth border, and outline quilting around the appliqués. It is bound in a red cotton strip.

This design with four spread eagles holding branches or stems of cherries in their beaks was popular in the last quarter of the nineteenth century and into the first two decades of the twentieth century, especially in Pennsylvania.[21] The long period of use for this quilt pattern may be due in part to later generations of quilt makers copying earlier examples. Over three dozen Eagle quilts have been identified.[22] The universal characteristics of these quilts include eagles with wide-open wingspans, fan-shaped tails, and shields as torsos. The quilt format consists of the four eagles on angle in the quilt's corners with a central motif of a wreath, crossed floral element, or circular concentric star (like a hex sign).[23] What the eagles carry in their beaks varies and includes leaves, sticks, single cherries, crackers, cherry stems, and baskets. Some beaks are empty. The patriotic pattern was undoubtedly popularized by the 1876 centennial of America's independence. Scholars have suggested that a printed source, as yet unlocated, must have inspired the design.[24]

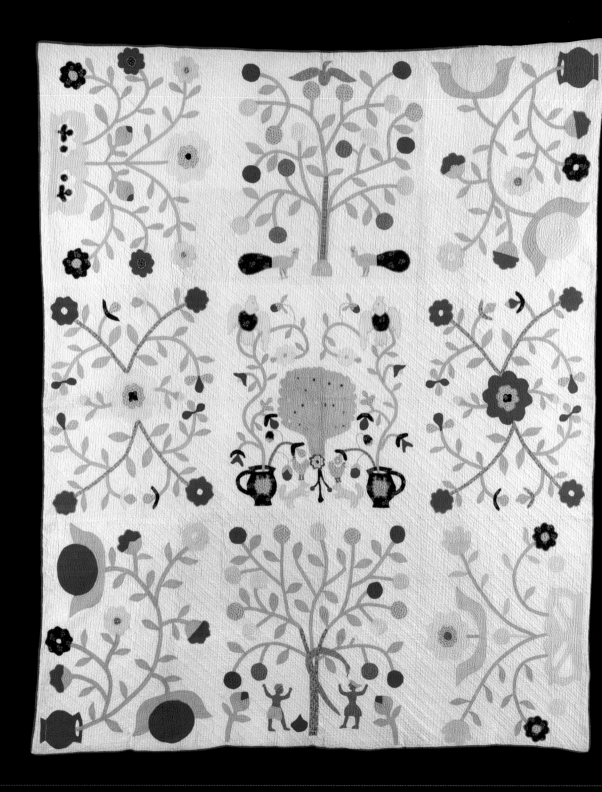

ADAM AND EVE QUILT FIGURE 111

MAKER UNKNOWN

PROBABLY PENNSYLVANIA, CA. 1890

COTTONS; COTTON EMBROIDERY THREADS

14 RUNNING STITCHES PER INCH

82½ X 67⅝ IN. (210 X 172 CM)

GIFT OF FOSTER AND MURIEL MCCARL, 1977.609.1

Eagle and Cherries Quilt Figure 112

Maker unknown

Probably Pennsylvania, 1875–1900

Cottons

7–8 running stitches per inch

80 x 80 in. (203 x 203 cm)

Gift of Foster and Muriel McCarl, 1979.60910

1   As is true of at least one other similar appliquéd bedcover, this one may have been inspired by a well-known quilt that is said to have been made about 1820 and was donated to the Art Institute of Chicago in 1919. An image and description of the quilt were published in the January 1922 issue of *Ladies' Home Journal*. The quilt pattern was available by mail. For more on the Art Institute of Chicago quilt (19.546), see Elizabeth Wells Robertson, *American Quilts* (New York: Studio Publications, 1948), 12, and Patsy and Myron Orlofsky, *Quilts in America* (New York: McGraw-Hill, 1974), 229 (overall but with tonalities reversed). Unlike Colonial Williamsburg's example, the Chicago bedcover was quilted in a variety of motifs such as stars, crescents, birds, floral sprays, and hearts. Another major difference between the two quilts is their construction. The Chicago example uses an early quilt construction technique in which the design is appliquéd on four large blocks with a border as an addition. The fruit tree appliqués face two directions. Colonial Williamsburg's quilt consists of a single piece of top fabric with the orientation of the four fruit trees facing four directions. The caption for the Art Institute of Chicago's quilt in the *Ladies' Home Journal* reads, "Especially colorful is the Cherry Tree design of 1820, from the Emma B. Hodge Collection . . . orange and scarlet birds fly through gray-green foliage or peck at bright cherries; the fox grapes and the vines are brown, the tulips, red and yellow" (31). The Denver Museum of Art owns a quilt made in 1936 based on the Chicago example (see Denver Art Museum, *Denver Art Museum Quilt Collection* [Denver, CO: Denver Art Museum, 1963], 44–45). Two other very similar quilts may have been based on the Chicago quilt (see Sotheby's, *Fine Americana*, October 26, 1991 [New York: Sotheby Parke Bernet, 1991], lot 13, and Sotheby's, *Fine Americana*, January 28–31, 1993 [New York: Sotheby Parke Bernet, 1993], lot 856). Also, a related quilt worked in four-block appliqué is in the collections of the Wisconsin Historical Society, Madison (1988.188); that quilt was made by Christina Nicoline Hansen of Wisconsin and Oregon, ca. 1922–1924 (see Maggi McCormick Gordon, *American Folk Art Quilts* [North Pomfret, VT: Trafalgar Square Books, 2007], 24–25).

2   The vendor from whom the quilt was purchased provided the following information: "My father, Andrew R. Denninger, bought this quilt in 1990 from two (2) spinster sisters living in the Ghent area of Norfolk, Va. They were in their mid 90's. They told my father that the quilt has always been in their family and was made by their great grandmother whose name was Fanny Butt." Andrea Lester to CWF object file 2007.609.1, March 30, 2007. Although several likely candidates by the name of Frances Butt were discovered, the quilt maker's identity is not confirmed.

3   For more information on the sampler, see Kimberly Smith Ivey, *In the Neatest Manner: The Making of the Virginia Sampler Tradition* (Austin, TX, and Williamsburg, VA: Curious Works Press and Colonial Williamsburg Foundation, 1997), 72, fig. 97.

4   The quilt design, however, is not unique. The identical pattern of repeating lyres with swags and tassels is found in at least one other quilt made up of pink, green, and yellow cottons. Julie Silber to author (Baumgarten), e-mail message, November 29, 2012.

5   The quilts were published in *Quilt Treasures of Yesteryear: Franklin County Quilt Documentation Project* (Chambersburg, PA: Chambersburg Quilt Guild, 2009), 28–29.

6   "Christian Rauch" on findagrave.com, Find a Grave memorial #26051584, record added April 16, 2008; "Ann Margaret Rauch" on findagrave.com, Find a Grave memorial #26051589, record added April 16, 2008; Jacob Hade marker, digital image as found on findagrave.com, Find a Grave memorial #27762415, record added June 23, 2008; Sarah Hade marker, digital image as found on findagrave.com, Find a Grave memorial #27762408, record added June 23, 2008; John E. Hade marker, digital image as found on findagrave.com, Find a Grave memorial #27762405, record added June 23, 2008; Sarah Hade household, 1860 U. S. census, Greencastle, Franklin, PA, page 311, National Archives and Records Administration (NARA) microfilm M653, roll 1111, digital image as found on Ancestry.com (2009); and Henry Ranch household, 1850 U. S. census, Antrim, Franklin, PA, page 479B, NARA microfilm M432, roll 782, digital image as found on Ancestry.com (2009).

7   A label stitched to the back side of the quilt is inscribed in red embroidery stitches: "Made by Ellen Ann Raywalt / in Steuben Co. N. Y. while teaching school / before Oct. 29 1857 / and quilted in Virginia, after her marriage / to A. H. Ansley, on above date." However, the quilted initials, "E A R," and date of "May 4th 1857" reveal that Ellen quilted the bedcovering prior to her marriage. Marriage date of October 28, 1857, provided by Ernest C. Ansley to author (Ivey) in letter dated September 4, 2000. Family members spell the name as "Rawalt." In census records the name appears in various spellings.

8   Ellen Ansley to her parents, January 22, 1858; and Ellen Ansley to Hannah Raywalt, March 20 and June 26, 1858, photocopies in CWF object file 2000.609.5. In both letters to her sister, Ellen discussed the need for carpets and her efforts in making them: "This week monday I washed & after getting out my weeks washing I ripped up four pair of old pants & an old [?] of Henry's & washed for carpet rags. I have cut and sewed a few" and "I shall keep right on cutting rugs as I get them."

9   In her unpublished memoirs, "Civil War Experiences," Ellen's younger sister-in-law, Catherine Cromwell Ansley, recalled the frightening events the Ansley family endured at the onset of the war. She wrote:

> When I was five years old my father, William Ansley, Jr., moved from Rushville, Yates Co., N.Y. to Fairfax Court House, Fairfax Co., Virginia. . . .
>
> I well remember when my father sat reading his paper when the first gun had been fired on Fort Sumpter, how he . . . said, "No matter what happens I will never turn traitor to my country." . . . It was our fortune or misfortune to be located in the very hotbed of the turmoil of the beginning of the Civil War. . . .
>
> My brother [Albert H. Ansley] put his things of most value into his lumber wagon put his wife [Ellen Raywalt Ansley, quilt maker] and two children on the spring seat, locked up his home and turned his horses heads toward the north. . . . There was no opportunity to sell anything in those exciting times, just simply start out with your lives in your hands and leave everything behind.
>
> My father thought we would try and stay a little longer. . . .
>
> . . . So a neighbor's boy who was still at home, came with a big covered wagon and we put in all the things we thought we would need the most and took what we could in our light spring wagon with our own horse which my mother drove and started for Washington. . . . I was only ten years old and I wanted to take my large doll with me but my mother said there was no room for nonsense like that. So I did it in its best and did its extra clothes in a package and laid them beside it on an ottoman. I heard afterwards that a Southern officer took them to send to his little girl.

10   "Ellen Ann Ansley" on findagrave.com, Find a Grave memorial #87128574, record added March 21, 2012; and "Albert Henry Ansley" (AFN:Z6K7-JV), Family Group Record, last updated March 22, 1999, www.familysearch.org.

11 A similar quilt worked in this method is illustrated in Florence Peto, *American Quilts and Coverlets* (New York: Chanticleer Press, 1949), plate 18.

12 According to the family history, Sarah and Harriet Robinson were the granddaughters of John Robinson Jr., treasurer of Virginia and Speaker of the House of Burgesses in Williamsburg, VA, from 1738 until his death in 1766. However, research did not reveal any relationship between the quilt makers and the Speaker. "Sarah Robinson" on findagrave.com, Find a Grave memorial #76827920, record added September 20, 2011; Samuel F. Gray household, 1900 U. S. census, Indianapolis, Marion, IN, enumeration district 59, page 6B, NARA microfilm T623, roll 388, digital image as found on Ancestry.com (2004); "Harriett Barbour" on findagrave.com, Find a Grave memorial #45867005, record added December 27, 2009; Samuel Barbour household, 1860 U. S. census, Indianapolis Ward 5, Marion, IN, page 404, NARA microfilm M653, roll 279, digital image as found on Ancestry.com (2009); Thomas Robinson household, 1850 U. S. census, District 97, Rush, IN, page 409B, NARA microfilm M432, roll 170, digital image as found on Ancestry.com (2009); and Thomas Robinson household, 1840 U. S. census, Noble, Rush, IN, page 142, NARA microfilm M704, roll 93, digital image as found on Ancestry.com (2010).

13 *Biographical Directory of the United States Congress, 1774–Present*, s.v. "Robinson, John Larne," accessed August 12, 2013, http://bioguide.congress.gov.

14 Samuel Barbour household, 1860 U. S. census, Indianapolis Ward 5, Marion, IN, page 404, NARA microfilm M653, roll 279, digital image as found on Ancestry.com (2009); Elizabeth Barbour household, 1900 U. S. census, Indianapolis, Marion, IN, enumeration district 59, page 6B, NARA microfilm T623, roll 388, digital image as found on Ancestry.com (2004); U. S. Social Security Death Index (SSDI), 1935–current, s.v. Violet Barbour, online database, Ancestry.com (2011); and SSDI, 1935–current, s.v. Louise Barbour, online database, Ancestry.com (2011). Blanche Louise was a telephone operator in France during World War I, and Anna Violet was an author and professor of English and European history at Vassar College.

15 For a full discussion of these quilts, see Connie J. Nordstrom, "One Pot of Flowers Quilt Pattern—Blossoming through Centuries," in *Uncoverings 2002*, ed. Virginia Gunn (Lincoln, NE: American Quilt Study Group, 2002), 31–64. Colonial Williamsburg's quilt is listed on p. 59 as no. 5 in Appendix A: Nineteenth-Century Quilts and Published Sources. Connie J. Nordstrom and author (Ivey), conversation, September 21, 2013.

16 Designs similar to this in Pennsylvania art are sometimes referred to as a *hex* or *hex sign*, a term that was not used until at least the 1920s. It was a common practice for the German Lutheran and Reformed settlers of Eastern Pennsylvania to decorate their everyday household items, such as quilts, furniture, and architecture, with colorful motifs. Many of the designs included distelfinks, hearts, tulips, flowering trees, and geometric designs imitating the stars, sun, and moon. In the mid-nineteenth century it was popular to paint enlarged images of these designs, especially stars within circles, on barns. Two schools of thought exist on the meaning of the hex signs: they were used to ward off evil, and they were simply decorative. Either way, some of the motifs do convey universal meanings, such as the heart for love, tulips for faith, sun for divine, and eagle for patriotism and strength. For more information on the history of the hex sign, see Dan Yoder and Thomas E. Graves, *Hex Signs: Pennsylvania Dutch Barn Symbols and Their Meaning*, 2nd ed. (Mechanicsburg, PA: Stackpole Books, 2000).

17 A full-size quilt with a center block in a coxcomb variation was made ca. 1850 by a member of the German Schmidt family of Ripley County, IN. See Jane Amstutz Harnden and Pamela Frazee Woolbright, eds., *Oklahoma Heritage Quilts: A Sampling of Quilts Made in or Brought to Oklahoma before 1940* (Oklahoma City, OK: Central Oklahoma Quilters Guild, 1990), 36.

18 A full-size quilt in the same pattern and in a private collection in the 1980s was also attributed to Alma Richter and the date of 1854. A search of Ripley County, IN, records failed to locate an Alma Richter around that date. However, the 1900 U. S. census for Adams Township, Ripley County, IN, includes one Alma Richter (1898–1984) living in the household of her parents along with Anna. Anna Richter was born in Germany in 1814. August Richter household, 1900 U. S. census, Adams, Ripley, IN, enumeration district 117, page 12B, NARA microfilm T623, roll 400, digital image as found on Ancestry.com (2004); and SSDI, 1935–current, s.v. Alma Richter, online database, Ancestry.com (2007).

19 Colonial Williamsburg's quilt was published in Carleton L. Safford and Robert Bishop, *America's Quilts and Coverlets* (New York: Weathervane Books, 1974), 204–205, figs. 307, 307a, 307b.

20 See Sotheby's, *Important Americana*, January 26–28, 1989 (New York: Sotheby Parke Bernet, 1989), lot 1237. At the top of the identical quilt, an eagle bears a banner with the inscription in gray running stitches "EQUAL RIGHTS AND LIBERTY 1891." Note that the catalog description has an incorrect date, and the inscription was cropped out of the image. Colonial Williamsburg curator Barbara Luck discovered the inscription on examination of the quilt. The design for the two quilts must have been derived from the same unidentified source.

21 Patricia T. Herr noted that there were probably published instructions on how to create these Eagle quilts, "which appear to nest in Pennsylvania." "What Distinguishes a Pennsylvania Quilt," in *In the Heart of Pennsylvania: Symposium Papers*, ed. Jeannette Lasansky (Lewisburg, PA: Oral Traditions Project, 1986), 35.

22 Jeannette Lasansky in *In the Heart of Pennsylvania: 19th and 20th Century Quiltmaking Traditions* (Lewisburg, PA: Oral Traditions Project, 1985) wrote: "As early as 1876 another phenomenon occurred here: the emergence of the *Eagle* appliqué as a favorite. Often thought by present quilt owners to be unique, it was anything but. Although a printed period source still eludes researchers, it must have existed because of the marked similarity in the eagle's basic body construction and layout and the consistent overall format of the three dozen 'unique' quilts seen" (14). For example, the International Quilt Study Center & Museum in Lincoln, NE, owns at least nine quilts in this pattern.

23 An exception to this format is an Eagle quilt in the International Quilt Study Center & Museum in Lincoln, NE (1997.007.0126). It consists of nine large repeating eagles with a border of twenty-four smaller repeating eagles.

24 Pieces of what appear to be home-produced patterns for the Eagle quilt have been located in two different private collections from Lancaster and Berks Counties, PA. Fold lines in the pattern for an outer circle of a center star motif indicate the paper was folded and cut, in the manner used to cut out a snowflake, to create the pattern. Barb Garrett to author (Ivey), e-mail message, October 7, 2011. The authors thank Barb Garrett for sharing images of the patterns with them.

CHAPTER 13

SIGNATURE ALBUM

CHAPTER 13

SIGNATURE ALBUM

One style of the compartmentalized format made of individual appliquéd or pieced blocks that became popular by the late 1840s was the album quilt. Album quilts could be worked entirely by one person but are best known as the product of group efforts, with different people contributing one or more of the individual blocks that compose the whole.

It was common for the creators of the quilt blocks to personalize their work with signatures, dates, place names, and other inscriptions. These signature, also called autograph, album quilts first appeared in the mid-Atlantic and were most popular in the East Coast states, Ohio, Tennessee, and Indiana between 1840 and 1855. They were probably influenced by the fashionable sentimental ideas of friendship during this time. Similar to autograph album books, which were introduced in the 1830s and a favorite pastime among schoolgirls and young ladies, signature album quilts were a collection of autographs and themes (fig. 113). Improved indelible inks at this time all but replaced the traditional method of inscribing or marking textiles with cross-stitch and opened new avenues for inscriptions.[1] Stencils and stamps designed specifically for personalizing quilt blocks were also available, making it easier for quilt makers to individualize blocks (figs. 114, 115). Poems, stories, and music on friendship published in *Godey's Lady's Book* and other fashion magazines of the day provided inspiration as well as verses for the quilt makers to copy. Religious and moralistic adages stitched by schoolgirls

on their samplers during the late eighteenth century were scribed in ink on mid-nineteenth-century album quilts.

Album quilts were often created to commemorate a special event or with the intention being the presentation of the item to an honored recipient, such as a bride, minister, or other respected member of a community. Because they were frequently a joint effort by a group of individuals and given in friendship, they are sometimes referred to as friendship quilts. The making of friendship quilts was most certainly influenced by westward migration and the wish to be remembered by loved ones left behind or by those leaving a community (see fig. 118).[2] As on schoolgirl samplers of the early nineteenth century, an echoing sentiment of many quilt blocks was the plea to be remembered (see fig. 116).

Popular among middle-class Americans, the giving of signature and friendship album quilts was an acceptable and appropriate method of showing respect, gratitude, or admiration by members of religious groups and social organizations. These groups enjoyed environments that made it easy to share quilt designs and labor. Many album quilts produced in Maryland and northern Virginia, for example, were created by women of the Methodist Church (see fig. 119). In fact, Gloria Allen and Nancy Tuckhorn stated that "in Maryland, the act of quiltmaking and the practice of Methodism seem to go hand in hand."[3] Women from other religious groups also joined together to produce album quilts; examples discussed here include Baptist and Quaker in addition to Methodist denominations.

Because many album quilts record signatures, place names, and dates, they can be attributed to specific times and places. The inscriptions also record connections between friends and family, revealing social and kinship networks (see fig. 117). Certainly friends and family en-joyed coming together to make the quilts, and the completed projects also served as a means to remember friends and relatives who had written or stitched their names on the textiles. The quilts themselves confirmed the importance of these social and kinship networks.

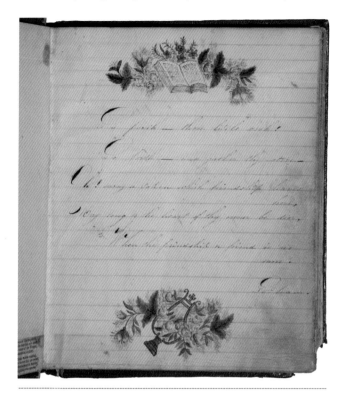

Figure 114 Oakford Family Textile Stencil, maker unknown, United States, ca. 1850, brass and blued steel, 2¾ x 2½ in. (7 x 6 cm), gift of Julie Stanton, 2008-20. Stencils, such as this one, made it easier to sign quilts and other textiles.

Figure 113 Sarah Folger's Autograph Album Book, Ohio and Indiana, 1826–1850, leather, paper, ink, and watercolor, 8 x 6 1/2 in. (20 x 16 cm), Museum Purchase, conserved with funds donated by the Miami Valley American Needlework Guild in memory of Doris G. Davis, 2005-16, 3. Collecting small drawings, watercolors, mottos, and autographs in paper album books was a popular pastime in the 1830s and 1840s for young ladies. As in this album book, many often contained sentiments of friendship and remembrance. Sarah Folger (1808–1871) continued to collect autographs and keepsakes in her memory book long after her marriage to Rufus Crane in 1829.[4] The album records about twenty signatures, including that of her sister and husband, and the locations of Cincinnati, Ohio, and Cambridge City, Indiana. The book, along with family Bibles, unfinished needlework projects, and a signed Cincinnati, Ohio, sampler dating 1820 by Sarah, descended in the family. The first page of the album book is embellished with a painted open book, flowers, and an inked inscription:

Go forth—thou little book!
Go forth—and gather thy store—
Oh! many a token which friendship leaves here,
May long to the heart of thy owner be dear,
When the friendship or friend is no more.

Figure 115 Jacob Bower Quilt Stamp, maker unknown, lead and fruitwood, United States, ca. 1850, 2 x 3 in. (5 x 8 cm), anonymous gift, 1971-2044. This stamp was probably used by female members of the Bower family to autograph and add inked embellishments to quilts.

Figure 116 Pieced Signature Quilt Blocks,[5] Sarah Murphy, Susanna D. Dennis, and possibly other makers, "Roseville," possibly Ohio, ca. 1844, cottons with ink inscriptions, 20 x 20 in. (51 x 51 cm), Museum Purchase, 1974.609.11. These pieced blocks originally may have been intended for a quilt, but it was never completed. A variation of Goose Tracks, this pattern lacks the square of white that is usually added between each block of the goose track. The blocks are backed in plain white cotton and bound in two strips of red printed cotton. They are not quilted. The piece was probably begun as a signature and friendship quilt. The name "Sarah Murphy" is inscribed in ink on a block near the top right. At bottom left is the signature "Susanna D. Dennis / March 4th   Roseville / 1844" and the verse, "Remmember me when thou doth sigh / And softly bend the knee / To ofer up thy prayer on high / Oh then remmember me."

ROLLINS FAMILY QUILT BLOCK

FIGURE 117

This pieced quilt block,[6] in a variation of the Mariner's Compass pattern, also called Noonday, Rising Sun, or Sunflower, records names of one New Hampshire family. The block may have been intended as a central medallion for a signature quilt. The unfinished block was not backed or quilted, and the edges were left unbound.

The block is notable for its elaborate calligraphy of inked inscriptions, gesturing hands, and well-defined leaves. The inked inscriptions include the dates of Ebenezer Rollins's birth on March 22, 1781, and his marriage to Betsey Rollins in 1807. Radiating out from the center are sixteen points that are inscribed with the names of their children and grandchildren.

ROLLINS FAMILY QUILT BLOCK FIGURE 117

FIGURE 118

An echoing theme of signature quilts, such as this one, is the sentimental request to be remembered. Seven of the 169 signed blocks that form this Delectable Mountains quilt request remembrance. One block provides the exact dates of the quilt (fig. 118a). The quilting in this cover follows the geometric outlines of the piecing; it is backed in white cotton. Two sides of the quilt were finished by turning the front to the back and stitching it in place. Two sides were left unfinished with the raw edges of the fabric exposed.

Figure 118a Detail. Though the time it took to create such a complicated project as a signature quilt is typically unknown, in this unusual instance an inscription informs: "This Bedquilt commenced in 1839 / And finished in 1847."

Organized and assembled by Ruth Ogden, the signatures imply that she may have been planning a move. The quilt pattern itself is suggestive of a pilgrim or pioneer who is attempting a great journey. The pattern name, Delectable Mountains, is taken from John Bunyan's Christian allegory, *The Pilgrim's Progress, from This World to That Which Is to Come,* published in 1678 and widely read for the next two hundred years. The Delectable Mountains are a rest haven for Bunyan's characters Christian and Hopeful and are a sign that they are nearing their destination as they make their perilous pilgrimage to the Celestial City. Bunyan described the mountains as "a most pleasant Mountainous Country, beautified with Woods, Vinyards, Fruits of all sorts, Flowers also, with Springs and Fountains, very delectable to behold."[7] Ruth's journey westward would have required travel through mountains that were both beautiful and hazardous, and like Bunyan's pilgrims, she too would have needed faith to see her through.[8]

Most of the quilt blocks were signed by Ruth, family members, and friends, some of whom lived as far away as Ohio and Georgia.[9] Twelve of the blocks contain male signatures, although it is most likely that the blocks were created by female friends or relatives. Two of the signers were Baptist ministers, one of whom was "Revd Charles J. Hopkins / Preached his farewell sermon in the / Baptist Ch in Bridgeton Sept 24th 1843 . . . / Removed to New York City." Some blocks indicate kinship with inscriptions such as "Dear Aunt" and "To my mother." However, one quilt block appears to have been made by a stranger; it is inscribed, "Dear Mrs Ogden / I have not the pleasure of a / personal acquaintance yet I have taken / the liberty of sending a small token of love / Eliza P. Grunzebach[?] / Pelham August 7th 1844."

About the QUILT MAKER Ruth was the wife of Curtis Ogden, a tailor, a year or so older than Ruth, who owned his own real estate in Bridgeton, New Jersey. In 1816, Curtis was appointed postmaster of the town and served until 1841, conveniently operating the post office from his tailor shop on Commerce Street. Three of the Ogdens' four children lived to adulthood. Ruth and Curtis were active members of the First Baptist Church of Bridgeton, where both are buried—Ruth in 1853 and Curtis in 1867, in addition to their young son Charlie, who died at the age of three.[10] A Bridgeton newspaper reported the Ogdens' loss: "The son [Charles] of Mr. Curtis Ogden, aged nearly four years, was suddenly ran over by a large wagon, and in a few minutes exchanged this mortal life, we trust, for a better, where pain, death and parting, are never known."[11]

Like pages from a scrap or album book, the individual blocks capture moments in Ruth's life. The parting of family members and friends, the uncertainty of life, a husband's birthday, and a son's love are all recorded on her quilt. The inscriptions provide a very personal glimpse into Ruth's world.[12]

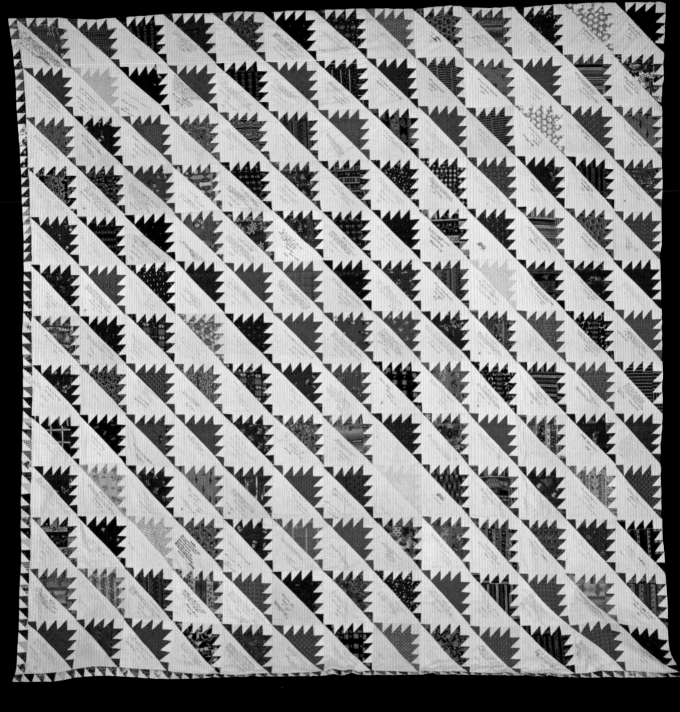

DELECTABLE MOUNTAINS ALBUM QUILT FIGURE 118

BLOCKS BY RUTH BOWER SWINNEY OGDEN (CA. 1788–1853)
AND FRIENDS AND FAMILY, ORGANIZED AND ASSEMBLED
BY RUTH BOWER SWINNEY OGDEN

BRIDGETON, NEW JERSEY, 1839–1847

COTTONS; INK INSCRIPTIONS

7–8 RUNNING STITCHES PER INCH

102 X 100 IN. (259 X 254 CM)

GIFT OF MR. AND MRS. ALEXANDER PURVES
AND HELEN OGDEN BARNARD, 1990.609.3

FIGURE 119

This album quilt top consists of thirty-six appliquéd blocks autographed by at least twenty-six individuals,[13] presumably parishioners of the Reverend William George Eggleston (1815–1908),[14] a traveling Methodist minister in Northern Virginia, Washington, D. C., and Maryland. Most of the blocks are dated and include the town of origin. In their signing, dating, and inscriptions, the blocks are scribed, stenciled, stamped, and stitched, representing the four principal methods that nineteenth-century women used to mark their quilts (figs. 119a–d).[15] The quilt top is unbacked, and the edges are turned to the reverse and machine stitched.

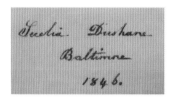

Figure 119a Detail. Scribed.

Figure 119b Detail. Stenciled.

Figure 119c Detail. Stamped.

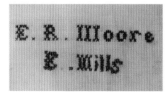

Figure 119d Detail. Stitched.

Figure 119e Detail. Several of the quilt blocks are inscribed for Mrs. W. G. Eggleston.

Following Methodist Church practice at the time, the Reverend Mr. Eggleston was transferred to a new congregation every two years. The quilt blocks record his circuit assignments and relocations from 1844 to 1847. They are corroborated by the traveling preachers file in the records of the United Methodist Historical Society (fig. 119f).[16]

Methodist women sometimes made quilts to present to their departing ministers.[17] However, it appears that the minister's wife, Frances Sanford Muse Eggleston, may have been responsible for the organization and assembly of this bedcover. Several of the squares are inscribed with the words "For Mrs. W. G. Eggleston" (fig. 119e). Apparently, Frances collected the signed quilt blocks to remember old friends and to ease the pain of constantly moving. She may have provided the fabric and designed the quilt blocks for her friends to inscribe, as the blocks have a uniform appearance.[18] In reference to Frances, the minister proudly recorded, "No man ever had a better wife." He married twice more after her death in 1862. Born in Baltimore in 1815, the highly esteemed Methodist pastor retired from the ministry in 1895, lived to be ninety-three, and was buried in Winchester, Virginia.[19]

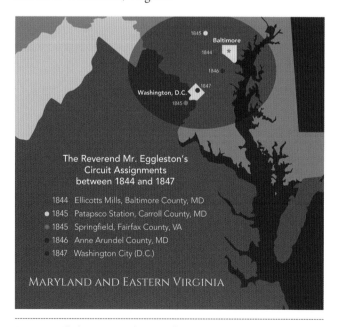

The Reverend Mr. Eggleston's
Circuit Assignments
between 1844 and 1847

1844 Ellicotts Mills, Baltimore County, MD
1845 Patapsco Station, Carroll County, MD
1845 Springfield, Fairfax County, VA
1846 Anne Arundel County, MD
1847 Washington City (D.C.)

MARYLAND AND EASTERN VIRGINIA

Figure 119f The Reverend Mr. Eggleston's Circuit Assignments, 1844–1847, courtesy James Armbruster.

Signature Album Quilt Top Figure 119

Blocks by friends of the Reverend and Mrs. William
George Eggleston, probably organized and assembled
by Mrs. William George Eggleston (1814–1862)

Vicinity of Washington, D. C., Northern Virginia,
and Baltimore, Maryland 1844–1847

Cottons; ink inscriptions; silk and cotton
embroidery threads

88¼ x 89¾ in. (224 x 228 cm)

Museum Purchase, 1999.609.2

FIGURE 120

This quilt successfully combines two distinct styles of appliquéd blocks. The first approach uses primarily red-and-green appliquéd motifs whose shapes are independent from the fabric from which the designs have been cut. Some of the shapes have been created using the same technique that a child uses to cut out snowflakes from a folded piece of paper. The second method, known as chintzwork, consists of appliquéd printed-cotton motifs whose realistic designs of fruit, wreaths, and flowers were cut out of their printed fabric. The chintzwork blocks are appliquéd in overcast and buttonhole stitches. The blocks are set on point with related cotton prints in a latticework pattern to create the sashing. The quilt is backed in off-white cotton and bound in a one-half-inch folded cotton tape, which has been stitched in place with a treadle sewing machine. At the time of the quilt's creation, sewing machines were expensive and highly desirable. Women occasionally showed off their new possession and their skill in using it by machine stitching visible areas in their quilts. In addition to outline, the bedcover is quilted in patterns of shells, tulip flowers, maple and oak leaves, feathers, and parallel lines.

According to family history, Sarah Chandlee Pidgeon assembled and quilted this friendship album quilt as a gift for her husband, Samuel Pidgeon (1817–1902) of Clarke and Frederick Counties, Virginia, shortly after their marriage in 1850.[20] Sarah collected the inscribed blocks from friends and family who belonged to meetings of the Religious Society of Friends in Virginia and Sandy Spring, Maryland, Sarah's hometown. Created by Sarah's friends and family in Maryland, the chintzwork blocks alternate with the red-and-green appliquéd blocks made by friends and family of Sarah's husband in Virginia. The only block to contain both chintzwork and red-and-green appliqué is the center block, which is inscribed "Eliza Chandlee," the name of Sarah's sister (figs. 120a, 120b).[21]

Many of the same signatures, which are inked, stamped, and embroidered, and one specific block design, the Apple

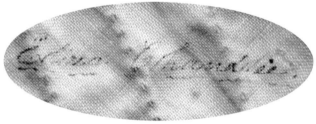

Figures 120a and 120b Details. The center block is inscribed "Eliza Chandlee" and "Friendship Offerings."

Pie Ridge Star, have been found on other quilts from northern Virginia.[22] At least eight Quaker quilts with overlapping signatures have been identified by Mary Robare.[23] It was not unusual in the nineteenth century for Quakers to travel distances to rotating meetings where members would spend time in the homes of friends and relatives. These occasions provided time for socializing, in addition to opportunities for sharing ideas, labor, and quilt blocks.[24] The recurring quilt signatures and Apple Pie Ridge Star motif help document the network of relationships within a community of Virginia and Maryland Quaker families before the American Civil War (fig. 120c).

Sarah's quilt descended through five generations of the Pidgeon family until it came to Colonial Williamsburg, partly as a gift.

Quaker Friendship Album Quilt Figure 120

Sarah Marshall Chandlee Pidgeon (1825–1886)
and her friends and family

Sandy Spring, Maryland, and Clarke and Frederick
Counties, Virginia, ca. 1850

Cottons; ink inscriptions; cotton embroidery threads

9–11 running stitches per inch

104 x 97 in. (264 x 246 cm)

Partial gift of Christopher and Mary Robare, 2009.609.2

Figure 120c Detail. The Apple Pie Ridge Star block, first identified as such on a circa 1858 Quaker quilt by a member of the Hollingsworth family, has been found on a number of quilts from the Winchester, Virginia, region. Apple Pie Ridge, outside of Winchester in the northern tip of the Shenandoah Valley, was named for the abundant apple orchards planted in the area during the eighteenth century. The fertile land attracted Quakers to settle there. The motif, however, is not exclusive to Winchester or Virginia. It is found on quilts from other regions and called by different names.

About the QUILT MAKERS

Sarah and her younger sister, Eliza, were the only daughters of Mahlon and Catharine Frame Chandlee, Quakers originally from Pennsylvania. The sisters grew up in a home called Brother's Content in a close-knit Quaker community of Sandy Spring, Maryland. Needlework was part of Sarah's life at a relatively young age. A sampler worked by her in 1837,

when she was twelve years old, attests to her needlework skills and education.[25] The sisters maintained a close relationship into adulthood. Eliza recorded her feelings of loss when Sarah, at the age of twenty-five, married Samuel Pidgeon in December 1850 and moved to Virginia: "The days of my childhood are forever gone. . . . During the past year there has been some changes which I have felt more visibly than any that have ever taken place during my short life; the one I will speak of was that of parting with my sister; she was married."[26]

Figure 120d Sarah Marshall Chandlee Pidgeon, courtesy Raymond Berry. This photograph was taken in the fall of 1885, several months before Sarah's death in January 1886. Sarah is seated in the middle of her family at Circle Hill, the Pidgeon family farm that spanned Frederick and Clarke Counties, Virginia.

SIGNATURE ALBUM QUILT

FIGURE 121

A variation of the Oak Leaf and Reel patterns, this quilt consists of twenty-five red-and-green blocks with inked signatures of twenty-three different people.[27] Two blocks are unsigned. The quilt is bound in a folded one-half-inch strip of red cotton printed with yellow and brown. It is backed in plain-woven cotton and quilted in a simple outline pattern.

Seven of the signatures bear the Rockafellow surname and four the Auten surname. The identified makers ranged in age from fourteen to thirty-three at the time they signed their blocks. Place names include Somerville, Flemington, and Readington, New Jersey. Several signatures appear to be those of sisters, and some of the makers were neighbors.[28] It is not known for whom the quilt was made or for what occasion.

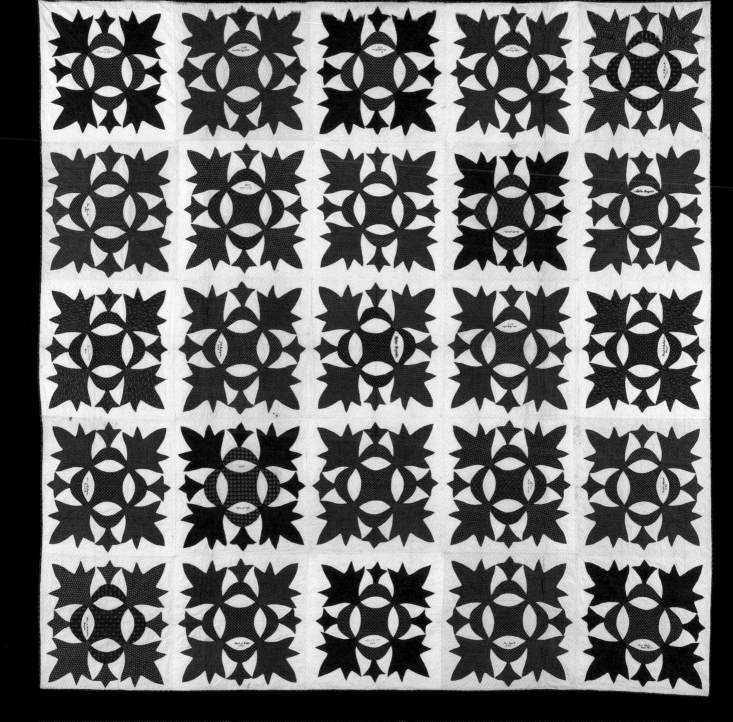

Signature Album Quilt Figure 121

Blocks signed by members of the Rockafellow and Auten families and others, organized and assembled by unknown maker

New Jersey, 1853

Cottons; ink inscriptions

8–10 running stitches per inch

88 x 88 in. (223 x 223 cm)

Gift of Mrs. Frederick G. Hammitt and family, 2002.609.3

BOTANICAL ALBUM QUILT

The number of individuals who worked on this unusual album quilt is unknown. The repetition of stitching details and the shared use of particular fabrics among motifs suggest that a small, closely knit group or perhaps even a single person created the quilt. The delicate designs are made up of layered and padded appliquéd swatches, some with the additions of silk ribbon and decorative embroidery stitches, all of which create a quilt with great dimensionality.[29] A few of the flower petals were padded, stitched in the round, and then applied to the quilt. The bedcover is quilted in clamshells, outlines, and squares on point. It is backed in white cotton and bound in a bias-cut green strip of cotton.

The appliqués include an array of realistic flowering plants not usually found on mid-nineteenth-century album quilts, including hanging baskets, ivy, and geraniums (fig. 122a). All of these plants were known in the United States by the time the quilt was made, and in fact the dates when these plants became popular in America assisted in the dating of the quilt. Geraniums, for example, were advertised for sale in America by the late eighteenth century.[30] Thomas Jefferson grew potted garden geraniums at the White House.[31] As with quilts and quilt makers, by the mid-nineteenth century the plant had made its way westward with the pioneers. The most unusual plants depicted on the quilt are the love-lies-bleeding, third from the top in the far right column; bleeding-heart, directly below the central wreath; and white- and magenta-colored fuchsia, second and fourth from the top in the far left column.[32]

"Love," "Remember me," and "Forget me not" are all inscriptions that tie this quilt to a strong mid-nineteenth-century interest in albums, both quilt and book varieties. In the center medallion, the quilt maker embroidered the complete text of the Lord's Prayer using red silk cross-stitches. Beneath the Lord's Prayer is another inscription, suggesting that the quilt was a gift to a girl named Emma: "To Emma / May you my child in virtue['s] way proceed   Her paths are pleasant and to heaven lead / Then when you leave this tenement of clay   Angels shall guide you to the realms of day." Judging from the pair of birds and the hearts featured prominently just above the center medallion and the word "Love" embroidered in one of the squares, this quilt may have been created for a woman about to embark on a new phase of her life, perhaps marriage or a move.[33] At center right, a tiny bird perched on a plant holds a nameplate with the inscription "Louise / Present," possibly meaning "Louise's present," but no other identification is known.

Figure 122a Detail. By the mid-nineteenth century, brightly colored geraniums were a popular bedding plant that filled Victorian gardens with masses of color.

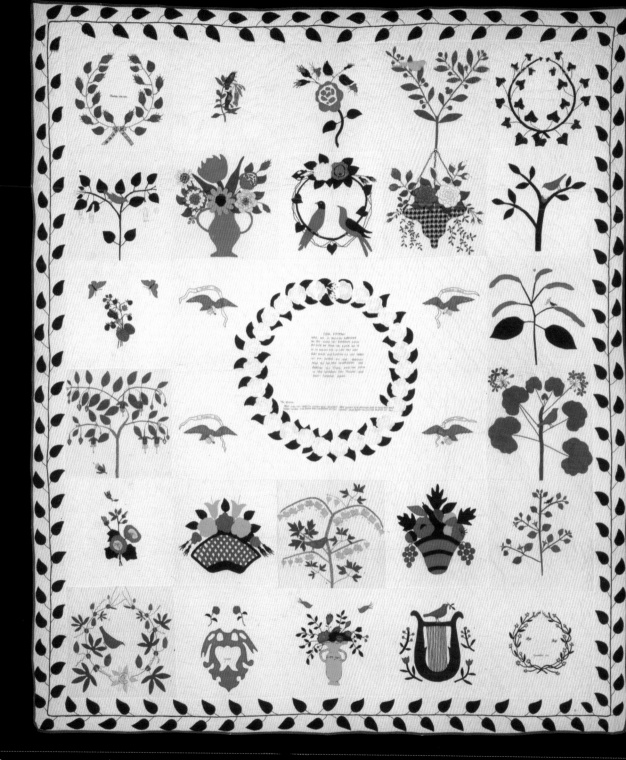

Botanical Album Quilt   Figure 122

Maker unknown

Probably Maryland or New York, ca. 1860

Cottons; ink inscriptions; silk ribbon; silk, wool, and cotton embroidery threads

8 running stitches per inch

81 x 70 in. (206 x 178 cm)

Museum purchase, 1985.609.5

1   A nonfugitive India ink made from a black pigment of lampblack mixed with a gelatinous substance became commercially available at this time. The ink, however, was corrosive to textiles, and the search for better permanent inks continued throughout the nineteenth and into the twentieth century. For further discussion, see Carolyn Ducey, *Chintz Appliqué: From Imitation to Icon* (Lincoln, NE: International Quilt Study Center & Museum, 2008), 35, 47, and Margaret T. Ordoñez, "Ink Damage on Nineteenth Century Cotton Signature Quilts," in *Uncoverings 1992*, ed. Laurel Horton (San Francisco, CA: American Quilt Study Group, 1993), 148–168.

2   Pat Ferrero, Elaine Hedges, and Julie Silber in *Hearts and Hands: The Influence of Women and Quilts on American Society* (San Francisco, CA: Quilt Digest Press, 1987) discussed the large numbers of friendship quilts made during the peak of westward migration and comment that carrying a friendship quilt on the overland trails was in a sense like bringing their loved ones with them (52).

3   Gloria Seaman Allen and Nancy Gibson Tuckhorn, *A Maryland Album: Quiltmaking Traditions, 1634–1934* (Nashville, TN: Rutledge Hill Press, 1995), 15.

4   Entries in the Folger family Bible, Colonial Williamsburg collection.

5   The blocks were published in Sandi Fox, *For Purpose and Pleasure: Quilting Together in Nineteenth-Century America* (Nashville, TN: Rutledge Hill Press, 1995), 139–140.

6   The block was published in Jane Bentley Kolter, *Forget Me Not: A Gallery of Friendship and Album Quilts* (Pittstown, NJ: Main Street Press, 1985), 70, and in Fox, *For Purpose and Pleasure*, 117. A similar pieced cotton block documenting the family of Daniel and Betsey Packard Hardy is owned by the New Hampshire Historical Society in Concord, NH (1968.59.113). For more on that block, see Patricia Cummings, *New Hampshire's Own Early Quilt Historian: Ellen Emeline (Hardy) Webster, (1867–1950): Her Amazing Quilt "Charts," Her Writings, and Her Life* (Concord, NH: printed by author, 2008).

7   John Bunyan, *The Pilgrim's Progress*, ed. N. H. Keeble (New York: Oxford University Press, 1998), 45.

8   For another New Jersey Delectable Mountains quilt with signatures and more on the Ogden quilt, see Fox, *For Purpose and Pleasure*, 83–89.

9   Signatures and place names on the quilt are Sarah Westcott, Bridgeton; Henry Charles Ogden, Philadelphia; Elisha S. Barrath, Ohio; M. S. Hann; Susan Lukens; Mary Elmer, Bridgeton; Agnes G. Mills, Bridgeton; Ursulla Slosvc[?]; Carline M. Titsworth, Shilo[h?]; M. B. Sheppard, Camden, NJ; Charles Ogden Barratt, Vienna Cross Roads, OH; Martha E. Elmer, Bridgeton; Ruth S.[?] Barrath; Mariah Swinney; Susan H. Nichols; David Swinney, Manayunk; Anna Lake Jenkins, Camden, NJ; Mrs. Rebecca Ann Lupton, Bridgeton; Andrew Jenkins; Therisa Wilson, Bridgeton; Maria O. Harra Lupton; Rosannah J. Swinney, Albany, GA; Jane O. Leake; Lydia Jenkins, Camden, NJ; Elizabeth Wood, Philadelphia; Eunice A. Swinney; Sarah Chatman; Andrew J. Swinney, Baker County, GA; Rachel S. Barratt, Bowentown; Ellen T. Taylor; Rebecca Mills; the Reverend Charles E. Wilson, Bridgeton; Daniel J. Swinney, Mansfield, OH; E. B. Westcott; Margaret Jane Swinney, Manayunk; E. H. Swinney; Carolene E. [W?]ood, Philadelphia; Janetta C. Swinney; Mrs. Abigail Murphey; Hannah Ann Barrath, Bowentown; E. Eliza Wilson, Bridgeton; Sarah E. Hunt; Fanny H. Jeffers; Mrs. Eliza Keiser, New Germantown, NJ; Abigail M. Ogden, Philadelphia; Jonathan Ogden, Philadelphia; Willis L. Ogden; Caroline Murphey, Philadelphia; Martha Murphey, Philadelphia; Mary Frances Murphey, Philadelphia; Ann Elizabeth Swinney, Shilo[h?]; Mrs. Ogden, Bridgeton; Mary Wilson, Bridgeton; Ethan B. Swinney, Hopewell; Sarah Seeley; Sarah L. Smalley, Plainfield,

NJ; Mary Budd Smalley, Bowentown; Hannah F. Smalley, Plainfield, NJ; W. A. Roy, Imlaystown; M. G. Hawns[?], Bridgeton; Martha N. Jeffers; Mrs. Harriet Roy; Charles E. Wilson Jr.; Margaretta C. Little, Bridgeton; Curtis Ogden; Clarissa Ann Whitaker; Charles Seeley Fithian; Jane Fithian; A.[?] H. Burt; Ruth B. Ogden; Henry S. Ogden, Philadelphia; Maria W. Smalley, New Rochelle; Mary E. Smalley, Brooklyn; Mrs. Mary G. Breuster[?], Bridgeton; Mrs. Harriet Davis Seeley; Sarah J.[?] Little, Bridgeton; Phebe Holmes McBride; Eleanor Harris; Abigail Whitaker; Eliza E. Sheppard; Ephraim Sheppard; Mrs. Harriet [S?]heppard; Cornelia Burt; Sara B. Sheppard; Jane L. Bush, Salem; Hannah Barker; Ruth S. Davis, Philadelphia; Eleanor Matilda Fithian; Mrs. Clarissa A. Swinney, Manayunk, PA; Phebe V. Swinney; Mary Louisa Phippen, Newburg, Orange County, NY; Charles Henry Brewster; Emeline Fuller, Bridgeton; Mrs. Rachel Whitaker; Jane M. Westcott; Cynthia Lupton; Ruth H[?]iller; Jane Davis, Shilo[h?]; Columbia Township; Mrs. Ruth B. Ogden, Bridgeton; William and Anne Lynn, Newark, NJ; Rebecca S. Gitsworth, Bridgeton; Ann Dempsey; Mary T.[?] Seeley; Mrs. Hannah Sheppard; Eliza F. Swinney; Mary G. Brewster; A. G. Hardy, Hopkinton, NH; Elisha Swinney, New Holland, PA; Robert Curtis Ogden, Philadelphia; Ann Maria Bath[?], Salem; Anna Matilda Crane, Bridgeton; the Reverend Charles J. Hopkins, Bridgeton and New York City; Sarah Jane Duffel; Nathaniel Reeve, Bridgeton; Harriet Holmes; Margarett M.[?] Satheld[?], Bridgeton; Lewis O. H[?]arrison; Lydia W. Dare, Bridgeton; Eliza P. Grunzebach[?], Pelham; Mary S. Johnston; Ruth S. Davis; Helen Maria Ogden, Philadelphia; A. E. Heilig; Hannah Burns[?]; Rhoda Harris; Maria D. Barber; Martha L.[?] Bush; Ellen M. Westcott; Lydia Garrison; John and Jane Sibley, Vine Street, Philadelphia; Sarah Sibley, Louisville, KY; Lydia B. Tomlinson, Bridgeton; Mary Johnston; Jane H. Swinney, New Holland, PA; Susan[?] M. Hopkins, Bridgeton; Sarah V. Hopkins, Bridgeton; Sarah Parvin; E. B. Fithian; Jane Bush; Hannah M. Simkins, Bridgeton; Curtis Ogden Jr.; Jane B. Barber; Mary A. Parvin, Bridgeton; Mary Elizabeth Lanning; Sarah H. Buesk[?]; Miss Prudence Riley; Ruth Ogden Swinney, Manayunk; Hannah P. Thompson; Jane W. Smalley, New Rochelle; Margaret Holmes, Bowentown; Thomas W. Stalling, Bridgeton; Elizabeth M. Reeve, Bridgeton; Elisabeth Hann; Elisa Cleaver, Bridgeton; Willson A Burrows; Mrs. Rachel Wood, Philadelphia; Henry L. Smalley, Bowentown; Sarah Cleaver, Bridgeton; Tabitha Smalley; Miss Mary Garrison, Philadelphia; John and Ann Heilig; and Ruth B. Ogden.

10 Sexton's book, Pearl Street Baptist Church, Bridgeton, NJ, as per Carl L. West, librarian, Cumberland County Historical Society, Greenwich, NJ, to Barbara Luck, March 25, 1991, CWF object file 1990.609.3; Thos. Cushing and Charles E. Sheppard, *History of the Counties of Gloucester, Salem, and Cumberland, New Jersey, with Biographical Sketches of Their Prominent Citizens* (Philadelphia: Everts & Peck, 1883), 587, 602–603; and Curtis Ogden household, 1850 U. S. census, Bridgeton, Cumberland, NJ, page 197A, National Archives and Records Administration (NARA) microfilm M432, roll 446, digital image as found on Ancestry.com (2009). Ruth Ogden's birth and death dates come from the sexton's book.

11 *Washington Whig* (Bridgetown, NJ), January 20, 1817.

12 Some examples include the following:
       Forget me not— but let my memory linger
       As a soft, shadowy twilight, in thy mind:
       And like a harp, touched by some fairy finger
       My voice shall whisper through the evening wind—.
          Forget me not:
       Susan Lukens.

When those we love are far away
How sweet to trace each sacred spot
Where they have roamed, which seem to say
    Forget me not
Margaret Jane Swinney
Manayunk Pa
1844

See yonder grave how green how fair
there rests the dew there smiles the sky
There sleeps your sisters dust and there
    you soon must lie
Robert Curtis Ogden
August 28 1843
Philadelphia

"Parted friends again may meet,
    From the toils of nations free;
Crown'd with mercy, oh! how sweet
    Will eternal friendship be!"
Elizth Wood
Phila.
Decr. 1843

To my mother,
    O never, never from my heart,
Dear mother shall thine in age fly,
    'Till feeling, thought, and life depart
And in the moment when I die!
Curtis Ogden Jr.
Nov 30th. 1843.

13 Signatures and place names on the quilt top are S. E. Piper; Susan A. Jenkins, Ellicotts Mills, MD; E. Wheary; M. L. Norris; Caroline Wheary; M. A. Pipe; Elizabeth Ann Culver, Patapsco Station; L. A. Martin; Margt. Iles, Ellicotts Mills; Catherine De La Curlette, Springfield, VA; E. R. Morre, E. Mills; Louia[?] E. Stanley, Washington City; Elizabeth Dunchcomb [or Dinchcomb]; Margaret Dushane, Baltimore; Maria Louisa Morcell, Washington City, DC; Julia D. Terrett, Washington, DC; C. A. Wheary; Sarah [?] Jones, Washington City; S. Wheary; Sarah Ann Fell; Rebecca M. Jones, Washington City; Martha E. Baldwin, Brotherton, A. A. County, MD; E. I. [J] Wheary; E. A. Isaac; Jane Iles, Ellicotts Mills; S[?] Dushane, Baltimore; E. R. Moore, E. Mills; E. Piper; E. A. Hughes; and M. A. Josnell.

14 William George Eggleston marker, digital image as found on findagrave.com, Find a Grave memorial #100815278, record added November 16, 2012. Birth and death dates for Mrs. Eggleston (Frances Sanford Muse Eggleston) come from J. Gray McAllister, *Family Records: Compiled for the Descendants of Abraham Addams McAllister and His Wife Julia Ellen (Stratton) McAllister, of Covington, Virginia* (Easton, PA: Press of the Chemical Publishing Co., 1912), 80.

15 See Fox, *For Purpose and Pleasure*, 26–33.

16 Preachers File, Archives of the Baltimore-Washington Conference, United Methodist Church, Lovely Lane Museum and Archives Library, Baltimore, MD.

17 For four album quilts made for Methodist ministers and now in the United Methodist Historical Society, Lovely Lane Museum and Archives, Baltimore, see Dena S. Katzenberg, *Baltimore Album Quilts* (Baltimore, MD: Baltimore Museum of Art, 1981), 82–83, 92–95, 104–105. These quilts date 1845–1848.

18 The ground fabric in one block in the bottom row is considerably

darker than the others. The cotton ground may not have been prewashed, leaving an original finishing process on the cotton to darken over the years.

19 See J. H. Light, "Rev. William George Eggleston," in *Minutes of the 125th Session, Baltimore Annual Conference, Methodist Episcopal Church, South* (Baltimore, MD: Methodist Episcopal Church, 1909), 84–88.

20 A handwritten label once attached to the quilt reads, "'Album Quilt' / Belonged to / Samuel L. Pidgeon / made about 1851." The note is believed to have been written by Susan Williams Pidgeon, daughter-in-law of Sarah Chandlee and Samuel Pidgeon. A later note written in 1981 by Dorothy Pidgeon Berry, Sarah's granddaughter, which accompanies the quilt, reads, "This is an 'autograph' quilt, so called because the squares were made by different people who frequently wrote their names on the squares. It was made for my grandfather, Samuel Pidgeon, of Circle Hill farm, Clarke Co., Virginia. My grandmother, Sara Chandlee Pidgeon, put the squares together and quilted it Dorothy Everett (Pidgeon) Berry." CWF object file 2009.609.2. Biographical information on Sarah Chandlee Pidgeon from Mary Holton Robare, "Cheerful and Loving Persistence: Two Historical Quaker Quilts," in *Uncoverings 2007*, ed. Joanna E. Evans (Lincoln, NE: American Quilt Study Group, 2007), 173. Samuel Pidgeon's birth and death dates from "Samuel L. Pidgeon" on findagrave.com, Find a Grave memorial #31860631, record added December 1, 2008.

21 Mary Robare noted that other patterns in the quilt's construction appear to be deliberate. In several blocks the quilting pattern emphasizes the relationship of the quilters, such as sisters-in-law using the same leaf quilting pattern. Other family members used the same printed cotton in their blocks. Robare to author (Ivey), e-mail message, June 21, 2012.

22 For example, a pieced quilt in a pinwheel pattern signed in the quilting "SGP May 6, 1836" for Susan G. Pidgeon, also on this quilt, is in a private collection. Sarah's quilt contains the following signatures and place names: M. L. S. (Mary Lea Stabler); Lucy Steer, Waterford; Eliza Ann Schooley; E. L. (Elizabeth Lee); Nancy C. Weatherill, Walnut Hill, VA; Sarah E. Kirk; Elizabeth S. Stone, Walnut Hill, VA; Eliz; Rachel Steer; Bettie S.[or L.] Pickrell[?], Mount Pleasant; Sarah Walker; B. I. L. (Beulah Iddings Lea); Eliza Chandlee; Deb Lea; [Rache]l J. Stone, Walnut Hill, VA; Lydia J. Hollingsworth, Retirement; Rachel A. Hough, Mount Pleasant, VA; Susan G. Pidgeon, Brucetown; M. S. (Mary Snowden) Tyson; Rachel Ellicott; Elizabeth J. [?]; Esther Ann Brown; Rachel [?]; R. R. (Rebecca Russell); Pidgeon, Brucetown; and Rachel A., Brucetown.

23 The story of Sarah and her quilt is the result of the methodical research by Mary Holton Robare. For in-depth discussions of this quilt and related quilts, see Mary Holton Robare, *Quilts and Quaker Heritage* (Winchester, VA: Hillside Studios, 2008); Robare, "Cheerful and Loving Persistence," 165–206; Bunnie Jordan, "Northern Virginia Region," in *Quilts of Virginia, 1607–1899: The Birth of America through the Eye of a Needle*, ed. Barbara Tricarico (Atglen, PA: Schiffer, 2006), 58–60; and Karen B. Alexander, "Shenandoah Valley Region," in Tricarico, *Quilts of Virginia*, 77–81.

24 See Jessica F. Nicoll, "Signature Quilts and the Quaker Community, 1840–1860," in *Uncoverings 1986*, ed. Sally Garoutte (Mill Valley, CA: American Quilt Study Group, 1987), 27–37.

25 Robare, "Cheerful and Loving Persistence," 175–176.

26 Eliza Chandlee, Journal, p. 2, Mary Elizabeth Pidgeon Family Papers, RG 5/123, Friends Historical Library of Swarthmore

College, Swarthmore, PA, as quoted in Robare, "Cheerful and Loving Persistence," 177.

27 Inscriptions on blocks: "Elizabeth Van ars Dale / 1853," "Sarah Rockafellow / 1853," "Sarah A. Harris / 1853," "Sally Vanetta / 1853," "Mary J. Hardcastle / 1853," "[?] Vandergraft," "Lemual B. Rockafellow / Flemington," "Emeline Stewart / 1853 / married same time," "Ann Sharp / White House," "Ann Quick / 1853," "Adetta A Van ars Dale / 1853," "Sarah F.[or S] Welter / 1853," "Annie M. Rockafellow / Readington," "Susan M. Rockafellow / Bound brook," "Elizabeth Rockafellow / 1853," "Jane Vannatta / 1853," "Sarah Auten / 1853," "J. S. Rockafellow / 1853," "Sametha T.[or J] Auten," "Ann Rockafellow / 1853," "Rebecca Van [?]," "Lydia S. Auten / 1853," and "Deborah Auten / Somerville NJ."

28 Census records for 1850 document a number of the quilt signers and offer clues to their relationships. Sisters Elizabeth and Adetta (Alletta) Van Arsdale were the teenage daughters of farmers Peter and Nancy Van Arsdale. Peter C. Van Arsdale household, 1850 U. S. census, Hillsborough, Somerset, NJ, page 408, NARA microfilm M432, roll 463, digital image as found on Ancestry.com (2005). Sisters Jane and Sarah Ann Vannatta lived in the household of hatter Aaron Vannatta. Living in the household next door were thirty-year-old Sarah Rockafellow and her husband, carpenter William Rockafellow; Sarah would have been about thirty-three when the quilt was made, the oldest of the known signers. William Rockafellow household, 1850 U. S. census, Bridgewater, Somerset, NJ, page 274, NARA microfilm M432, roll 463, digital image as found on Ancestry.com (2005). The youngest quilt signer, Susan M. Rockafellow, was the daughter of blacksmith Andrew Rockafellow and his wife, Maria; Susan Maria was eleven at the time of the 1850 census. Andrew Rockafellow household, 1850 U. S. census, Bridgewater, Somerset, NJ, page 242, NARA microfilm M432, roll 463, digital image as found on Ancestry.com (2005). See also research report by Sarah Reeder in CWF object file 2002.609.3.

29 Some appliquéd flowers consist of four layers of fabric and others are heavily padded. The quilt appears as #6 on p. 95 in Elly Sienkiewicz, *Dimensional Appliqué: Baskets, Blooms and Baltimore Borders* (Lafayette, CA: C & T Publishing, 1993).

30 *New-York Daily Gazette* (New York City), November 14, 1791.

31 Thomas Jefferson to Margaret Bayard Smith, March 6, 1809, in *The Papers of Thomas Jefferson*, Retirement Series, vol. 1, *4 March to 15 November 1809*, ed. J. Jefferson Looney, (Princeton, NJ: Princeton University Press, 2004), 29.

32 Loves-lies-bleeding was in the American colonies by the eighteenth century. Joan Parry Dutton, *Plants of Colonial Williamsburg: How to Identify 200 of Colonial America's Flowers, Herbs, and Trees* (Williamsburg, VA: Colonial Williamsburg Foundation, 1979), 122–123. Discovered as early as 1810, bleeding-heart became fashionable in Britain about 1846, and by 1877 it was a popular cottage-garden plant in America. David Stuart and James Sutherland, *Plants from the Past* (New York: Viking, 1987), 126. By 1868, when Joseph Paxton's *Botanical Dictionary* was published, several hundred named fuchsia species were well-known in England and had been in cultivation there from the early nineteenth century. Samuel Hereman, *Paxton's Botanical Dictionary, Comprising the Names, History, and Culture of All Plants Known in Britain; with a Full Explanation of Technical Terms* (London: Bradbury, Evans, 1868), s.v. "fuchsia." The authors are indebted to M. Kent Brinkley for providing information about the plants.

33 For more appliquéd album quilts of this type, see Kolter, *Forget Me Not*, 26–41. A related, but distinct, tradition of friendship quilts is described by Linda Otto Lipsett, *Remember Me: Women and Their Friendship Quilts* (San Francisco, CA: Quilt Digest Press, 1985).

CHAPTER 14

Baltimore Album

CHAPTER 14

BALTIMORE ALBUM

S ome of the most highly treasured nineteenth-century quilts are the distinctive and elaborately conceived appliquéd album quilts produced in Baltimore and nearby counties between 1845 and 1860.[1] The third largest city in the United States during the 1840s, Baltimore boasted the largest seaport and had a strong textile industry. Besides those made locally, literally hundreds of different fabrics from around the world, including New England, Germany, France, England, Holland, and India, were available to Baltimore women. Religious movements and social organizations, such as the Independent Order of Odd Fellows and the Freemasons, created environments within the city and its nearby counties that made it easy to share quilt designs, fabrics, and labor.[2] Ships arriving in the port city not only carried a huge selection of textiles but also brought an influx of German and Irish immigrants, especially after the mid-1840s.[3] Their cultural traditions and aesthetics were reflected in the quilts created in the region.[4] Baltimore's prosperous years, however, came to a standstill with the worldwide financial panic of 1857, the rise of anti-immigration sentiments, and the divide over the slavery question. The album quilt fashion passed and was replaced with new fads, such as Berlin woolwork and, in time, crazy quilts.

Like other album quilts, Baltimore album quilts were made of individual blocks decorated with intricate designs appliquéd to a ground fabric. Block motifs were created by layering multiple swatches of fabric to create realistic foliage, fruit, birds, and baskets. In some instances the artistic layering of the appliqué imitated the naturalistic chintzwork that had been popular earlier in the century (see fig. 127). A hallmark of Baltimore album quilts was the use of underlaid, or reverse, appliquéd patches in which two or more layers of fabric were basted together and areas of the top layer were cut away to reveal the fabric beneath. Frequently, the raw edges of the appliqué swatches were folded under and sewn with blind, or hidden, stitches. Sometimes the edges were fastened with more decorative buttonhole stitches. Some appliquéd designs were further ornamented with inked, embroidered, or corded details. Dimension was added with padding and ruching, or gathered appliqué.

The sophisticated suggestion of texture and dimension through the careful choice and placement of printed fabric swatches was another noteworthy trademark of these quilts. Various small-patterned printed calicoes were used in a number of ingenious ways to give the illusion of shading, the suggestion of texture, and the imitation of detail. Perhaps the best examples were prints of graduating color intensities, called *rainbow*, which were used to create a contoured or shaded effect for images such as marble monuments (see fig. 130a).

As with most album quilts, after the quilt blocks were decorated and assembled, the bedcover was usually layered

Figure 123 Maryland Album Quilt, Addie Thayer Adams (later Mrs. William Henry Ruark) (1839–1911), Somerset County, Maryland, ca. 1860, cottons, 13–14 running stitches per inch, 86 x 85 in. (218 x 216 cm), gift of Mrs. William Hooper Ruark, 1983.609.2. In contrast to the work of most Baltimore album quilt makers, who assembled multiple varied designs for their quilt tops, Addie Adams limited the field of her quilt to the repetition of two alternating symmetrical motifs without intermediate bands of fabric, or sashing.[5] Characteristic of a number of mid-nineteenth-century American quilts are the red-and-green color scheme and the use of classically inspired swags and bowknots. The blocks and border were quilted separately in patterns of squares on point. The quilt is bound in a green printed strip of one-half-inch folded cotton. Addie, who married late in life, probably had to wait some time to use her beautiful quilt as a newlywed. Family tradition states that Addie Adams completed this quilt prior to her marriage to William Henry Ruark, which was probably during or shortly after 1880.[6]

with batting and backing and quilted through all the layers using running stitches. The actual quilting in many of these examples, however, is of secondary importance to the intricate and colorful appliquéd blocks. Some were quilted in simple diamond, square, or outline patterns.

Many variables figured into the length of time required to construct such elaborate quilts, including the number of stitchers, their dedication and proficiency, and the availability of time and raw materials. A quilt made by Eliza Jane Baile that is related to Baltimore album quilts in terms of composition, fabrics, quilting, and appliqué techniques is inscribed "commence'd June 1850" and "Finished October 30 1851."[7] This amount of time seems quite reasonable considering that modern-day quilters report that a single appliqué block requires forty to sixty hours to create.[8]

Appliquéd floral and fruit wreaths, birds, baskets, and urns were popular motifs in the skillfully created blocks. The designs stemmed from many sources, such as contemporary magazine, book, and print illustrations. Fashionable forms in the decorative arts also influenced the shapes found on Baltimore album quilts. For example, baskets in several variations, including reticulated and overflowing, were popular designs that decorated the surfaces of silver, ceramics, architecture, furniture, theorems, and other textile arts such as samplers and embroidered pictures. Paper album books and German-influenced fraktur and scherenschnitte cut-paper designs were also important design influences.

A number of album quilts made in Baltimore and the immediately adjacent counties featured complex blocks of architectural motifs that captured civic monuments and buildings found in Baltimore and nearby Washington, D. C. Interestingly, during the first half of the nineteenth century, other decorative arts produced in the city, such as seating furniture and samplers, were decorated with painted or stitched buildings (see fig. 124). By the late 1820s the skyline of Baltimore was indeed dotted with church steeples, monuments, and the rooftops of impressive architectural structures. After 1827, Baltimore became known as the Monumental City, so-called by President John Quincy Adams during his visit to the city that year.

Baltimore album quilts combined traditional quilt-making processes with a new era of commercialism and work force specialization of the art not seen before in American quilts. The many similar or almost identical appliquéd blocks found in these quilts suggest common design sources (see figs. 125, 126). It is now believed that prefabricated blocks consisting of precut and basted cotton pieces for appliqué were available for purchase from at least several enterprising businesswomen in the city.[9] The blocks were presumably sold as kits for quilt makers to assemble and could be mixed and matched with the maker's own designs.

Figure 124 Baltimore Hospital Sampler, Margery Jane McGuire, Baltimore, Maryland, ca. 1842, wool and silk on cotton, 25 x 25 in. (63.5 x 63.5 cm), ex. coll. Betty Ring, Museum Purchase, 2012-65. Margery Jane McGuire's circa 1842 sampler is the latest of an important group of Baltimore building samplers that depict the Baltimore Hospital and a twin-towered building. Built in the 1790s originally to take care of yellow fever victims, the Baltimore Hospital was of great interest to visitors and townspeople alike.

Based on the techniques and designs of the blocks, at least three distinct styles have been recognized by quilt scholars. Within each style there may have been more than one designer at work, and individual Baltimore album quilts may contain blocks of more than one designer's style (see fig. 130). The designer may not necessarily have been the maker of the quilt; the maker may or may not have been the designer of the blocks.

The classic Baltimore high style is characterized by swag borders, intricate woven baskets and vases of flowers, spread eagles, white roses, floral wreaths, important urban buildings, and civic monuments (see fig. 129). Other characteristics include the use of rainbow fabrics, finely layered appliqué, delicate inked inscriptions and details, and triple-lobe bowknots. Over the years quilt scholars have given the style various attributions, including a young Baltimore woman named Mary Evans (ca. 1833–1916), an unnamed "Designer I," and "Style I."[10] Most recently blocks in this style have been attributed to Anna Maria Heidenroder Simon (1808–1877), also known simply as Mary Simon. New genealogical research suggests, however, that Mary Simon, a recent immigrant from Bavaria, may have been involved only in the cutting and basting of squares possibly for sale and not the designer.[11]

A second style identified in Baltimore album quilts is distinguished by a predominantly red-and-green palette (see fig. 130). Three-dimensionality is created by the addition of padding, ribbons, ruching, and embroidery rather than by the careful choice, placement, and layering of fabrics as seen in the classic Baltimore high style. Wool and silk embroidery threads are used for detail, especially in the flowers where the petals are defined by the embroidery. William Rush Dunton, an early quilt scholar, attributed the wool embroidery to a German influence.[12] Most flowers have a cookie-cutter and somewhat symmetrical silhouette. The Ringgold monument block is also included in the vocabulary of this style (see fig. 130a).

A third style of Baltimore album quilts, which is not represented here, has been associated with a group of quilts made by women of the Jewish faith. Characterized as "in the style of German folk art," the quilts feature stylized and often exotic flowers and animals, especially deer and horses. Designs were created with layered appliquéd swatches with details embroidered in wool yarns.[13]

Baltimore album quilts are unique to a specific time and place in American history and culture. Expressions of patriotism, friendship, and virtue, they reflect the interests of the quilt makers and the popular American culture of the time. A blend of the old and the new, Baltimore album quilts represent the interweaving of quilt traditions with

the mass design and production of appliquéd blocks assembled by individual as well as groups of quilt makers. Many Baltimore album quilts were created as gifts for men and in some instances reveal the recipient's affiliation with a particular organization, such as a church or fraternal group. Yet, other Baltimore album quilts were made as keepsakes, like a paper album book filled with inscriptions and memories.

Figure 125 Detail from Baltimore Album Quilt, figure 130.

Figure 126 Detail from Baltimore Album Quilt, figure 129. These two almost identical blocks from two different quilts are in the classic Baltimore style. The blocks were probably sold as prefabricated cutout designs for the quilt maker(s) to assemble.

FIGURE 127

This large counterpane was decorated with flowers, leaves, and fruit cut out of block-printed cotton chintz, reassembled, and stitched to the ground fabric with cotton threads. The technique of cutting chintz motifs and using them for appliqué is often known today by the terms *chintz appliqué* or *chintzwork* (see chap. 8). The ground of this counterpane, a woven quilted textile called *Marseilles quilting*, is an unusual choice for an appliquéd bedcover (fig. 127a). The textile was purchased by the yard and seamed together prior to the appliqué process. Unlike a true quilt, this bedcover was not layered with batting or quilted. The counterpane is bound with white cotton pattern-woven tape.

The center panel depicting a bowl of fruit was printed in England about 1815 and was intended for use on appliquéd quilts. It appears at the center of a number of other American quilts, including a Petersburg, Virginia, quilt stitched by the Boyle sisters (see fig. 72). Achsah Wilkins herself used the same panel on at least four other counterpanes.[14] The textile panels were printed with additional floral groupings in the four quadrants, which many quilters would cut apart and use elsewhere on the quilt. In this example, Achsah did not reuse the wreath or pineapple quadrants, perhaps saving them for another project.

About the QUILT MAKERS   Achsah Goodwin Wilkins is often cited for the technical excellence of the appliquéd counterpanes she designed, in which even the most delicate stems were carefully turned under and closely blindstitched, but Achsah may not have done any of the stitching. She used the skilled help of African American stitchers. Her granddaughter reported that Achsah had a skin condition that prevented her from working with the needle, so she enlisted female African American servants to hand stitch the appliqué motifs, which Achsah had first designed and pinned in place.[15] The Wilkins family did, in fact, have two female "free colored persons" living in the household in 1820. One was under age fourteen and the other over forty-five, though census records do not note their names.[16] (At that date, census records listed the name of the head of household only.) This stunning bedcover tells the story of two worlds working side by side in Baltimore.

An influential figure in the early development of Baltimore appliquéd quilts, Achsah Wilkins is credited with at least ten counterpanes using similar materials and appliqué technique. Achsah was noted for the artistry of her designs and her organizational skills as the spearhead and supervisor of quilting groups within her adopted Methodist Church.[17] She was married in Baltimore to Dr. William Wilkins Jr. in 1794. Widowed around 1832, she lived more than twenty years after her husband's death.[18]

Figure 127a Detail. The ground is woven Marseilles quilting, similar to that discussed in chapter 6. The appliqué is carefully turned under and neatly blindstitched.

Baltimore Chintz Appliquéd Counterpane FIGURE 127

ATTRIBUTED TO ACHSAH GOODWIN WILKINS (1775–1854)
AND UNIDENTIFIED AFRICAN AMERICANS

BALTIMORE, MARYLAND, CA. 1820

COTTONS

106¾ X 128½ IN. (271 X 326 CM)

MUSEUM PURCHASE, 2009.609.1

FIGURE 128

This quilt was made from thirty-six individually appliquéd blocks, most of which were signed and dated by one of at least twenty-six women.[19] In addition to signatures, some blocks include dates and place names. One block is marked "Baltimore," nine are dated "1846," and several refer to "Friendship."[20] The inscriptions were stamped, inked, or cross-stitched. The block motifs were created with layered and underlaid appliquéd fabrics. The addition of padding in some motifs and embroidery stitches in the birds' eyes, beehive, and all-seeing eye provide further dimension. Chintz borders are characteristic of some early album quilts produced in the Baltimore region. This exact one appears on at least one other Baltimore album quilt.[21] The addition of such borders may be a carryover from earlier in the century when it was fashionable to use printed floral textiles in the creation of appliquéd counterpanes (see fig. 127). Chintz borders may have influenced the appliquéd vine and floral borders found on many Baltimore album quilts (see figs. 129, 130, 131, 133). This bedcover was quilted primarily in parallel diagonal lines with a few areas of contour quilting around the applied motifs. The white cotton backing was brought to the front to form a narrow edge finish.

Several of the blocks feature imagery associated with the Independent Order of Odd Fellows, a benevolent and fraternal society founded in Baltimore in 1819. The social organization, also known as the Three Link Fraternity, was a mutual benefit association that provided aid to its members in times of need due to illness, unemployment, death, and the like. It also was the first fraternity to accept both men and women when in 1851 it formed the Daughters of Rebekah.[22] One block near the top center of the quilt includes an image of the all-seeing eye, representing the omniscience of God, as well as other symbols of the Odd Fellows. In another block near the lower center of the quilt is a heart within an open hand, representing sincerity. The beehive, hourglass, globe, bow and arrows, tent, crescent moon, and serpent are other symbols that appear in Odd Fellows imagery (fig. 128a).

At least one block may be associated with current events. The potted cactus plants in the fifth block on the bottom row may allude to the U. S.-Mexican War (1846–1848).

Figure 128a This quilt block is filled with Odd Fellows imagery, including a beehive representing the power of association, order, and industry and the three links of friendship, love, and truth.

About the QUILT MAKERS Six of the women who signed this quilt have been identified as living in Ward 7 of Baltimore.[23] However, the purpose for their project, its relationship if any to the Odd Fellows, and its intended recipient are not yet known. Interestingly, Thomas Wildey, who is credited with establishing the first American lodge of the Independent Order of Odd Fellows in Baltimore in 1819, lived in nearby Ward 5 (fig. 128b).[24]

Figure 128b Thomas Wildey and four other members of the English Order of the Odd Fellows held their first meeting in North America in Baltimore on April 26, 1819. "Chart of Odd Fellowship," courtesy Library of Congress.

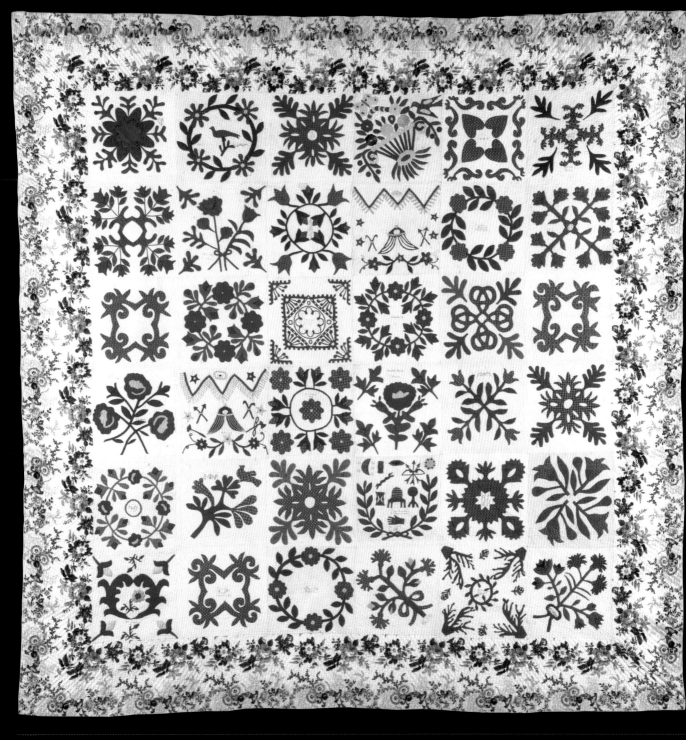

Baltimore Album Quilt Figure 128

Blocks by various makers, quilter(s) unknown

Baltimore, Maryland, 1846

Cottons; ink inscriptions; wool braid; cotton
and silk embroidery threads

9 running stitches per inch

103⅓ x 104 in. (262 x 264 cm)

Museum Purchase, 2009.609.3

FIGURE 129

The finest examples of classic Baltimore album quilts, like the one shown here, are noted for their elaborately conceived appliquéd blocks, which suggest texture and dimension through the careful choice and placement of printed fabric swatches, such as shaded, or rainbow, prints.[25] The appliquéd motifs in this quilt were created using multiple layers of applied and underlaid fabric swatches. No additional stuffing was required to give them a sense of dimension. Details were added in ink to indicate tendrils, seeds, leaf and petal veins, insect antennae, bird feet, window sashes, and cords on flagpoles. The top ground was pieced from at least two different fabrics, the top and side borders being markedly darker than the bottom border and interior. The quilt is backed in white cotton and edged with a black-and-green calico with solid-red cording at the inside edge.

A number of Baltimore album quilts feature complex blocks of architectural motifs representing monuments found in Baltimore and nearby Washington, D. C. Here, the center medallion of four public buildings represents a historic snapshot recording what was important to Baltimore's community. The lower left block depicts the Washington Monument in Baltimore, which was designed by Robert Mills (fig. 129a).[26] In 1815 the Freemasons presided over the laying of the cornerstone for the building, which was the earliest structure in the New Republic planned to honor the first president.

The lower right block features the U. S. Capitol in its pre-1856 state (fig. 129b). The building was well-known from the many published views. Charles Bulfinch was the official architect of the structure from 1817 to 1829, and it is his dome, which was in place from 1825 to 1856, that appears on this quilt's version of the building.[27]

A brick building in the upper left block probably represents Seamen's Bethel Mission (fig. 129c).[28] Over the years researchers have attributed a number of identifications to it, including the Baltimore Merchant's Exchange Building, Baltimore City Hall, and the Basilica of the National

Shrine of the Assumption of the Blessed Virgin Mary (the Baltimore Cathedral) prior to its addition. The semblance of bricks in this block was created by couching a thin white cotton tape over red cotton fabric.[29]

Figure 129a Detail. Washington Monument, Charles Street, Baltimore.

Figure 129b Detail. U. S. Capitol in Washington, D. C.

The Battle Monument in Baltimore, designed by architect Maximilian Godefroy and built in the center of what is now known as Monument Square in 1815–1825, is seen in the upper right block (fig. 129d).[30] The fifty-two-foot-high marble monument honors those slain in the Battle of North Point during the War of 1812. The battle occurred in September 1814 when the British attacked Baltimore by both land and sea. The monument is depicted on the city's seal, which was adopted in 1827, and also appears in the center of the state's flag. In this version, gas lights flank the Battle Monument, suggesting progress and the wealth of the city.

The undulating floral border is unusual in that it features four different corner motifs of floral sprigs and a dove. Notably placed in the center of the bottom border is an appliquéd beehive with a swarm of embroidered bees, suggesting the idea of industry, or busyness. Although the actual quilting in many Baltimore album quilts is of secondary importance to the intricate and colorful appliquéd blocks, here the border of the quilt features princess feathers and hearts, stuffed to give them added dimension and interest, against a background of parallel diagonal lines (fig. 129e). The sixteen appliquéd blocks are quilted in parallel diagonal lines radiating in four directions, doubled squares set on the diagonal, and pear, or heart, motifs.

It is, however, the stylistic consistency that distinguishes this spectacular quilt. Many related Baltimore album quilts incorporate a variety of styles among their blocks (see fig. 130).[31] These range from the sophisticated, relatively naturalistic representation of forms, seen in this quilt, to far simpler, more abstract images made up of fewer, plainer fabrics. Nevertheless, the uniform vision that shaped this quilt may not necessarily be credited to a single maker, or even designer. A group conceivably might have achieved such results, depending on its members' compatibility and cohesiveness. The blocks in this quilt, identified by quilt scholars as Style I, Designer I, or high style, are characterized by swag borders, intricate baskets and vases of layered flowers, spread eagles, floral wreaths with three-lobed bowknots, important urban buildings, and civic monuments.[32]

Other than the inked inscription "E Pluribus Unum" that appears in a banner in the eagle's beak over the Washington Monument, no inscriptions are found on the quilt. It was discovered in the Wilmington, Delaware, and Chester, Pennsylvania, area, and at one time was owned by Mrs. William Peto.

Figure 129c Detail. This brick building probably represents Seamen's Bethel Mission.

Figure 129d Detail. Battle Monument, Calvert and Fayette Streets, Baltimore.

Figure 129e Detail. The appliquéd floral swag border is further enhanced with quilted feathers and hearts that have been stuffed for additional interest.

Figures 129f and 129g Details. Intricate baskets with multiple layers of fabric are a hallmark characteristic of Baltimore album quilts created in the high style.

Baltimore Album Quilt Figure 129

Maker(s) unknown

Baltimore, Maryland, region, ca. 1850

Cottons; ink inscription; cotton tape; silk embroidery
threads

10–12 running stitches per inch

90½ x 91½ in. (230 x 232 cm)

Gift of Foster and Muriel McCarl, 1976.609.6

FIGURE 130

Like other Baltimore album quilts, this quilt consists of elaborately created blocks of appliquéd wreaths, baskets, and urns in addition to motifs representing urban buildings and civic monuments.[33]

The blocks reflect at least three levels of sewing skill and complexity.[34] The motifs were created with layered and underlaid appliquéd swatches of printed, plain, and rainbow fabrics. Some flowers are padded while others have been ruched to give them added dimension. Embroidery threads are used for supplemental detail as well as to outline or secure in buttonhole stitches some of the appliqués.[35] Inked inscriptions and details contribute to the overall impressiveness of the quilt.[36] The border of bright-red rosebuds and green leaves is echoed in the center-medallion wreath, creating a sense of cohesiveness in the quilt despite the multiple levels of skill found in the different blocks. The bedcover is quilted in a wide variety of floral and foliage shapes, pinwheels, hearts, parallel diagonal lines, and ovals. It is backed in white cotton and bound with a strip of printed red cotton with white dots.

Inscribed "Ringgold," the second block in the top row depicts a memorial tribute to Major Samuel Ringgold, a brave Maryland soldier who died on May 11, 1846, in the Battle of Palo Alto, the first engagement of the Mexican War (figs. 130a, 130b). He became an instant hero, particularly in his home town of Baltimore. A temporary monument for him was erected in the Merchant's Exchange Building, where he was laid in state in December 1846. Memorials to him appear on at least eight other stylistically related quilts.[37] The building next to the Ringgold block represents the U. S. Capitol in Washington, D. C., prior to the addition of the wings after 1850 (see also fig. 129b).

Figure 130a Detail. The monument memorializing the death of Major Samuel Ringgold is found on other Baltimore album quilts although usually not quite as embellished. In addition to the four ruched roses, great texture is created in this block with the choice of tiny pattern–printed green calico to imitate grass and leaves and brown rainbow-printed cotton to mimic the veining of marble. The monument is further enhanced with the inscription "Ringgold," which is outlined in cut-steel beads and decorated with inked eagles. Appliquéd crossed flags and stacked guns pay further tribute to the fallen warrior. Perched atop the monument is a blue dove, perhaps symbolic of the upward flight of the hero's spirit.

Figure 130b Death of Major Samuel Ringgold, of the Flying Artillery, at the Battle of Palo Alto, May 8, 1846, courtesy Library of Congress. One of Baltimore's best-loved heroes of the Mexican War, Major Samuel Ringgold was shot through both legs by a cannonball and mortally wounded at the Battle of Palo Alto.

About the QUILT MAKER Family tradition provides a detailed account of the quilt. Sarah Anne W. Lankford's older brother Henry Smith Lankford (1823–1905) is said to have purchased the individual quilt blocks "at a Masonic conclave in Baltimore, where the blocks were auctioned."[38] Henry lived in Baltimore between 1847 and 1869, during which time he was initiated into King David's Lodge, No. 68, in Baltimore on May 21, 1850.[39] The story continues that Henry presented the blocks to his sister Sarah, who assembled and quilted the cover, finishing in 1850. The oral history cannot be verified in every respect, but the cross-stitched initials, "S. A. W. L.," in the center of the lower left apple wreath certainly suggest that Sarah had a role in the construction of the quilt sometime prior to her marriage in 1853 to Samuel Griffin Miles (fig. 130d).[40] Based on stylistic differences, the prefabricated blocks were probably the work of several professional artists. Sarah may also have been responsible for some or all of the simpler blocks and for the vine that forms a border on all four sides.

Although it is not known if Sarah intended the quilt to be a gift to her brother, the bedcover did descend to Henry's granddaughter and eventually to the family member who made a gift of it to Colonial Williamsburg.

Figure 130c Lankford Family, Somerset County, Maryland, 1885. Four generations of the Lankford family are represented in this photograph. Henry S. Lankford stands on the right.

Figure 130d Detail. Cross-stitched in the center of the apple wreath are the initials SAWL for Sarah Anne W. Lankford, who assembled and quilted this dramatic and rare quilt.

Baltimore Album Quilt Figure 130

Blocks by Sarah Anne W. Lankford (1830–1898) and unknown makers, assembled and quilted by Sarah Anne W. Lankford

Baltimore and Princess Anne County, Maryland, ca. 1850

Cottons; ink inscriptions; metal and glass beads; wool, silk, and cotton embroidery threads

13 running stitches per inch

99¾ x 84 in. (253 x 213 cm)

Gift of Miss Marsha C. Scott, 1979.609.14

The rich complexity of this album quilt is derived from the multitude of different plain, glazed, and printed cottons found in the appliquéd blocks. For example, several printed purple cottons are used in the grape border although these small swatches at a distance look very similar. The layering of fabrics in the appliqué, in addition to using underlaid appliquéd patches to add highlights of color, further enhances the intricacy of the design. The orientations of the blocks are inconsistent; some blocks face upward, others downward, and some sideways, depending on how the quilt is positioned. Most blocks have fine details embroidered in wool or cotton, as does the grapevine border. Some blocks also include appliquéd motifs stitched with open buttonhole stitches around the edges in a chintzwork technique sometimes referred to as *broderie perse*. The blocks are quilted in seven-eighth-inch squares on point with outline quilting around the appliqué. The border is quilted in diagonal parallel lines. The white cotton backing is turned to the front and hemmed to form a narrow finished edge.

The red, white, and blue sashing of this album quilt is an arresting and relatively rare feature. Two similar quilts are banded only in blue and white, but sashing composed of a single fabric seems to have been most common in mid-nineteenth-century America. Perhaps not coincidentally, this quilt and both related blue-and-white-banded bedcovers include blocks of the unusual motif of a flowering cactus (fig. 131a).[41] The cactus plant became popular in America as a result of the U. S.-Mexican War (1846–1848).

In addition to the blooming cactus, floral sprigs, and wreaths of flowers, the quilt blocks in this example include a cornucopia, the Masonic emblems of a compass and square (fig. 131b), birds, and an open Bible with inked verse from Ecclesiastes 12:1: "Remember now thy / Creator in the days / of thy youth, while / the evil days come / not, nor the years / draw nigh, when thou / shalt salt [sic] say, I have / no pleasure in them" (fig. 131c).

Figure 131a Detail. The flowering cactus is found on other album quilts from the Baltimore region and reflects the popular interest in the U. S.-Mexican War.

Figure 131b Detail. The compass and square are symbolic motifs associated with the Freemasons and Odd Fellows.

About the QUILT MAKERS The album quilt descended in the Danner family of Maryland[42] and is believed to have been made by three sisters-in-law, two of whom were living in the same household at the time. One of the blocks is signed and dated in ink "Julia A Danner / Feb 14th / 1856" (fig. 131c). Julia Engel married Henry Danner in 1853, three years before the date on the quilt. She gave birth to her first child less than two months after she signed and dated the quilt. Julia and Henry Danner lived on Wilderness Farm, near Lisbon in Howard County,

Maryland. Deborah Ecker married Daniel Danner, Henry's brother, in 1838. They lived near Unionville, in neighboring Frederick County. Eve Danner, the men's sister, married late and was a single woman living with Daniel and Deborah when the quilt was made. Eve married George Washington Dudderar sometime after 1860. In 1870, Eve and George along with two of his children from his first marriage were living in Frederick County next to Daniel and Deborah. By 1880, Eve was widowed and living with her brother Henry and his wife, Julia, in Howard County.[43]

Figure 131c Detail. Julia Engel Danner inscribed "Feb 14th / 1856" in ink below a Bible verse encircled by appliquéd flowers. Her first child was born less than two months later.

MARYLAND ALBUM QUILT FIGURE 131

EVE DANNER (CA. 1811–AFTER 1880), DEBORAH ECKER DANNER
(1819–1876), AND JULIA ENGEL DANNER (1825–1907)

FREDERICK AND HOWARD COUNTIES, MARYLAND, CA. 1856

COTTONS; INK INSCRIPTIONS; SILK, WOOL, AND COTTON

9–12 RUNNING STITCHES PER INCH

95⅝ X 97 IN. (242 X 246 CM)

MUSEUM PURCHASE MADE POSSIBLE BY DONATED FUNDS, 1979.609.15

FIGURE 132

This quilt uses blocks of layered and underlaid appliqué designs similar to those on Baltimore album quilts and sets them on point within wide diagonal sashing, creating a bold and striking design. When viewed flat in a photograph or museum exhibit case, the quilt's sideways motifs may seem disconcerting. However, when used on a bed and seen from various directions, the design would be far easier to comprehend and appreciate. The quilting was done in double rows of parallel lines and a wide variety of abstract and stylized designs, including leaves and flowers. The quilt is backed in white cotton, which is turned to the front to create a narrow edge finish. Wool embroidery threads create a vine of olive green in one block featuring a wreath with green leaves and red-and-yellow flowers (fig. 132a).[44]

Figure 132a Detail.

Another block incorporates symbols associated with the Independent Order of Odd Fellows, although no connection between the maker's family and that organization has yet been established.[45] Seen within a block on the lower right, the heart within an open hand represents sincerity, and the three links represent friendship, love, and truth in Odd Fellows symbolism (fig. 132b). The bow and arrows, pair of compasses, Bible, olive branch, and crescent moon also appear in Odd Fellows imagery.[46] The Independent Order of Odd Fellows was established in Baltimore in 1819 as a benevolent and social society.

Attribution of the quilt to Lydia Naomi Covington Palmatary is based on family tradition and the quilt's line of descent.

Figure 132b Detail. The open hand with a heart is sometimes associated with charity and the giving with the hands and from the heart. In the Odd Fellows vocabulary, it most often is representative of honesty, candor, and sincerity—the open hand has nothing to hide.

About the QUILT MAKER   On February 25, 1831, Lydia Naomi Covington married John Thomas Palmatary (1810–1890), a farmer at Duck Creek Hundred in Kent County, Delaware. The couple's first four children were born at Duck Creek Hundred. By 1850, the family had moved about fifty miles to Kent County, Maryland, where their remaining three children were born.[47] Presumably the quilt was created around this time. The quilt was handed down to Lydia's eldest daughter and continued to descend in the female line of the family until it was acquired by Colonial Williamsburg.

MARYLAND ALBUM QUILT FIGURE 132

LYDIA NAOMI COVINGTON PALMATARY (1812–1900)

KENT COUNTY, MARYLAND, 1845–1855

COTTONS; WOOL EMBROIDERY THREADS

6–7 RUNNING STITCHES PER INCH

104 X 100 IN. (264 X 254 CM)

MUSEUM PURCHASE, 1973.609.3

MARYLAND ALBUM QUILT

FIGURE 133

The counties surrounding Baltimore are known for their fine album quilts. Made near Annapolis in the county just south of Baltimore, this quilt is composed of twenty-five appliquéd blocks that relate to those in Baltimore album quilts, yet these are more delicately designed and executed, some with embroidered details in chain and outline stitches. Underlaid appliquéd patches in some blocks add further color. Blocks of wreaths, floral and fruit crosses, and pots of flowers are separated by narrow red sashing and are carefully assembled for visual symmetry when viewed as a bedcovering. The four heavier matching motifs anchor the outer corners while the other blocks are arranged and directed toward the center. A narrow outer border of shallow meandering vines with embroidered tendrils completes the composition. A few of the original pencil lines for the embroidery pattern, as well as for the quilting pattern, can still be seen in the border. The bedcover is quilted in outline around the appliquéd motifs and in additional designs of double diagonal lines, feather wreath, checkerboard, and four-lobed crosses (fylfots). It is backed in off-white cotton and bound with a one-inch folded strip of red cotton.

About the QUILT MAKER The quilt is said to have belonged to John and Sarah Carr of Fairview in Anne Arundel County. Although oral history ascribes the making of the quilt to a woman named Worthington, the family may have confused the names because Sarah Carr's maiden name was Whittington, not Worthington. John Carr and Sarah Whittington married in Anne Arundel County in February 1843.[48] It is possible that Sarah made the quilt or received it as a gift prior to her marriage.

Figure 133a Detail.

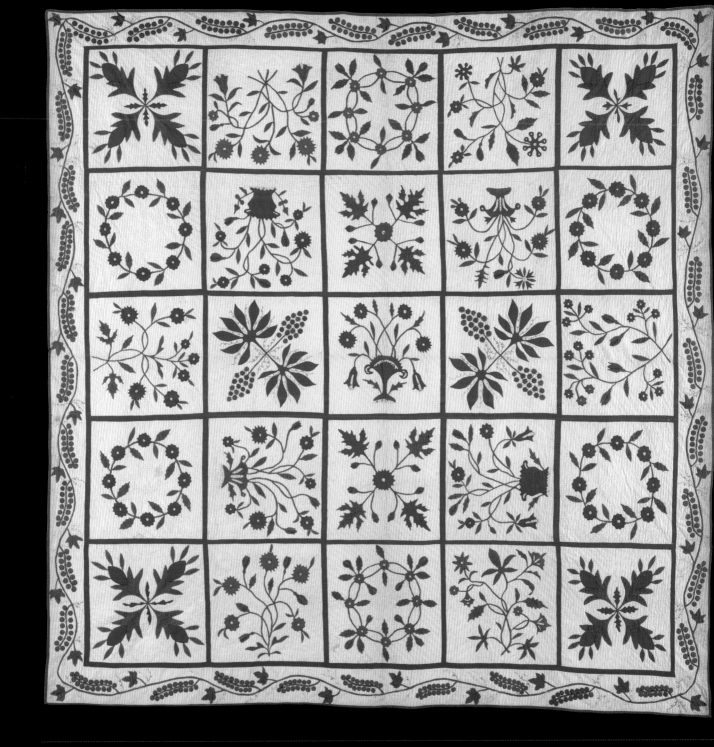

Maryland Album Quilt Figure 133

Member of the Carr, Whittington, or Worthington family, possibly Sarah Whittington Carr

Anne Arundel County, Maryland, 1840–1850

Cottons; wool and silk embroidery threads

9–11 running stitches per inch

105½ x 103 in. (268 x 261 cm)

Museum Purchase, the Friends of Colonial Williamsburg Collections Fund, 2008.609.4

1   Dena S. Katzenberg, Jennifer Faulds Goldsborough, and Elly Sienkiewicz remain some of the best overall references for the study of these impressive Baltimore-area mid-nineteenth-century album quilts. Katzenberg's information on fabrics and designs provides critical insights regarding the rich array of fabrics available to these quilt makers and the stitchers' artful manipulation of these fabrics to create images of extraordinary subtlety, depth, and detail (17–47). Dena S. Katzenberg, *Baltimore Album Quilts* (Baltimore, MD: Baltimore Museum of Art, 1981); Jennifer Faulds Goldsborough, *Lavish Legacies: Baltimore Album and Related Quilts in the Collection of the Maryland Historical Society* (Baltimore: Maryland Historical Society, 1994); Jennifer F. Goldsborough, "An Album of Baltimore Album Quilt Studies," in *Uncoverings 1994*, ed. Virginia Gunn (San Francisco, CA: American Quilt Study Group, 1995), 73–110; and Elly Sienkiewicz, *Baltimore Beauties and Beyond: Studies in Classic Album Quilt Appliqué*, vols. 1 and 2 (Lafayette, CA: C & T Publishing, 1989 and 1991).

2   It has been said that Baltimore holds a unique place in the religious history of the nation. It is considered the birthplace of Methodism in America; at a conference held at the Lovely Lane Meeting House in Baltimore on December 27, 1784, the Methodist Church in the United States was born. The Baltimore Cathedral, which was completed in 1821, was planned by John Carroll, the first Roman Catholic bishop in the country. Har Sinai Congregation, the first Jewish congregation founded on Reform principles in the United States, was organized in Baltimore in 1842. Francis F. Beirne and Carleton Jones, *Baltimore: A Picture History*, 3rd ed. (Baltimore, MD: Bodine & Associates and Maclay & Associates, 1982), 11.

3   As the westernmost port in the United States, Baltimore was a favored entry point for immigrants. The opening in 1828 of the Baltimore-Ohio Railroad, the nation's first commercial steam railway, provided immigrants with a direct route west. Irish and German immigrants flooded Fell's Point, Baltimore's port. Their numbers greatly increased in the 1840s due to the 1848 German political uprisings, unemployment, and the Irish potato famine of the mid-1840s. By the late nineteenth century, Baltimore was the second leading point of entry to the United States, surpassed only by Ellis Island.

4   Katzenberg, *Baltimore Album Quilts*, 46. Katzenberg wrote, "Baltimore's ties with the Germans in Western Maryland and Pennsylvania were strong, and the influences of that folk art are easily recognized on the Baltimore quilts."

5   Compare Addie's quilt to two red-and-green Maryland appliquéd quilts with repetitive blocks dated ca. 1850 and ca. 1845–1855 in Goldsborough, *Lavish Legacies*, 48–51.

6   The family recalled the marriage as being ca. 1872, but census records indicate it must have occurred during or shortly after 1880. Addie and William Ruark were living in King William, VA, in 1900 and 1910. Both were buried in the Manokin Presbyterian Church cemetery in Princess Anne, Somerset County, MD. William Ruark household, 1880 U. S. census, Fairmont, Somerset, MD, enumeration district 71, page 322D, National Archives and Records Administration (NARA) microfilm T9, roll 515, digital image as found on Ancestry.com (2010); William Ruark household, 1900 U. S. census, West Point, King William, VA, enumeration district 45, page 10B, NARA microfilm T623, roll 1714, digital image as found on Ancestry.com (2004); Wm. H. Ruark household, 1910 U. S. census, West Point, King William, VA, enumeration district 48, page 3A, NARA microfilm T624, roll 1633, digital image as found on Ancestry.com

(2006); and Manokin Presbyterian Church Cemetery, Somerset Cemeteries Project, entries for "Adams, Addie Thayer" and "Ruark, William Henry," accessed December 2, 2011, http://www.rootsweb .ancestry.com/~mdsomers/scp/manokin.htm.

7   See Doris M. Bowman and Joan Stephens, *The Smithsonian Treasury: American Quilts* (Washington, DC: Smithsonian Institution Press, 1991), 50–51.

8   See Sienkiewicz, *Baltimore Beauties and Beyond*, 1:108.

9   Among the quilt scholars and authors is Ronda McAllen who suggested that professional female needle artists designed and produced basted blocks to sell, possibly through fancy dry goods or millinery stores. To support her theory, she pointed to an 1849 Baltimore advertisement for a Miss Chase who offered for sale handsome album squares. McAllen and author (Ivey), conversation, September 20, 2013.

10 Goldsborough in "Album of Baltimore Album Quilt Studies" provides a concise description of the three styles, distinguishing them as Designer I, Designer II, and Designer III (81–82). Marylou McDonald in her 2008 calendar "Baltimore Album Quilt" with Jan Whitlock also provides brief descriptions of the three styles, preferring to call them Style 1, Style 2, and Style 3 because each style probably represents the work of more than one designer. The classic Baltimore high style (Designer I or Style 1) was attributed to a young Baltimore woman named Mary Evans by Katzenberg based on a photograph of an appliquéd quilt block, which was said to have belonged to Mary Evans, and notes of it taken early in the twentieth century by Dr. William R. Dunton Jr. (Katzenberg, *Baltimore Album Quilts*, 62). The square was one of seven precut and basted appliquéd blocks that were found in a trunk that had belonged to Mary Evans. The squares were unseen by scholars until 1990 when they were acquired from the family by the Maryland Historical Society. For more, see Goldsborough, *Lavish Legacies*, 112–117.

11 In 1850, a young Baltimore woman named Hannah Trimble described in her diary several visits to see quilts, including, "then out [to] Mrs. Simon's in Chesnut St. The lady who cut & basted these handsome quilts—saw some pretty squares." Diary of Hannah Mary Trimble, February 1, 1850, MS2517, Manuscripts Division, Maryland Historical Society, Baltimore. Remarkably, the two quilts that Hannah saw survive and have been identified as classic Baltimore album quilts in the high style (Style 1 or Designer I). Mrs. Simon has been identified as Maria Anna Heidenroder Simon, wife of carpet weaver Philip Simon, who lived on French and Chestnut Streets. Born in Bavaria, she immigrated to America in 1844, after the earliest dated Baltimore quilt squares of 1842 were produced. Goldsborough, "Album of Baltimore Album Quilt Studies," 97–100. See also Virginia Vis, "Conformity and Diversity in Baltimore Album Quilts," in *Eye on Elegance: Early Quilts of Maryland and Virginia*, Alden O'Brien with Virginia Vis (Washington, DC: DAR Museum, 2014), 39.

12 William Rush Dunton Jr., *Old Quilts* (Catonsville, MD: published by author, 1946), 18.

13 For a full discussion of Baltimore Jewish women and their quilts, see Ronda McAllen, "Jewish Baltimore Album Quilts," in *Uncoverings 2006*, ed. Joanna E. Evans (Lincoln, NE: American Quilt Study Group, 2006), 187–217.

14 Dunton, *Old Quilts*, 184, 186, 189, 196.

15 Ibid., 187–188.

16 William Wilkins household, U. S. 1820 census, Ward 8, Baltimore, MD, page 294, NARA microfilm M33, roll 42, digital image as found on Ancestry.com. (2010).

17 Achsah Wilkins continued to work on quilts most of her life, sometimes with her mother and sister. McAllen and author (Ivey), conversation, March 19, 2014. "A. Wilkins," possibly this quilt maker, appears as a signature in the border of an album quilt from 1847–1848 in the collections of the United Methodist Historical Society, Lovely Lane Museum and Archives, Baltimore; the quilt also bears the names of a number of other women. See Katzenberg, *Baltimore Album Quilts*, 94, 120.

18 Genealogical information for Achsah Goodwin Wilkins has been widely published, including in Dunton, *Old Quilts*, 187–189, 202–203, and Katzenberg, *Baltimore Album Quilts*, 34, 44, 59, 63–65. For marriage record, see "Maryland Marriages, 1655–1850," s.v. "William Wilkins," online database, Ancestry.com (2004).

19 Signatures are E. Conaway, M. G[?], Pascal, C. R. LaRley, Miss Rebecca Taylor, P. H. A., Ann Carmine, A. M. Yance, Ann Delia Y[?]lift, Georgina Eltonhedos, C. A. Nice, S. Callender, E. F. Thomas, Mary Ann Laffaty, A. E. Sameny, Maroelleaner Personet, L. M. Willis, Rose Ann Dunn, Margarett A. Mullett, Sarah A. Deluhay, Laura J. Decker, Augusta Camp, G. Louisa Wise, Sopia Nice, Nanisey Hol[?], and M. S. Phillips.

20 Two other blocks have the inscriptions "Bultmor" and "Balti[?]," presumably for Baltimore.

21 See Amanda M. Porter's quilt dated 1849 in Goldsborough, *Lavish Legacies*, 68–69. For another pre-1850 Baltimore album quilt with a chintz border, see ibid., 80–81; this quilt contains several blocks related to CWF's quilt, including an identical floral wreath block in the top row, fourth in. A fourth quilt, dated 1847 with a chintz border and associated with the Reverend Robert M. Lipscomb, is in the collections of the United Methodist Historical Society, Lovely Lane Museum and Archives, Baltimore. See also fig. 72 for an identical chintz border on a Petersburg appliquéd quilt.

22 Inspired by the biblical Rebekah, the organization stressed the primary duty of doing good. Originally only wives and daughters of Odd Fellows were accepted. Imagery associated with the Daughters of Rebekah and found on Baltimore album quilts includes the beehive, representing cooperative industry; moon and seven stars, symbolizing the never failing order of God's universe; the dove, embodying peace; and the lily, signifying purity.

23 The women are Margaret A. Mullet, Mary Ann Laffaty (or Lafferty), Laura J. Decker (or Delcher), Catherine A. Nice, Sophia Nice, and Margaret S. Phillips. Thomas Mullet household, 1850 U. S. census, Ward 7, Baltimore, MD, page 279B, NARA microfilm M432, roll 283, digital image as found on Ancestry.com (2009); John W. Delcher household, 1850 U. S. census, Ward 7, Baltimore, MD, page 297B, NARA microfilm M432, roll 283, digital image as found on Ancestry.com (2009); and William B. Philip household, 1850 U. S. census, Ward 7, Baltimore, MD, page 269B, NARA microfilm M432, roll 283, digital image as found on Ancestry.com (2009).

24 Thomas Wildey household, 1860 U. S. census, Ward 5, Baltimore, MD, page 309, NARA microfilm M653, roll 460, digital image as found on Ancestry.com (2009).

25 The quilt appears in the following publications: Elly Sienkiewicz, *Baltimore Album Quilts: Historic Notes and Antique Patterns* (Lafayette, CA.: C & T Publishing, 1990), figs. 40–42 on 104, 105, and front and back of dust jacket; Carleton L. Safford and Robert Bishop, *America's Quilts and Coverlets* (New York: Weathervane Books, 1974), 148–149; Jane Bentley Kolter, *Forget Me Not: A Gallery of Friendship and Album Quilts* (Pittstown, NJ: Main Street Press, 1985), 2 (shown upside down); and Cynthia Elyce Rubin, *Southern Folk Art* (Birmingham, AL: Oxmoor House, 1985), 189.

26 For other examples of appliqués of the Washington Monument, see Katzenberg, *Baltimore Album Quilts*, 114–115, and Sienkiewicz, *Baltimore Beauties and Beyond*, 1:19.

27 This maker's simplified version of the U. S. Capitol is missing the pediment front over the central columns and has fewer columns in the wings. For other Baltimore album quilts depicting the U. S. Capitol, see fig. 130; Sienkiewicz, *Baltimore Beauties and Beyond*, 1:91; and Alden O'Brien, *Historic Quilts of the DAR Museum* (Brownsboro, AL: Martha Pullen, 2011), 78–81.

28 The attribution is based on an 1835 engraving of Seamen's Bethel Mission that was found on a web archive by Elly Sienkiewicz. Elly Sienkiewicz to author (Ivey), e-mail message, March 11, 2014.

29 The same materials and technique were used in the Seamen's Bethel Mission block on the Reverend Hezekiah Best Baltimore album quilt in the collections of the United Methodist Historical Society, Lovely Lane Museum and Archives, Baltimore. Debby Cooney to author (Baumgarten), e-mail message, December 17, 2007. For an illustration of this quilt, see Katzenberg, *Baltimore Album Quilts*, 82–83.

30 For other examples of appliqués of the Battle Monument, see Katzenberg, *Baltimore Album Quilts*, 88–89, and Sienkiewicz, *Baltimore Beauties and Beyond*, 1:91.

31 This quilt and the quilt in fig. 130 share three blocks that are very similar in form: a compote of fruit, including a cut watermelon; the U. S. Capitol; and a flying bird with a flower spray in its beak centered in a floral wreath with a three-lobed bow. The two quilts also share many of the same fabrics, not only in these three analogous blocks but in other motifs as well.

32 For similar blocks and border, see Goldsborough, *Lavish Legacies*, 60–61.

33 The quilt appears in the following publications: Elly Sienkiewicz, *Design a Baltimore Album Quilt: A Teach-Yourself Course in Sets and Borders* (Lafayette, CA: C & T Publishing, 1992), 49; Goldsborough, *Lavish Legacies*, 18; Sandi Fox, *For Purpose and Pleasure: Quilting Together in Nineteenth-Century America* (Nashville, TN: Rutledge Hill Press, 1995), 58; and Beatrix T. Rumford and Carolyn J. Weekly, *Treasures of American Folk Art from the Abby Aldrich Rockefeller Folk Art Center* (Boston: Little, Brown, 1989), 134.

34 The quilt is a combination of styles incorporating blocks in the high style, characterized by multiple layers of finely appliquéd fabrics, images of monuments and urban buildings, and a three-lobed bowknot motif, and blocks in Style 2, which features three-dimensionality created by padding and ruching and embroidered details. A less-sophisticated third style uses the green-and-red color scheme with less padding and layering of fabrics. Virginia Vis categorizes the large center block as the work of yet a fourth designer. Vis, "Conformity and Diversity," 44.

35 Most appliqués, however, were turned under and secured with overcast stitches.

36 Above the depiction of the U. S. Capitol building is an ink-drawn bird with a banner in its beak reading "Cha's / W / Carter." Charles W. Carter's identity and his connection with the makers of the quilt remain undetermined. In the second block on the bottom row is an ink-drawn monument with a banner beneath it reading "Stranger." Other inked details include plant tendrils, watermelon seeds, butterfly antennae, and bird feet.

37 For other quilt blocks with memorials to Major Samuel Ringgold,

and Dennis Duke and Deborah Harding, eds., *America's Glorious Quilts* (New York: Park Lane, 1989), 283. An almost identical monument on a block inscribed "To the Memory of / Col W. H. Watson" appears on a quilt in the collection of the Los Angeles County Museum of Art (see Fox, *For Purpose and Pleasure*, 52, 55). Colonel W. H. Watson, a fellow Baltimorean, was killed leading a battalion of Baltimore volunteers in a charge near Monterrey, just four months after the death of Ringgold. Fox is aware of eleven quilt blocks with this monument (61n6). It is unclear how many memorialize Ringgold and how many Watson.

38   The story is familiar to present-day family descendants; its basic elements were published in a newspaper article believed to have appeared in 1948. A photocopy of the article, which is the source of the quote in the text, is in the CWF object file. The exact date and name of the newspaper are unknown.

39   Henry S. Lankford obituary, *Baltimore (MD) Sun*, November 7, 1905; and Stanley R. Uppercue, grand secretary of the Maryland Masons, to E. Preston Parks, secretary of Manokin Lodge No. 106, July 21, 1980, CWF object file 1979.609.14. In his letter, Uppercue stated: "Our files reveal one H. S. Lankford, initiated in King Davids Lodge No. 68, Baltimore, May 21, 1850; demitted May 20, 1862; affiliated with Lafayette Lodge No. 111, Baltimore, November 1, 1862 and suspended there from for non-payment of dues on April 28, 1873."

40   Henry Smith Lankford and Sarah Anne W. Lankford were born to Benjamin and Susan Lankford of Somerset County, MD. Henry married twice, first in 1851 to Martha Ann Riggin of Somerset County, MD, and second in 1853 to Mary D. Pinckard of Northumberland County, VA. Henry and both wives were buried in the Antioch Methodist Church cemetery in Somerset County. Sarah Anne was born August 30, 1830, the fifth of nine children. By 1856, when Samuel Miles joined Henry Lankford in the wholesale grocery business, the couple was established in Baltimore. Sarah died in 1898 and was buried alongside Samuel and his first wife in St. Paul's Episcopal Church cemetery in Somerset County. The quilt donor speculated that the initial W stood for the name *Whittington*, which appears with some frequency as a family name in records. Note that no relationship between the Lankford family and Sarah Whittington Carr, owner of the Baltimore album quilt in fig. 133, has been established. "Maryland Marriages, 1667–1899," s.v. "Samuel G. Miles," online database, Ancestry.com (2000); Woodrow T. Wilson, *Thirty-Four Families of Old Somerset Co., Maryland* (1974; Baltimore, MD: Gateway Press, 1977), 175–176; Sarah A. Miles funeral notice, *Baltimore (MD) Sun*, September 21, 1898; and Sarah A. Miles obituary, *Baltimore (MD) Sun*, September 21, 1898.

41   In addition to the sashing format and the cactus plant motif, the three quilts are similar in their loose floral arrangements and vine border. For the blue-and-white-banded quilts, see Dunton, *Old Quilts*, 170–175. The quilts sold at Sotheby's Auction in 1984 (Sotheby's, *American Folk Art, Furniture and Decorations*, June 30, 1984 [New York: Sotheby Parke Bernet, 1984], lot 252). One was later published in Michael M. Kile, ed., *The Quilt Digest*, vol. 4 (San Francisco, CA: Quilt Digest Press, 1986), 53, and in Judith Reiter Weissman and Wendy Lavitt, *Labors of Love: America's Textiles and Needlework, 1650–1930* (New York: Knopf, 1987), 71.

42   The family history states that the quilt descended from Deborah

Ecker Danner to her son Edward Delevan Danner to his son (Edward Lindsay Danner) to his daughter (Mary Danner Dudderar) of Unionville, MD.

43   Daniel Danner household, 1850 U. S. census, District 8, Frederick, MD, page 428B, NARA microfilm M432, roll 293, digital image as found on Ancestry.com (2009); Daniel Danner household, 1860 U. S. census, Liberty, Frederick, MD, page 84, NARA microfilm M653, roll 474, digital image as found on Ancestry.com (2009); "Maryland Marriages, 1667–1899," s.v. "Henry Danner," online database, Ancestry.com (2000); "George Washington Danner" on findagrave.com, Find a Grave memorial #49725469, record added March 15, 2010; "Maryland Marriages, 1655–1850," s.v. "Daniel Danner," online database, Ancestry.com (2004); Geo W Duderar household, 1870 U. S. census, Liberty, Frederick, MD, page 355B, NARA microfilm M593, roll 587, digital image as found on Ancestry.com (2009); Henry Danner household, 1880 U. S. census, Howard, MD, enumeration district 104, page 415A, NARA microfilm T9, roll 511, digital image as found on Ancestry.com (1999); "Julia A. Danner" on findagrave.com, Find a Grave memorial #86619285, record added March 11, 2012; and "Deborah Danner" on findagrave.com, Find a Grave memorial #97179442, record added September 16, 2012.

44   The quilt appears in Sienkiewicz, *Design a Baltimore Album Quilt*, 8.

45   According to Floyd O'Hern, grand secretary, Grand Lodge of Maryland, John T. Palmatary's name does not appear in existing Independent Order of Odd Fellows records for Maryland (which are, however, incomplete). Floyd E. O'Hern to Barbara Luck, October 30, 1992, CWF object file 1973.609.3. The degree of Rebekah was instituted for wives, daughters, and mothers of Odd Fellows in 1851. However, O'Hern stated that the first Rebekah lodges to appear in Maryland were the Colfax Lodge No. 1 at Cumberland and the Queen Esther Lodge No. 2 at Baltimore, instituted on June 21 and June 22, 1886, respectively. Thus, it would seem that Lydia Palmatary was not personally involved in the order at the time of the quilt's fabrication.

46   The bird may be a dove, a symbol of the degree of Rebekah. See Barbara Franco, *Fraternally Yours: A Decade of Collecting* (Lexington, MA: Museum of Our National Heritage, 1986), 21, 44, 45. See also Aaron B. Grosh, *The Odd-Fellow's Manual* (Philadelphia: H. C. Peck and Theo Bliss, 1858), 104–109, 130–133, 142; and John D. Hamilton, curator of Collections, Museum of Our National Heritage, to Barbara Luck, August 31, 1992, CWF object file 1973.609.3.

47   "Delaware Marriage Records, 1744–1912," s.v. "John T. Palmatary," online database, digital image as found on Ancestry.com (2008); John Palmatary household, 1830 U. S. census, Kent, DE, page 232, NARA microfilm M19, roll 12, digital image as found on Ancestry.com (2010); John Palentery household, 1840 U. S. census, Duck Creek Hundred, Kent, DE, page 52, NARA microfilm M704, roll 33, digital image as found on Ancestry.com (2010); and John Palmertory household, 1850 U. S. census, District 3, Kent, MD, page 298B, NARA microfilm M432, roll 294, digital image as found on Ancestry.com (2009). The 1850 census lists John as a farmer having five thousand dollars' worth of real estate.

48   "Maryland Marriages, 1655–1850," s.v. "John Carr," online database, Ancestry.com (2004).

CHAPTER 15

MENNONITE & AMISH

CHAPTER 15

MENNONITE & AMISH

The Mennonite and Amish peoples share a heritage that began in sixteenth-century Europe with the religious movement known as Anabaptism, whose believers advocated adult baptism, including rebaptizing those who had been baptized as infants in the Catholic Church. Named for the Dutch religious reformer Menno Simons (1496–1561), the Mennonites believed in nonviolence and strictly following the teachings of Jesus Christ as outlined in the Bible. In the 1690s, doctrinal differences led to a split. A more conservative group, known as the Amish, led by Swiss-born Jacob Amman (ca. 1644–ca. 1730), separated from the Mennonites.

The Mennonite and Amish faiths spread around the world although most of the immigrants to America were German-speaking people from Europe. Over the years, both the Mennonites and the Amish have retained their strong Christian faith, worn relatively plain clothing, and held to beliefs in nonviolence and service to the community. However, from the beginning, Mennonite settlers in America tended to assimilate into the broader cultural group. In contrast, the Amish avoided assimilation. They gathered in tightly knit communities and advocated a life of strict separation from worldly influences that might engender pride or result in a loss of faith. Their conservative dress, mostly agrarian lifestyle, strong sense of group cohesion, and avoidance of most modern conveniences such as electricity and automobiles have kept them relatively isolated from the mainstream.

Both groups made quilts. Mennonite women's quilts were varied and sometimes reflected styles fashionable in the broader culture, including both pieced and appliquéd techniques (see fig. 134).[1] Although some conservative Mennonite women made quilts similar in appearance to those of their Amish neighbors, Mennonites more often selected printed textiles and up-to-date patterns.

Amish women more often avoided the popular appliqué techniques and patterns as too showy and wasteful of cloth, preferring piecing instead. Still, Amish women began making pieced quilts much later than their Mennonite, English, and Welsh neighbors, who have longer quilting traditions and did piecing early on. Prior to the second quarter of the nineteenth century, Amish bedcoverings usually consisted of feather ticks and woven coverlets. The earliest references to American Amish quilts are the few that appear in inventory listings of the 1830s, and dated extant examples suggest that these were probably made in a wholecloth technique.[2] Not until relatively late in the nineteenth century did Amish women begin making the pieced quilts for which they became famous—but by that time their styles of quilting were old-fashioned and conservative by the standards of mainstream culture. The more conservative Amish women adopted certain quilting styles only after they were discarded by mainstream groups because they then considered it safe to accept the style without threat of disruptive outside influences.[3] By the twentieth century, some Amish women embraced a variety of quilt patterns and styles.[4]

Figure 134 Appliquéd Quilt, attributed to Barbara Seitz (1808–1848), Lancaster County, Pennsylvania, ca. 1840, cotton, 39 x 37 in. (99 x 94 cm), Museum Purchase with funds from an anonymous donor. The Mennonite quilt maker assembled appliquéd hearts to form starlike medallions on this charming crib quilt.

Amish women, especially those from Lancaster County, Pennsylvania, are best known for a distinctive bold geometric manner of piecing, often combined with skillfully stitched quilting that includes undulating feather borders and central medallions that can be traced back to the eighteenth century (see wholecloth quilts in chapter 5). Inspiration for piecing and quilting probably came from a variety of sources. Some scholars point to the centralized diamonds on the bindings of eighteenth-century Amish hymnals as a possible design source.[5] It is even more likely that the Pennsylvania Amish borrowed ideas from Welsh settlers living nearby. Nineteenth-century Welsh wool quilts often had large-scale patterns pieced with center diamonds, bars, and center squares, sometimes quilted with medallions, fans, and cables like those on some Amish and Mennonite quilts (see fig. 135).[6]

By the time quilt making began in Amish areas, home spinning and weaving were no longer being done. Amish women purchased factory-made textiles, including quilting materials, from traveling salesmen or large mail-order companies, such as Sears or Montgomery Ward. The Amish typically selected for their quilts the rich dark colors found in their clothing, often doing the piecing with a treadle sewing machine. Pennsylvania Amish quilts were often constructed of thin, fine wool or cotton-wool mixtures while Midwest Amish quilts were typically made of cotton. After the development of rayon, nylon, and polyester blends, Amish women did not hesitate to adopt the newer, easy-care materials.[7] Quilting was done by hand with running stitches using dark cotton thread.

Although Amish communities shared an overarching conservatism and insularity, they (and their quilts) were not all alike. Not governed by a parent organization, the religious leaders of each community set the rules for appropriate behavior and styles for their group. Regional differences in quilts can be detected among Amish communities. While most avoided the use of printed textiles on quilt fronts, some Amish women used small-scale prints on the back, and a few, especially those in Iowa and Indiana, used prints, lighter colors, and embroidery on quilt tops.[8]

Amish quilts are very difficult to date and attribute to specific makers accurately. Self-effacing Amish women typically declined to sign or date their quilts, though the name of the recipient was sometimes included. Amish quilt makers retained styles for decades, making it impossible to date the quilts based on fashion, and avoided large-scale printed textiles that can be easily dated. Further, many modern Amish women began making traditional quilts for sale to the general public, sometimes using old textiles, especially after Amish quilts were recognized as important folk art following a landmark exhibit at the Whitney Museum of American Art in 1971 titled "Abstract Design in American Quilts." The intense saturated colors and bold geometry of Amish quilts appealed then—and still do—to modern artists, scholars, collectors, and quilt lovers.

Figure 135 Center Diamond Quilt, maker unknown, Wales, 1875–1900, wool and cotton-wool with linen quilting threads, 4 stitches per inch, 91 x 86 in. (231 x 218 cm), Museum Purchase, 2013.609.5. Pennsylvania Amish women, especially those from Lancaster County, may have been inspired by the traditional bold piecing done by Welsh quilt makers who resided in nearby communities. Although the pieced designs are similar, many of the stitch patterns differ between the two groups. This quilt is stitched with coiling spirals that are typical of Welsh products but not seen in Pennsylvania Amish quilts.

Log Cabin Variation Crib Quilt

FIGURE 136

This visually dynamic pieced quilt features radiating strips of fabric that combine to form a pattern usually known as Windmill Blades, a variant of the widely used Log Cabin pattern (for another example of the Log Cabin pattern, see fig. 143). While most Amish quilt makers confined their use of printed textiles to backings, Mennonite makers were freer in their selection of patterned fabric, such as the woven plaids and printed dots in this example. This quilt also includes solid plain-woven and corded wools, cotton-wool mixtures, and one cotton fabric, all pieced by hand. The backing is pieced together of two different late nineteenth-century printed cottons in compatible red, black, and white patterns (fig. 136a). The hand-quilting stitches, which follow the pattern design, are not readily visible on the front.

Collectors purchased the quilt from the DeLong family estate in Shartlesville, Pennsylvania. The DeLongs were not Mennonites, but they may have purchased the quilt from a Mennonite quilt maker nearby.

Figure 136a Detail of the printed design on two different backing textiles.

Sawtooth Diamond Quilt

FIGURE 137

The sawtooth variation of the Center Diamond pattern boldly showcases two contrasting solid colors of cotton, yet the finely executed quilting designs, including hearts, undulating feathers, and cables, add subtle decorative appeal (fig. 137a). According to the oral history told to the donors, the quilt was a wedding gift from her mother to Frances L. Bieler,[9] whose satin-stitched initials and the date 1920 are worked at the center of the diamond. The quilt was said to have been made about 1900 and given to Frances at the time of her wedding twenty years later. The quilting must have been completed after the embroidery was done, as the quilting is carefully worked around the initials.

Two-color quilts with elaborate initials embroidered at the center of a Sawtooth Diamond have been attributed to Mennonites in northern Lancaster County, Pennsylvania, especially in Elizabeth and Warwick Townships. Ephrata, the presumed home of this quilt maker, shares a border with Warwick Township. Although Amish quilt makers in Lancaster County occasionally pieced in this design, they typically used wool and omitted the signatures.[10]

Figure 137a Quilting pattern.

Log Cabin Variation Crib Quilt FIGURE 136

MAKER UNKNOWN, PROBABLY MENNONITE

PROBABLY SHARTLESVILLE VICINITY, BERKS COUNTY,
PENNSYLVANIA, 1890–1910

WOOLS, COTTON-WOOL MIXTURES, COTTONS

5 RUNNING STITCHES PER INCH

48 X 47 IN. (122 X 119 CM)

MUSEUM PURCHASE, 1986.609.3

Sawtooth Diamond Quilt   Figure 137

Mennonite maker, attributed to the Bieler family

Probably Ephrata, Pennsylvania, 1920

7–8 running stitches per inch

81½ x 80½ in. (207 x 204 cm)

CENTER DIAMOND QUILT

Judging from the number of surviving Center Diamond quilts, this pattern was a favorite, especially in Lancaster County, Pennsylvania.[11] In fact, few other designs better exemplify Amish style while also appealing to modern taste. From afar, the dramatic geometric quilt compares favorably to minimalist paintings of the 1960s and 1970s. The spare design was appropriate for a conservative group intent on avoiding showy excesses. The quilting stitches, however, reveal intricate patterning in stark contrast to the simple pieced design (fig. 138a). At the center of the large diamond is an eight-pointed star enclosed in a medallion circle of feathers, or plumes. Quilted maple leaves, geometric inner borders enclosing curved four-armed crosses similar to the traditional Pennsylvania German fylfot, realistic roses and tulips, and undulating feather vines extend outward from the center. Amish quilting patterns in many ways resemble the outlines of colorful appliquéd motifs on quilts made by their more liberal Pennsylvania

German neighbors; Amish women did not avoid decoration but rather incorporated it in a way that was acceptable to their group.[12]

The quilt is made of solid-colored twill, sateen, and crepe wools, filled with thin cotton batting, and backed with a small-scale cotton print, all quilted with black cotton. The binding was machine stitched to the front and whipstitched to the back.

Figure 138a Quilting pattern.

SUNSHINE AND SHADOW QUILT

Small squares of bright and dark solid textiles were sewn together to form concentric diamonds that create a light and dark effect known in the Amish community as Sunshine and Shadow. (Mennonite and English quilters called it Trip Around the World.) Amish quilt makers typically confined the pieced sections within a central square surrounded by solid wide borders, as in this example. The pattern was especially popular for wedding quilts.[13] Here, the quilting incorporates twenty-four baskets of flowers that alternate with hearts in the wide outer border, reinforcing the concept that this quilt may have served as a wedding gift (fig. 139a).

The quilt front was made from a variety of twill, crepe, sateen, and plain-woven wools, cotton-wool mixtures, and

cottons; backed with dark-blue plain-woven cotton; and stitched with dark-brown cotton quilting threads.

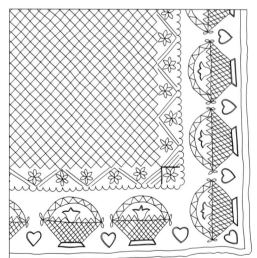

Figure 139a Quilting pattern.

Center Diamond Quilt Figure 138

Unknown Amish maker

Lancaster County, Pennsylvania, 1920–1940

Wools, cottons

10–12 running stitches per inch

76⅛ x 75¾ in. (194 x 192 cm)

Museum Purchase, 1974.609.31

Sunshine and Shadow Quilt Figure 139

Unknown Amish maker

Probably Lancaster County, Pennsylvania, 1935–1955

Wools, cotton-wool mixtures, cottons

8 running stitches per inch

79 x 78 in. (201 x 198 cm)

Museum Purchase, 1980.609.2

STAR QUILT

FIGURE 140

Numerous variations of this dramatic central-star pattern exist (see figs. 91, 93, 148). Usually called Lone Star, Star of Bethlehem, or Starburst, the designs originated in non-German-speaking communities but were later adapted by Mennonite and Amish quilt makers and executed in dramatic, solid colors.[14]

A star pattern this large requires great precision to cut and piece, especially since the diamond-shaped pieces have stretchy bias sides. If the piecing is not done evenly, the star points will be irregular or the pieced section will not lie flat. It is even more challenging to piece a star quilt with a sewing machine, which was the case with this example. Amish and Mennonite women did not hesitate to acquire treadle sewing machines when the labor-saving devices became available. Although many women pieced by machine, they inevitably quilted by hand.

Block initials HL are quilted into two corners, but the identity of the quilt maker (or the recipient) is not known. Certain features of the quilt suggest a Pennsylvania Mennonite or possibly Midwest Amish origin. The bedcover is all cotton, not the fine wools used by early Pennsylvania Amish quilt makers; Pennsylvania Mennonites and Midwest Amish more often selected cotton for their quilts. The undulating feather quilting pattern in the bedcover is related to that used on Pennsylvania Amish quilts, but the hearts, large curving leaves, fanlike flowers, and bulbous tulips suggest a non-Amish, possibly Mennonite, origin (fig. 140a). Finally, the narrow binding is more typical of a Pennsylvania Mennonite or Midwest Amish quilt; Pennsylvania Amish bindings tend to be wider.

The quilt is backed with the same green cotton as that in the front borders and is quilted with green cotton.

Figure 140a
Quilting pattern.

NINE PATCH VARIATION QUILT

FIGURE 141

Pieced in a variation of Nine Patch, this quilt has vibrant contrasting solid colors that enliven the simple building block of three rows of three squares each. The pieced center is worked with both hand and machine stitches and is contained within a narrow inner border and a wide outer border that are typical of Amish design. The bedcover is quilted with black running stitches in parallel diagonal lines, fans, and scallops, or clamshells. The quilting is not as finely drawn or executed as it is in most Amish examples. The backing is solid-purplish cotton, now faded to beige, brought to the front to form an edge binding.

Artist Michael Oruch, the previous owner, purchased the quilt in Clark, Missouri, an Amish community founded in the 1950s.[15] The apparent early date of the textiles and colors (especially the yellow-orange color sometimes known as "cheddar") suggests that the quilt was made well before the 1950s, probably in Ohio or Pennsylvania, and brought to Missouri when an Amish family moved west.

Numbers and initials, some backwards, worked with quilting stitches into the inner border are not entirely decipherable. They may refer to an unknown recipient and a date of 1910.

Star Quilt Figure 140

Unknown Mennonite or Amish maker

Pennsylvania or Ohio, 1920–1960

Cottons

8–9 running stitches per inch

89 x 88 in. (226 x 224 cm)

Museum Purchase, funded by the Antique Collector's Guild
1979.609.2

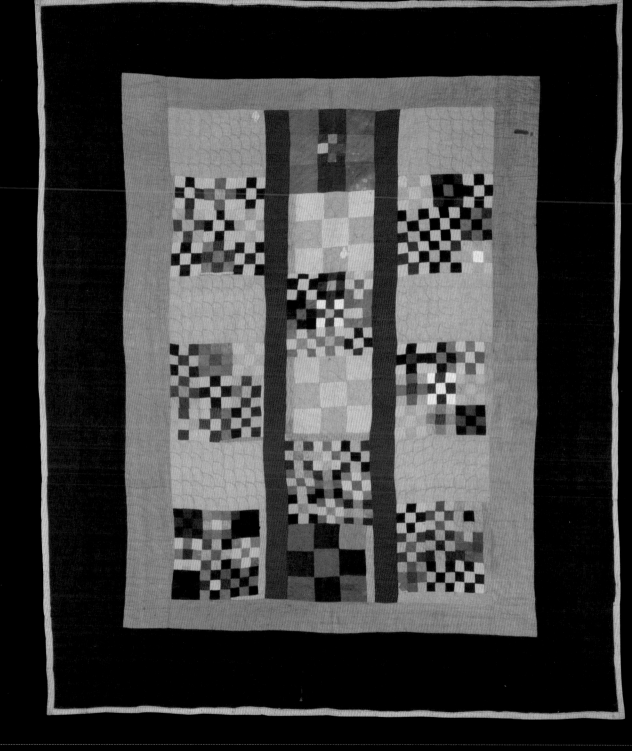

NINE PATCH VARIATION QUILT   FIGURE 141

Fans Quilt

FIGURE 142

This quilt achieves great visual impact through eccentric patterns and contrasting bright and dark hues in which multicolor fans stagger diagonally against a two-color ground with undulating feather quilting in the areas between fans (fig. 142a). Adding to the lively effect are remnants of pink thread stuck in the seams, suggesting that the outlines of the fans were once embroidered. This combination of pieced fans with embroidered outlines occurs in two documented Indiana quilts dating 1924 (fig. 142b) and circa 1934.[16]

It seems out of character for an Amish quilt maker to create such a bold design outlined with bright-pink needlework, a style that seems more suited to nineteenth-century silk show quilts (see chap. 20). By the time this quilt was likely made, however, embroidered show quilts had gone out of fashion, and the conservative Amish quilt maker felt comfortable embracing portions of the older style.

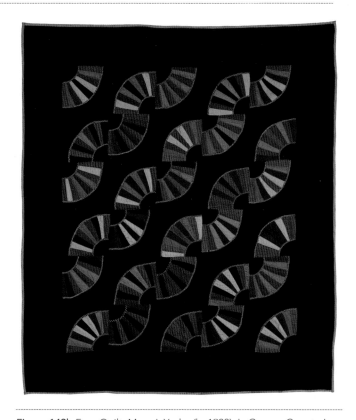

Figure 142b Fans Quilt, Mary J. Yoder (b. 1903), LaGrange County, Indiana, 1924, wools, 77¾ x 67½ in. (197 x 171 cm), courtesy Fort Wayne Museum of Art, Indiana, 1992.22.6. Mary Yoder's quilt still retains the decorative embroidery outlining the fans.

Figure 142a The quilting pattern follows the outlines of each fan and includes undulating feathers in the border and between diagonal rows of fans.

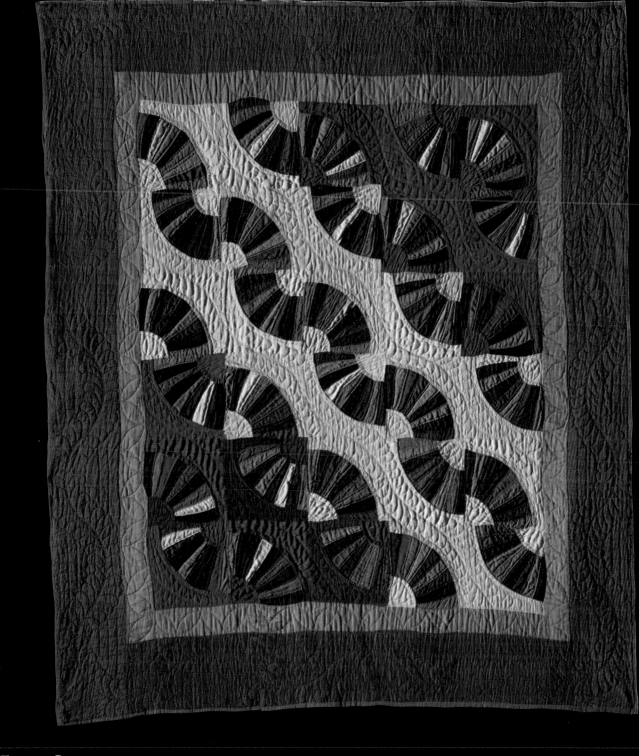

FANS QUILT   FIGURE 142

UNKNOWN AMISH MAKER

PROBABLY INDIANA, 1920–1935

WOOLS, COTTON-WOOL MIXTURES, COTTONS;
SILK EMBROIDERY THREADS (REMNANTS)

8 RUNNING STITCHES PER INCH

88½ X 74 IN. (225 X 188 CM)

MUSEUM PURCHASE, 1980.609.1

1   See Patricia T. Herr, "Bouquet of Applique," chap. 12 in *Quilting Traditions: Pieces from the Past* (Atglen, PA: Schiffer, 2000); and Clarke Hess, "Pieced Textiles: Quilts, Rugs, and Animals," chap. 12 in *Mennonite Arts* (Atglen, PA: Schiffer, 2002).

2   Eve Wheatcroft Granick, *The Amish Quilt* (Intercourse, PA: Good Books, 1989), 25–26, 29–31.

3   Granick, *Amish Quilt*, 31; and Janneken Smucker, Robert Shaw, and Joe Cunningham, *Amish Abstractions: Quilts from the Collection of Faith and Stephen Brown* (San Francisco, CA: Pomegranate Communications with Fine Arts Museums of San Francisco, 2009), 13–14. For more on Amish quilts, see Janneken Smucker, Patricia Cox Crews, and Linda Welters, *Amish Crib Quilts from the Midwest: The Sara Miller Collection* (Intercourse, PA: Good Books, 2003) and Rachel and Kenneth Pellman, *A Treasury of Amish Quilts* (Intercourse, PA: Good Books, 1990).

4   Janneken Smucker, *Amish Quilts: Crafting an American Icon* (Baltimore, MD: Johns Hopkins University Press, 2013).

5   Robert Bishop and Elizabeth Safanda, *A Gallery of Amish Quilts: Design Diversity from a Plain People* (New York: E. P. Dutton, 1976), 23.

6   Dorothy Osler, *Amish Quilts and the Welsh Connection* (Atglen, PA: Schiffer, 2011). See also Jen Jones, *Welsh Quilts: A Towy Guide* (Carmarthen, Wales, UK: Towy Publishing, 1997).

7   Nao Nomura and Janneken Smucker, "From Fibers to Fieldwork: A Multifaceted Approach to Re-examining Amish Quilts," in *Uncoverings 2006*, ed. Joanna E. Evans (Lincoln, NE: American Quilt Study Group, 2006), 123–156.

8   Granick, *Amish Quilt*, 79, 129, 137; and Bishop and Safanda, *Gallery of Amish Quilts*, 15–17.

9   Frances L. Bieler has not yet been located in Ephrata records.

10 A red-and-green cotton Mennonite quilt made for Ada R. Brubaker by her mother is discussed and illustrated in Herr, *Quilting Traditions*, 145. Another red-and-green cotton quilt made by Mary L. Landis and dated 1888 is published in Rachel and Kenneth Pellman, *A Treasury of Mennonite Quilts* (Intercourse, PA: Good Books, 1992), 33. See related but unsigned quilts made by the Amish King sisters in Donald B. Kraybill, Patricia T. Herr, and Jonathan Holstein, *A Quiet Spirit: Amish Quilts from the Collection of Cindy Tietze and Stuart Hodosh* (Los Angeles, CA: UCLA Fowler Museum of Cultural History, 1996), 138–139. Two similar, unsigned wool Amish examples are published in Bishop and Safanda, *Gallery of Amish Quilts*, 31, 37.

11 See examples in Patricia T. Herr, *Amish Quilts of Lancaster County* (Atglen, PA: Schiffer, 2004).

12 Bishop and Safanda, *Gallery of Amish Quilts*, 23.

13 Herr, *Quilting Traditions*, 57.

14 See related star pattern quilts in the following publications: Herr, *Quilting Traditions*, 98–104, Lone Star quilts made by Amish, Mennonite, and Church of the Brethren women in Pennsylvania; and Kraybill, Herr, and Holstein, *Quiet Spirit*, 204, 205, 208, 209, Ohio Star quilts.

15 The quilt was in Michael Oruch's collection at the time it was published by Eve Granick in *Amish Quilt* (34).

16 In addition to Mary Yoder's quilt (fig. 142b), see the embroidered fans quilt made by Lydia Whetstone of Shipshewana, IN, ca. 1934 in Kraybill, Herr, and Holstein, *Quiet Spirit*, 220–221. The authors thank Jim and Connie Thompson of Williamsburg, VA, and Leah Reeder of the Fort Wayne Museum of Art for assistance in researching this quilt design.

AFRICAN AMERICAN

CHAPTER 16

AFRICAN AMERICAN

Like those of other Americans, the quilts of African Americans vary considerably depending on the date, the location or community, the purpose for which the quilt was made, and the personal artistic vision of the quilt maker. Few quilts survive from the period of slavery in America. Nevertheless, surviving records make it clear that enslaved people made quilts for their own use, and some African Americans worked on quilts intended for white households (see fig. 127).

During the seventeenth century and the first half of the eighteenth century, bed quilts were expensive and relatively uncommon in almost all American households, whether white or black, free or enslaved. For warm bedding, the majority of colonists purchased woolen blankets produced in Britain or woven from the wool of local sheep.

Quilted clothing was more common than bed quilts in the earliest years of American settlement. Like most women, enslaved women sometimes wore quilted petticoats, or skirts, a fashion that continued throughout most of the eighteenth century until the advent of slim, neoclassical silhouettes in the 1790s made full petticoats obsolete. Newspaper advertisements for runaways are good sources for detailed descriptions of typical clothing. In 1735, eighteen-year-old Diana ran away in South Carolina wearing "an oznabrigs [coarse linen] jacket & quilted petticoat." In 1740, another eighteen-year-old, named Phillis, also combined a coarse linen jacket with a quilted petticoat: "Had on when she went away an Oznabrig Jacket, and a very old Silk quilted Petticoat." In 1775, a Virginia runaway named Road, born in New England, was described as someone who "affects gaiety in dress." The twenty-eight-year-old had on or took with her "a homespun striped jacket, a red quilted petticoat, a black silk hat, a pair of leather shoes, with wooden heals, a chintz gown, and a black cloak." It is not known whether these women had quilted their own petticoats or obtained ready-made imported English examples as new or secondhand goods, but there is ample evidence that enslaved women had the needle skills to do quilting. For example, a woman who ran away from a South Carolina subscriber in 1761 was described as being "an exceeding good seamstress," and another enslaved Charleston woman, named Molly, was "an extraordinary Needle-Woman, used to the Millinery Business."[1]

One advertisement for a runaway man suggests that the technique of appliqué was also known in the African American community at an early date, possibly brought over from Africa. An Angola-born man had on an unusual suit described as "white negro cloth [a substantial woolen fabric] jacket and breeches, with some blue between every seam, and particularly on the fore part of the jacket, a slip of blue in the shape of a serpent."[2] Suits of livery provided by slaveholders as uniforms sometimes combined two colors of woolen fabrics, such as this white with blue color combination. The serpent motif is not typical of livery, however, and the runaway may have decorated the suit himself, choosing to use the symbolic African snake.

By the nineteenth century, there is evidence for communal quiltings in the quarters, both to make bedcoverings and to socialize. Two enslaved house servants at Rose Hill in Cecil County, Maryland, attended a quilting party during the traditional Christmas holidays. On December 26, 1838, plantation owner Martha Ogle Forman wrote in her diary that "Harriet and Rebecca had a quilting party." Harriet, or Harriot, Batton and Rebecca Gilmore were about twenty-nine and twenty-six years old, respectively.[3] In Mississippi, another enslaved woman, named Martha Watkins, took part in a social event during the winter of 1861 that included quilt making as one of the activities: "We had a fine time last night with just our own people and Payton to play the violin and banjo, and Simon played on the tambourine. Susan had a quilting and after we got the quilt out they had to dance instead of a supper." Quiltings were often associated with hospitality and food. Martha Watkins continued, "John's barrel of flour has not arrived from St. Louis. I have sent for a barrel too. I will have my quilting next Saturday night. I want my flour to come so I may have a supper."[4]

While it is abundantly clear that enslaved and free African Americans made quilts, there is no evidence from period sources that they used quilts to relay secret signals or codes on the Underground Railroad. The suggestion of a secret quilt code appears to have come to the attention of historians in the second half of the twentieth century. Author-photographer Roland Freeman heard about a connection between quilts and the Underground Railroad in the 1950s when he was a boy.[5] Scholar Gladys-Marie Fry briefly mentioned the use of quilts for communication in her 1990 book, stating, "Quilts were used to send messages. On the underground railroad, those with the color black in them were hung on the line to indicate a place of refuge (safe house)."[6] In 1993, Deborah Hopkinson wrote a children's book, *Sweet Clara and the Freedom Quilt*, that told the story of a quilt that was used to help slaves escape to freedom. Shortly after that, author Jacqueline Tobin met a Charleston African American quilt seller named Ozella Williams who told a similar story about quilts being used to communicate on the Underground Railroad. Williams subsequently elaborated on her story and described secret meanings attached to quilt squares. Based in part on Ozella Williams's accounts, Tobin teamed with Raymond Dobard to write the book *Hidden in Plain View*.[7]

Since the 1990s, however, a new generation of scholars has been unsuccessful in corroborating the story of an Underground Railroad quilt code through historical evidence, including histories of the Underground Railroad and first-person written accounts of escaped slaves. The same scholars argue that the belief in the quilt code is myth.[8] But myths carry truth in symbolic form. The Underground Railroad quilt code speaks of larger truths: that enslaved people did make quilts for functional warmth and as an artistic outlet; that quilts were often hung outdoors, perhaps to air or to dry after washing; that quilts often held meanings and symbols, sometimes known only to the maker or to the immediate group; and that many enslaved individuals did escape to freedom through personal and communal efforts.

Many African American quilts survive from the late nineteenth and twentieth centuries, and others remain to be identified through family histories and genealogical research. The quilts cannot be identified by appearances alone, however. Although African Americans often produced everyday, practical quilts made from strips, or "strings," of reused textiles assembled in asymmetrical or improvisational designs and tied together or quilted with long stitches, similar quilts were also made by white women in the United States, Great Britain, Australia, and elsewhere. Utilitarian quilts responded more to scarcity and expediency than to cultural norms or design ideas (see chap. 17).[9]

Because the biographies and work of many African American quilt makers have now been published, scholars are beginning to identify groups of African American quilts that share design relationships.[10] The distinctive narrative quilts of Harriet Powers, born near Athens, Georgia, may have been part of a regional style influenced by remembered or passed-down African textile designs.[11] Dora Smith's quilt (fig. 150), believed to have been made in nearby DeKalb County, Georgia, shares similarities of technique and iconography with Harriet Powers's two surviving works in their use of appliquéd symbolic elements, including abstract human figures, crescent moons, crosses, and eye motifs.

Twentieth-century quilts from the vicinity of Gee's Bend, Alabama, form another distinctive group. Gee's Bend quilts are especially well documented and famous for their strong designs, innovative use of color and pattern, asymmetry, and free adaptation of traditional quilt patterns (see figs. 146–148). Many African Americans of Gee's Bend trace their ancestry back to antebellum workers on the plantation owned by Mark Pettway, who assigned his name to all of the enslaved, whether they were related to each other or not.

LOG CABIN QUILT TOP

FIGURE 143

Log Cabin quilts are considered foundation piecing, in which the individual pieces making up the top are stitched to a foundation textile that forms a base and is eventually covered by the pieces (fig. 143a). In Log Cabin, the quilt maker works from the center out to the edges of each smaller unit, building up the design with carefully chosen rectangles of fabric that represent the logs of the cabin. This unfinished quilt top was constructed of 110 small foundation squares, each having a red or pink square center. The quilt maker carefully chose and assembled the colors to create a stunning design of dark and light diamonds. The textiles are mostly patterned dress silks, along with some upholstery fabrics and ribbons.

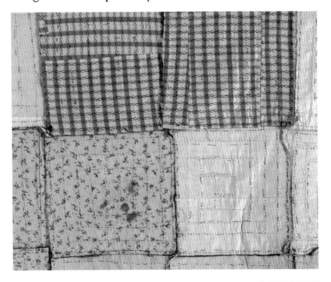

Figure 143a A detail of the back of the Log Cabin quilt top shows the cotton foundation squares onto which the silk pieces were stitched.

About the QUILT MAKER The quilt was made and descended in an African American family whose members lived in Illinois, Missouri, and Ohio. The last family member to own the quilt was Helen Edmonia McWorter Simpson of Cleveland, Ohio. Helen sold the quilt to Jean Jackson in the 1970s, at which time Helen was moving to an assisted living facility. The Jackson family helped their widowed neighbor undertake the move.[12]

Helen McWorter Simpson's ancestors can be traced back to enslaved families, although the quilt was made after slavery was outlawed. The most well-known family member was her great-grandfather, a former slave named "Free Frank" McWorter, who founded the town of New Philadelphia, Illinois.[13] The quilt was probably made by Helen's mother or one of her grandmothers. Her mother, Edmonia V. Parker, was born about 1869 and married John E. McWorter in 1892 in Missouri. The paternal grandmother, Frances Jane Coleman, married Solomon McWorter in 1863; the couple worked as farmers in Illinois.[14]

In all likelihood, however, the quilt maker was Helen's maternal grandmother, Anna Jane Parker, who was born about 1841 in North Carolina. By 1860, she was the wife of Charles E. Parker and living in St. Louis. According to Helen, her grandmother Parker "sewed beautifully" and worked as a seamstress. Anna Jane was still working as a dressmaker in 1910, at which time she was a widow living with Edmonia and John McWorter, her daughter and son-in-law. Helen, their daughter and a teenager at the time, probably observed her grandmother's craftsmanship firsthand. Anna Jane would have had the sewing skills and access to dress silks for creating the colorful quilt.[15]

Log Cabin Quilt Top Figure 143

Relative of Helen Edmonia McWorter Simpson
(Mrs. Gordon Henry Simpson), possibly Anna Jane Parker,
(Mrs. Charles E. Parker) (b. ca. 1841)

Missouri or Illinois, 1875–1900

Silks, cottons

78½ x 74 in. (199 x 188 cm)

Gift of Jean and Jerry Jackson, 2012.609.1

APPLIQUÉD COUNTERPANE

This dynamic bedcover is an expressive example attributed to an African American stitcher. Composed as a collage of cotton and silk textiles with lace, braids, beads, buttons, and shade pulls, the bedcover borrows baskets of flowers and wreaths from traditional American album quilts, blends them with motifs and colors that relate to African textile arts, and arranges them in a manner suggestive of fashionable late nineteenth-century crazy quilts. Gladys-Marie Fry, who once owned the quilt, suggested that many of the motifs reflect African cosmology. Fry believed that the angels beneath the central cross memorialized two young African American sisters who died in one of the epidemics of the early twentieth century. Their white faces symbolize the fact that they are no longer living.[16]

The bedcover lacks any batting or quilting stitches. The diverse materials are fastened to white cotton ground fabric using a variety of stitching methods, including traditional appliqué with slip stitches, chain and running stitches worked close to the edges, and machine stitching. Some of the cotton shapes were gathered up prior to being stitched to the ground, creating texture and depth. Yellow cotton satin backing was brought to the front to form a wide border.

FIELD OF DIAMONDS QUILT

FIGURE 145

Although eight-pointed stars appear in the design of this quilt, Emma Russell called it the "Field of Diamonds." Because of her choice of colors, the stars seem to fade and reappear, creating ambiguity as to whether the stars or the diamonds predominate. This rhythmic placement of colors gives variety to an otherwise symmetrical design. The quilting is worked with running stitches through a white backing.

About the QUILT MAKER   Emma Russell, the daughter of quilter Phoeba Johnson, grew up in Mississippi and moved to Bienville, Louisiana, after her marriage to Will Henry Russell. She made this quilt for Clayton Pierce, a New Jersey collector. Her handwritten letter to him on a piece of lined paper torn from a spiral notebook states:

> This is your quilt, the Field of Diamonds, in Puff Pieces. [I] hope you will like it. Will and I both are up, and doing very well at Present, Thanks to our Lord. I just keep Buisy, with My sewing. Hope you get this package, and let me know if you are satisfied with it. Greetings from the two of us. . . .
>
> P. S. I havent' heard from the Bank, since I cashed the check, from N. J.[17]

Emma reported to scholar Roland L. Freeman that Will helped her to quilt on occasion. Emma is also known for pictorial appliquéd quilts that tell stories of her memories and speak of her religious beliefs.[18]

Appliquéd Counterpane   Figure 144

Unknown African American maker

Possibly Baltimore or New York State, ca. 1920

Cottons, silks; lace, braid, beads, shade pulls,
Buttons; wool embroidery threads

88 x 70 in. (224 x 178 cm)

Museum Purchase, 2000.609.7

FIELD OF DIAMONDS QUILT FIGURE 145

EMMA RUSSELL (MRS. WILL HENRY RUSSELL) (1908–2004)

BIENVILLE, LOUISIANA, 1987

COTTONS, POLYESTERS

6–7 RUNNING STITCHES PER INCH

89 X 74½ IN. (226 X 189 CM)

MUSEUM PURCHASE, 2005.609.1

HOUSETOP QUILT

The Housetop pattern of concentric squares was a favored motif in the community of Gee's Bend. Rita Mae Pettway combined solid fabrics with polka dots, a Southwest-inspired print, and printed teddy bears.[19] The bedcover is hand quilted and backed with white that was brought to the front to form a narrow edge finish.

About the QUILT MAKER Rita Mae Pettway, known as Rabbit, was reared by her grandparents Annie E. and Ed O. Pettway after her mother's death when Rita Mae was only four years old. Annie and Ed also helped to rear their great-grandchildren, including Louisiana P. Bendolph, who later recalled memories of her childhood on the farm and having to work in the cotton fields: "My mom [Rita Mae] worked hard to make our life better than hers. . . . She was a single mom with five kids by then, and we had to work in order to survive. Life was hard, but we did what we had to."[20]

Despite a life of hard physical labor, the women found time to quilt and pass their knowledge to the next generation. When she was about six or seven years old, Louisiana and her siblings played under the quilt while their mother, their great-grandmother, and two aunts all joined in stitching together: "We would sit under the quilt and I would watch the needle going in and out of the fabric. I loved watching and playing under the quilts."[21]

Rita Mae approached her quilt making with an artist's eye. She recounted that she would hang quilts on the line in the yard to analyze their design: "During the summertime when I'm making them, that's when I used to hang them out there and just stand out in the yard. And sometime I walk down the road and look at them from the opposite side, then back on that side. . . . I was looking for a design that I had put in it. A lot of times when you're making a quilt, you can't really see the design in it until you get a good piece away from it, or either after you finish it."[22]

COAT OF MANY COLORS QUILT

Arlonzia Pettway grew up and quilted in the community of Gee's Bend, Alabama. Arlonzia combined rectangles of cotton and silk velvets, textured polyester double knits, plain-woven cottons patterned with flowers and geometrics, plaids, fragments of a printed dashiki from the late 1960s, and a print incorporating portions of the phrases "Coca-Cola" and "It's the real thing," the Coke motto from 1969. The rectangles are set on angles to create a lively zigzag pattern. The quilt is backed with two different machine-quilted fabrics, and quilted by sewing machine through all the layers. Holes have been patched with pieces of red fabric.

About the QUILT MAKER Arlonzia Pettway was one of the founding quilters in the Freedom Quilting Bee, a sewing and quilting cooperative established in 1966

to help poverty-stricken Gee's Bend residents earn money using their skills. Their quilts were sold in New York at auction and later at Bloomingdale's. Arlonzia quilted for the bee during its first five years but found the requirement for standardization too confining: "Used to worry me to death trying to make every quilt just like this, just like that, but I did."[23]

Arlonzia learned to quilt from her mother, Missouri. Arlonzia was a teenager when she helped make a memory quilt using the clothing of her deceased father, Nathaniel Pettway. "It was when Daddy died. I was about seventeen, eighteen. He stayed sick about eight months and passed on. Mama say, 'I going to take his work clothes, shape them into a quilt to remember him, and cover up under it for love.'" Arlonzia recalled tearing up her father's pants and shirts and cutting them to shape for her mother's quilt.[24]

Housetop Quilt   Figure 146

Rita Mae Pettway (b. 1941)

Gee's Bend, Alabama, ca. 1990

Cotton, polyester

5 running stitches per inch

73 x 78 in. (185 x 198 cm)

Museum Purchase, Dr. and Mrs. T. Marshall Hahn Jr. Fund, 2008.609.10

Coat of Many Colors Quilt FIGURE 147

ARLONZIA PETTWAY (1923–2008)

GEE'S BEND, ALABAMA, CA. 1970

COTTONS, SYNTHETICS

MACHINE QUILTED

91 X 81½ IN. (231 X 207 CM)

MUSEUM PURCHASE, DR. AND MRS. T. MARSHALL HAHN JR. FUND
2008.609.11

Indiana Bendolph Pettway selected a standard Lone Star pattern for this quilt but adapted the traditional design in dramatic black and white, with small additions of geometric-patterned printed cotton shading from grey to blue. Beneath the white areas of relatively thin double knit can be seen older printed cotton used as a filling. The quilt is backed with a daisy print in yellow, orange, brown, and white that was brought to the front to form the narrow edge finish.

About the QUILT MAKER   Indiana Pettway grew up in poverty in Gee's Bend, Alabama, an isolated community consisting mostly of rural African Americans descended from enslaved families (fig. 148a). Her sister Nettie Jane later recorded in an interview how she and Indiana had learned to quilt: "Mama started me out making quilts. I done it with my sister three years older than me. Her name was Indiana, same as Mama. Mama and Indiana and me was the ones making quilts. Papa used to buy what they call quilt rolls for Mama to make quilts out of. It was scrap cloth. All sort of mixed-up stuff. We used old clothes sometime, if they wore out but was still fittin' to put in a quilt."[25]

Figure 148a In this photograph of the Patrick and Indiana Bendolph family from Gee's Bend, Alabama, daughter Indiana, the maker of the Lone Star quilt, is second from the left. Photo by Arthur Rothstein, 1937, Library of Congress, Prints and Photographs Division, FSA-OWI Collection.

LONE STAR QUILT FIGURE 148

INDIANA BENDOLPH PETTWAY (1913–1996)

GEE'S BEND, ALABAMA, CA. 1970

COTTON, POLYESTER

3–4 RUNNING STITCHES PER INCH

80 X 79½ IN. (203 X 202 CM)

MUSEUM PURCHASE, DR. AND MRS. T. MARSHALL HAHN JR. FUND, 2008.609.8

FIGURE 149

With its abstract geometry and free running stitches, this quilt relates to some examples made at Gee's Bend in Wilcox County, which is adjacent to Dallas County, where this quilt maker lived. The quilt is pieced in an asymmetrical design based on rectangular strips of cloth, a style sometimes called a *string quilt*. The strips include plaid and solid textiles made of wool, cotton, and synthetics in a startling combination of subdued and brilliant colors. The bright-yellow strips placed at a ninety-degree angle at the corner are echoed by the small patch of yellow that adds sparkle to the more subdued blue and brown plaids. The white cotton hand-quilting stitches seem to deliberately ignore the outlines of the piecing and are, instead, arranged in random vertical, horizontal, and slanted rows. Blue cotton backing is brought to the front to form a binding at the top and bottom. The coarse batting in the quilt consists of unrefined cotton from the local gin, with fragments of seeds and stalks still present.

About the QUILT MAKER Alberta Miller[26] (fig. 149a) made this quilt as a high-school graduation gift for her employer's young white neighbor Olivia Alison, who took it to college with her. Alberta worked for about twenty years as a housekeeper and babysitter for the Sam and Carol Sommers family, who lived next door to the Alisons.

Figure 149a Quilt maker Alberta Miller, probably 1970s, courtesy Carol Sommers.

FIGURE 150

The maker of this appliquéd quilt incorporated initials ("DS") and letters that spell out words ("CATS," "DOGS," "BOYS," and "GIRL") and names ("LIZA," "AMOS," "RUTH," and "TOBY") inside circles on the quilt blocks. Appliquéd motifs were also taken from domestic life and the environment, including scissors, a kettle, stars, the moon, crosses, snakes, abstracted human figures, a hand, and an eye. The quilt maker turned under the raw edges of the appliqué motifs and fastened them to the ground textile with running stitches about one-eighth inch from the edges. The quilting is worked with running stitches through cotton batting and white cotton backing. The embroidered numbers "01" in the center of the "DS" panel may refer to the year 1901 (fig. 150a).

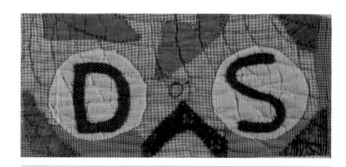

Figure 150a Detail.

About the QUILT MAKER Dora Smith's identity as the quilt maker comes from the initials DS appliquéd on the bottom right panel and longtime oral tradition. James Allen, the dealer from whom Colonial Williamsburg acquired the quilt, noted that it came from "a black family in Decatur, DeKalb County, Georgia. The maker's name is

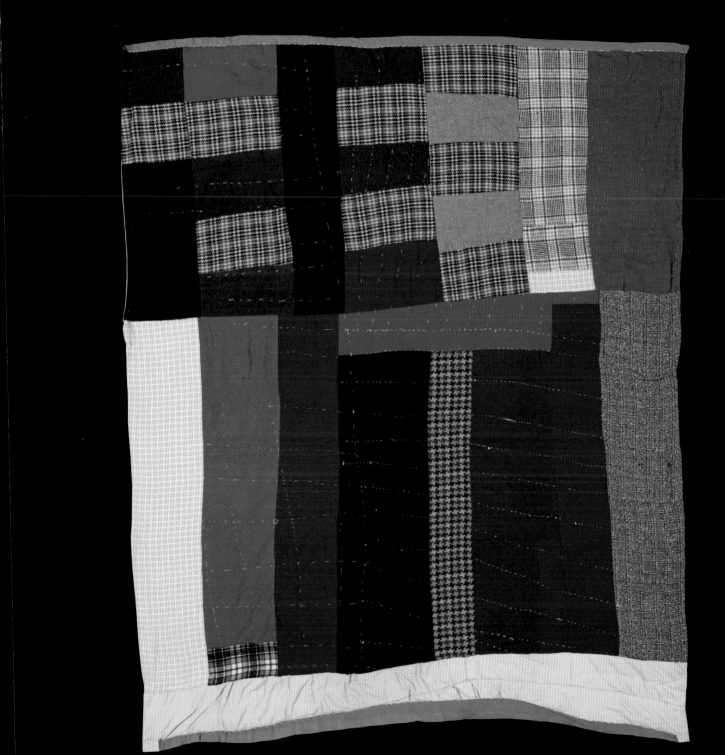

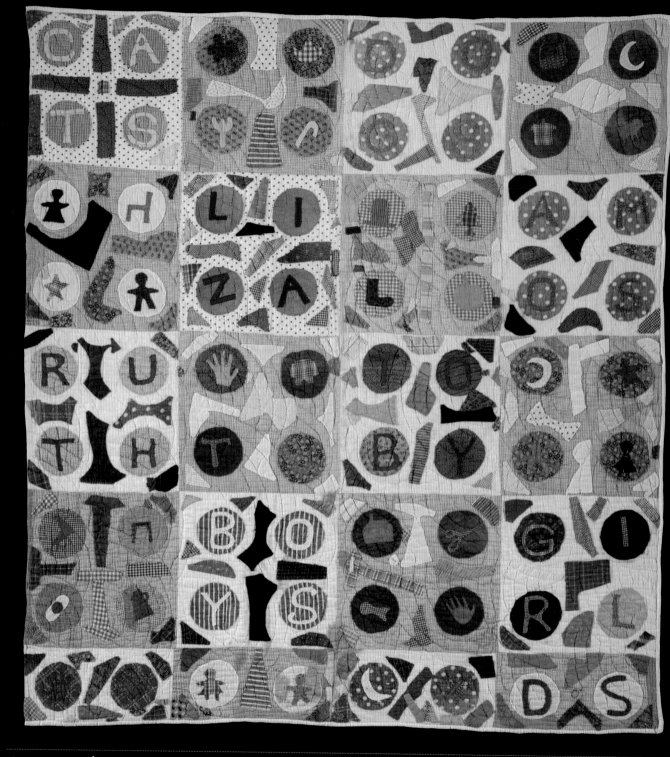

Appliquéd Quilt Figure 150

Dora Smith

DeKalb County, Georgia, probably 1901

Cottons

5–6 running stitches per inch

73 x 67 in. (185 x 170 cm)

Museum Purchase, 1996.609.1

Dora Smith."[27] Allen had purchased the quilt twenty years earlier, after it had passed from the original owner's family through the hands of two different dealers. The tradition passed down with the quilt is that the names were those of the quilt maker's children. Although genealogical research reveals the existence of several African American women living in Georgia with the name Dora Smith, none of the women located thus far had children named Liza, Amos, Ruth, or Toby.

Although the life details of Dora Smith are still a mystery, her quilt reveals her literacy and artistry. Her technique and designs bear a resemblance to those of the more-famous quilt maker Harriet Powers, also from northern Georgia. The quilts of Harriet Powers retold biblical stories she must have heard in church. Dora Smith's quilts were less obviously religious in nature. Nevertheless, both women shared the use of celestial motifs, such as stars and moons, in addition to motifs of snakes, human hands, eyes, and simplified human figures.[28]

notes for AFRICAN AMERICAN

1   *South-Carolina Gazette* (Charleston), July 19, 1735, September 20, 1740, April 18, 1761, and December 21, 1769; and Pinckney's *Virginia Gazette* (Williamsburg), June 15, 1775.

2   *South-Carolina and American General Gazette* (Charleston), December 11, 1770.

3   *Plantation Life at Rose Hill: The Diaries of Martha Ogle Forman, 1814–1845*, ed. W. Emerson Wilson (Wilmington: Historical Society of Delaware, 1976), 404, 449.

4   Martha Watkins to Mary "Molly" Watkins, January 27, 1861, in E. Grey Dimond and Herman Hattaway, eds., *Letters from Forest Place: A Plantation Family's Correspondence, 1846–1881* (Jackson: University Press of Mississippi, 1993), 197–198. Martha Watkins was an enslaved servant. Sarah Watkins, the mistress of the household, served as scribe for Martha in this letter to Molly, Sarah's daughter.

5   Roland L. Freeman, *A Communion of the Spirits: African-American Quilters, Preservers, and Their Stories* (Nashville, TN: Rutledge Hill Press, 1996), 15.

6   Gladys-Marie Fry, *Stitched from the Soul: Slave Quilts from the Ante-Bellum South* (New York: Dutton Studio Books, 1990), 65. Fry does not provide a source for her information.

7   Jacqueline L. Tobin and Raymond G. Dobard, *Hidden in Plain View: The Secret Story of Quilts and the Underground Railroad* (New York: Doubleday, 1999).

8   Laurel Horton, "The Underground Railroad Quilt Code: The Experience of Belief," in *Uncoverings 2007*, ed. Joanna E. Evans (Lincoln, NE: American Quilt Study Group, 2007), 207–216; and Barbara Brackman, *Facts and Fabrications: Unraveling the History of Quilts and Slavery* (Lafayette, CA: C & T Publishing, 2006).

9   See Bets Ramsey, "The Land of Cotton: Quiltmaking by African-American Women in Three Southern States," in *Uncoverings 1988*, ed. Laurel Horton (San Francisco, CA: American Quilt Study Group, 1988), 22–23. Pieced cotton utilitarian quilts made by Acadians in Louisiana, originally of French descent by way of Canada, are described and illustrated by Jenna Tedrick Kuttruff, "Three Louisiana Acadian Cotonnade Quilts: Adding Pieces to a Puzzle," in *Uncoverings 1999*, ed. Virginia Gunn (Lincoln, NE: American Quilt Study Group, 1999), 63–86. Australian waggas were utilitarian patchwork quilts made of humble fabrics, such as flour sacks or scrap woolen clothing and blankets. Their abstract designs relate to African American utilitarian quilts. See Annette Gero, *Historic Australian Quilts* (New South Wales, AUS: Beagle Press for the National Trust of Australia, 2000), 84–95; Annette Gero, "The Folklore of the Australian Wagga: A Distant Cousin of the Pennsylvania Hap," in *Pieced by Mother: Symposium Papers*, ed. Jeannette Lasansky (Lewisburg, PA: Oral Traditions Project of the Union County Historical Society, 1988), 61–67; and Annette Gero, "The Fabric of Waggas and Wonderful Stories," in *The Fabric of Society: Australia's Quilt Heritage from Convict Times to 1960* (Sydney, AUS: Beagle Press, 2008), 198–231. For British examples of utilitarian quilts, see Janet Rae, "In the Frame," and Margaret Tucker, "The Quiltmakers," in Janet Rae, et al., *Quilt Treasures of Great Britain: The Heritage Search of the Quilters' Guild* (Nashville, TN: Rutledge Hill Press, 1995), 26, fig. 18, and 143, fig. 112.

10 See Fry, *Stitched from the Soul*; Freeman, *Communion of the Spirits*; Maude Southwell Wahlman, *Signs and Symbols: African Images in African-American Quilts* (New York: Studio Books, 1993); and John Beardsley, William Arnett, Paul Arnett, and Jane Livingston, *The Quilts of Gee's Bend* (Atlanta, GA: Tinwood Books, 2002).

11 Fry, *Stitched from the Soul*, 84–91; and Sandi Fox, *Wrapped in Glory: Figurative Quilts and Bedcovers, 1700–1900* (New York: Thames and Hudson; Los Angeles, CA: Los Angeles County Museum of Art, 1990), 136–141.

12 Jean Jackson subsequently gave the quilt to Helen Brewster, her sister-in-law, who decided it was too rare and fragile to hang in her house and returned it to Jean. Helen Simpson's only child, Helen Eugenie Simpson (1934–1972), was advertising, promotion, and publicity manager for an NBC-owned television station in Cleveland. She was found shot in her car in 1972, and the case was never solved. "Top Woman at Cleveland TV Station Found Slain," *Jet* 42, no. 24 (September 7, 1972): 44; and U. S. Social Security Death Index (SSDI), 1935–current, s.v. Helen Simpson, online database, Ancestry.com (2011).

13 Free Frank had been born into slavery in 1777 in South Carolina, sent to Kentucky, and eventually purchased his own freedom and that of his wife, Lucy (b. 1771), his children, and several grandchildren. He left enough money to purchase the freedom of the remaining grandchildren after his death in 1854. He had moved his family to Illinois in the winter of 1830–1831 and became a successful farmer and the founder of the town of New Philadelphia, now a National Historic Landmark. He eventually petitioned to take a last name, McWorter, which was granted by an act of the Illinois state legislature in 1837. The order reads, "On the 19th day of January was approved an act of the Legislation of the State of Illinois . . . changing the name of Free Frank to that of Frank McWorter

and also providing that all the children of said Free Frank should thereafter take the name of their father as changed and provided for by said act." Helen McWorter Simpson, *Makers of History* (Evansville, IN: Laddie B. Warren, 1981), I, 11. See also Juliet E. K. Walker, *Free Frank: A Black Pioneer on the Antebellum Frontier* (Lexington: University Press of Kentucky, 1983).

14 Simpson, *Makers of History*, 2, 15, 37; Carles E. Parker household, 1880 U. S. census, Saint Louis, MO, enumeration district 130, page 294D, National Archives and Records Administration (NARA) microfilm T9, roll 729, digital image as found on Ancestry.com (2010); John E. McWorter household, 1900 U. S. census, Ward 26, St. Louis, MO, enumeration district 397, page 2B, NARA microfilm T623, roll 900, digital image as found on Ancestry.com (2004); and Walker, "Descendants (Partial) of Free Frank and Lucy McWorter," in *Free Frank*.

15 Simpson, *Makers of History*, 43; Chas E. Parker household, 1860 U. S. census, Ward 8, St. Louis, MO, page 714, NARA microfilm M653, roll 652, digital image as found on Ancestry.com (2009); and John E. McWorter household, 1910 U. S. census, Ward 26, St. Louis, MO, enumeration district 415, page 1A, NARA microfilm T624, roll 822, digital image as found on Ancestry.com (2006). The census taker misidentified Edmonia as "Edwina."

16 Conversation with author (Baumgarten), December 16, 2004.

17 Emma Russell to Clayton Pierce, [1987], CWF object file 2005.609.1.

18 Freeman, *Communion of the Spirits*, 38–39, 42. For examples of Emma Russell's religious quilts, see ibid., 91–92. See Freeman also for more biographical information and a photograph of Emma and Will H. Russell. For Emma's birth and death dates, see SSDI, 1935–current, online database, Ancestry.com (2011).

19 The Milwaukee Art Museum, WI, has a similar quilt made by Rita Mae Pettway that uses identical Southwest-inspired printed cotton (M2003.85).

20 Louisiana P. Bendolph, "A New Generation of 'Housetops,'" in *Gee's Bend: The Architecture of the Quilt*, ed. Paul Arnett, Joanne Cubbs, and Eugene W. Metcalf Jr. (Atlanta, GA: Tinwood Books, 2006), 189–190.

21 Ibid., 189.

22 Ibid., 215.

23 Arlonzia Pettway in Beardsley et al., *Quilts of Gee's Bend*, 31–32.

24 Arlonzia Pettway in Jane Livingston, "Work Clothes," in *Gee's Bend: The Women and Their Quilts* (Atlanta, GA: Tinwood Books, 2002), 73.

25 Nettie Jane Kennedy in Beardsley et al., *Quilts of Gee's Bend*, 110.

26 Alberta Miller's birth and death dates are from the SSDI, 1935–current, online database, Ancestry.com (2011).

27 Invoice, James E. Allen to Abby Aldrich Rockefeller Folk Art Center, August 15, 1996, CWF object file 1996.609.1.

28 Gladys-Marie Fry first pointed out the relationship between the quilts of Harriet Powers and this one by Dora Smith. Conversation with author (Baumgarten), December 16, 2004.

CHAPTER 17

Make Do

MAKE DO

Textiles and the materials for making quilts could be expensive, and frugal housewives have often mended, patched, remade, and recycled old clothing and home furnishings. Petticoats were one item of clothing often quilted (see fig. 151), and when fashion made them obsolete, they were sometimes incorporated into bed quilts. Women saved bed sheets and old coverlets to use as backings for newly made quilts and covered worn quilts with new textiles to extend their useful lives. Miss Eliza Leslie's *Lady's House-Book* even instructed readers to recover white Marseilles counterpanes after they became worn, thus repurposing the original machine-woven materials into a new role as the filling for a handmade quilt: "The surface of a Marseilles quilt, being fine and thin, soon wears off. They may afterwards be covered with an outside of fine, white, thick muslin, and quilted over again."[1] Women who made paper-template quilts recycled old letters and newspapers for the purpose, sometimes leaving the papers inside for additional insulation.[2] By the early twentieth century, many women used fabric flour or feed sacks to make quilts and other useful items, such as dish towels, underwear, and children's clothing.

Utilitarian and "make do" quilts range from works of artistry to practical warm coverings. Although some of them are fragile and ragged, they tell stories of survival, hard work, and frugality, and they often exhibit enduring beauty that can be appreciated years after they have served their original function.

Figure 151 Petticoat, Abigail Trowbridg, Connecticut, 1750, silks and wools, 18–21 half backstitches per inch in border design areas, 12 running stitches per inch in upper portion, length 36 in. (91 cm), circumference 130½ in. (331 cm), Museum Purchase, 1952-19. Despite the modern connotations of the term, petticoats were not necessarily underwear but rather women's skirts intended to be visible through the open-front gowns fashionable at the time. The several yards of material in the garment could contribute to a handsome bed quilt. This quilted petticoat features animals, human figures, and a coat of arms, typical of motifs used in a group of quilted petticoats from Connecticut around the middle of the eighteenth century (see fig. 152).

Bed Quilt made from a Petticoat

FIGURE 152

This bed quilt tells an interesting story of change over time. Full skirts and quilted petticoats fell out of fashion after styles shifted to slim skirts just before 1800. Sometime in the late eighteenth or early nineteenth century, the enterprising owner of a quilted petticoat made this bed quilt from her old-fashioned garments. She cut the petticoat in two and restitched the pieces together with the hems abutting. Scraps left over from a damask gown became flounces to drape the sides of the bed. Made of material originally imported from China, the damask gown was certainly out of fashion by the time the quilt was assembled, but the silk was still strong and potentially useful. Loose threads on one of the narrow extensions suggest that a third ruffle was once stitched in place on the quilt to hang over the foot of the bed.

The petticoat making up the center of the bedcover is part of a group of distinctive and unusual wholecloth quilted pieces that appear to be unique to Connecticut and Rhode Island.[3] Most of the surviving examples are petticoats with fine silk or worsted-wool fronts quilted through wool batting with relatively heavyweight woolen backing fabrics (see fig. 151). What makes these New England products truly extraordinary are the lively and varied quilted animals, many with large circles for eyes and parallel quilted channels on their bodies, giving them a skeletal appearance. The distinctive designs were probably the work of a professional pattern drawer or schoolteacher.[4] The teacher or pattern drawer must have been trained in traditional English needlework patterns of the late seventeenth century because many of the designs can be traced back to needlework and published design sources from that period.

The quilting is distinctive not only in design but also in technique. Rather than using running stitches, quilters of the New England animal-motif group used backstitches spaced a short distance apart in the intricate borders. The spaced backstitch, also called *half backstitch,* allows for tighter curves and denser designs than does the running stitch (see fig. 3). In most examples in this group, the grids above the petticoat borders are worked with running stitches because simple linear designs do not require time-consuming backstitching to delineate them.

The quilted portion of this bedcover is beige plain-woven silk, quilted with yellow silk using half backstitches in the dense design areas and running stitches elsewhere. The natural-color wool batting and light-brown wool backing added warmth and weight to the delicate silk face. The complex design includes a modified version of the British lion and unicorn royal arms. The arms are dwarfed by a large basket of flowers above. Flowering branches and a cornucopia coexist with playful animals, birds, and a pear tree with a man and his dog beneath. The date 1761 is stitched into the branch of the pear tree (fig. 152a).

The quilt was found around 2005 in the attic of a Providence, Rhode Island, house owned by a member of the Goddard family.

Figure 152a Drawing of the petticoat panels that were cut apart and reassembled to make the quilt. The short vertical line at the top of the right panel was the original slit for giving access to a pocket worn under the petticoat; the slit is now sewn shut.

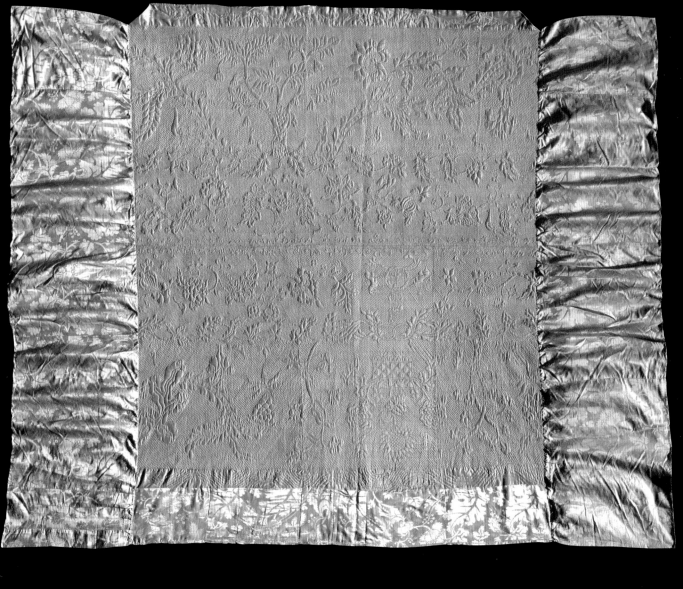

Bed Quilt made from a Petticoat Figure 152

Maker unknown

Connecticut or Rhode Island, 1790–1830, petticoat 1761

Silks, wools

14–16 half backstitches and running stitches per inch

85½ x 105 in. (217 x 267 cm)

Museum Purchase, 2006-58

Petticoat made from a Bed Quilt

FIGURE 153

While some bed quilts incorporated quilted petticoats as part of their fabric (see fig. 152), this remarkable petticoat was actually made from one end of a bed quilt that originally had a wide border on all four sides. Sometime in the eighteenth century, the creative seamstress cut one end of the flat quilt to skirt length, sewed the left and right outer edges together to form a center back seam, and pleated the skirt to a narrow waistband. Although the resulting garment included the areas where the quilt's border turned the corners, this design anomaly would have been worn at the back, hidden by a gown's skirt, which typically covered the sides and back of a petticoat, leaving the border design visible only at the center front.

The fine satin of the face is quilted to a backing of rich blue plain-woven glazed worsted, and the batting is a thin layer of wool fibers. The piece is quilted with silk running stitches.

The last owners of the petticoat, Jean Chichister Hollerith Case and her family, from whom Colonial Williamsburg acquired it, believed it descended through their Beverley ancestors, the Virginia side of the family. Subsequent research, however, revealed that the quilted two-handled vases, sunflowers, abstracted fan shapes, and peaked scallops in the borders closely resemble the motifs on other pieces made in Philadelphia's Quaker community around the middle of the eighteenth century that may have been drawn by a schoolteacher or professional designer (see also fig. 23).[5] This research led curators to reattribute the garment to the Philadelphia Quaker branch of the family. The original owner of the quilt (later the petticoat) may have been Philadelphian Elizabeth Mickle, who married Joseph Fox, the son of Justinian Fox, the family patriarch, in 1746.[6]

Figure 153a Drawing of the quilting design on the petticoat made from one end of a cut-up bed quilt. Note that the quilt's design turns at the outer edges; these areas were joined to create a center-back seam on the petticoat and would have been hidden by the gown skirt.

Petticoat made from a Bed Quilt FIGURE 153

Member of the Fox family, possibly Elizabeth Mickle Fox (Mrs. Joseph Fox) (1729–1805)

Philadelphia, Pennsylvania, probably 1770–1790, bed quilt probably 1750–1765

Silks, wools

11–12 running stitches per inch

Length 39½ in. (100 cm), circumference 96¼ in. (244 cm)

Partial gift of Jean H. Case, Sarah H. Nietsch, and Lucia B. Lefferts, 2005-299

RESIST BLOCK QUILT

FIGURE 154

This charming quilt is a good example of how frugal early Americans recycled old materials. The indigo-resist linen floral pattern and the block-printed cotton border were imported to America and probably originally used as fashionable bed curtains and coordinating edge bindings. After the curtains had faded or gone out of fashion, a family member made a simple block-pattern quilt by piecing two sizes of square indigo prints to rectangles of white cotton and quilting them in a diamond pattern. The white cotton backing was brought to the front to form the narrow edge binding.

The quilt descended from Joseph Davison (1754–1842)[7] or his son William of Franklin County, Pennsylvania.

QUILT WITH EARLIER PLATE-PRINTED BACKING

FIGURE 155

Textile furnishings for tall-post bedsteads contained many yards of valuable material that could be reused when the hangings became outdated or one panel was damaged. This quilt maker reused old bed hangings to back her pieced quilt. Printed in the China-blue technique using copperplates, the large-scale pattern of pheasants and other birds with flowers and peacock feathers can be identified as English and dated to the late eighteenth century because of the presence of blue threads in the selvages.[8] According to British law at the time, blue threads in the selvages indicated that the textile was all cotton and printed in England between 1774 and 1811. Careful examination reveals that the maker reused two double-wide bed curtains, without removing their original linen seaming stitches or quarter-inch turned-up hems. Each curtain contains two selvage widths of the original textile stitched together with linen thread and measures about 48½ inches wide by about 77 inches long. Because the curtain panels were too small to cover the entire quilt back, the maker added smaller pieces of the same textile at the edges. The later seams and quilting stitches were worked with cotton, typical of nineteenth-century threads. The printed textile was brought around the edges to the front to form a narrow edging.

The pieced face of the quilt combines multicolor roller-printed cottons in an assortment of floral, geometric, and plaid designs alternating with white cotton, forming an Irish Chain pattern (fig. 155a). A single eight-pointed star anchors each of the four corners. The quilting stitches follow the piecing but also include six-petal flowers within the white squares. The border has an undulating linear design combined with six-petal flowers, leaf shapes, and triangles. The pencil lines are still visible, clearly traced around a circular shape that was used as a drawing template.

Colonial Williamsburg purchased the quilt from Timothy and Betsy Trace, dealers in New York.

Figure 155a Detail of quilt face.

Resist Block Quilt   Figure 154

Member of the Davison family

Franklin County, Pennsylvania, textiles 1750–1780, probably pieced and quilted 1800–1830

Linens, cottons

8 running stitches per inch

83½ x 83¼ in. (212 x 211 cm)

Gift of Sandra F. Fisher, 2005-329

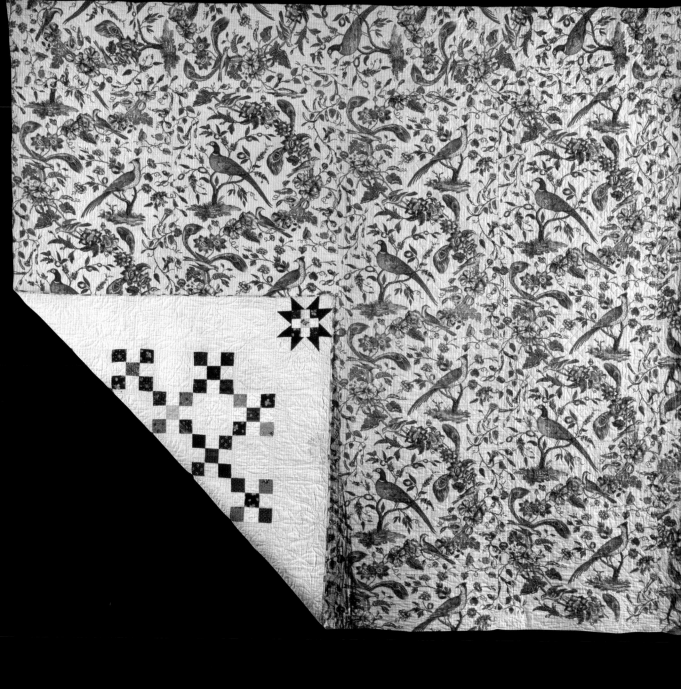

QUILT WITH EARLIER PLATE-PRINTED BACKING   FIGURE 155

MAKER UNKNOWN

ENGLAND OR UNITED STATES, 1840–1850, BACKING 1790–1800

COTTONS, LINEN

8–10 RUNNING STITCHES PER INCH

90 X 103¾ IN. (229 X 264 CM)

MUSEUM PURCHASE, 1966–80

Quilt with Printed Counterpane Backing

FIGURE 156

On one side, this colorful quilt consists of fifty-six squares set on point, each pieced from squares and triangles of blue and brown cottons and alternating with cotton in a bright orange-yellow color sometimes referred to as "cheddar." The quilting is worked with white and dark-brown running stitches in a concentric fan pattern, and the quilt is finished with straight-grain binding. Although the quilt maker must have been proud of her newly fashionable pieced quilt with its bright colors, the reused backing consisting of an old printed bedcover is of considerably more interest to scholars today.

Examples of early American block printing are rare. The printed counterpane that survives as the quilt's backing reflects the patriotism of early nineteenth-century Americans in its use of the country's national symbol—spread eagles in three different sizes—alternating with starlike medallions. The printing is crude, unlike that of the sophisticated imported textiles available at the time (see fig. 54a), yet the printer assembled smaller printing blocks in a creative way to make a one-of-a-kind bedcover for his client. The ground textile consists of three fabric widths, seamed before printing. Because the printed counterpane was slightly too small to back the finished quilt, the maker added plain and checked cotton strips to the edges.

The person who sold the quilt to Colonial Williamsburg acquired it from a dealer, who had in turn purchased it from an unnamed ninety-three-year-old woman living in Greensboro, North Carolina. The North Carolina history of this example is strengthened by the existence of a related printed counterpane also found in that state.[9]

Paper-Backed Quilt Top

FIGURE 157

An unknown Texas quilt maker cut up old Fort Worth newspapers to use as templates for the multisided pieces of her cotton bedcover; the square pieces in the center of each design unit, however, were apparently not supported with paper. Never completed or quilted, the pieced textile survives with most of the fragile acidic papers still intact (fig. 157a). The newspapers disclose a slice of life in the region, revealing women's fashions, news features, and cartoons from the years 1913 and 1914. The maker selected fragments of everyday ginghams, stripes, and prints for the quilt top, which is based on a pattern of encroaching hexagons with squares on point at the centers. Despite the fact that an organized pattern can be detected, many of the pieces are, in turn, pieced up themselves, creating an abstract effect that is not unlike that of a crazy quilt.

The donor received the quilt top from her sister, who got it from a friend in Virginia. It is not known who made the quilt or how it got to Virginia.

Figure 157a Detail. The back shows the Fort Worth, Texas, newspapers used as templates or inexpensive filling.

Quilt with Printed Counterpane Backing   Figure 156

Maker unknown

North Carolina, 1860–1880, backing 1800–1830

Cottons

4–5 running stitches per inch

89 x 80½ in. (226 x 204 cm)

Museum Purchase, 1982-172

Paper-Backed Quilt Top Figure 157

Maker unknown

Vicinity of Fort Worth, Texas, 1913–1914

Cotton, newspapers

76 x 68 in. (193 x 173 cm)

Gift of Carol E. Harrison, 2007.609.4

Work-Clothes Quilt

FIGURE 158

Few quilts exemplify the concept of "making do" better than this practical, sturdy, and warm denim quilt. The thrifty maker cut apart old denim overalls and jeans, removed the pockets to reveal less-faded colors underneath, and reassembled the flattened pieces to make a quilt top. She tied the quilt through heavy cotton batting and backed it with fertilizer sacks with barely legible words turned to the inside of the quilt. Under infrared lighting, the primary words can be deciphered as "[PLA]NTERS / . . . PLANT FOOD / . . . MIXTURE / . . . 10-6" and "PLANTERS / CORRECT PLANT FOOD / SPECIAL MIX[TURE] / 3-12-6" (fig. 158a).

This work-clothes quilt is not unique. Several rural African American women from Alabama also made them (see fig. 202).[10] A textile dealer found this quilt in Elizabethtown, Kentucky, and donated it to an art auction charity, where it was purchased and kept for many years by a private owner. Eventually, the purchaser took the quilt back to the original dealer to resell, at which time Colonial Williamsburg purchased it.

Figure 158a Detail. Infrared photography reveals faint stamped words on old fertilizer sacks used as the quilt backing. The writing was turned to the inside of the quilt, but the photograph has been flipped to make the words more legible. Photograph by John Watson.

Pieced Quilt

FIGURE 159

This quilt top is constructed from a wide variety of checked, striped, and solid cottons and cotton-wool mixtures in blues, light browns, and off-whites and backed with larger-scale plaid cotton of blue and brown. The pieces document important but ephemeral utilitarian textiles once used for clothing and household furnishings. The quilting is worked with black running stitches in a pattern of concentric fans through thick cotton batting.

Although fragile and much worn, the charming quilt documents the popular Alamance plaids made in that county of northern North Carolina since the mid-1850s.

In 1880, seven mills in Alamance County were producing the popular cotton plaids, and by 1884, the Southern Plaid Manufacturers' Association represented 2,300 plaid looms. By the early 1890s, the textiles were exported throughout the southern states and as far away as New York, California, and Wisconsin.[11] The quilt itself is utilitarian in its choice of materials and design, making use of scraps and small pieces stitched together in a slightly haphazard pattern that echoes the popular crazy quilts of the day.

The quilt descended from the donor's grandparents Edwin H. Hines and Margaret Gurley Hines, who married in 1877. They were Quakers and farmers in Wayne County, North Carolina.[12]

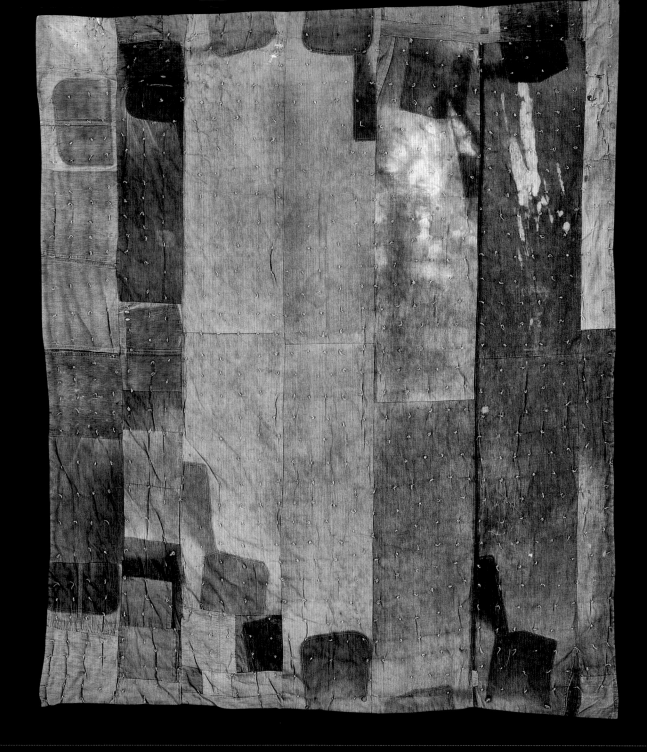

WORK-CLOTHES QUILT FIGURE 158

MAKER UNKNOWN

KENTUCKY, PROBABLY ELIZABETHTOWN, 1930–1950

84 X 69½ IN. (313 X 177 CM)

MUSEUM PURCHASE, DR. AND MRS. T. MARSHALL HAHN JR. FUND,
2008.609.9

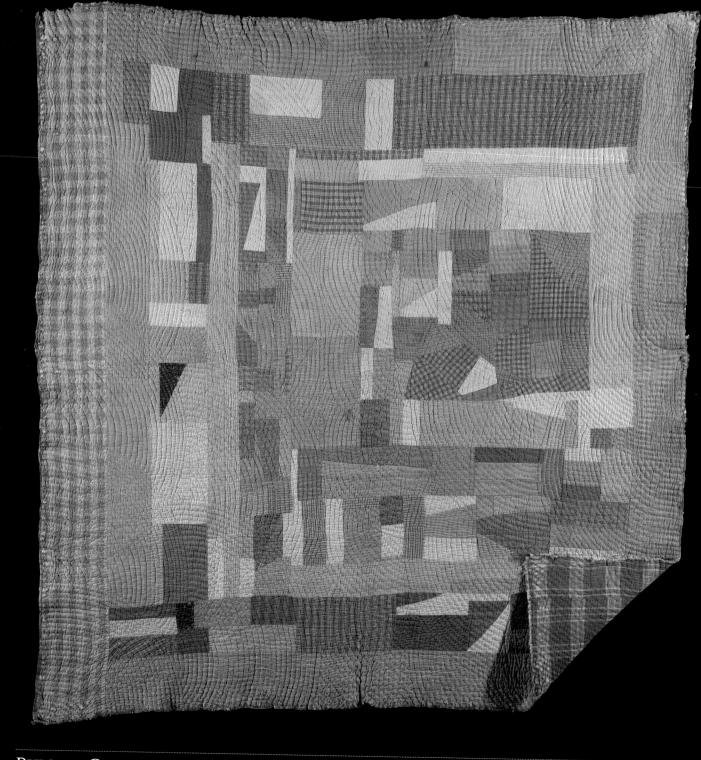

Pieced Quilt Figure 159

Member of the Gurley or Hines family, probably
Margaret Gurley Hines (Mrs. Edwin Hines) (b. ca. 1852)

Wayne County, North Carolina, 1880–1910

Cottons, cotton-wool mixtures

4 running stitches per inch

76½ x 74 in. (194 x 188 cm)

Gift of Mrs. Robert (Faye) Kilpatrick, 2012.609.3

1   [Eliza Leslie], *Miss Leslie's Lady's House-Book; A Manual of Domestic Economy* (Philadelphia: A. Hart, late Carey & Hart, 1850), 311.

2   Cuesta Benberry suggested that newspaper templates were used in the African American community, sometimes serving as inexpensive batting. *A Piece of My Soul: Quilts by Black Arkansans* (Fayetteville: University of Arkansas Press, 2000), xiv–xv.

3   For a complete discussion of the quilted objects and their design sources, see Linda Baumgarten, "The Layered Look: Design in Eighteenth-Century Quilted Petticoats," *Dress* 34 (2007): 7–31. Other examples related to the group are found in these museum collections: Colonial Williamsburg Foundation (1951-445, 1994-88, and 1951-150, 2); Historic Deerfield, MA, published in Lynne Z. Bassett, *Telltale Textiles: Quilts from the Historic Deerfield Collection* (Deerfield, MA: Historic Deerfield, 2003), 12–13; Los Angeles County Museum of Art, CA, several details published in Sandi Fox, *Wrapped in Glory: Figurative Quilts and Bedcovers, 1700–1900* (London: Thames and Hudson; Los Angeles, CA: Los Angeles County Museum of Art, 1990), figs. 9–10; Yale University Museum Art Gallery, New Haven, CT (1949.137); Rhode Island School of Design, Providence, a petticoat fragment reused as the center of a bed quilt, published in Linda Welters, "A Petticoat Quilt," in *Down by the Old Mill Stream: Quilts in Rhode Island,* ed. Linda Welters and Margaret T. Ordoñez (Kent, OH: Kent State University Press, 2000), 197–200; and Connecticut Historical Society, Hartford, (1959.54.2) published in Susan P. Schoelwer, *Connecticut Needlework: Women, Art, and Family, 1740–1840* (Hartford, CT: Connecticut Historical Society, 2010), 60–61.

4   Lynne Z. Bassett suggested that the petticoats were "probably made by girls under professional tutelage in a southeastern Connecticut school in the mid-18th century." *Telltale Textiles,* 12.

5   Bed quilts and petticoats closely related to this design include the following: quilt attributed to Mary Norris Dickinson or another family member, Stenton, James Logan's historic house in Philadelphia (1969.3.1); quilt owned by a member of the Emlen family, possibly Sarah, collection of Dr. and Mrs. Donald Herr; quilt that descended in Mifflin family, Winterthur Museum, Garden & Library, Delaware (1960.0787); quilt said to be a 1752 wedding gift to Hannah Trotter Elfreth, Elfreth's Alley, Philadelphia (80.11); Waln family quilt, Ryerss Museum & Library, Philadelphia (27-007-01); quilt associated with Ann Skyrin, International Quilt Study Center & Museum, Lincoln, NE (2006.056.0017); petticoat owned by Jane Richardson McKinly,

Delaware Division of Historical and Cultural Affairs, Dover (1964.74); petticoat said to be the 1752 wedding petticoat of Hannah Cooper (later Mrs. Charles West), Philadelphia Museum of Art (P1947-8-1); and petticoat made and worn by Ann Marsh, Chester County Historical Society, West Chester, Pennsylvania (1992.644). The designs may be the work of mother and daughter Elizabeth and/or Ann Marsh, Quaker schoolteachers in Philadelphia. See Linda Baumgarten, "Vase-Pattern Wholecloth Quilts in the Eighteenth-Century Quaker Community," in *Uncoverings 2015,* ed. Lynne Zacek Bassett (Lincoln, NE: American Quilt Study Group, 2015), 7–34.

6   Jean H. Case and author (Baumgarten), telephone conversation, April 26, 2011; William Wade Hinshaw and Thomas Worth Marshall, *Encyclopedia of American Quaker Genealogy* (Ann Arbor, MI: Edwards Brothers, 1938), 2:364, 527, 596; and *The Diary of Elizabeth Drinker,* ed. Elaine Forman Crane (Boston: Northeastern University Press, 1991), 3:2150–2151.

7   "Pennsylvania, Veterans Burial Cards, 1777–1999," s.v. Joseph Davison, online database, digital image as found on Ancestry.com (2010).

8   A textile with the same design is found in the collections of the Winterthur Museum in Delaware. See Florence M. Montgomery, *Printed Textiles: English and American Cottons and Linens, 1700–1850* (New York: Viking Press, 1970), 253, fig. 253.

9   Colonial Williamsburg 1979-391. The linen-cotton counterpane is printed with a floral design. It was found in Snow Camp, NC.

10   See Joanne Cubbs, "A History of the Work-Clothes Quilt," in *Gee's Bend: The Architecture of the Quilt,* ed. Paul Arnett, Joanne Cubbs, and Eugene W. Metcalf Jr. (Atlanta, GA: Tinwood Books, 2006), 66–89.

11   Erma H. Kirkpatrick, "A Study of 'Alamance Plaids' and Their Use in North Carolina Quilts," in *Uncoverings 1988,* ed. Laurel Horton (San Francisco, CA: American Quilt Study Group, 1989), 45–56. See also Ruth Haislip Roberson, ed., *North Carolina Quilts* (Chapel Hill: University of North Carolina Press, 1988), 12–15, 19, 23–24.

12   Edwin H. Hines household, 1880 U. S. census, Fork, Wayne, NC, enumeration district 293, page 479A, National Archives and Records Administration (NARA) microfilm T9, roll 986, digital image as found on Ancestry.com (2010); and "North Carolina, Marriage Collection, 1741–2004," s.v. "Eddin Hines," online database, digital image as found on Ancestry.com (2007).

CHAPTER 18

POLYNESIAN

CHAPTER 18

POLYNESIAN

The geographic area known as Polynesia encompasses a number of islands in the South Pacific, including Samoa, Easter Island, the Cook Islands, New Zealand, the Hawaiian Islands, and French Polynesia, including Tahiti. Quilts made in Hawaii are perhaps the best known of the Polynesian types and most often represented in American quilt collections.

Although women in Hawaii have quilted in a number of styles, including piecing and crazy quilts, the classic Hawaiian quilt is unmistakable in appearance, usually consisting of a single large appliquéd symmetrical design of a tropical flower or foliage that covers the surface of the quilt. The appliqué is formed by folding a large piece of textile into fourths or eighths and cutting a preplanned design through all the layers, not unlike cutting a paper snowflake (see figs. 160, 161). The most typical color scheme consists of two solid colors, often a bright color on a light or white ground. After carefully basting the large motif to the ground textile, the quilter turns under and slip-stitches the raw edges to the ground. Once layered with batting and backing, the quilting often takes the form of contour, or echo, quilting of running stitches in parallel rows or waves that follow the outline of the appliquéd motif. Hawaiian quilts were the result of native culture blending with and responding creatively to contact with missionaries, merchants, and sailors from the West, in what has been called a "collision of Western and Polynesian worlds."[1]

Before contact with Westerners, Hawaiians and other Polynesians used their sewing and fiber arts skills to create bark-cloth textiles from the felted fibers of the paper mulberry tree. Used for clothing and bedding, these textiles were called *kapa* in Hawaii and *tapa* elsewhere in Polynesia. Westerners introduced woven textiles that were quickly adopted by native Hawaiians and other Polynesians. Westerners also brought sewing and quilting styles that eventually evolved into the classic Hawaiian appliquéd quilt by the middle of the nineteenth century. A number of influences went into the evolution of the Hawaiian quilt, among them album quilts with symmetrical folded-and-cut paper patterns that were especially fashionable on the mainland in the 1840s and 1850s (see fig. 162). Although the concept of using folded paper or textiles to create appliqué patterns may have come from outside, Hawaiian women themselves adapted the technique and made it uniquely theirs by greatly enlarging the scale and selecting designs inspired by tropical plants. Traditionally, Hawaiian women made quilts as gifts to commemorate family events, such as weddings and anniversaries, imbuing each quilt with a sense of tradition and love of family.[2]

The popularity of Hawaiian quilts in the twentieth and twenty-first centuries meant that more people wanted to purchase finished quilts or patterns to make their own quilts, and women sought to learn the techniques outside of Hawaii. What was once an intimate family-oriented process unique to the Hawaiian Islands took on international and even commercial characteristics. To meet the demand, some Hawaiian women made quilts to order, and others cut and basted patterns for sale. Eventually, Hawaiian-style quilts were copied in the Philippines and elsewhere for sale around the world.[3]

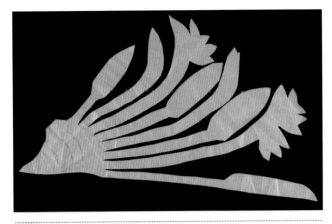

Figure 160 Paper Pattern, Agnes Kahoe (b. ca. 1891),[4] Hawaii, 1920s, 38½ in. wide (98 cm), gift of Lisa Noelani Tam-Hoy Robbins, 2012.609.7, 1. This paper pattern is one-eighth of a design for the center of a quilt. The quilt maker folded a large textile intended for the design into eighths, traced the paper pattern onto the folded textile, and then cut through all of the layers of the textile. When unfolded, the textile was ready to be appliquéd to the ground fabric of the quilt top. Below is a drawing showing the design as it might have looked at the center of a Hawaiian quilt (fig. 161). The paper pattern is inscribed in pencil "Bird Paradaiso," suggesting that the maker knew the design by the name of the flowering plant called bird-of-paradise. Agnes Kahoe was a traditional Hawaiian quilt maker who taught her daughter, Rose, to quilt (see figs. 163–166).

Figure 161 Drawing of Agnes Kahoe's Bird Paradaiso design as it would be seen on a quilt.

Other Polynesian Islands developed related traditions of quilt making. Scholar Phyllis Herda suggested that there was "an Eastern Polynesian quilting aesthetic" that was based on "the distinctive four-way symmetry of appliquéd quilts" in the region. The Cook Islands were the source of distinctive textiles sometimes confused with the better-known Hawaiian products. Women there made large-scale appliquéd panels that shared similarities in their construction with Hawaiian quilts: large pieces of fabric were cut from folded paper or fabric patterns, resulting in symmetrical designs that were first basted and then slip-stitched to the contrasting ground fabric. In the Cook Islands, however, no battings or backings were applied, despite the fact that the products were referred to as quilts or by the native term *tivaevae*. *Tivaevae* held ceremonial and social meaning and were presented at such events as births, first-birthday celebrations, weddings, and ceremonies to honor visiting dignitaries, where *tivaevae* were wrapped around the dignitaries' shoulders.[5]

Figure 162 Appliquéd Quilt Top, Sarah Elizabeth Haines Dunham (ca. 1837–ca. 1916) and Theodore Runyon Dunham (ca. 1834–ca. 1892),[6] Newark, New Jersey, ca. 1855, cotton, 84 x 77 in. (213 x 196 cm), gift of Mrs. John D. Green, 1972.609.3. Quilts appliquéd with designs from folded-and-cut paper templates may have influenced Hawaiian quilts.

Figure 163 Photograph of Rose Lokelani Lum Tam-Hoy, at left wearing hat, with Master Quilter Deborah "Kepola" Umiamaka Kakalia, Honolulu, Hawaii, probably 1970s, courtesy Lisa Noelani Tam-Hoy Robbins.

Figures 164, 165, and 166 Quilt Squares in Three Stages of Construction, Rose Lokelani Lum Tam-Hoy (1923–2011),[7] Honolulu, Hawaii, 1960–1995, cottons, polyesters, 6 and 8 running stitches per inch, 18¼ to 22½ in. square (46 to 57 cm), gift of Lisa Noelani Tam-Hoy Robbins, 2012.609.6, 1–3. Rose Lokelani Lum Tam-Hoy of Honolulu learned to quilt from her mother, Agnes Kahoe (see fig. 160). Rose taught traditional quilting at the Mission Houses Museum (now the Hawaiian Mission Houses Historic Site and Archives) in Honolulu, and squares such as these may have been used as demonstration projects. The green pineapple–design square survives with the needle still in position where it was abandoned during the appliqué process.

Appliquéd Quilt, Pōpō Lehua O Pana'ewa

Figure 167

This striking quilt is appliquéd in the Hawaiian style with solid-red cotton cut in a large-scale overall symmetrical design of scrolling leaves and flowers with a diagonal X running from corner to corner, a design that has been identified as *Pōpō Lehua O Pana'ewa*, depicting the flower *Ixora casei*.[8] Typical of Hawaiian products, the quilting is worked in concentric lines of stitching that follow the outline of the appliquéd motif, a technique called *contour quilting*.

Because the large design was cut in one piece from the folded textile, the approximately thirty-one-inch-wide red textile was first stitched together to create a piece large enough for the pattern. The quilt is backed with the same white cotton textile as the front and bound at the edges with red.

The quilt was found on the mainland with no known provenance. However, the word "Grewell" inked on a back corner suggests possible ownership. Genealogical and historical records reveal that several people with that name lived in or visited Hawaii.[9]

Appliquéd Ceremonial Tivaevae

Figure 168

The strong central motif of a radiating compass and the peace eagle corner spandrels in this appliquéd textile were achieved by carefully folding and cutting a solid-red cotton fabric that was then stitched to a white cotton ground fabric. The bold, large pattern and cutting technique reflect Polynesian aesthetics and a strong indigenous tradition.

The appliquéd coverlet descended in the family of Vice Admiral William C. Cole (1868–1935). A label written by a Cole family member and attached to the textile states, "When Rear Admiral Wm Carey Cole landed in Honolulu . . . a Hawaiian chief draped this around his shoulders" (fig. 168a). Admiral Cole did travel to Hawaii with the U. S. Navy, corroborating part of the family history. In 1908, he served as navigator on the battleship USS Kansas when it sailed to Honolulu and eventually on to New Zealand, where the sailors were greeted with much fanfare "as heroes."[10]

Despite the family history of a Honolulu origin for this textile, research suggests that the story may not be entirely accurate. A group of presentation textiles, or *tivaevae*, with American eagle motifs similar to the ones on this piece, has been identified from eastern Polynesia, especially the Cook Islands.[11] It is possible that the family correctly remembered only part of the ceremonial textile's story and that Admiral Cole received it while visiting the Cook Islands or New Zealand during the same journey that his ship also stopped at Honolulu.

Although these ceremonial coverlets were never intended to be quilted, they were nevertheless called "quilts" in the Cook Islands.[12]

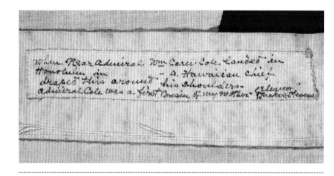

Figure 168a Detail. A handwritten cloth label attached to the appliquéd textile alleges that Admiral Cole received the ceremonial textile in Honolulu, where it was draped around his shoulders. It is more likely, however, that he received it in the Cook Islands or New Zealand, where nonquilted *tivaevae* were sometimes presented in this manner to honored guests.

Appliquéd Quilt, Pōpō Lehua O Pana'ewa Figure 167

Maker unknown

Hawaiian Islands, 1950–1975

Cottons

6 running stitches per inch

85½ x 83½ in. (217 x 210 cm)

Museum Purchase, Dr. and Mrs. T. Marshall Hahn Jr. Fund, 2011.609.6

Appliquéd Ceremonial Tivaevae   Figure 168

Maker unknown

Polynesia, probably Cook Islands, ca. 1908

Cottons

109½ x 99¼ in. (278 x 253 cm)

Museum purchase, Dr. and Mrs. T. Marshall Hahn Jr. Fund,
2003.609.1

1   Linda Boynton Arthur, *The Hawaiian Quilt: A Unique American Art Form* (Waipahu, HI: Island Heritage Publishing, 2010), 6.

2   Ibid., 21, 24–27.

3   Loretta G. H. Woodard, "Communities of Quilters: Hawaiian Pattern Collecting, 1900–1959," in *Uncoverings 2006*, ed. Joanna E. Evans (Lincoln, NE: American Quilt Study Group, 2006), 1–28.

4   Kealoka Kahoe household, 1940 U. S. census, Honolulu, HI, enumeration district 2-74, page 12A, National Archives and Records Administration (NARA) microfilm T627, roll 4585, digital image as found on Ancestry.com (2012).

5   Phyllis Herda, "*Tivaevae:* Women's Quilting in the Cook Islands," in *Uncoverings 2011*, ed. Laurel Horton (Lincoln, NE: American Quilt Study Group, 2011), 55–78, esp. 58 and 65. For more information on Polynesian quilts, see Joyce D. Hammond, *Tifaifai and Quilts of Polynesia* (Honolulu: University of Hawaii Press, 1986).

6   Theodore R. Dunham household, 1880 U. S. census, Newark, Essex, NJ, enumeration district 30, page 221A, NARA microfilm T9, roll 776, digital image as found on Ancestry.com (2010).

7   SSDI, 1935–current, s.v. Rose L. Tamhoy, online database, Ancestry.com (2011). Rose L. Tam-Hoy's life history is courtesy Lisa Noelani Tam-Hoy Robbins.

8   Woodard, "Communities of Quilters," 12. The authors thank Laurie Woodard and Julie Silber for identifying this pattern. Woodard located three quilts with the design when registering Hawaiian quilts. Julie Silber to author (Baumgarten), e-mail message, November 29, 2011.

9   Although the ink inscription could be a laundry mark, it may well be the name of a past owner. A woman named Jean Farriel Grewell, a resident of Hawaii, married Colorado resident Daniel Edward Leemaster on September 3, 1972. The quilt could have been a wedding gift to the couple from Hawaiian friends. Another possibility is that Illinois resident Bess Grewell could have brought the quilt back to the mainland during her sea voyage to Honolulu in April 1951. "Nevada Marriage Index, 1956–2005," s.v. Jean Farriel Grewell, online database, Ancestry.com (2007); and "Honolulu, Hawaii, Passenger and Crew Lists, 1900–1969," s.v. "Bess Grewell," online database, digital image as found on Ancestry.com (2009).

10 "Dictionary of American Naval Fighting Ships," Naval History and Heritage Command, Department of the Navy, s.v. "Kansas II" and "William C. Cole," accessed June 29, 2013, http://www.history .navy.mil/danfs/k1/kansas-ii.htm and http://www.history.navy.mil /danfs/w8/william_c_cole.htm.

11 Pamela Fitz Gerald, *Warm Heritage: Old Patchwork Quilts and Coverlets in New Zealand and the Women Who Made Them* (Auckland, NZ: David Bateman, 2003), 126. The textile published by Fitz Gerald has a peace eagle in each corner, similar to fig. 168; the piece published by Fitz Gerald was made in Rarotonga, the largest of the Cook Islands. Residents of the Cook Islands traveled freely between their home and New Zealand. See also Loretta G. H. Woodard, "Exploring Polynesian Design: Hawaiian, Tahitian, and Cook Island Quilts," *Blanket Statements* 84 (Spring 2006): 1, 3–5. The large coverlets were called *tifaifai* in Tahiti and *tivaevae* in the Cook Islands. The authors thank Dr. Phyllis Herda, Loretta Woodard, Gwen Wanigasekera, and Paula Karkkainen for sharing their research and for helpful correspondence about this group of ceremonial textiles.

12 Herda, "*Tivaevae,*" 58.

Red & White

CHAPTER 19

RED & WHITE

In the second half of the nineteenth century, red-and-white quilts became especially fashionable. Women featured the color scheme in quilts using a variety of construction techniques, including appliqué, piecing, and outline embroidery. The most desirable materials for the popular quilts were threads and textiles dyed Turkey red, the name given to the brilliant red in cotton textiles that had been dyed using a special process to make them color-fast. Turkey red was especially popular for items that had to be washed or immersed, including towels, bandana-style handkerchiefs, children's clothing, bathing suits, and, of course, quilts.

Believed to have been developed in India and adopted in the eastern Mediterranean, including areas controlled by Turkey, the Turkey-red process used the natural dyestuff madder and, later, synthetic alizarin. To achieve the brilliant color and fastness, the cotton had to be put through a lengthy process that included impregnation with oil and treatment with additional substances, one of which was the metallic salt alum, which served as a mordant, or color fixative. By the second half of the eighteenth century, French and later British dyers adopted the technology to produce Turkey-red cotton threads, and by the early years of the nineteenth century, they were able to produce finished cotton cloth dyed with the technique. The development of synthetic alizarin in 1868 eventually brought

the price down, though the complexity of the dye process still caused Turkey-red fabrics to be more expensive than ordinary, less-colorfast reds.[1]

An offshoot of the Turkey-red fashion was outline embroidery using colorfast red cotton floss to embroider onto white cotton or linen. Especially popular from about 1876 to 1930, outline embroidery embellished a wide variety of household furnishings: doilies, splashers tacked up to protect the wall behind washbasins, children's bibs, and bed quilts. Although some women drew their own designs to be embroidered, ladies' magazines and pattern companies also provided designs to be pounced or ironed onto white cotton or linen grounds. The iron-on transfer technique was developed in the 1870s and continued in use into the twentieth century.[2] Some companies sold squares with prestamped designs that were ready to embroider and make into quilts.

Red outline embroidery was sometimes known as Kensington or South Kensington embroidery, named for the Royal School of Art Needlework located in South Kensington, London. Embroidered textiles made by Royal School needleworkers were displayed in America at the 1876 Centennial Exhibition in Philadelphia and inspired a new generation of embroiderers to produce their own adaptations of the popular South Kensington products.

REDWORK OUTLINE EMBROIDERY DOLL QUILT

FIGURE 169

This quilt, sized for a doll's bed, features nine unrelated motifs spaced three across and three down. The designs came from commercial patterns transferred to the cloth through ironing or pouncing and tracing. The designs of the seated girl at the center and the girl jumping rope were sold by *Ladies' Home Journal* as perforated patterns ready for pouncing.[3] Simple linear designs in playful patterns such as these were considered suitable for children as their first embroidery projects. Some companies produced patterns and stamped pieces called *kindergarten squares* intended especially for children. This quilt, signed "Hattie. E. Mory / 5 Yrs. 8 Months / 1891," may well have been embroidered by Hattie and then quilted into a doll's bedcover by her mother. The embroidery is less skilled in execution than the quilting and binding.

About the QUILT MAKERS   Hattie E. Mory was the daughter of farmer John F. Mory and Ida M. Mory, his wife, of Salisbury Township, Pennsylvania. Hattie was born in May 1886.[4]

REDWORK OUTLINE EMBROIDERY QUILT

FIGURE 170

The maker of this child's quilt selected seventy-two small-scale patterns purchased from commercial sources either as pre-stamped squares or made to be transferred to the cloth through ironing or tracing. The squares include sunbonnet-wearing girls (Sunbonnet Sue or Sunbonnet Babies) performing tasks for the days of the week and celebrating the seasons. The Sunbonnet Baby designs match those offered for sale as prestamped squares in the early 1920s by the Ladies Art Company, which labeled the designs "Stamped Outline Embroidery Blocks for Nursery Quilts" (fig. 170a).[5] The quilt also includes nursery rhymes, flowers, animals, and birds. At the bottom of the quilt, a block showing a horse drinking from a water trough is labeled "A Temperance drink." The red of the cotton outline embroidery is given greater prominence by the precisely pieced narrow red sashing that forms a regular grid unifying the diverse embroidered designs.

Although the maker and provenance of the quilt are not known, the initials L and LWF are probably those of the maker, and the initials NYC positioned below a train suggest the origin of the quilt.

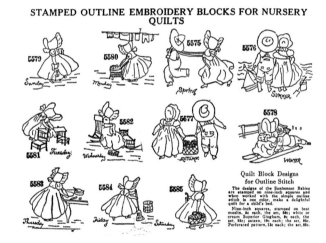

Figure 170a "Stamped Outline Embroidery Blocks for Nursery Quilts," Ladies Art Company, ca. 1922, courtesy the Deborah Harding Redwork Collection at the Michigan State University Museum, East Lansing. The quilt contains these designs of Sunbonnet Babies working and enjoying the four seasons of the year. Numerous patterns and prestamped blocks were available for purchase by embroiderers who chose not to draw their own designs.

Within the embroidery: *Hattie. E. Mory / 5 Yrs. 8 Months / 1891*

Redwork Outline Embroidery Doll Quilt   Figure 169

Hattie E. Mory (b. 1886) and Ida M. Mory (Mrs. John F. Mory)
(b. ca. 1863)

Pennsylvania, 1891

Cottons; cotton embroidery threads

7–10 stitches per inch

25¼ x 23¼ in. (64 x 59 cm)

Museum Purchase, funds donated in memory
of Gilbert and Irene Baumgarten, 2011.609.2

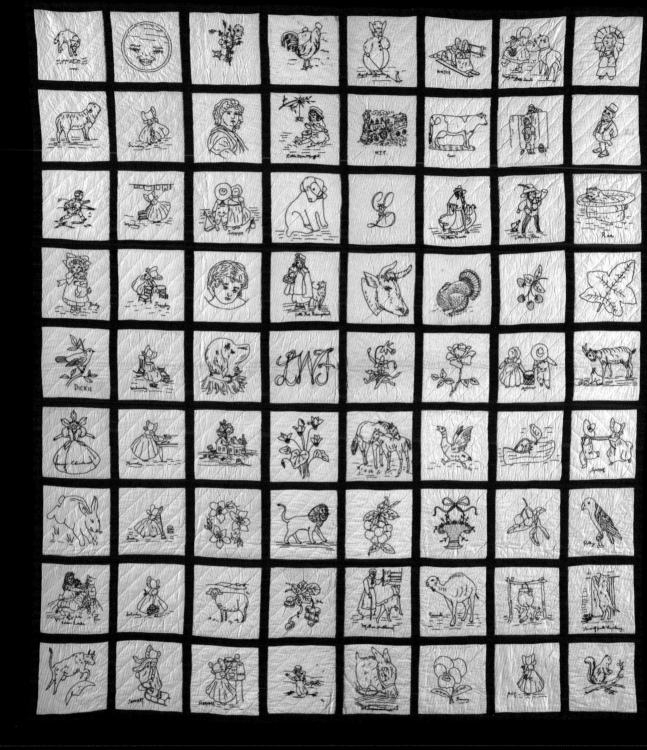

Redwork Outline Embroidery Quilt FIGURE 170

PROBABLY "LWF"

POSSIBLY NEW YORK, CA. 1925

COTTONS; COTTON EMBROIDERY THREADS

7–8 RUNNING STITCHES PER INCH

77 x 70 in. (196 x 178 cm)

MUSEUM PURCHASE, FUNDS DONATED IN MEMORY

DELECTABLE MOUNTAINS QUILT

FIGURE 171

Bright-red cottons are pieced together with white cottons into an array of jagged "mountains" that radiate from the center of the quilt, forming a design known as Delectable Mountains, used by many quilt makers throughout the nineteenth century (see figs. 118, 185, 186, 188, 189). The precisely spaced piecing and the bold two-color scheme create a visually stunning textile. To make the quilt more functional for use on a bed, the quilt maker lengthened the originally square design by adding an extra row of peaks at the top and at the bottom. The cover is hand quilted through thin batting and white cotton backing using running stitches in parallel lines and scallops. White cotton binding cut on the straight grain forms the edge finish.

The quilt descended in the donor's family, probably on her mother's side. The family was originally located in Galion, Ohio, before moving to Pittsburgh, Pennsylvania.

SCHOOLHOUSE QUILT

FIGURE 172

Schoolhouse quilts became popular between 1875 and 1920, when one-room schools were gradually fading from use and people began to look back on them with sentimental fondness. The twenty-five classic red schoolhouses in this quilt look haphazardly positioned at first glance. However, the buildings are arranged so they read correctly when laid on a bed: the two outside columns on either side of the quilt have their roofs facing toward the middle of the bed, with the middle column of houses alternating left and right lengthwise down the center of the bed. The lively arrangement gives added visual interest to the quilt. The quilting is worked in parallel rows through very thin batting to white cotton backing. Faint pencil lines show beneath the quilting stitches. The top, left side, and bottom are finished with bias binding; the right side is turned under and stitched but not bound, possibly indicating that the quilt has been repaired along that edge or cut down slightly.

SCHOOLHOUSES IN DIAMONDS QUILT

FIGURE 173

The popular schoolhouse quilts were made in a wide variety of designs. The twelve buildings in this quilt are set upright within diamonds created by angled narrow sashing. Instead of being made of solid-red cotton, the buildings here are cut from cotton printed in a geometric design that suggests bricks and shingles. The quilting, which was first drawn with pencil, is worked in curving lines that suggest lily flowers within the diamonds, and the border is quilted in waves.

DELECTABLE MOUNTAINS QUILT   FIGURE 171

MAKER UNKNOWN

PROBABLY PENNSYLVANIA OR OHIO, CA. 1900

COTTONS

9–11 RUNNING STITCHES PER INCH

78¾ X 70¾ IN. (200 X 180 CM)

GIFT OF MRS. MARSHALL STEEL JR., 2003.609.6

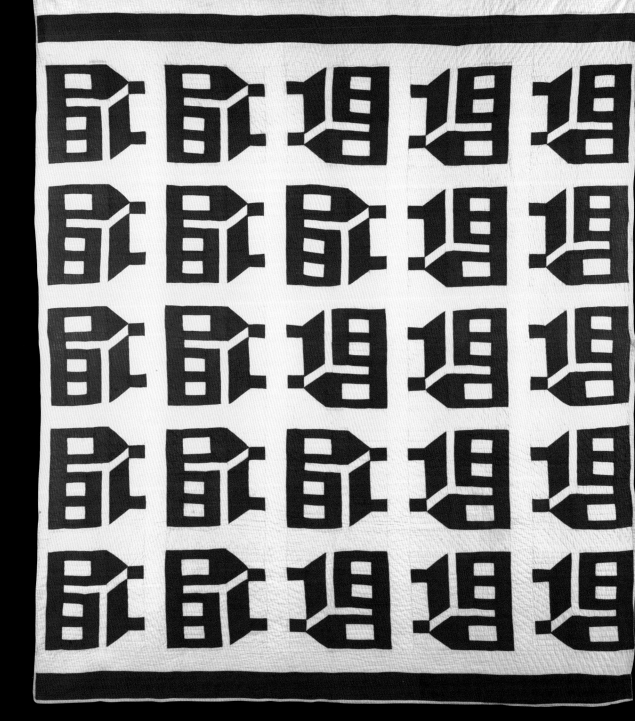

Schoolhouse Quilt Figure 172

Maker unknown

Probably New England, 1875–1890

Cottons

7 running stitches per inch

80¾ x 69¾ in. (205 x 177 cm)

Museum Purchase, gift funds in memory of Catherine M. Weekley, 2009.609.4

Schoolhouses in Diamonds Quilt Figure 173

Maker unknown

Probably New Jersey, 1900–1930

Cottons

5–6 running stitches per inch

71¼ x 74 in. (180 x 100 cm)

Museum Purchase, 2009.609.5

1   Deryn O'Connor, "Four Aspects of Turkey Red: The Process and Early History," *Quilt Studies* I (1999): 27–33. See also Barbara Brackman, *America's Printed Fabrics, 1770–1890* (Lafayette, CA: C & T Publishing, 2004), 62–65.

2   Deborah Harding, *Red and White: American Redwork Quilts and Patterns* (New York: Rizzoli, 2000), I:26.

3   Ibid., 53.

4   John F. Mory household, 1900 U. S. census, Salisbury, Lehigh, PA, enumeration district 49, page 34B, National Archives and Records Administration (NARA) microfilm T623, roll 1429, digital image as found on Ancestry.com (2004).

5   Harding, *Red and White*, 33.

CHAPTER 20

Show

CHAPTER 20

SHOW

In the last quarter of the nineteenth century when home beautification was a primary duty of Victorian housewives, the interest in show quilts reached its zenith. Most of these decorative quilts were smaller than bed-size quilts and generally intended more for show and admiration than for practical use. Frequently part of the decorative furnishings of the parlor—the Victorian woman's arena where she displayed her good taste and held court—show quilts were more likely to cover a table or piano than a sleeping family member! If used on a bed, they were not tucked in but laid on top over a more ordinary cover.

Show quilts were usually composed of silks and other fine fabrics. The seams of many were covered with fancy embroidery stitches in silk, filoselle, arrasene, and gold threads (see fig. 174).[1] Most show quilts, however, are not quilts in the truest definition of the word in that they rarely contain batting or quilting stitches.

Today, the most familiar show covers are crazy quilts, which were made primarily between 1880 and 1920. Actually, the term *crazy* is misleading. Despite the hodgepodge of irregularly shaped fabric swatches traditionally used in them, these types of covers were not composed haphazardly. The construction of a crazy quilt was usually well thought out and designed, and many quilts were the result of systematically arranged fabric shapes on a foundation within precise blocks.[2] The asymmetrical arrangements reflected the influence of the aesthetic movement in art

and design popularized at the 1876 Centennial Exhibition in Philadelphia and the stylish influence of Asia, especially that of Japan.[3] Originally referred to as Japanese bedspreads, the quilts, with their irregular designs, may have been inspired by Japanese ceramics with a cracked glaze, called *crazed* or *crackle*.

Numerous crazy quilts were further embellished with painted images, ribbons, lace, beads, sequins, and three-dimensional forms. Favorite motifs included spiders and webs, butterflies, flowers such as pansies and lilies, fans, Japanese vases, peacock feathers, symbolic images such as horseshoes and anchors, and Kate Greenaway figures. Some crazy quilts were not as elaborate, however, and were made using patches of sturdy wool and cotton fabrics with home-inspired motifs (see figs. 178, 179).

The fad for crazy quilts was an indicator of the country's economic prosperity at the close of the nineteenth century. Retailers offered for sale bags of silk swatches and pre-embroidered motifs for the creation of crazy quilts. Patterns and instructions for designs and stitches were also readily available.[4] Popular women's magazines such as *Peterson's Magazine* and *Godey's Lady's Book and Magazine* encouraged their readers to create crazy quilts, in addition to other highly decorative show quilts and home accessories.

Like other types of quilts, some crazy quilts were created as presentation quilts or in memory of loved ones (see fig. 177). And like album and friendship quilts, crazy quilts were also produced as a group effort with individuals contributing one or more blocks (see fig. 176). Some were made from fabrics worn by the person for whom the quilt was intended and/or contained symbols of the person, favorite flowers, special dates, outlines of hands, ribbons from meetings attended, and so on.

Figure 174 Detail of Virginia Album Crazy Quilt (fig. 177).

In their attempt to be fashionable, ardent housewives zealously stitched crazy quilts, attended crazy quilt shows, held crazy teas, and read short stories and newspaper articles about them. The *Decatur (IL) Morning Review* reported on April 23, 1891, "that a young lady living in the northern part of the city has a lovely crazy quilt made out of pieces taken from the pants of young gentlemen callers. Her father's dog is the cloth collector in the case, and he always takes his samples to his young mistress."[5] Poems were also written about crazy quilts. This poem satirizing the craze appeared in the magazine *Good Housekeeping* on October 25, 1890:

Oh, say, can you see by the dawn's early light,
　　What you failed to perceive at the twilight's last gleaming;
A crazy concern that through the long night
　　O'er the bed where you slept was so saucily streaming;
　　　　The silk patches so fair,
　　　　Round, three-cornered and square,
　　　　Gives proof that the lunatic bed-quilt is there.
Oh, the crazy-quilt mania triumphantly raves,
And maid, wife and widow are bound as its slaves.

On that quilt dimly seen as you rouse from your sleep
　　Your long-missing necktie in silence reposes.
And the filoselle insects that over it creep,
　　A piece of your vest half-conceals, half-discloses;
　　　　There is Kensington-stitch
　　　　In designs that are rich,
　　　　Snow-flake, arrasene, point russe and all sich.
Oh, the crazy-quilt mania, how long will it rave?
And how long will fair woman be held as its slave?

And where is the wife who so vauntingly swore
　　That nothing on earth her affections could smother?
She crept from your side at the chiming of four
　　And is down in the parlor at work on another.
　　　　Your breakfasts are spoiled,
　　　　And your dinners half-boiled,
　　　　And your efforts to get a square supper are foiled
By the crazy-quilt mania that fiendishly raves,
And to which all the women are absolute slaves.

And thus it has been since the panic began,
　　In many loved homes it has wrought desolation,
And cursed is the power by many a man,
　　That has brought him so close to the verge of starvation.
　　　　But make it she must,
　　　　She will do it or bust,
　　　　Beg, swap, and buy pieces, or get them on trust.
Oh, the crazy-quilt mania, may it soon cease to rave
In the land of the free and the home of the brave.
　　　　　　　　　　　　—Unidentified.

CRAZY QUILT

FIGURE 175

This crazy quilt is filled with popular motifs of the period, such as flowers, fans, birds, a spider web, insects, and paisley shapes, that reflect the then-fashionable interests in nature, gardening, and Japan. Embroidered in the bottom right corner is the monogram "ACP," probably for the unknown maker or owner of the quilt. One block contains the German inscription "NICHT REICHIHUM SONDERN ZUFRIEDEN HEIT," which translates roughly as "not riches but contentment" (fig. 175a).[6] In the top left corner is the message "Silken rest / lie all thy / cares up" (fig. 175b). Decorative embroidery stitches and techniques including buttonhole, chain, couched, cross, double cross, fly, French knots, herringbone, lazy daisy, satin, and Turkey work embellish the throw as well as cover the seams. The quilt is bound with a wide border of green silk velvet and backed in a gold pattern-woven silk. It is not quilted.

Nothing is known of the quilt's provenance or if the German inscription indicates that the maker was of Ger-

man heritage. The donors purchased many of their quilts and coverlets in Pennsylvania.

Figure 175a Detail. The German inscription "NICHT REICHIHUM SONDERN ZUFRIEDEN HEIT" roughly translates as "not riches but contentment." It is unusual to find a German inscription on a crazy quilt.

Figure 175b Detail. The inscription reminds us that a good night's rest is priceless.

CRAZY QUILT FIGURE 175

MAKER UNKNOWN

POSSIBLY PENNSYLVANIA 1883

SILKS; SILK RIBBON; BEADS; SILK, CHENILLE,
AND METALLIC EMBROIDERY THREADS

65½ X 54½ IN. (166 X 138 CM)

GIFT OF FOSTER AND MURIEL MCCARL, 2006.609.12

FIGURE 176

This dynamic crazy quilt consists of twenty blocks of applied asymmetrical silk textiles and fan shapes on cotton foundations. The blocks are overlaid with embroidery stitches forming names and initials, flowers, a star and moon, butterflies, a horseshoe, a spider web, and other insects.[7] Reflecting an interest in nature, embroidered, painted, and appliquéd birds, fish, insects, and four-footed creatures were popular motifs on crazy quilts. Of particular interest on this one is the raised-work mouse that at first glance appears real enough to be scampering across the throw (fig. 176a). (A quilt maker in Missouri actually did put two real stuffed chipmunks on her crazy quilt.)[8] The quilt is bordered with ribbons and textiles cut to points at the edges. It has tied quilting with a thin cotton batting and cotton backing.

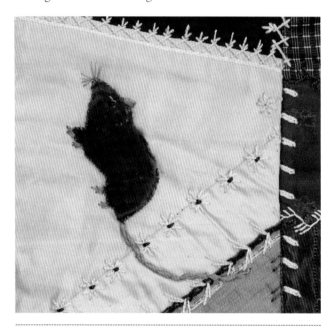

Figure 176a Detail. Reflecting an interest in nature, four-footed rodents, such as this stuffed velvet mouse, are just some of the creatures that appear in various techniques on crazy quilts.

About the QUILT MAKERS

The quilt was made in 1886 by the ladies of the Presbyterian Missionary and Aid Society of Reedsburg, Wisconsin, which was organized by Mrs. Oliver W. Winchester. Her husband was pastor of the church from 1880 to 1886. Twenty women,

ranging in age from twenty-four to seventy-five, joined forces to create the quilt, which was intended as a gift for the Winchesters. For some reason, despite all the work already done, the quilt was never finished; unbacked, it still retains basting stitches around the edges of the cut silks. According to a church member, the unfinished quilt was presented to the pastor and his wife in 1886.[9] If so, it did not remain with his family. A woman named Mildred Perry owned it and gave it to her friend and neighbor Eleanor Luehrsen. Mrs. Luehrsen returned it to the church in 2004.[10] No one ever completed the borders or backing.

Although some of the ladies stitched only their initials into their quilt pieces, their identities are known from the church and genealogical records.[11] In the 1880s, women were assumed to be housewives; only their husband's occupations are given in the records:

Sarah Ann Stewart Sallade (widow of Nathaniel, physician)
Lavina Reed Green (widow of Joseph, postmaster)
Cornelia Lusk De Vor (wife of John, woolen mill president)
Helen Neely Perry (wife of Ralph, banker)
Mary Meyers Rudd (wife of David, lumberman)
Belle Ward Morse (wife of George T., banker)
Estella Stewart Howland (wife of Franklin, lumberman)
Sarah Ann Dornick Stewart (wife of John, merchant)
Mary E. Mackey Finch (wife of Mortimer, harness maker)
M. Ghastin (unknown)
Lucy Mallory Gale (wife of James Willis, hardware dealer and flour mill operator)
Eleanor Burnett O'Dell (wife of Ed, occupation unknown)
Lydia Herrick Grove Dwinell (widow of Solomon, minister)
Harriet Pixley (wife of William, jeweler)
Vanelia Crocker Rood (wife of Charles A., physician)
Laura Martindale Hunt (widow of Abner, farmer)
Ursula Ann Noyes Merriman (wife of Edward, store clerk)
Mary Smith Hunt (wife of Henry, merchant)
Harriet Marquisee Mackey (wife of Safford, lumber business owner and miller)
Francis Smith Harris (wife of Abner, merchant and postmaster)

Unfinished Album Crazy Quilt   Figure 176

Ladies of the Presbyterian Missionary and Aid Society,
First Presbyterian Church

Reedsburg, Wisconsin, 1886

Silks, cottons; silk ribbon; silk, chenille, and metallic
embroidery threads

77 x 74 in (196 x 188 cm)

Museum Purchase, 2007.609.3

Virginia Album Crazy Quilt

Order is imposed in this crazy quilt by breaking the whole into twenty-five large quilt blocks, evidently each the work of a single seamstress as most blocks are signed or initialed in some fashion.[12] One inscription reads "'Old Lady' Bill" and another "Should auld / acquaintance / be forgot. / Bettie." (fig. 177a). The only complete name that appears is that of "Lucie Knight." The blocks are embellished with painted decoration and a large variety of embroidery stitches including blanket, chain, couched, cross, feather, fern, herringbone, knots, lazy daisy, long-arm cross, outline, satin, and straight. The cotton backing is machine quilted in an approximate one-inch diamond pattern. The throw is edged with braid and eighteen tassels consisting of wooden balls covered in maroon and olive-green silks. Other types of edging found on crazy quilts include fringes, ruffles, scallops, and sawtooth patterns.

Made at the height of the crazy fad, this example was created in celebration of the September 25, 1888, marriage of Walter Harris Robertson and Lelia Graham Eggleston of Farmville and Henrico County, Virginia, parents of the donor. Walter worked as a fertilizer manufacturer in Farmville, Virginia, where the couple lived in 1900. Their household included Walter's widowed mother, his younger brother, a nurse, a cook, and their two children, Lelia E. and Paul. By 1910, the family had settled in Norfolk, Virginia, where Walter eventually became president of his own fertilizer manufactory. Once again, Lelia and Walter's home was filled with extended family members including Walter's aging mother, a nephew, a border, a cook, twenty-year-old Lelia and seventeen-year-old Paul.[13] The quilt was surely a cherished possession within this active home, for it survives in pristine condition.

Figure 177a Detail. Some of the blocks are signed or initialed. One includes an inscription.

Virginia Album Crazy Quilt Figure 177

Friends and family of Walter Harris Robertson (ca. 1859–1931)
and Lelia Graham Eggleston Robertson (1862–1939)

Probably Prince Edward and Henrico Counties, Virginia,
1888

Silks, cottons; silk ribbon; wooden balls; paint;
silk, chenille, and metallic embroidery threads

90 x 55¼ in. (229 x 140 cm)

Gift of Miss Lelia E. Robertson, 1979.609.5

MAINE CRAZY QUILT

FIGURE 178

Most surviving crazy quilts are made of silks and velvets for use as parlor throws. This one is more utilitarian in its approach, consisting of forty-two blocks of woolen and cotton flannels and sturdy fabrics with a backing of plaid flannelette. It was intended for everyday use as a bed quilt. Despite the practical materials, the makers incorporated fancy embroidery stitches similar to those in more expensively fashioned crazy quilts.[14] They also included some very charming motifs, such as the Statue of Liberty and a prominent rooster (fig. 178a), both in the third row from the top, and a baseball game in the second row, fifth block in. The cover is bound with a three-fourths-inch folded strip of brown cotton. It is not quilted.

About the QUILT MAKERS   One block in the bottom right corner is stamped with the makers' name of Coffin. Family tradition recalls that Lena Coffin and her mother, Augusta Coffin, created the quilt before Lena's marriage in 1895 to Emery Farnsworth (1876–1961), a fisherman and farmer of Maine.[15] The couple operated a berry farm and, from 1905 to 1915, a small canning factory in eastern Maine, near the town of Jonesport. It was a family-run business; Lena, as well as their children, assisted in the fields and with the canning of blueberries and clams. Lena would also bicycle six miles to the nearest town to sell the berries. The quilt descended in the family of Lena's great-grandson, who donated it to the museum.

Figure 178a Detail. The embroidered motif of the Statue of Liberty, which was dedicated on October 28, 1886, helped in dating the quilt.

MAINE CRAZY QUILT FIGURE 178

LENA COFFIN (LATER MRS. EMERY FARNSWORTH) (1876–1951)
AND AUGUSTA L. GARDNER COFFIN (1838–1909)

MAINE, CA 1891

WOOLS, COTTONS; SILK EMBROIDERY THREADS

86½ X 73½ IN. (220 X 187 CM)

GIFT OF MR. AND MRS. RUSSELL J. EDMUNDS, 2011.609.5

VIRGINIA CRAZY QUILT

Jane Savin Kent's crazy quilt is an excellent example of how quilt making and story-telling go hand in hand. Unlike many crazy quilts that were based on published patterns and sources, this example is filled with original motifs and symbolism. The quilt also differs from most crazies in the choice of fabrics. Rather than the expensive silk brocades and velvets that are usually found in parlor throws, some of the textile swatches were taken from coverlet and blanket materials, as well as mixtures of silk-and-wool and cotton-and-wool fabrics. The quilt is backed in floral-printed cotton and bound on three sides in a one-fourth-inch folded maroon wool strip with a strip of the backing fabric on the right side. Each of the forty-nine pieced and appliquéd blocks is worked on a foundation of either plain cotton or linen. Embroidery stitches and techniques include blanket, chain, coral knot, couched, cross, fern, herringbone and variations, needle weaving, spider web, stem, and straight. The cover is not quilted.

and future sister-in-law, John Richard Savin (b. 1877) and Maggie Ethel, on December 25, 1902. The quilt descended to their daughter Elsie Savin Haynie (1912–1980) and then to Elsie's son and Jane's great-nephew Donald Haynie, who donated the quilt to Colonial Williamsburg.[16]

Figure 179b Detail. Most, if not all, of the appliquéd motifs in this crazy quilt appear to be original designs by the maker. This block features a schoolhouse and teacher, a reminder of schooldays.

Figure 179a Jane Savin Kent, courtesy Donald Haynie. Seated outside her home in Northumberland County, Virginia, Jane wears a homemade dress of printed cotton. Known as a great storyteller, Jane made all of her own clothes, cultivated flowers for sale to a local inn, and raised vegetables for canning.

About the QUILT MAKER Jane R. Savin Kent (fig. 179a), described as a great storyteller, lived her entire life in Lancaster and Northumberland Counties in Virginia's Northern Neck. The donor, her grandnephew, recalled that most of the supplies at that time came from Baltimore, Maryland, by way of steamship down the Chesapeake Bay to Wicomico Landing, near the family's home. Jane created the quilt as a wedding gift for the marriage of her brother

Don remembered as a young boy of about six or seven listening to his great-aunt Jane and grandmother Maggie tell stories about the quilt's blocks. Many of the appliquéd motifs held special meaning for the family. Several blocks depicting the American flag celebrate the Fourth of July. Another with cherry stems recognizes George Washington's birthday. One block with bells, called the "wedding block," commemorates the marriage of John and Maggie Savin. Another showing a small house and woman's figure represents a schoolhouse and teacher (fig. 179b). A block depicting a cross and heart is known as the "holiday block" for its references to Easter and Saint Valentine's Day. Jane's "stitched stories" reflect her sense of patriotism as well as celebrate certain rites of passage, providing a snapshot of her life.

Virginia Crazy Quilt Figure 179

Jane R. Sayin Kent (Mrs. William H. Kent) (1872–1958)

Lancaster County or Northumberland County, Virginia, 1902

Wools, cottons, silk-wool mixtures, cotton-wool mixtures,
linens; silk embroidery threads

73½ x 73½ in. (187 x 187 cm)

Gift of Donald Haynie, 2012.609.2

Combining odd-shaped pieces with pictorial elements and embroidered details in chain, couched, and straight stitches, this tile quilt can be compared to late nineteenth-century crazy quilts. In this example, however, each appliquéd piece is separated from its neighbor by a narrow quarter-inch band of white muslin ground fabric showing through, resembling grout between broken ceramic tiles or the mortar between pavers or stones. The effect is one of vitality within an organized framework. This quilt design is sometimes called Boston Pavement or Stonewall but is most often referred to as a tile quilt. Only about twenty-five original quilts of this unusual pattern have been documented; all date roughly to the last quarter of the nineteenth century.[17]

The interior of this quilt is composed of sixteen blocks of appliquéd abstract shapes as well as figures, including that of an African American man with horse and whip, a snake, and birds. The figures and motifs appear primitive and quite charming, implying that the designs were the creation of the unknown quilt maker. Yet, at least one motif has been found on another quilt, suggesting that this design, and possibly others, was taken from a publication such as a contemporary ladies' magazine. A block in the third row depicts a charismatic yellow cat riding a brown dog (fig. 180a). This same domestic pair appears on a Massachusetts appliquéd and pieced quilt attributed to Minnie Burdick (1857–1951).[18]

The undulating vine and floral border has been appliquéd by sewing machine.[19] Details in the flowers and animal figures are worked in silk and cotton embroidery stitches. Unlike most show quilts, this bedcover is quilted, in a ran-

dom four-petal flower motif pattern. It is bound with a red cotton tape and backed with cotton printed in a small-scale geometric design.

Figure 180a Detail. An identical motif of a cat and dog appears on a Massachusetts pieced and appliquéd quilt, suggesting that both quilt makers used the same published design source.

There is still much to learn about tile quilts. Are they indicative of a certain region, religious group, and/or socioeconomic level? Most identified examples appear to have been created in New England, especially Connecticut. This type of appliquéd design may have been more popular with British quilt makers, with whom it is associated earlier in the nineteenth century.[20] Can a direct relationship between American tile quilts and a similar quilt form in Great Britain be made?

Very little is known about this quilt's provenance. A Tennessee antique dealer who collected from the South sold it at an Ohio auction.

TILE QUILT FIGURE 180

MAKER UNKNOWN

AMERICA, 1875–1910

COTTONS; SILK AND COTTON EMBROIDERY THREADS

11 RUNNING STITCHES PER INCH

70 X 68 IN. (178 X 173 CM)

MUSEUM PURCHASE, 2006.609.2

FANS SHOW QUILT

FIGURE 181

This jewel-tone quilt features thirty repeated half-open fans, each facing the same direction yet constructed of slightly different silks and outlined with a wide variety of fancy embroidery stitches.[21] The resulting cover relates to crazy quilts made about the same time, but the organized and regularly repeated fans give a greater sense of unity within the variety that was so fashionable. Reflecting the interest in Japan, fans were a popular decorating item in the last quarter of the nineteenth century. Used in tasteful decors, the fan motif could also be found painted, appliquéd, pieced, and embroidered on quilts. This cover was likely intended for show and may have originally graced a parlor table, settee, or piano. It is bound with a wide border of red satin silk, mitered at the corners, and backed in a silk damask. It is not quilted.

About the QUILT MAKER   A handwritten tag sewn to the face of the quilt states that it was made in 1886 by Anna E. B. Clark. Named after her maternal grandmother, Anna was the seventh child of Captain Benjamin Duval Clark (ca. 1810–1873) of Baltimore and his Virginia-born wife, Octavia Augusta Ball Clark (1827–after 1910).[22] In 1880, living in Baltimore, Maryland, with her widowed mother and two brothers James and Fayette Ball, Anna likely had easy access to sewing supplies as James was a dry goods salesman and Fayette a notions salesman.[23] The unmarried Anna continued to live with family members until at least 1940.[24]

SHOW QUILT

FIGURE 182

Constructed of rich-colored silk solids, plaids, textured weaves, and velvets, this small throw has the additional embellishment of feather stitches. Quilt makers in the late nineteenth century often used silks edged with fancy stitches to create wildly asymmetrical pieced crazy quilts. In this example, the design is more organized and symmetrical than that of crazy quilts; it consists of 323 square blocks with the repeating pattern of a centered appliquéd scalloped diamond.[25] Each small block measures only about 3¾ inches square. The edges of each scalloped diamond are covered in feather stitches, which connect to the feather stitches on adjacent blocks to form circles (fig. 182a). Accentuated by the jewel tones of the fabric, the visual result is reminiscent of the Cathedral Windows pattern, although the technique is different. The throw is bound on all four sides with red satin ribbon, with a bow of the same material in the bottom right corner. It is backed with a rose-colored silk satin; it is not quilted.

The last owner recalled that the quilt was given to her mother by Jane Ault, her mother's great-aunt, whose family was from Galion, Ohio, and Pittsburgh, Pennsylvania.

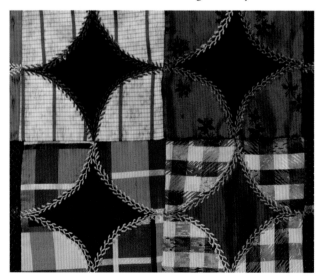

Figure 182a Detail. Feather stitches worked in silk threads cover the edges of each scalloped square.

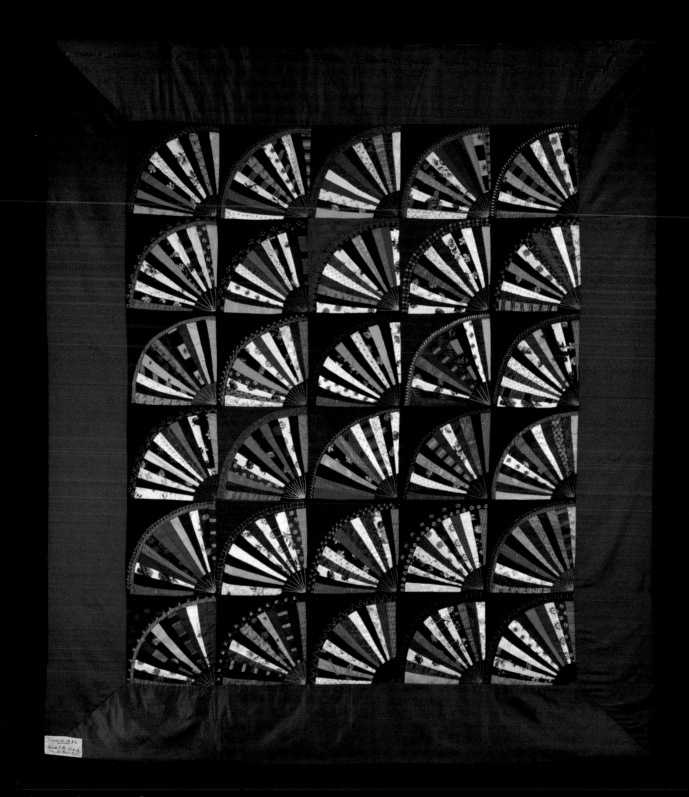

Fans Show Quilt Figure 181

Anna Eliza Blackwell Clark (ca. 1859–after 1940)   86 x 75 in. (218 x 191 cm)

Baltimore, Maryland, 1886   Gift of Dr. William Lehman Guyton, 2008.609.12

Silks; silk embroidery threads

Show Quilt   Figure 182

Attributed to Jane Ault

Possibly Pennsylvania or Ohio, ca. 1900

73½ x 65½ in. (187 x 166 cm)

Gift of Mrs. Jane Steel, 2003.609.5

1 Filoselle is an inferior silk thread sometimes couched and clipped to create fuzzy piles on the quilt's surface. Arrasene can be either of silk or wool fibers and is somewhat crinkled in appearance. Popular stitches found on crazy quilts include herringbone, chain, cross, feather, and Kensington, a stem or outline stitch that derives its name from the practice of outlining published designs from the Kensington Royal School of Needlework.

2 Barbara Brackman, *Clues in the Calico: A Guide to Identifying and Dating Antique Quilts* (McLean, VA: EPM, 1989), 145. She stated, "Nearly all Crazy Quilts are constructed on a foundation which is visible only on unbacked or damaged examples." Virginia Gunn in "Crazy Quilts and Outline Quilts: Popular Responses to the Decorative Arts/ Art Needlework Movement, 1876–1893" related the construction of crazy quilts to that of Log Cabin–patterned quilts: "However, crazy quilts were not made by cutting irregular templates. Instead, the technique used on the well-known log cabin quilts was adapted. Traditional quiltmakers were very familiar with the pressed patchwork method of fashioning log cabin quilts by adding strips of wool, cotton or silk to a foundation or background fabric. It would be easy to understand how an asymmetrical arrangement of silk strips around an irregular center might be considered a Japanese effect. If combined with embroidery and art needlework designs, all the fashionable decorating trends could be incorporated in one unique grass roots interpretation." *Uncoverings 1984*, ed. Sally Garoutte (Mill Valley, CA: American Quilt Study Group, 1985), 143.

3 Gunn, "Crazy Quilts and Outline Quilts," 131–152. The article describes the influence of the 1876 Centennial Exhibition in Philadelphia on the "art craze" that moved through America in the last quarter of the nineteenth century creating societies and magazines dedicated to the advancement of art, including the needle arts. Decorating one's home was an important element of this influence, which had roots in the aesthetic movement that originated in England in the 1860s. It was felt that a good home, especially one that was beautiful, helped create successful individuals. The movement incorporated elements from nature and was influenced by the graceful arts of Japan, which opened trade with the West in the 1860s. Crazy quilts were part of the new art needlework movement that put heavy emphasis on surface embroidery and scorned the patchwork and calico quilts of yesteryear.

4 Some quilt makers assembled sample books of stitches and designs. For example, Eleanor Royster Iden, of Raleigh, NC, compiled a ca. 1895 "Book of Crazy Stitches," now in the collection of the Museum of Early Southern Decorative Arts, Old Salem Museums & Gardens, Winston-Salem, NC (3567). She included some of the popular crazy quilt motifs such as fans and butterflies in her notebook. See Paula W. Locklair, *Quilts, Coverlets & Counterpanes: Bedcoverings from the MESDA and Old Salem Collections* (Winston-Salem, NC: Old Salem, 1997), 69.

5 Quoted by Sue Reich, *Quilting News of Yesteryear: Crazy as a Bed-Quilt* (Atglen, PA: Schiffer, 2007), 134.

6 No other crazy quilt with a German inscription has been recorded by Colonial Williamsburg. A figured and fancy woven coverlet in the collection of the Colorado Springs Pioneers Museum contains in its corner block the German inscription "ZUR RUHE," which roughly translates as "good night's sleep." Jan Thomas to author (Ivey), e-mail message, February 19, 2008.

7 Embroidery stitches include blanket, chain, couched, cross, double feather, fern, herringbone, knots, lazy daisy, outline, satin, and straight.

8 Mrs. David McWilliams of St. Louis, MO, included two taxidermic chipmunks at the bottom of her ca. 1882 crazy quilt (Collection of Missouri Historical Society/Missouri History Museum). For an image of the quilt, see Penny McMorris, *Crazy Quilts* (New York: E. P. Dutton, 1984), 51, and online at http://collections.mohistory.org /object/OBJ:1944+033+0004, accessed September 14, 2013.

9 A typed and handwritten paper by Mildred Perry with the provenance information and list of makers' names was pinned to the quilt.

10 Further information about the quilt provenance was provided by Donna Lange, a church member, in a report dated July 24, 2004. CWF object file 2007.609.3.

11 See ibid.

12 Painted or stitched onto various swatches are the following: "L C I / age 81," "H," "A L N," "Carrie," "S. H," "B," "Sister," "Should auld / acquaintance / be forgot. / Bettie.," "m C," "Lucie Knight," "S K B," "L," "A B D," "'Old Lady' Bill," "C B," "F. H.," "N P," "E B," "A J B," "Belle," "M," and "Martha."

13 Lelia E. Robertson, note to CWF object file 1979.609.5, no date; "W H Robertson" on findagrave.com, Find a Grave memorial #93516126, record added July 13, 2012; "Lelia G Robertson" on findagrave.com, Find a Grave memorial #93516103, record added July 13, 2012; Walter H. Roberson household, 1900 U. S. census, Farmville, Prince Edward, VA, enumeration district 74, page 6A, National Archives and Records Administration (NARA) microfilm T623, roll 1723, digital image as found on Ancestry.com (2004); Worten H. Robinson household, 1910 U. S. census, Ward 3, Norfolk, VA, enumeration district 30, page 10B, NARA microfilm T624, roll 1637, digital image as found on Ancestry.com (2006); Walter H. Robertson household, 1930 U. S. census, Norfolk, VA, enumeration district 95, page 2A, NARA microfilm T626, roll 2472, digital image as found on Ancestry.com (2002); J. G. Eggleston household, 1880 U. S. census, Henrico County, Richmond, VA, enumeration district 83, page 164D, NARA microfilm T9, roll 1371, digital image as found on Ancestry.com (2010).

14 Embroidery stitches include blanket, chain, cross, feather, fern, herringbone, knots, outline, satin, and straight.

15 "Augusta Laura Coffin" on findagrave.com, Find a Grave memorial #83454529, record added January 14, 2012; "Lena Mabel Farnsworth" on findagrave.com, Find a Grave memorial #83451949, record added January 14, 2012; "Emery Fletcher Farnsworth" on findagave.com, Find a Grave memorial #83444266, record added January 14, 2012; and "Maine, Marriage Records, 1713–1937," s.v. "Emery F Farnsworth," online database, Ancestry.com (2010).

16 Jane R. Kent marker, Wicomico Baptist Church Cemetery, Remo, VA, photograph supplied by Don Haynie, April 2012; Lebanon Baptist Church Cemetery, Lancaster County, VA, Elsie Savin Haynie marker, digital image as found on findagrave.com, Find a Grave memorial #54851161, record added July 12, 2010; and "World War I Draft Registration Cards, 1917–1918," s.v. John Richard Saven, online database, digital image as found on Ancestry.com (2005).

17 Bobbi Finley to author (Ivey), e-mail message, February 14, 2012. For more information on and other images of tile quilts, see Carol Gilham Jones and Bobbi Finley, *Tile Quilt Revival: Reinventing a Forgotten Form* (Lafayette, CA: C & T Publishing, 2010).

18 Minnie Burdick's "Centennial Album" quilt is in the collection of the Shelburne Museum, Shelburne, VT (1987-040). For more on this quilt, including an image, see Lynne Zacek Bassett, ed., *Massachusetts Quilts: Our Common Wealth* (Hanover and London: University Press of New England, 2009), 138–140, and for a detail, Sandi Fox, *Cats on Quilts* (New York: Harry N. Abrams, 2000), 49. Although hers is not a tile quilt, Minnie Burdick was probably

familiar with the style since a quilt by her younger sister, Hattie Burdick (b. 1861), in the collection of the International Quilt Study Center & Museum at the University of Nebraska, Lincoln, is in the tile quilt style. The authors are indebted to Bobbi Finley and Carol Gilham Jones for bringing these quilts to our attention.

19 Jones and Finley have documented three tile quilts with borders; only this one has an appliquéd border (*Tile Quilt Revival,* 8).

20 Kimberly Wulfert in her reproduction fabric review of the New England Quilt Museum's Collage Collection suggested that this type of appliqué was more common in England than in America (accessed March 7, 2012, http://www.antiquequiltdating.com /New_England_Quilt_Museum%27s_Collage_Collection.html). She pointed to two earlier British examples in Dinah Travis's chapter "Appliqué, Embellishments and Embroidery," in *Quilt Treasures of Great Britain: The Heritage Search of the Quilters' Guild* (Nashville, TN: Rutledge Hill, 1995), 51, fig. 40, and 55, fig. 44. See also Janet Rae, *The Quilts of the British Isles* (London: Constable, 1987), 86–87 for a chintz scrap appliquéd quilt in the collection of the Highland Folk Museum, Newtonmore, SCOT. In this quilt, largely irregular shapes and patterns of printed cottons have been applied to a white ground fabric with space around each patch somewhat like a tile quilt.

21 Embroidery stitches include coral, couched, cross, feather, fern, herringbone, knots, outline, and straight.

22 Horace Edwin Hayden, *A Genealogy of the Glassell Family of Scotland and Virginia, also of the Families of Ball, Brown, Bryan, Conway, Daniel, Ewell, Holladay, Lewis, Littlepage, Moncure, Peyton, Robinson, Scott, Taylor, Wallace, and Others, of Virginia and Maryland* (Baltimore, MD: Southern Book Co., 1959), 129; Walter L. Clark household, 1940 U. S. census, Baltimore City, MD, enumeration district 4-259, page 2A, NARA microfilm T627, roll 1518, digital image as found on Ancestry.com (2012); and Benjamin Clark household, 1860 U. S. census, Ward 15, Baltimore, MD, page 420, NARA microfilm M653, roll 464, digital image as found on Ancestry.com (2009).

23 Jas. B. Clark household, 1880 U. S. census, Baltimore, MD, enumeration district 105, page 24C, NARA microfilm T9, roll 501, digital image as found on Ancestry.com (2010).

24 Octavia Clark household, 1900 U. S. census, Ward 13, Baltimore City, MD, enumeration district 161, page 12B, NARA microfilm T623, roll 613, digital image as found on Ancestry.com (2004); Octavia A. Clam household, 1910 U. S. census, Ward 11, Baltimore, MD, enumeration district 174, page 12A, NARA microfilm T624, roll 556, digital image as found on Ancestry.com (2006); Walter L. Clarke household, 1920 U. S. census, Ward 11, Baltimore, MD, enumeration district 177, page 1A, NARA microfilm T625, roll 661, digital image as found on Ancestry.com (2010); Anna Clark household, 1930 U. S. census, Baltimore, MD, enumeration district 152, page 12A, NARA microfilm T626, roll 855, digital image as found on Ancestry.com (2002); and Walter L. Clark household, 1940 U. S. census, Baltimore City, MD, enumeration district 4-259, page 2A, NARA microfilm T627, roll 1518, digital image as found on Ancestry.com (2012). No records were found for Anna Clark after 1940.

25 Barbara Brackman identified a similar pattern as "Windows and Doors." See no. 2655 in *Encyclopedia of Pieced Quilt Patterns* (Paducah, KY: American Quilter's Society, 1993), 326–327.

CHAPTER 21

MEET THE MAKERS

Chapter 21

MEET THE MAKERS

O f the more than 150 quilts presented from Colonial Williamsburg's collection, over half have the names of their makers or owners linked with them through provenance or because the quilts and/ or blocks are marked in some way. Although not all of the makers have been identified, they clearly represent a diverse group of religious and cultural traditions, including Mennonite, Methodist, Lutheran, Baptist, Congregationalist, Presbyterian, Polynesian, African American, Irish, English, French, Asian, Indian, and northern European. Three distinct types of quilts—a wholecloth, an album, and a pieced—are represented by the Society of Friends (Quakers) (see figs. 23, 120, 159). Perhaps a reflection of their modest demeanor, most of our Amish and Pennsylvania German quilt makers preferred to remain anonymous, rarely signing or dating their quilts, unless it was for the recipient. Although most of our twentieth-century African American quilt makers have been identified, the names of the enslaved people who assisted their white owners in the quilting of earlier bedcovers will probably never be known.

At least three men contributed to the making of a quilt in the Colonial Williamsburg collection. Jewett Washington Curtis created his pieced bedcover from tiny scraps of wool, while teenager Louis Phillippi assisted his four sisters in their hexagonal quilt top, and Theodore Dunham cut the pattern templates for his wife's quilt (see figs. 2, 61, 162). Unlike these men, the names of most male professional embroiderers and quilters will never be known.

Some quilt makers, such as Jemima Prentice and Virginia Alsop Chewning Waite, quilted throughout most of their lives. Young Hattie Mory was "5 Yrs 8 Months" when she embroidered her name, age, and date on a redwork quilt, which her mother probably quilted (see fig. 169). On the other end of the spectrum, Amelia Lauck proudly proclaimed in quilting stitches that she had created a quilt for her son and daughter-in-law in her "62nd year" (see fig. 188), and Jemima Prentice pieced covers well into her eighties, if not nineties. Sixteen-year-old Kate H. Tupper completed her Chimney Sweep quilt shortly before her marriage to a successful southern lawyer (see fig. 81). Family tradition says Deborah Bunting Middleton was only twelve years old when she made her Flying Geese quilt (see fig. 80). Although it is more probable that she finished it at a later date, Deborah did wait until she was forty-five to use it as a newlywed.

In addition to the anonymous professional quilt makers of the late seventeenth and early eighteenth centuries, at least two of our nineteenth-century makers—the Boyle sisters of Petersburg, Virginia—worked as professional quilters, evidenced by two skillfully appliquéd and quilted covers they made for local clients (see figs. 71, 72). At least one of our quilters was a schoolteacher, although Ellen Ann Raywalt of New York happily gave up teaching "young hopefuls" to become the wife of Albert Ansley and a homemaker in northern Virginia at the onset of the American Civil War. How appropriate that her appliquéd quilt completed four months before her marriage featured honeysuckle, a symbol of love's bond and devotion (see fig. 106). Most of the quilt makers, however, were nonprofessionals whose primary occupations were homemakers.

Just as diverse as the makers were the reasons for creating the quilts. Many quilts were made in celebration or remembrance of special occasions such as weddings and graduations (see fig. 183). Twenty days before her marriage in 1801, Lucy Daniel of Middlesex County, Virginia, finished her white stuffed-work quilt, probably as part of her wedding trousseau (see fig. 53). Jane Savin Kent of the Northern Neck of Virginia stitched a crazy quilt filled with symbolic motifs for the marriage of her brother and future sister-in-law in 1902 (see fig. 179). According to tradition, a Mennonite mother created a Sawtooth Diamond quilt as a wedding gift for her daughter (see fig. 137). An African American housekeeper in Alabama in the early 1970s, Alberta Miller, fashioned a strip quilt as a special high-school graduation gift for the daughter of her employer's neighbor (see fig. 149).

Some quilts were created to remember or to be remembered by family and friends. Ruth Ogden collected 169 inscribed blocks for her Delectable Mountains quilt, though she never did leave her hometown of Bridgeton, New Jersey (see fig. 118). The parishioners of Methodist traveling

Figure 183 Quilt made from Wedding and Trousseau Dresses, Mary Cook Page (Mrs. John Page), Massachusetts, 1798–1825, cottons and linen, 6–7 running stitches per inch, 99¼ x 92 in. (252 x 234 cm), bequest of Mrs. Jason Westerfield, 1974-366.[1]

minister the Reverend William Eggleston presented signed blocks to his wife, Frances Muse Eggleston, who assembled them into a quilt top presumably to assuage the grief of constantly leaving friends behind (see fig. 119). Quilts were made as gifts for family and friends including nephews, future husbands, brothers, sisters-in-law, and children. They were made for show as well as for the basic necessity of keeping warm (see figs. 181, 202).

Not surprisingly, an intertwining theme throughout this collection is the bond of sisterhood. It transcends generations, religions, and cultures. Indiana Pettway of Gee's Bend, Alabama, quilted with her younger sister Nettie Jane Pettway (see fig. 148). Spinster sisters Christiann and Ann Margaret Rauch of Franklin County, Pennsylvania, marked two appliquéd quilts with their initials and the date 1849 for their two young nephews, the sons of their widowed younger sister (see figs. 104, 105). The Boyle sisters lived and worked together in Petersburg, Virginia, creating at least two quilted covers for sale (see figs. 71, 72). Three sisters-in-law in the Danner family of Frederick, Maryland, created an elaborate album quilt in the mid-1850s (see fig. 131). A large Star of Bethlehem and Le Moyne Star quilt was pieced by Sarah and Emily Sands of Annapolis, Maryland, who also created other needlework projects (see fig. 93). The sisters lived together their entire lives, and when they died within a year of each other in the early twentieth century, their obituaries noted their needlework skills.[2] Created as a gift for her husband, Sarah Chandlee Pidgeon's album quilt combines inscribed blocks from both her family and her husband's family (see fig. 120). Each family's blocks used distinct appliqué techniques. Only the center block inscribed "Eliza" for Sarah's beloved sister was worked in both techniques, as if uniting the families.

Even when a quilt is signed and dated, it is unusual to find much personal information about the maker and even rarer to have an image of the quilter. Fortunately, this is not the case with Amelia Heiskell Lauck (1760–1842), Jemima Parmalee Prentice (1773–1865), Nancy Virginia Alsop Chewning Waite (1834–after 1910), and Susana Allen Hunter (1912–2005), who created quilts throughout most of their lives. The life stories of these four quilters represent the scope and variety of quilting activities during the nineteenth and twentieth centuries.

(1760–1842)

AMELIA HEISKELL LAUCK

Just as individual cabinetmakers and other artisans influenced the trades of particular regions, one prolific quilter could also have a profound influence on the quilt making in a community. Take for example Amelia Heiskell Lauck and the quilts she artfully designed and skillfully stitched in her hometown of Winchester, Virginia, during the second decade of the nineteenth century. On the Great Valley Road and at the northern tip of the Shenandoah Valley, Winchester and its adjacent county of Frederick were areas of diverse cultures. Trade networks from the east brought influences from Washington, D. C., and Baltimore. German settlement from the north brought its own set of aesthetics and traditions. These factors helped shape the format, designs, and colors that gave Amelia's quilts their distinctive look.

At least four quilts made by Amelia have survived: two are in the Colonial Williamsburg collection and two are owned by the Daughters of the American Revolution Museum (figs. 185, 186).[3] Three of these quilts were inscribed by Amelia as gifts for her children. She likely made other quilts that are yet to be located.[4]

The surviving quilts are remarkably similar in their design and fabrics. All four are configured in a framed center-medallion format with concentric borders of alternating stuffed-work quilting and pieced Delectable Mountains. Sawtooth and zigzag patterns like Delectable Mountains were popular with quilters in the Shenandoah Valley. Eight-pointed stars appear in the corners of the pieced borders. All use the same printed floral cottons in the appliquéd flowers and red or pinkish-red printed cottons in the Delectable Mountains borders. A trademark of Amelia's quilts is the intricate quilting patterns that were given added dimension with cotton stuffing. The designs consist of an endless number of flowers (each one slightly different), vines, feathers, leaves, and clusters of grapes.

Presumably, it was Amelia's quilt-making influence that is seen in at least two other quilts created in the Shenandoah Valley. Margaret Barnhart Barley's Winchester quilt is constructed in a framed center-medallion format with appliquéd flowers and a basket in the center. Like Amelia's quilts, Margaret's borders alternate between Delectable Mountains and white quilted strips. The fine quilting in her circa 1847 quilt consists of vines of flowers, diagonal lines, and cross-hatching, some only an eighth of an inch apart.[5] The choice of a center-medallion design for the quilt may attest

Figure 184 *Amelia Heiskell Lauck*, Jacob Frymire, Winchester, Virginia, 1801, oil on canvas, 29½ x 24½ in. (80 x 62 cm), Collection of the Museum of Early Southern Decorative Arts, Old Salem Museums & Gardens, 3406. Seated in a Windsor chair with a book in her hand, perhaps suggestive of the sitter's literacy, the image of Amelia Heiskell Lauck evokes a sense of serenity and gentility. Perhaps the artist captured a rare moment in Amelia's life when she was not employed in quilt making, child rearing, or overseeing some aspect of the tavern that she and her husband, Peter, operated.

to Amelia's quilt-making influence at a time when album or compartmentalized quilts were becoming so popular. The influence of Amelia's quilt making can also be seen in another Winchester quilt, created by Harriet Ann Richards in 1840 (see fig. 92). Similar to Amelia's quilts, Harriet's quilt is signed and dated in quilting stitches and displays deftly executed quilting stitches that form beautiful, intricate floral designs.

Amelia Heiskell Lauck was the second of six children born to German immigrant Christopher Heiskell and his wife, Eve. In the mid-eighteenth century, the family relocated from Pennsylvania to Winchester, Virginia. A prominent landowner, Christopher Heiskell was also one of the original founders of the Old Stone Lutheran Church in Winchester.[6]

In 1779, at age nineteen, Amelia (also known as Emily and Milly to her family) married Peter Lauck (1753–1839), whose family had also resettled in Winchester from Pennsylvania. Amelia and Peter had eleven children together, six of whom survived into adulthood. Peter had served in Lord Dunmore's War of 1774 and later enlisted with his younger brother, Simon Lauck, in the American Revolutionary War under Daniel Morgan in his company of riflemen.[8] A member of Morgan's Raiders, Peter was severely wounded in late December 1775 in the Battle of Quebec, captured, and imprisoned.[9]

Upon Peter's release and return to Winchester, he was active in the community as a Mason, county constable, and member of the Lutheran church. He and Amelia were successful proprietors of the Red Lion Inn, a fine stone establishment that still stands today on the corner of Cork and Loudoun Streets in downtown Winchester (fig. 187). From about 1800 to 1835, the Lauck family lived at Edgehill, a brick home that Peter had built on a hill overlooking the town. At the time of Peter's death in 1839, Amelia and he were living back at the Red Lion Inn.[10] In addition to

Figure 185 Appliquéd Framed Center-Medallion and Pieced Quilt, Amelia Heiskell Lauck (1760–1842), Winchester, Virginia, 1823, cottons, 7–9 running stitches per inch, 112 x 109 in. (284 x 277 cm), Daughters of the American Revolution Museum, gift of the Ann Arundel (Maryland) Chapter, 87.50. Amelia Lauck created this quilt for her only surviving daughter, Rebecca (b. 1787), who married John Cunningham.[7] The initials RC and JC, in addition to the inscription "Made / By / Amilia Lauck in / the 62 Year of her / Age April 15th / 1823" appear on the quilt.

Figure 186 Appliquéd Framed Center-Medallion and Pieced Quilt, Amelia Heiskell Lauck (1760–1842), Winchester, Virginia, ca. 1823, cottons, 9–11 running stitches per inch, 87 x 85 in. (221 x 216 cm), Daughters of the American Revolution Museum, gift of Sally Lauck Harris, 2006.3.1. Embroidered in the banner in the eagle's beak "Presented by their Mother to W & E Lauck," this quilt was given by Amelia to her son William and his wife, Eliza Sowers, who wed on November 9, 1830.[11] As with Morgan's quilt (fig. 188), the outer border of this quilt was removed at some point, evidenced by a 1920s photograph in which it is intact.[12]

nine quilts valued at a total of eight dollars and a blanket at seventy-five cents—all of which may have been used as bedding for tavern clients—the inventory and appraisement of the estate of Peter Lauck taken in July 1840 lists "3 calico quilts & one blanket" valued at seventeen dollars. Compared to the Lauck's desk and bookcase valued at five dollars and eight chairs at four dollars, the value of the calico quilts

Figure 187 Red Lion Inn, Cork and Loudoun Streets, Winchester, Virginia, courtesy Virginia Department of Historic Resources.

is relatively high, suggesting that they had special merit.[13] These three quilts were not likely the ones marked by Amelia as gifts to her children, for the gifts were given long before the inventory was taken. Still, the calico quilts might have been Amelia's work.

For Amelia Lauck, the making of quilts appears to have been an individual effort, perhaps as an attempt to present each of her children with a keepsake. Yet, Amelia likely received help in creating her quilts, not from her daughter Rebecca or other female relatives and friends, but rather from the female slaves in the Lauck household. In fact, a number of southern quilts were probably the result of the work of both mistress and slave hands. Newspaper advertisements testify to the sewing skills of slaves. For example, one 1768 advertisement described a Virginia runaway as "she is very knowing about house business, can spin, weave, sew, and iron, well."[14] In 1820 Peter owned five female slaves between the ages of sixteen and twenty-six.[15] Although they probably worked in the tavern in various cleaning, washing, and cooking capacities, they also may have assisted with quilt making. Peter Lauck's estate inventory of 1840 gives names to some of these enslaved women, calling out Mime, Lucy, Bet, and Pat.[16]

APPLIQUÉD FRAMED CENTER-MEDALLION AND PIECED QUILT

FIGURE 188

The uniform and symmetrical design of this exceptional framed center-medallion quilt consists of finely cutout printed cottons that have been skillfully stitched in place (fig. 188a). The precise piecing of the red printed cottons in sawtooth patterns form Delectable Mountains, a pattern often seen on quilts produced in Virginia's Shenandoah Valley (see fig. 92). At some time in the quilt's history, the outer border was removed and presumably used in the creation of at least one pillow cover, which survives with the quilt (fig. 188b). The outer edge of the quilt, where the border was removed, was bound in a narrow one-fourth-inch binding machine stitched in place. The quilt is backed in white cotton.

Figure 188a Detail. The center medallion consists of finely cutout and stitched printed cottons.

APPLIQUÉD FRAMED CENTER-MEDALLION AND PIECED QUILT FIGURE 188

The intricate quilting pattern consists of floral, vine, grape, and feather designs that have been given added dimension with cotton stuffing. One-fourth-inch diagonal quilting lines create a puckered effect everywhere else on the quilt's surface (figs. 188c, 188d).

Amelia created the quilt as a wedding gift for her eighth child, Morgan Adolphus Lauck (1796–1826), and his bride, Ann Maria Ott, the daughter of Jacob Ott of Shenandoah County, Virginia, who married on May 26, 1824.[17] The quilt is marked in backstitches with the inscription "A present by Amelia Lauck to her S.[son] & D.[daughter] Morg. & M. Lauck / made in 62nd year." The couple lived in Shenandoah County, Virginia, where Morgan and his brother Joseph were partners in a tannery and mercantile business. Just two years after his marriage, Morgan died, leaving his widowed Ann Maria to raise their only child, Emily Maria (also known as Amelia Ann).[18] The quilt descended through Emily's children.

Figure 188b Pieced Pillow Cover, Amelia Lauck and unknown later maker, probably Winchester, Virginia, piecing and quilting 1822, pillow cover after 1840, cottons, 10–12 running stitches per inch, 16⅝ x 26¼ in. (41 x 67 cm), Museum Purchase, 2006.609.1B. The pillow cover was likely made from the outer border of the quilt, which was removed at some point in the quilt's history. The cover is backed in plain white cotton and machine stitched.

Figures 188c and 188d Detail of quilt and quilting pattern. Intricate quilting patterns in the borders are hallmark characteristics of Amelia's quilts.

APPLIQUÉD FRAMED CENTER-MEDALLION AND PIECED QUILT

FIGURE 189

This framed center-medallion quilt is surrounded by five consecutive borders of stuffed work and pieced Delectable Mountains. Unlike Morgan's quilt (fig. 188), this one retains its original outermost border, although the quilt itself is not as vibrant due to fading. It is backed in pieced white cotton that was brought to the front on three sides and hemmed in overcast stitches. A fourth side is edge bound in a separate strip of white cotton.

The intricate patterns of stuffed work stand out on this quilt. For example, the outer white border of stuffed work features exquisitely executed feather and wreath motifs alternating with grape clusters. A variety of stuffed flowers and leaves, each one unique, can be found elsewhere throughout the quilt.

Although not signed by Amelia Lauck, this quilt can confidently be attributed to her. It includes many of the same printed cottons in its appliquéd and pieced motifs and quilting designs that she used in her other quilts. Like the three signed quilts, perhaps this one too was intended as a gift for one of her children. Several unidentified quilts found in the Winchester area depict similar designs, color schemes, and stuffed-work quilted patterns and may have been the work of Amelia or inspired by her quilt making.

Appliquéd Framed Center-Medallion and Pieced Quilt Figure 189

Amelia Heiskell Lauck (1760–1842)

Winchester, Virginia, ca. 1805

Cottons

8 running stitches per inch

108 x 96 in. (274 x 244 cm)

Partial gift of Charles W. and Susan G. Bousliman, 2000.609.6

(1773–1865)

Jemima Parmalee Prentice

Jemima Parmalee Prentice created quilts throughout most of her life. A small scrap of paper in her handwriting records the astounding number of eighty quilts that she made during her lifetime. Her entries describe a large variety of quilt types such as "fine quilted silk bed quilts," "crib quilts," "sofa quilts for common use in the family," "nice sofa quilts, each child one," and "a common comfortable." Jemima made quilts for her children and grandchildren, pastors, friends, and those in need, including one "for a young widow of a poor Minister left with her babe." She also made quilts for sale to benefit Sunday schools on the frontier; scribbled in the margin of the paper, she recorded, "I have been as blest with health, that I have got 200 and 25 Dollars into the Missionary Society by silk pieces."[19] Three of her quilts descended through her family to her great-great-grandsons, who donated them to Colonial Williamsburg.

Jemima was a remarkable woman distinguished for her intelligence, order, hospitality, and religion. Born February 23, 1773, in Newport, New Hampshire, to Ezra and Sybil Hill Parmalee, in 1794 she married Sartell Prentice, a merchant in the fur trade. Together they had eight children, two of whom died in childhood.[20]

In October 1816, the family moved from Alstead, New Hampshire, to their new home in Canton, New York. Their three-week journey was similar to those of other pioneers who pushed west during this time seeking opportunity and fortune. Jemima and her three daughters, then nine, six, and two, traveled by covered wagon drawn by horses while oxen drew the household furniture and other freight. In a diary she kept en route, Jemima documented the difficulties her family encountered during the trek across the Connecticut River, through Vermont and New York counties, across the lower part of Lake Champlain, and through the Adirondack Mountains. In her first entry, dated October 24, 1816, Jemima wrote, "For you my dear friends all as one do I take my pen, hoping it will be some small gratification to hear of our situation daily. . . . I have parted from a number I highly prize."[21]

Jemima's three sons, ages eighteen, sixteen, and thirteen, traveled separately with the cattle. On October 29, she expressed her apprehension for their well-being when she wrote, "Some concerned about the boys who are with the cattle and team, and if nothing has happened have crossed the mountains today. Do not expect to see them again till we get to Keene, if well, and feel as if it would in reality be of the mercy of God if we are carried through

Figure 190 *Jemima Parmalee Prentice,* artist unknown, probably New York, ca. 1855, oil on canvas, 36 x 30 in. (91 x 76 cm), courtesy Graham and Sally N. Lusk. Living to the ripe old age of ninety-two, Jemima was known for her quilt making, excellent memory, sympathetic understanding, and good judgment.

safe." The following day Jemima, still worrying about the safety of her boys, wrote of her youngest child, Lucy Candace, whose nickname was Fan: "Fan . . . has been quite unwell, but is better this evening. . . . Fan rides in a little chair all the way. I am less tired than I expected. If I could hear that Mr. Wentworth and the boys are well and nothing happened unfavorably, should feel more at rest. Have Fan at my elbow very much when I write, which must be an excuse for matter and manner." Two days later on November I, they "crossed the lake today, with children crying, and clinging at first, afraid all the way: was not very afraid myself. . . . I do not wish any of you to come to see me the way I have come."[22]

Figure 191 Detail of figure 193.

Jemima conveyed her discontent a few days later when she wrote, "Here I am, my dearly beloved friends, sitting in the wagon two miles in the woods, while Mr. P. is gone back after the coat which was forgotten." It was worth the inconvenience, for in the coat pocket was a note for fifty-five dollars! In one of her final entries, Jemima wrote on November 9 of her disgust in her lodging accommodations: "My dear relatives, while you, I hope, are worshipping in the house of God, I am sitting on the bridge of the rapid River of St. Regis in the long woods. Last night I lay on the floor as the night before, in my clothes: the house was so full I had as good undressed in a meeting house."[23]

Shortly thereafter, the entire family safely arrived in Canton, where Sartell Prentice opened a mercantile establishment. Although the small village quickly grew by attracting enterprising inhabitants, by 1823 Sartell had given up the business. He and Jemima remained in Canton until about 1835, when they moved to Albany, New York, with their two unmarried daughters, Sybil Pamela and Lucy Candace (Fan). They lived at Mount Hope in a home overlooking the Hudson River that was built for them by their sons Ezra and John.[24]

Jemima's later years as a widow were spent in Brooklyn, New York, where she continued to make and sell quilts, using the profits to found Sunday schools in small villages springing up on the American frontier. Her granddaughter Ida Prentice Whitcomb described these activities in a brief memorial: "With bits of silk given her, she matched the colors, cut her triangles, and with deft fingers sewed them together. . . . When the cover was completed and interlining and lining basted under, quilting bars were brought and, seated before the form, she beeswaxed her thread and tied in tufts of silk or sometimes quilted the whole. Lute-string ribbon finished the work." The quilts were sold for the average price of $3 each with more than $225 collected this way and sent to the mission of Jemima's choice. Ida continued, "He [the missionary] was instructed to purchase four things, namely, a Bible, a small library, a baptismal font and a communion service—and with every such outfit in some new settlement a 'Prentice Sunday-school' sprang into being."[25]

Jemima Parmalee Prentice died in Brooklyn on November 19, 1865, at the age of ninety-two. The Reverend Dr. William B. Sprague described her in his funeral sermon as a woman "of great and retentive memory, of a godly life, taken from her Bible; a habit of private devotion that nothing interfered with, useful in life, endeavoring to imitate her divine Master and of strong faith, employing her musical powers on Watts's hymns, to relieve despondency, and all to God's glory."[26]

SILK DIAMOND AND NINE PATCH QUILT

FIGURE 192

The striped, checked, and solid silks in this quilt are pieced in alternating blocks of Diamond and Nine Patch. Diamonds are a shape frequently employed in quilt making. Here, Jemima Prentice has placed a square within each diamond. The fundamental design of Nine Patch consists of three rows of three squares each. It is a popular patch design because, once mastered, the quilter can progress to more intricate patterns. The quilt is backed with roller-printed cotton in a floral stripe and bound in a folded one-half-inch green silk.

This bedcover is likely one of the quilts Jemima described when she noted, "Made 7 fine quilted silk bed quilts . . . in Canton, St. Lawrence Co., NY / the Date is on them."[27] It is quilted with running stitches in geometric, flower and leaf, square, and clamshell patterns. One square is marked in the quilting "LCP / 1835," probably for Lucy

Candace Prentice, Jemima's youngest daughter (fig. 192a). Known as Fan, she was twenty-one that year.[28]

Figure 192a Detail. Marked in fine quilting stitches are the initials LCP and date 1835.

FLYING GEESE SILK QUILT OR COMFORTER

FIGURE 193

This colorful pieced quilt is made up of red, blue, and white silk triangles arranged in rows to form a variation of the Flying Geese pattern. Tufts of the red, blue, and white silk are used at points to tie the layers of the bedcover together. It is backed with pink-and-white roller-printed cotton in a stripe and paisley design and bound with a salmon-colored silk ribbon (fig. 193a).

Jemima continued to piece into her old age. In 1852, at the age of seventy-nine, she created this bedcover for her son James Hill Prentice (1817–1890), who was thirty-five and unmarried at the time.[29] A paper label once attached to the quilt reads: "Made for James Hill Prentice by his / Mother in the Eighteth year of her age / Brooklyn N Y October I[?]th 1852" (fig. 193b). James married Eloise Washington Valiant in 1859,[30] and the three quilts now in the Colonial Williamsburg collection descended through their family.

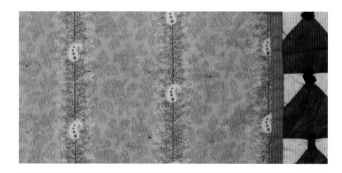

Figure 193a Detail. Reverse of quilt showing printed cotton backing.

Figure 193b Paper label once attached to the quilt.

Flying Geese Silk Quilt or Comforter Figure 193

Jemima Parmalee Prentice (1773–1865)

Brooklyn, New York, ca. 1852

Silks, cotton; silk ribbon

98½ x 93 in. (250 x 236 cm)

Gift of James and Janet Lusk, 2005.609.3

Family history states that Jemima pieced this quilt from silk dress samples from her relatives' dry goods business in Brooklyn, New York. Notice that the rectangular silk blocks appear in more than one colorway. In a typical quilt, the face fabric, inner batting, and backing are held together by stitches worked in decorative patterns. Instead of quilting stitches, this comforter is tied together with multicolor silk ribbons that keep the layers in place and create decorative tufts (fig. 194a). It is backed with brown-and-white silk check and bound with a bright-blue silk tape.

The comforter may be the last that Jemima pieced. She received help from her daughters Jemima Calista and Lucy Candace and from her daughter-in-law Eloise Washington Valiant Prentice,[31] who was at that time the young bride of Jemima's youngest son, James Hill Prentice. Eventually Eloise presented the quilt to her granddaughter and namesake, Eloise B. Prentice. A paper label, penned by Eloise W. V. Prentice and dated October 30, 1911, once attached to the silk cover records: "This quilt given to Eloise B[?] Prentice / on her fourth birthday by her grand / mother for whom she was named. / The quilt was made in 1862 before / Eloise's father was born – when her / great grandmother [Jemima Prentice] was 92 years old / & was tied by her grandmother – & her / two Great Aunts" (fig. 194b).[32] Eloise may have incorrectly remembered the date, as Jemima was ninety-two in 1865, not 1862.

In addition to the three in the Colonial Williamsburg collection, a fourth pieced silk bedcover still resides with the Prentice family. It is marked "E B P '07," presumably for Eloise B. Prentice who was born in 1907. Her grandmother, Eloise W. V. Prentice, may have made it for her.

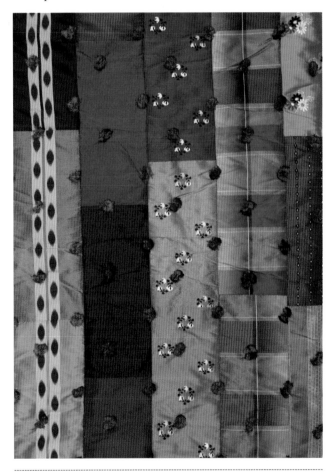

Figure 194a Detail. Decorative silk ribbon tufts hold together the three layers of this cover. The silks appear in different colorways.

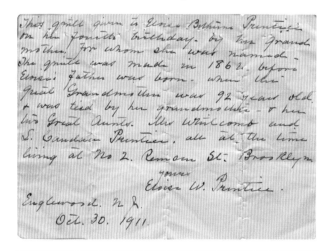

Figure 194b A paper label once attached to the silk comforter says that this quilt was the joint effort of mother, daughters, and daughter-in-law.

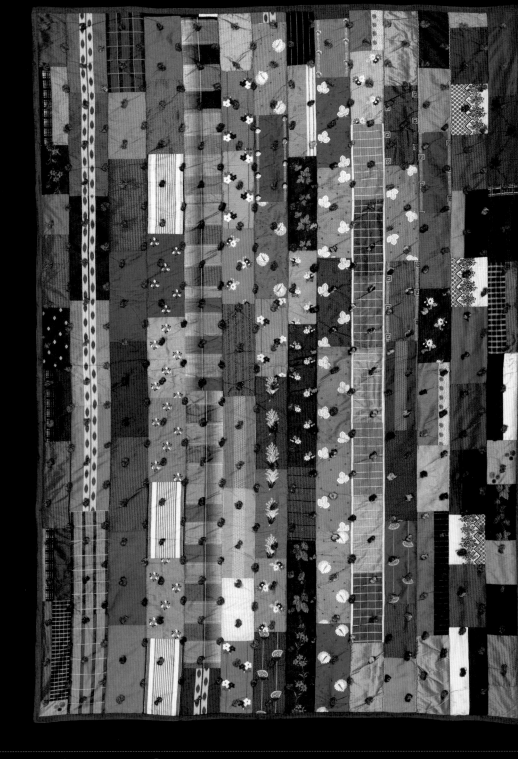

SILK SAMPLE QUILT OR COMFORTER FIGURE 194

JEMIMA PARMALEE PRENTICE (1773–1865) WITH JEMIMA CALISTA
PRENTICE WHITCOMB (1810–1894), LUCY CANDACE PRENTICE (1814–
1898), AND ELOISE WASHINGTON VALIANT PRENTICE (1842–1923)

BROOKLYN, NEW YORK, PROBABLY 1865

SILKS; SILK RIBBON AND TAPE

68¼ X 48½ IN. (173 X 123 CM)

GIFT OF GRAHAM AND SALLY N. LUSK IN MEMORY
OF ELOISE PRENTICE LUSK, 1998.609.2

VIRGINIA ALSOP CHEWNING WAITE

Virginia Alsop was born in May 1834, one of at least eight children in the Stafford County, Virginia, household of William Alsop (b. ca. 1792) and Manissa Harding Alsop (b. ca. 1795).[33] She was christened Nancy Virginia but was known to her family as Virginia or Jenny. When she was still a teenager, she made two quilts, each using the same bold-yellow printed cottons. Virginia signed the larger quilt with an embroidered picture of a bird and her unmarried initials VA. Later family members speculated that "Aunt Jenny" drew the bird as a subtle reference to her nickname, Jenny Wren.

Perhaps the unmarried teenager made two related quilts with matching fabrics, one large and one child size, because she was preparing for her upcoming wedding. She may also have anticipated the births of children who would eventually sleep under the crib quilt. In 1853 at the age of nineteen, Virginia married Joseph Chewning (b. ca. 1830), a farmer from Spotsylvania County. She bore three daughters—Fannie, Alice, and Emma—between the years 1854 and 1859.

Joseph died in Spotsylvania County in 1865.[34]

Virginia married again in 1869 to William Waite, who was a neighbor of Joseph Chewning's parents. Virginia likely knew William prior to Joseph's death. In 1870, thirty-year-old William was farming in Spotsylvania County while Virginia kept house. The household included Virginia's daughters from her first marriage, aged ten to fifteen, and a one-year-old daughter named Carrie.[35] Despite a blended family and busy life as a farmer's wife, Virginia continued making quilts in bold colors and energetic pieced patterns. A red-and-white quilt is marked VW in the quilting, initials that document her second marriage.

Virginia Alsop Chewning Waite died sometime in or after 1910, probably in Spotsylvania County, Virginia.[36] Her quilts, which share several of the same fabric patterns, bear witness to the skills of a young Virginian who began quilting as an unmarried girl and continued to make quilts years later as a remarried widow. Colonial Williamsburg's three quilts descended together in the maker's family.

Figure 195 Virginia Alsop Chewning Waite, courtesy Jane V. Van Leeuwen. A photograph dating to the early twentieth century shows Virginia about age seventy, a slight smile on her lips and bright eyes behind her glasses.

DOUBLE IRISH CHAIN QUILT

FIGURE 196

This bold quilt completed by Virginia Alsop prior to her first marriage combines alternating blocks of twenty-five small squares of various printed cottons and blocks of yellow printed cotton with red squares in each corner. The diagonal pattern created is often known as Double Irish Chain. The large size of the quilt would have fit a full-size bed, extending almost to the floor on the sides. Virginia embroidered her initials, "V.A," and the figure of a bird into one of the quilt blocks (fig. 196a). Family tradition holds that the bird is a reference to her nickname, Jenny Wren. The quilt is backed in plain-woven white cotton and bound in a one-half-inch folded strip of the same printed yellow cotton that is found in most of the yellow blocks. The cover is quilted in three colors of thread in a pattern of diagonal rows spaced about one-half inch apart.

Figure 196a Detail. Virginia marked her quilt with her initials VA and the figure of a bird, possibly in reference to her nickname of Jenny Wren.

PIECED FOUR PATCH AND APPLIQUÉD CRIB QUILT

FIGURE 197

Teenager Virginia Alsop made her crib quilt with the same yellow printed cotton as her full-size quilt in a Double Irish Chain pattern (fig. 196). The basic Four Patch squares are separated by printed pink sashing strips, but she added an unexpected appliquéd floral and leaf motif in the center. Although both quilts have squares of the identical yellow textile, Virginia designed the blocks on the crib quilt to be smaller, in keeping with the diminutive size of a crib quilt (fig. 197a). The small quilt is backed in red, brown, and white printed cotton and bound in a one-half-inch strip of brown printed cotton. The quilting pattern consists of parallel lines in the Four Patch areas with clamshell in the center block and outline in the appliqué.

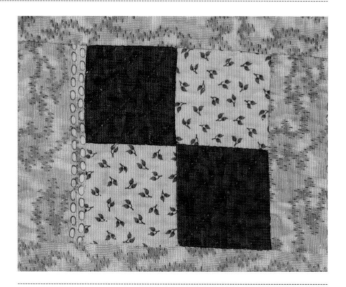

Figure 197a Detail. Virginia used the identical printed yellow cotton in both quilts.

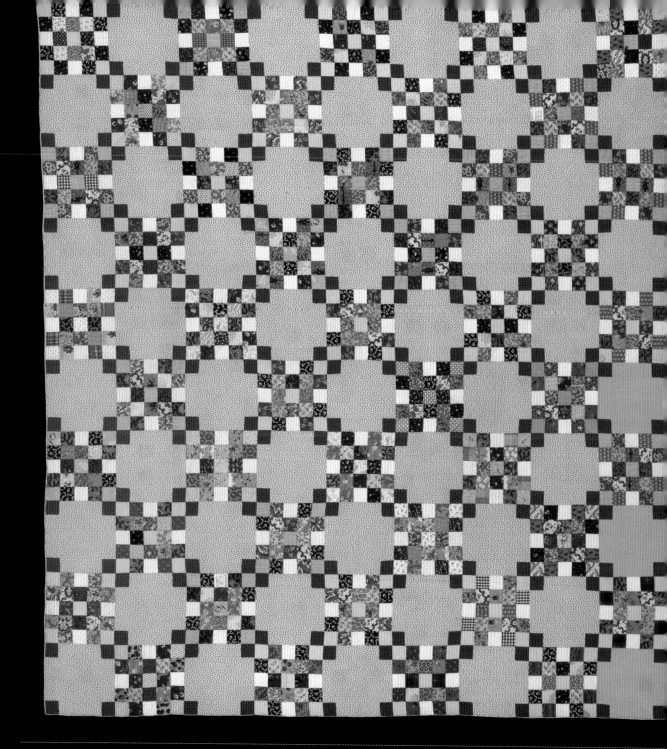

Double Irish Chain Quilt Figure 196

Virginia Alsop (1834–after 1910)

Stafford County, Virginia, ca. 1850

Cottons; cotton embroidery threads

5–7 running stitches per inch

103 x 115 in. (262 x 292 cm)

Museum Purchase, 2000.609.3

Pieced Four Patch and Appliquéd Crib Quilt Figure 197

Virginia Alsop (1834–after 1910)

Stafford County, Virginia, ca. 1850

Cottons

6–7 running stitches per inch

49½ x 45½ in. (126 x 116 cm)

Museum Purchase, 2000.609.2

ROBBING PETER TO PAY PAUL QUILT

FIGURE 198

Virginia combined a red floral stripe with white cotton in a Robbing Peter to Pay Paul pattern in this quilt. The name is derived from the visual effect created by the circular patterns of the quilt. Pie shapes cut, or "robbed," from one square were recombined with the contrasting color to form an abstract design that seems to alternate between circles and crosses. By the time she began piecing the zigzag border, Virginia had run out of the floral stripe fabric, and she finished with two different red prints (fig. 198a). The substitutions are hardly noticeable among the bold colors and pattern of the quilt. Virginia signed the quilt at the center top with her initials VW in running stitches. The quilt is backed in white cotton and has a thin batting. A solid-red cotton strip is used as the binding. The quilting pattern consists of diagonal lines spaced one-half inch to three-fourths inch apart with straight lines in the border.

Figure 198a Detail. Virginia pieced the zigzag border out of three different printed cottons of red, probably having run out of the red floral stripe she had used elsewhere.

ROBBING PETER TO PAY PAUL QUILT FIGURE 198

VIRGINIA ALSOP CHEWNING WAITE (1834–AFTER 1910)

SPOTSYLVANIA COUNTY, VIRGINIA, CA. 1875

COTTONS; COTTON EMBROIDERY THREADS

5–6 RUNNING STITCHES PER INCH

85½ X 97½ IN. (217 X 248 CM)

MUSEUM PURCHASE, 2000.609.4

(1912–2005)

SUSANA ALLEN HUNTER

Susana Allen Hunter was a prolific quilter who combined pragmatism and creativity to produce scores of distinctive improvisational quilts. Born in 1912 in a rural area of Alabama, Susana grew up in a large family headed by Tobe and Mary Allen, farmers in Wilcox County. By 1920, seven-year-old Susana was one of nine children at home ranging in age from two to twenty-two, and the Allens' children eventually increased to at least eleven in number.[37]

Susana married Julius Hunter (1909–1996) about 1928, and the couple raised two children, Lillie Bell and Paul, as well as grandson Tommie Hunter, after his mother left to find work in the city. Susana and Julius began their married life in Boykin, Dallas County, Alabama, but had moved to Wilcox County, Alabama, by the 1950s.[38] There they spent about twenty years as tenant farmers, occupying a two-room house with newspaper stuck to the walls for insulation and handmade quilts on the beds for warmth. Judging from the sacks used as backings on Susana's quilts, the Hunters bought sugar and animal feed by the hundred-pound bag (fig. 201a).

Around 1970, the Hunters moved about eight miles to Minter in Dallas County, and Susana remained there after Julius's death, occupying herself by making more quilts and gardening. Daughter Lillie Bell, who had moved away to work in New York, returned to Alabama after her retirement and settled next door to her mother. After Lillie Bell's death in 2005,[39] Susana moved to the home of grandson Tommie and his wife, Susie, and Susana Allen Hunter died there the same year. Colonial Williamsburg's quilts came from the collection of Tommie and Susie Hunter.

Susana Allen Hunter left a legacy of at least a hundred quilts. Despite her poverty—or perhaps because of it—she expressed herself by making warm, useful quilts for her family, using whatever textiles were available, from worn-out denim work clothes to synthetic curtains and dresses. At first glance the selection of textiles and colors on the quilts appears random, yet further study reveals subtle balance in the finished products. A textile is often added in just the right place to balance the composition or give an unexpected pop of color. The quilts show improvisational creativity and clever reuse and recycling, resulting in artistically stimulating and significant artifacts.

Of the five quilts in the Colonial Williamsburg collection, four of which follow, one has a batting of thick cotton, and the other four have no batting;[40] three are quilted with long running stitches, and two are tied with yarn.

Figure 199 Susana Allen Hunter with grandson Tommie Hunter and his wife, Susie, ca. 1987, courtesy Tommie and Susie Hunter.

PIECED STRIP QUILT

FIGURE 200

Various sizes and shapes of textiles are pieced into five long strips that are stitched together to form the final geometric design. Despite the apparent lack of planning, the colors are arranged to create subtle balance within an otherwise asymmetrical arrangement. The long quilting stitches are worked through thick cotton batting to a backing of coarse white cotton feed sacks. Although one of the feed sacks has been slit lengthwise to fit the space needed for the backing, the head of a mule can be matched to an intact hundred-pound feed sack used as the backing of Susana's Housetop Quilt (fig. 201a).

HOUSETOP QUILT

FIGURE 201

Beginning with solid green, Susana Hunter built up her quilt's central square by means of lengthening strips of textiles in a multitude of wovens, prints, and stripes. Visually related to the Log Cabin pattern, this version was usually known as Housetop in the African American communities around Dallas and Wilcox Counties, Alabama. Square and rectangular pieces fill out the rest of the quilt. At some time in the quilt's history, Susana added newer textiles over older floral prints that had disintegrated with laundering or use. A faded area across the center of the quilt, undoubtedly caused by drying over a clothesline in the sunshine, adds character and visual interest by breaking up the solid-green center square with an abstract line of gold that is picked up by the outer yellow and gold patches.

Although the quilt has a fascinating array of textiles on the front, the backings are of equal interest. Cotton sacks used to package sugar and animal feed were opened out and stitched together to back the quilt. Susana turned the sacks so that the wording faces inside, although it is still mostly legible. One of the sacks reads, "100 LBS. NET / PURE / REFINED SUGAR / FINE GRANULATED / CANE SUGAR / MANUFACTURED BY / [not legible] / PHILIPPINES / 100 LBS. NET WT." The other sack features the head of a toothy, grinning mule and the words "100 LBS. NET / SPECIAL / MANUFACTURED BY / COTHRAN FEED CO. / SELMA, ALA" (fig. 201a).

The bedcover is quilted with running stitches but has no batting.

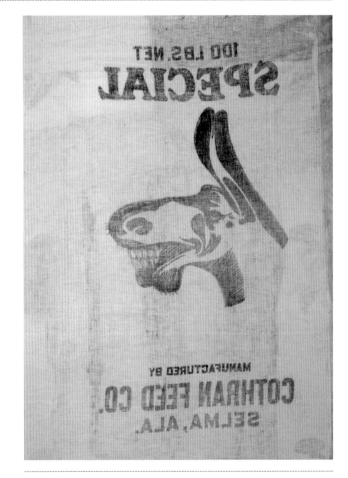

Figure 201a Detail of quilt back showing feed sacking with words turned to the inside.

Pieced Strip Quilt Figure 200

Susana Allen Hunter (1912–2005)

Wilcox County or Dallas County, Alabama, 1950–1970

Cotton, wool, synthetics

2–3 running stitches per inch

80¼ x 67½ in. (204 x 171 cm)

Museum Purchase, 2013.609.1

HOUSETOP QUILT FIGURE 201

Susana Allen Hunter (1912–2005)

Wilcox County or Dallas County, Alabama, 1960–1970

Cotton, wool, synthetics

3–6 running stitches per inch

84½ x 66½ in. (215 x 169 cm)

Museum Purchase, the Friends of Colonial Williamsburg Collections Fund, 2013.609.4

DOUBLE-SIDED WORK-CLOTHES QUILT

FIGURE 202

One side of this sturdy quilt consists primarily of khaki pants and denim work clothes, reversing to a variety of colors and textiles, including khaki, denim, printed cottons, and solid-brown and pink-red textiles. Susana Hunter went to some trouble to prepare the clothing for her quilt by taking out seams and hems and removing the pockets to reveal the less-faded denim underneath. Although it is not clear whether the unfaded pocket areas were accidentally positioned or deliberate, their placement adds a lively sense of rhythm to the utilitarian fabrics on the plainer side of the quilt. An unexpected choice for a work-clothes quilt is the inclusion of small patches of white synthetic taffeta dress or lining material. The quilt maker's use of bleached denim for the more brightly colored side of the quilt seems to blend with the cotton printed with irregular stripes in two different colorways of blue with yellow and orange with brown.

The quilt was made not as separate front and back joined around the edges but rather as a unified whole, with many of the pieces folded over at the edges to continue on the opposite side. Although running stitches hold the textiles together, there is no filling or batting.

TIED HOUSETOP QUILT

FIGURE 203

Susana Hunter combined a wide variety of colorful printed and woven textiles from dresses and women's suits with utilitarian feed sacking and tied the whole together with evenly spaced bright-green synthetic yarn that breaks up the large blocks of dark textiles and picks up the fresh green color in some of the smaller pieces. One of the textiles features purple elephants on dotted orange ground, a print taken from a dress designed and labeled by Suzy Perette in the 1960s (fig. 203a).[41]

The quilt is backed with sheeting stamped with the words "West Seneca State School," a residential school for developmentally challenged youth in West Seneca, New York; the institution held that name from 1962 to 1974.[42] How would a rural Alabama quilt maker acquire sheets used in New York State for the backing of her quilt? According to family members, Susana's daughter, Lillie Bell, worked for a doctor in New York for many years before retiring back home to Alabama. The daughter may have sent her mother sheets discarded after the West Seneca State School had changed its name. Judging from her other quilts, it would have appealed to Susana's thrifty nature to salvage used but still useful textiles. The presence of a textile so far from its origin serves as a caution for those researching a quilt's provenance based on the origins of the textiles. It is possible that some of the textiles on the front of the quilt came from Lillie Bell's New York wardrobe after the dresses had gone out of fashion.

The edges are finished by bringing the white backing to the face in some areas and by turning the face fabrics to the back in other areas.

Figure 203a Detail of dress designed by Suzy Perette in the 1960s. Susana Hunter used the same elephant print fabric in her Tied Housetop Quilt. Courtesy SwaneeGRACE.

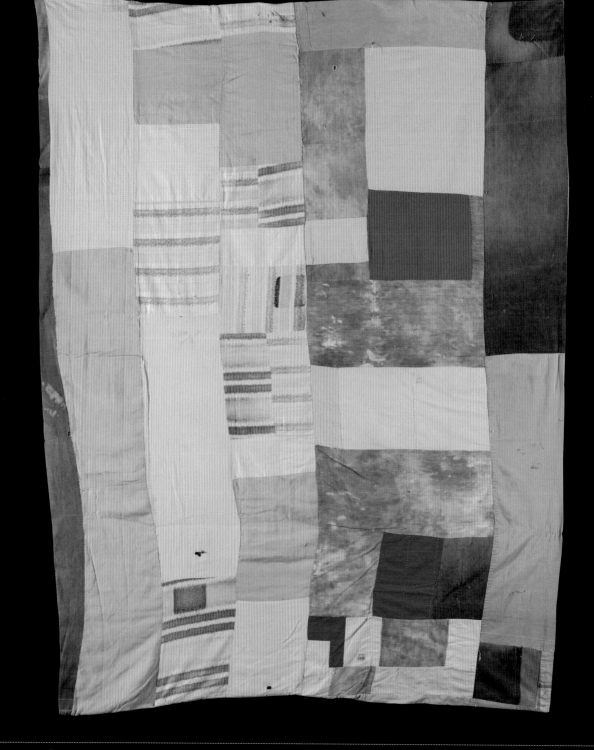

Double-Sided Work-Clothes Quilt Figure 202

Susana Allen Hunter (1912–2005)

Wilcox County or Dallas County, Alabama, 1960–1970

Cotton, wool, synthetics

2–4 running stitches per inch

85 x 65½ in. (216 x 166 cm)

Museum Purchase, Dr. and Mrs. T. Marshall Hahn Jr. Fund, 2013.609.2

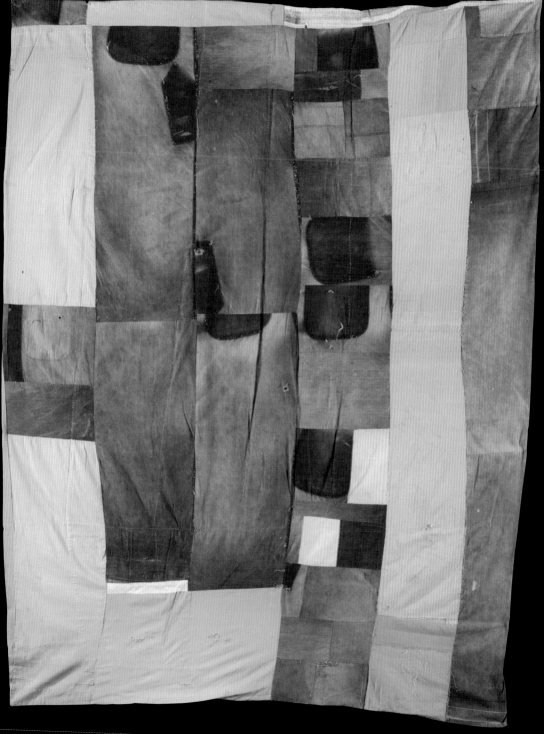

TIED HOUSETOP QUILT   FIGURE 203

SUSANA ALLEN HUNTER (1912–2005)

WILCOX COUNTY OR DALLAS COUNTY, ALABAMA, 1965–1975

COTTON, WOOL, SYNTHETICS

84 X 73½ IN. (213 X 187 CM)

MUSEUM PURCHASE, DR. AND MRS. T. MARSHALL HAHN JR. FUND
2013.609.3

1 A paper label originally stitched to this quilt states, "In 1793 Miss Mary Cooke, of Groton, Mass. rode on horseback to Boston, crossing the Charles River by ferry" to purchase fabrics in preparation for her upcoming marriage to John Page. Massachusetts marriage records document the wedding as occurring in 1798 at Lunenburg, about eight and a half miles from Groton. According to the label, Mary Cook Page made this quilt from her dresses, perhaps after they had gone out of fashion. The lighter block-printed floral cotton is believed to have been her wedding gown, and the dark cotton a dress from her trousseau. Mary quilted the wide strips with abstract leaf motifs and the triangles with repeated hearts through thin cotton batting and linen backing. CWF object file 1974-366; and Massachusetts, Town and Vital Records, 1620–1988, online database, digital image as found on Ancestry.com (2011).

2 See Gloria Seaman Allen, *A Maryland Sampling: Girlhood Embroidery, 1738–1860* (Baltimore, MD: Maryland Historical Society, 2007), 55.

3 For further discussion of the quilts in the DAR Museum collection, see Alden O'Brien, *Historic Quilts of the DAR Museum* (Brownsboro, AL: Martha Pullen Co., 2011), 34–37. The authors are indebted to Alden for sharing her research and thoughts on this group of quilts.

4 Alden O'Brien suggested that Amelia may have created a quilt for each of her surviving children. *Historic Quilts of the DAR Museum*, 35.

5 Margaret Barley's Winchester quilt, in the Virginia Quilt Museum collection, is published in Joan Knight, *Virginia Quilt Museum* (Charlottesville, VA: Howell Press, 2002), 17. The authors are indebted to Alden O'Brien for first bringing this quilt to our attention.

6 Linda Crocker Simmons, *Jacob Frymire: American Limner* (Washington, DC: Corcoran Gallery of Art, 1975), 28; and O'Brien, *Historic Quilts of the DAR Museum*, 34–35.

7 Simmons, *Jacob Frymire*, 42.

8 Simon Lauck was a gunsmith, as was at least one of his sons, Jacob. A ca. 1820 American long rifle, which carries the mark of Jacob Lauck, is in the Colonial Williamsburg collection (1998-164).

9 Simmons, *Jacob Frymire*, 28; O'Brien, *Historic Quilts of the DAR Museum*, 35; and Garland R. Quarles, *Some Worthy Lives: Mini-biographies, Winchester and Frederick County* (Winchester, VA: Winchester-Frederick County Historical Society, 1988), 140–142. Images of the Lauck family are well documented in the portraits by Jacob Frymire and Charles Willson Peale; see Simmons, *Jacob Frymire*, 10, 21–22, 28–30, 32–33, 38, 42–43.

10 Garland R. Quarles, *The Story of One Hundred Old Homes in Winchester, Virginia*, rev. ed. (Winchester, VA: Winchester-Frederick County Historical Society, 1993), 133.

11 "Virginia, Marriages, 1740–1850," s.v. "Eliza J. Sowers," online database, Ancestry.com (1999).

12 O'Brien, *Historic Quilts of the DAR Museum*, 37.

13 "Inventory and Appraisement of the Estate of Peter Lauck, deceased, real, personal and mixed taken the 3rd day of July 1840," Will Book 20, pp. 456–457, Frederick County Court, Winchester, VA.

14 Purdie & Dixon's *Virginia Gazette* (Williamsburg), October 20, 1768.

15 Peter Lank household, 1820 U. S. census, Winchester, Frederick, VA, page 45, National Archives and Records Administration (NARA) microfilm M33, roll 138, digital image as found on Ancestry.com (2010).

16 "Inventory and Appraisement of the Estate of Peter Lauck."

17 See Simmons, *Jacob Frymire*, 22. Also, "Virginia, Marriages, 1710–1850," s.v. "Morgan Lauch," online database, Ancestry.com (1999).

18 Simmons, *Jacob Frymire*, 22.

19 Photocopy of handwritten note in CWF object file 1998.609.1.

20 William Kelly Prentice, *Eight Generations: The Ancestry, Education and Life of William Packer Prentice* (Princeton, NJ, 1947), 68–79, 88–89; and C. J. F. Binney, *The History and Genealogy of the Prentice, or Prentiss Family, in New England, etc., from 1631 to 1883*, 2nd ed. (Boston: published by the editor, 1883), 67–68.

21 As transcribed in Prentice, *Eight Generations*, 70.

22 As transcribed in ibid., 71–72.

23 As transcribed in ibid., 73–74.

24 Ibid., 89.

25 As transcribed in ibid., 77–78.

26 As quoted in Binney, *History and Genealogy of the Prentice, or Prentiss Family*, 67.

27 See note 19.

28 See Prentice, *Eight Generations*, 70.

29 Binney, *History and Genealogy of the Prentice, or Prentiss Family*, 68, 115; and "James H. Prentiss" on findagrave.com, Find a Grave memorial #100471416, record added November 10, 2012.

30 Binney, *History and Genealogy of the Prentice, or Prentiss Family*, 115.

31 Binney, *History and Genealogy of the Prentice, or Prentiss Family*, 68, 115; James H. Prentice household, 1880 U. S. census, Brooklyn, Kings, NY, enumeration district 93, page 452D, NARA microfilm T9, roll 846, digital image as found on Ancestry.com (2010); Green-wood Cemetery, Brooklyn, NY, Burial Index, entry for Eloise W. Prentice, online database, accessed July 25, 2013, www.green-wood.com /burial_search/; "Menands, New York, Albany Rural Cemetery Burial Cards, 1791–2011," s.v. "Lucy Candace Prentice," online database, digital image as found on Ancestry.com (2011); and "Jemima C. Prentice Whitcomb" on findagrave.com, Find A Grave memorial #39723144, record added July 21, 2009.

32 Eloise B. Prentice (1907–1985) was the daughter of James Howard (1865–after 1930) and Sophia C. McCartee Prentice. Eloise married Louis Tiffany Lusk in 1933. The quilts descended to their sons, James and Graham Lusk. James H. Prentice household, 1910 U. S. census, Englewood Ward 2, Bergen, NJ, enumeration district 11, page 11A, NARA microfilm T624, roll 868, digital image as found on Ancestry.com (2006); James Prentice household, 1930 U. S. census, Englewood, Bergen, NJ, enumeration district 56, page 15A, NARA microfilm T626, roll 1311, digital image as found on Ancestry.com (2002); "Minnesota, Death Index, 1908–2002," s.v. "Eloise Prentice Lusk," online database, Ancestry.com (2001); Louis Lusk household, 1940 U. S. census, Norwalk, Fairfield, CT, enumeration district 1-118, page 6A, NARA microfilm T627, roll 498, digital image as found on Ancestry.com (2012); and "Other Weddings," *New York Times*, December 28, 1933.

33 William Waite household, 1900 U. S. census, Livingston, Spotsylvania, VA, enumeration district 82, page 11A, NARA microfilm T623, roll 1728, digital image as found on Ancestry.com (2004); William Alsop household, 1850 U. S. census, Eastern District, Stafford, VA, page 47B, NARA microfilm M432, roll 978, digital image as found on Ancestry.com (2009); and Wm. Alsop household, 1860 U. S. census, Stafford, VA, page 944, NARA microfilm M653, roll 1375, digital image as found on Ancestry.com (2009).

Perhaps Morgan was named in honor of Morgan's Raiders, in which his father and uncle were heroic members.

34 "Virginia Marriages, 1851–1929," s.v. "Joseph E. Chewning," online database, Ancestry.com (2000); "Virginia, Deaths and Burials Index, 1853–1917," s.v. "Joseph Chewing," online database, Ancestry.com (2011); and Wm. L. Waite household, 1870 U. S. census, Livingston, Spotsylvania, VA, page 404A, NARA microfilm M593, roll 1679, digital image as found on Ancestry.com (2009).

35 Wm. H. Waite household, 1860 U. S. census, Berkeley, Spotsylvania, VA, page 245, NARA microfilm M653, roll 1380, digital image found on Ancestry.com (2009); and Wm. L. Waite household, 1870 U. S. census.

36 William L. Waite household, 1910 U. S. census, Livingston, Spotsylvania, VA, enumeration district 117, page 9A, NARA microfilm T624, roll 1649, digital image as found on Ancestry.com (2006). Virginia does not appear in later censuses.

37 Tabitha Montgomery to author (Baumgarten), e-mail messages, January 28, 2013, and July 18, 2013; Tobe Allen household, 1920 U. S. census, Acherville, Wilcox, AL, enumeration district 183, page 7A, NARA microfilm T625, roll 43, digital image as found on Ancestry.com (2010); and U. S. Social Security Death Index (SSDI), 1935–current, s.v. Susana Hunter, online database, Ancestry.com (2011). Additional biographical information for Susana Hunter came from personal communications with Jeanine Head Miller, curator at the Henry Ford Museum, Dearborn, MI, who delivered a paper on Susana Allen Hunter's quilts for Colonial Williamsburg's symposium "Influences on American Quilts: Baltimore to Bengal," November 8–10, 2012. Miller personally interviewed grandson Tommie and incorporated his recollections into her presentation and the biography online at thehenryford.org. According to Miller's research, there were at least eleven children in the Allen family. The Henry Ford Museum has more than thirty of Susana's quilts, which were part of a one-woman exhibit in 2008 titled "Art from Everyday Life: The Quilts of Susana Allen Hunter." The Hunter collection at the Henry Ford is accessible online at http://collections.thehenryford.org/Collection.aspx?keywords=susana+allen+hunter, accessed February 8, 2013.

38 SSDI, 1935–current, s.v. Julius Hunter, online database, Ancestry.com (2011); and Julius Hunter household, 1930 U. S. census, Boykins, Dallas County, AL, enumeration district 29, page 2A, NARA microfilm T626, roll 14, digital image as found on Ancestry.com (2002). There was a mistake in recording Susana's name in the 1930 census because Sarah, not Susana, was listed as Julius's wife. The daughter's name was Lil, almost certainly referring to Lillie Bell.

39 SSDI, 1935–current, s.v. Lillie B. Hunter, online database, Ancestry.com.

40 Although many of Susana Hunter's bedcovers were made of two layers without battings, she and the family apparently referred to them as "quilts."

41 The vintage dress was located on http://lolavintage.blogspot.com/2009/08/novelty-print-of-day-elephants-oplenty.html, accessed 1/29/2013. "Novelty Print of the Day—Elephants O'Plenty: 60's Suzy Perette Dress," *Lola Vintage*, August 27, 2009.

42 Oral History Project, Center for Disabilities Studies, University at Buffalo, State University of New York, accessed February 11, 2013, http://disabilitystudies.buffalo.edu/oralhistory.php. In 1974 the name of the school was changed to the West Seneca Developmental Center.

Closing Remarks

CLOSING REMARKS

I t is mid-July 2012. The authors are talking with Colonial Williamsburg's decorative arts librarian, Susan Shames, who was immensely helpful in the time-consuming genealogical research of the quilt makers. We are discussing the underlying theme of sisterhood that weaves throughout many of our quilt stories. Susan becomes pensive. Looking up she quietly informs us, "I quilt with my sister, too" (see fig. 204).

Susan's words so succinctly reinforce the significance of quilts and why it is important to study them today. Quilt making transcends time. In addition to their warmth and beauty, quilts symbolize the unique experiences and contributions of women—both past and present. As connectors, or, if you will, direct highways, to the past, other cultures, and other peoples, quilts are important historical documents. They are a wealth of information, as informative as a history class, and certainly more beautiful and enjoyable to study. Through the study of quilts, we learn about the evolution of styles and fashion; social, political, and economic issues of particular times and places; and the importance of family and community ties (see fig. 205). Mensie Lee Pettway, twentieth-century African American quilt maker from Alabama, said, "A lot of people make quilts just for your bed, for to keep you warm. But a quilt is more. It represents safekeeping, it represents beauty, and you could say it represents family history."[1]

Most, if not all, of the quilts presented in this book elicit a response from the viewer whether it's because of

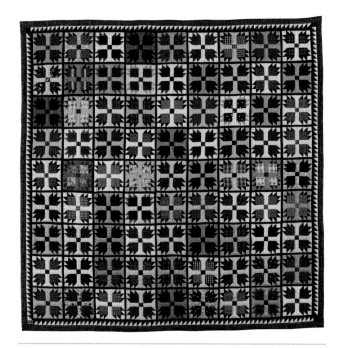

Figure 204 Bear Paw Quilt, Susan Shames and Alice J. Patteson, James City County, Virginia, 2004, cottons and polyester, 12–13 running stitches per inch, 83½ x 83½ in. (212 x 212 cm), courtesy Susan Shames. As a young bride, Susan was inspired by a magazine illustration of a Bear Paw quilt pattern to create one of her own. Decades later, with four completed quilts under her belt and her four children grown, she finally had the space and time in her life to design and finish her interpretation of the favorite pattern. Susan's sister, Alice Patteson, assisted in the quilt-making process, as she did with Susan's other quilts, by cutting out the swatches of colorful fabric. Many of the pieces were unused scraps from previous sewing projects: Susan's childhood bedroom curtains, her grandmother's plaid dress, a blouse from the 1960s, her mother's red-and-black printed dress, and fabric bits from other quilt projects. Each of Susan's quilts tells a story. Some were made with stories in mind; stories developed around others as they were pieced and quilted.

their beauty, the skill with which they were created, or their vibrant color, remarkable condition, known provenance, and so on. They are made from cloth—the most intimate medium, for we are swaddled in it at birth, married in special clothing, and at death are wrapped in it. Many quilts actually take the viewer into the sublime. They make you feel something you might not have felt otherwise. This is what makes many quilts a form of art and not simply a craft with the function of providing warmth. Through the study of quilts, quilt making, and quilt makers, we become interested in the life outside of our own and, thus, less self-centered and better citizens of the world.

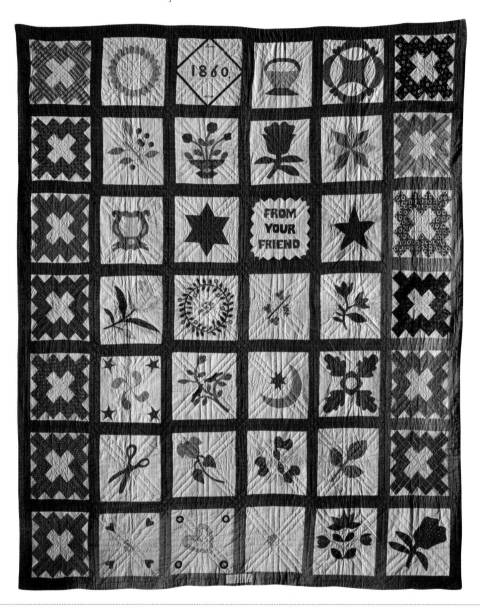

Figure 205 Album Quilt, "From Your Friend," Louisa Beebee (later Mrs. Newton Darrow) (1843–1910) and friends, Waterford, Connecticut, 1860, cottons and wool with ink inscriptions and cotton and silk embroidery threads, 6 running stitches per inch, 92½ x 75½ in. (248 x 192 cm), Museum Purchase from the estate of Foster and Muriel McCarl, 2012.609.5. A group of female neighbors joined together to create this pieced and appliquéd album quilt intended to be a gift "FROM YOUR FRIEND," according to the words appliquéd into one of the squares. A twentieth-century typed label sewn to the textile reads, "This quilt was made by Mrs F. Newton / Darrow and Friends in 1860. / Property of Rev. and Mrs E. W. Darrow." In addition, several of the quilt makers embroidered, stamped, or stenciled their names onto the individual blocks: "Louisa," "M Addie Chappell," and "Cornelia Mei[g?]s." The women can be traced to the community of Waterford in New London, Connecticut. In 1870, Louisa Beebee Darrow was the twenty-seven-year-old wife of Newton Darrow, a farmer. Louisa was about seventeen years old when she worked on the quilt.[2] Addie Chappell, who signed the "FROM YOUR FRIEND" block, has been identified as Adaline Chappell. She was twelve in 1860 when she signed her quilt square.[3]

1   John Beardsley, William Arnett, Paul Arnett, and Jane Livingston, *Gee's Bend: The Women and Their Quilts* (Atlanta, GA: Tinwood Books, 2002), 384.

2   Newton F. Darrow household, 1870 U. S. census, Waterford, New London, CT, page 847, National Archives and Records Administration (NARA) microfilm M593, roll 114, digital image as found on Ancestry.com (2003); and "Louise C. Darrow," on findagrave.com, Find a Grave memorial #54751136, record added July 10, 2010.

3   Eleazur Chappell household, 1860 U. S. census, Waterford, New London, CT, page 149, NARA microfilm M653, roll 91, digital image as found on Ancestry.com (2009).

Acknowledgments

ACKNOWLEDGMENTS

Four Centuries of Quilts: The Colonial Williamsburg Collection would not have become a reality without the generous support of Mary and Clint Gilliland of Menlo Park, California, through the Turner-Gilliland Family Fund of the Silicon Valley Community Foundation, which funded research, pattern drawing, design, and printing. We very much appreciate our shared interests, good conversations, and the friendship that has developed over the years.

Many individuals and families have entrusted their quilts into the care of the Colonial Williamsburg Foundation. We are pleased to share their treasured quilts with our readers and visitors now and years into the future and proudly list donors' names with the quilt entries.

We extend our sincerest thanks to our colleagues, past and present, who have given their time and skills to help make this project possible. We are especially indebted to curator emeritus Barbara Luck, who added numerous important artifacts to the collection and meticulously researched and documented them. We constantly relied on her groundwork with the folk art collection. Ronald Hurst, vice president for Collections, Conservation, and Museums and Carlisle H. Humelsine Chief Curator, encouraged us in our research and acquisitions. Ron also served as a reader and contributor and made excellent suggestions. We are grateful for his leadership. Photographer Craig McDougal and retired photographer Hans Lorenz provided the high-quality images of our quilt collection that

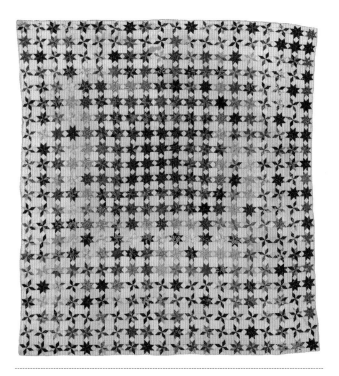

Figure 206 Le Moyne Star Quilt, Jane Pelton Burdon (Mrs. Theophilus R. Hyde Jr.) (1857–1925),[1] New York or Waterbury, Connecticut, ca. 1875, cottons, 7 running stitches per inch, 97½ x 87 in. (248 x 221 cm), gift of Beatrix T. Rumford, 2006.609.6. Four hundred forty eight-pointed stars, each consisting of eight diamonds, were used in the construction of this charming pieced quilt. The swatches represent an array of colorful printed cottons. The bedcover is quilted in random squares, diamonds, and parallel lines and bound with a one-fourth-inch-wide pattern-woven cotton tape. Made by Jane Pelton Burdon of New York and Waterbury, Connecticut, the quilt descended through the family to her great-grandniece, who donated it to Colonial Williamsburg.

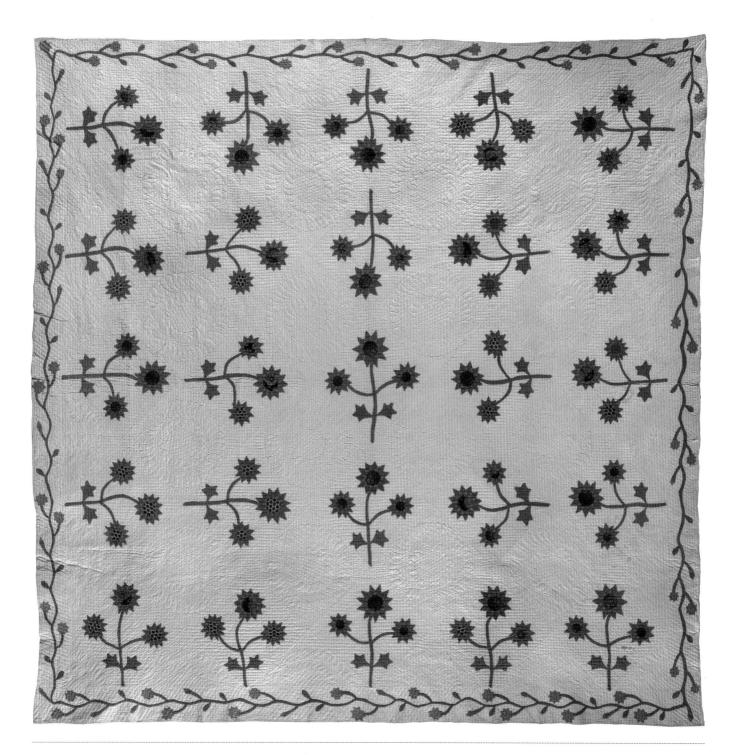

Figure 207 Sunflower Quilt, Carrie May Dyche (1871–1956),[2] West Virginia or Virginia, 1880–1907, cottons, 7–10 running stitches per inch, 103 x 104¼ in. (262 x 265 cm), gift of Betty Dyche Lough Gorin, 2013.609.6. The quilt maker stitched her initials CMD on the back, indicating that she made the quilt prior to her marriage to George Thrush in 1907.[3]

make this book so visually stunning. Craig accommodated many last-minute requests with good cheer and collegiality. Angelika Kuettner, associate registrar for imaging and assistant curator of ceramics, coordinated the hundreds of images and assisted in numerous aspects of the photography. John Watson, associate curator of musical instruments and conservator of instruments and mechanical arts, lent skill, ingenuity, and out-of-the-box thinking to capture quilt patterns using computer-assisted design techniques, which author Linda Baumgarten used to create the line drawings in this publication. Loreen Finkelstein, conservator of textiles, treated the quilts with expertise and sensitivity toward preserving all evidence embedded in their fibers, while meeting even the most challenging deadlines. Amanda Keller, assistant curator of historic interiors, and Beth Gerhold, textile refurnisher, provided cheerful support and assistance with routine requests and appointments, freeing up time for the authors to devote time to quilt research and writing. Our many other curatorial, conservation, museum, and registrar colleagues stepped in whenever needed with help and encouragement. Sarah Houghland, director of Development Services, was especially supportive. Additionally, the staff at the John D. Rockefeller, Jr. Library was always helpful with retrieving books, special orders, and queries.

Our colleagues in the Productions, Publications, and Learning Ventures Division made our words and photographs come together in the beautiful publication you see here. Paul Aron, director of the Publications Department, led the Publications team and coordinated the many aspects of the project. The striking book design was the inspiration and dedicated work of Shanin Glenn, who combined talent with enthusiasm for the project. Editor Amy Watson made us better writers and researchers by asking all the right questions. The clarity and accuracy of the book owes much to her exhaustive and thorough work. Tom Austin and Lael White in the Photographic Services Department produced the printed images for color correction under a tight deadline.

Special thanks to Collections librarian Susan Shames, who offered her time and considerable expertise with genealogical research. Susan relentlessly pursued the written records to unearth the details of our quilt makers' lives.

As you have seen in figure 204, she is also a talented quilter in her own right.

Our dedicated corps of textile volunteers and interns eased our task by providing numerous hours of assistance. In addition to their work in textile storage, they did research and helped with cataloging and examining quilts, conservation, and color proofing. We thank Ellen Armstrong, Kathie Ballentine, Ashley Deluce, Morgan Flaherty, Carol Harrison, Nan Losee, Trudy Moyles, Lorraine Phillips, Sarah Reeder, and Julie Stanton. Florine Carr helped produce the line drawings showing the quilting patterns and assisted with fiber identification.

The following institutions were helpful in providing images, research, and access to collections: Connecticut State Library, Hartford; Cumberland County Historical Society, Greenwich, New Jersey; Daughters of the American Revolution Museum, Washington, D. C.; Fort Wayne Museum of Art, Fort Wayne, Indiana; Frederick County Circuit Court, Winchester, Virginia; Friends Historical Library, Swarthmore College, Swarthmore, Pennsylvania; Library of Congress, Washington, D. C.; Museum of Early Southern Decorative Arts, Winston-Salem, North Carolina; United Methodist Historical Society of the Baltimore-Washington Conference, Baltimore, Maryland; Victoria and Albert Museum, London, England; and Winterthur Museum, Garden & Library, Winterthur, Delaware. The Royal Ontario Museum, Toronto, provided research funding and access to collections through a Veronika Gervers Research Fellowship awarded to Linda Baumgarten. The International Quilt Study Center & Museum, Lincoln, Nebraska, funded Linda Baumgarten's research fellowship to study quilts in their collections, resulting in an exhibit at the museum titled "The Whole Story."

Many individuals shared their time and expertise: Warren Q. Adams, Olivia Alison, Gloria Allen, Lynne Z. Bassett, Mary Baumgarten, Kathryn Berenson, Barbara Brackman, Angela Burnley, Jean H. Case, David Cleggett, Debby Cooney, Dr. Patricia Crews, Rosemary Crill, Jill D'Allessandro, Hilary Davidson, Sheryl DeJong, Amy Marks Delaney, Christopher Densmore, Deepali Dewan, Kathy Dirks, Carolyn Ducey, Linda Eaton, Ellen Endslow, Bobbi Finley, Sandra F. Fisher, Joan Foster, Sandi Fox, Dr. Gladys-Marie

Fry, Barbara Garrett, Jennifer Graham, Jonathan Gregory, Titi Halle, Marin Hanson, Kristina Haugland, Meghan Hays, Dr. Phyllis Herda, Don and Trish Herr, Jan Hiester, Ann Horsey, Laurel Horton, Tommie and Susie Hunter, Jean Jackson, Susan Jerome, Peter Kaellgren, Paula Karkkainen, Corey Keeble, Laura Keim, Deborah Kraak, Carol Kregloh, Ned Lazaro, Sally Lusk, Edward Maeder, Ronda McAllen, Diane Mikonowicz, Jeanine Head Miller, Martha Moffat, Tabitha Montgomery, Jeffrey Nash, Susan Newton, Connie J. Nordstrom, Alden O'Brien, Dorothy Osler, Alexandra Palmer, Janet Price, Leah Reeder, Mary Robare, Beatrix Rumford, Susan Schoelwer, Jerry Seagrave, Robert W. Shindle, Elly Sienkiewicz, Julie Silber, Carol Sommers, Kathy Staples, Callie Stapp, Tora Sterregaard, Kristen Stewart, Damon Talbot, Jim and Connie Thompson, Gwen Wanigasekera, Kirk Whittle, Leigh Wishner, Lorie Woodard, and Wendell Zercher.

We are most appreciative of the support and love of our families. Families are like quilts—they provide color, texture, warmth, and comfort to our lives. Linda thanks John Watson, beloved husband, friend, and colleague, for his support and creative ideas that resulted in many hours of fascinating conversation. His input vastly improved the book. Kim thanks her husband, Gordon, and son, Gordon, for their support and good humor throughout the writing and editing of the book, which resulted in many canceled family outings and time together. Gordon and Gordon's patience in listening to the telling and retelling of numerous quilt stories and their understanding of the significance of these stories reinforced the importance of quilt study.

Figure 208 Album Quilt, Amanda Leonard Williams (Mrs. Thomas R. Williams) (1842–1912),[4] Maryland or Virginia, ca. 1860, cottons and ink, 6–8 running stitches per inch, 86 x 70 in. (218 x 178 cm), gift of Donald Haynie, 2013.609.7. Created about ten years after the enthusiasm for Baltimore album quilts reached its zenith, this album quilt illustrates the enduring popularity of the quilt style. The quilt consists of twenty blocks of appliquéd motifs, some with embroidered embellishments. Many are similar to blocks found on high-style Baltimore album quilts, although overall they are not as sophisticated and lack the layering of fabrics and careful choice and placement of printed cottons that give appliquéd motifs on Baltimore album quilts their depth and texture. This quilt was quilted in outline, squares, and squares on point and originally bound with a three-fourths-inch-wide white strip of cotton. Born in Maryland, Amanda Leonard married Thomas R. Williams of Northumberland County, Virginia. The quilt descended through the family of one of their three children.

1   Jane Pelton Burdon Hyde marker, digital image as found on findagrave.com, Find a Grave memorial #119526317, record added October 30, 2013.

2   Dyche family Bible; and Maryland, "Department of Health, Division of Vital Records and Statistics (Death Record, Index, Counties), 1945–1968," SE8, online database, Maryland State Archives, (http://guide.mdsa.net/viewer.cfm?page=topviewed : accessed April 16, 2014), entry for Carrie May Thrush, July 26, 1956, p. 3306.

3   "West Virginia, Marriages Index, 1785– 1971," s.v. Geo O Thrush, online database, Ancestry.com (2011).

4   Amanda L. Williams marker, digital image as found on findagrave.com, Find a Grave memorial #84599699, record added February 6, 2012.

Index

redwork outline quilts, 275, *275–277*. *See also* embroidered quilts

ribbons, 234, *235*, 284, 298, *300*, 317, *317–318*

Richards, Harriet Ann (later Mrs. George R. Long), 134, 307

Richter, Alma, 163

Richter, Anna, 163, *165*

Richter family, 163

Ringgold, Samuel, 202, *202, 204*

Robertson, Lelia Graham Eggleston (Mrs. Walter Harris Robertson), 290

Robertson, Walter Harris, 290

Robinson, Harriet (later Mrs. Samuel Barbour), 160

Robinson, Sarah (Mrs. Thomas Robinson), 160

Robinson family, 160

Rockafellow family, 182, *183*

Rollins family, 174, *175*

Royal School of Art Needlework, 274

ruching, 190

ruffles, 290

rugs, rag, *158*, 169n8

Russell, Emma (Mrs. Will Henry Russell), 236

S

sacks, flour or feed, 250, 261, *262*, 326, *326*, 329, *332*

Saint-Aubin, Charles Germain de, 64, 66

sampler quilts, 111, *113*

samplers, 136, 152, *152*, 172, *192*

Sands sisters (Emily and Sarah), 136, 305

sashing
  angled, 278, *281*
  diagonal, 208, *209*
  lattice-patterned, 100, *100–102*, 180, *181–182*
  printed cotton, 104, *105*, 120, *121*, 127, *129*, 138, *139*, 180, *181–182*
  red, white, and blue, 205, *205–207*
  solid-color, 152, *153*, 210, *210–211*

scripture quilts, 122n5

Seamen's Bethel Mission, 198, *199, 201*, 213n28, 213n29

Seitz, Barbara, *217*

sequins, 284

sewing machine, 110, 180, 217, 225. *See also* stitching, machine

shalloon, 52, 62n1

Shames, Susan, 336, *336*

Shenandoah Valley quilts, 98, *99*, 134, *134–135*, 148n4, 306, *307–311*

Sherwin, William, 32

show quilts, 228, *284–300*, 284–302

signature quilts, 8, 120, 171–188, *174–185*

signatures and initials
  cross-stitched, x, xi, 5, 74, *74*, *124*, *155*
  embroidered, 5, 127, *127*, 134, *134*, 180, *180–181*, 219, *221*, 286, *287–289*, 307, 320, *320*, *337*
  ink signed, x, xi, 5, 106, *107*, *172*, 174, *175–183*, 178, 180, 182, 206, *206*
  ink stamped, 5, 172, *173*, 178, *178–181*, 180
  pieced, 6
  quilted, 225, *226–227*, 314, *314–315*
  stitched, 5, 53, 158, *159*, 178, *178–179*, 323

Simon, Anna Maria "Mary" Heidenroder, 193, 212n11

Simpson, Helen Edmonia McWhorter, 234

Smith, Abby, 35

Smith, Dora, 244, 247

Smith, Emily Hannah Badger (Mrs. Levi Bull Smith), 77, *77*

Smith, Julia Evelina, 35

Smith, Levi Bull, 77, *77*

Smythe, Thomas, 16

stamps, 5, 172, *173*, 178, *178–181*, 180, *337*

Starke, Sarah, x

star quilts, 131–148, *133–147*

stencils, 5, 141, *141–142*, 172, *173*, 178, *178–179*, *337*

stitches
  appliqué, used in
    blanket, 95, 166, *167*
    blind, 160, *162*, 190
    buttonhole, 95, 96, *97–99*, 98, 100, *100–103*, 180, *180–181*, 190, 202, *204*, 205, *207*
    chain, 236, *237*
    overcast, 166, *167*, 180, *180–181*, 213n35
    running, 236, *237*
    slip, 104, *105*, 236, *237*
  embroidery
    blanket, 290, *290–291*, 294, *294–295*

bullion knots, 45, *45*
  buttonhole, 95, 286, *286–287*
  chain, 13, *14*, 16, *16–17*, 160, *162*, 286, *286–287*, 290, *290–291*, 294, *294–295*
  coral knot, 294, *294–295*
  couching, 45, *45–46*, 286, *286–287*, 290, *290–291*, 294, *294–295*
  cross-stitch, 5, 286, *286–287*, 290, *290–291*, 294, *294–295*
  double cross, 286, *286*, 287
  feather, 290, *290–291*, 298, *299–300*
  fern, 290, *290–291*, 294, *294–295*
  fly, 286, *286–287*
  French knots, 43, *43–46*, 45, 64, *65*, 286, *286–287*
  herringbone, 96, *97*, 286, *286–287*, 290, *290–291*, 294, *294–295*
  Kensington, 274, 301n1
  knots, 290, *290–291*
  lazy daisy, 286, *286–287*, 290, *290–291*
  long-arm cross, 290, *290–291*
  needle weaving, 294, *294–295*
  outline, 96, *97*, 290, *290–291*
  padded satin, 43, *43–44*
  running, 43, *43*, 44
  satin, 43, *43–46*, 45, 160, *162*, 286, *286–287*, 290, *290–291*
  spider web, 294, *294–295*
  split, 43, *43–46*, 45
  stem, 43, *43–44*, 294, *294–295*
  straight, 43, *43–44*, 290, *290–291*, 294, *294–295*
  Turkey work, 286, *286–287*
  piecing, used in, 83, *83*
  quilting, used in, 4, *4*, 14, *14–15*, 251, *252*

stitching, machine
  appliqué, used for, 236, 296
  backings and bindings, used for, *151*, 178, 180, 222, 308, *310*
  piecing, used for, 217, 225
  quilting, used for, x, xi, 239, *241*, 290
  See also sewing machine

string quilts, 233, 244, *245*

stuffed-work patterns and motifs
  berries, 164, *164*
  birds, 77, *79*
  cornucopias, 77, *79*
  feathers and plumes, 116, *116–117*,